IBM's Token-Ring Networking Handbook

J. Ranade Series on Computer Communications

ISBN	AUTHOR	TITLE
0-07-060360-X	Spohn	*Data Network Design*
0-07-019022-4	Edmunds	*SAA / LU6.2 Distributed Networks and Applications*
0-07-054418-2	Sackett	*IBM's Token-Ring Networking Handbook*
0-07-004128-8	Bates	*Disaster Recovery Planning: Networks, Telecommunications, and Data Communications*
0-07-020346-6	Feit	*TCP / IP: Architecture, Protocols, and Implementation*
0-07-005075-9	Berson	*APPC: Introduction to LU6.2*
0-07-005076-7	Berson	*Client / Server Architecture*
0-07-012926-6	Cooper	*Computer and Communications Security*
0-07-016189-5	Dayton	*Telecommunications*
0-07-016196-8	Dayton	*Multi-Vendor Networks: Planning, Selecting, and Maintenance*
0-07-034242-3	Kessler	*ISDN*
0-07-034243-1	Kessler/Train	*Metropolitan Area Networks: Concepts, Standards, and Service*

OTHER RELATED TITLES

ISBN	AUTHOR	TITLE
0-07-051144-6	Ranade/Sackett	*Introduction to SNA Networking: A Guide for Using VTAM / NCP*
0-07-051143-8	Ranade/Sackett	*Advanced SNA Networking: A Professional's Guide to VTAM / NCP*
0-07-033727-6	Kapoor	*SNA: Architecture, Protocols, and Implementation*
0-07-005553-X	Black	*TCP / IP and Related Protocols*
0-07-005554-8	Black	*Network Management Standards: SNMP, CMOT, and OSI*
0-07-021625-8	Fortier	*Handbook of LAN Technology*
0-07-063636-2	Terplan	*Effective Management of Local Area Networks: Functions, Instruments, and People*
0-07-004563-1	Baker	*Downsizing: How to Get Big Gains from Smaller Computer Systems*

IBM's Token-Ring Networking Handbook

George C. Sackett
ASAP Technologies, Inc.
Rutherford, New Jersey

McGraw-Hill, Inc.
New York San Francisco Washington, D.C. Auckland Bogotá
Caracas Lisbon London Madrid Mexico City Milan
Montreal New Delhi San Juan Singapore
Sydney Tokyo Toronto

Library of Congress Cataloging-in-Publication Data

Sackett, George C.
IBM's token-ring networking handbook / George C. Sackett.
p. cm. — (J. Ranade series on computer communications)
Includes index.
ISBN 0-07-054418-2
1. IBM Token-Ring Network (Local area network system) 2. Local area networks (Computer networks)—Management. I. Title. II. Series.
TK5105.8.I24S23 1993
004.6'8—dc20 93-20462
CIP

1 2 3 4 5 6 7 8 9 0 DOC/DOC 9 9 8 7 6 5 4 3

ISBN 0-07-054418-2

The sponsoring editor for this book was Jerry Papke, the editing supervisor was Joseph Bertuna, and the production supervisor was Pamela A. Pelton.

Printed and bound by R. R. Donnelley & Sons Company.

To my wife Peg and daughter Chelsea, no greater love have I found than the love you give me and I give you in return.

Contents

Preface xiii

Chapter 1. Introduction to Local Area Networking 1

1.1 WHAT IS THE NETWORK? 2
1.2 LOCAL AREA NETWORKS 3
1.3 COMPARING LAN AND PBX 4
1.4 LAN AND WAN 6
1.5 CAPABILITIES AND BENEFITS OF A LAN 8
1.6 PLANNING A LAN 8

Chapter 2. Token-Ring Network Architecture 11

2.1 SYSTEMS NETWORK ARCHITECTURE 11
2.1.1 The Seven Layers of SNA 13
2.2 UNDERSTANDING OPEN SYSTEMS INTERCONNECTION 14
2.2.1 The Seven Layers of OSI 16
2.2.2 The Importance of Open Systems and Standards 16
2.3 LOGICAL LINK CONTROL SUBLAYER 18
2.3.1 LLC Protocol Data Unit 19
2.4 MEDIUM ACCESS CONTROL SUBLAYER 27
2.4.1 MAC Frame Format 28
2.5 SUMMARY 38

Chapter 3. IBM's Token-Ring Network Concepts 41

3.1 LAN TOPOLOGIES 42
3.1.1 Mesh Topography 42
3.1.2 Star Topography 43
3.1.3 Bus Topography 44
3.1.4 Ring Topography 45
3.1.5 MultiSegment 47
3.2 TOKEN-RING ADDRESSING 49
3.2.1 Individual and Group Addressing 50
3.2.2 Universal and Locally Administered Addresses 50

3.2.3 Null Address 51
3.2.4 All-Stations Broadcast Addresses 51
3.2.5 Functional Addresses 51

3.3 BRIDGING AND ROUTING 52
3.3.1 Source Routing Bridge 52
3.3.2 Transparent Bridge 55
3.3.3 Spanning Tree Algorithm 56
3.3.4 Parallel Routes 59
3.3.5 Source Routing Transparent Bridge 59
3.3.6 Routers 60

3.4 TOKEN PASSING RING PROTOCOL AND TOKEN CLAIMING 61
3.5 ACTIVE MONITOR 64
3.6 NEIGHBOR NOTIFICATION 64
3.7 ACCESS PRIORITY 65
3.8 RING ATTACHMENT PROCESS 66
3.9 SUMMARY 67

Chapter 4. Token-Ring Components 69

4.1 TOKEN-RING MEDIA 70
4.1.1 Cable Types 71
4.1.2 Patch Cables 75

4.2 IBM's 8228 MULTISTATION ACCESS UNIT 75
4.3 IBM's 8218 COPPER REPEATER 76
4.4 IBM's 8219 OPTICAL FIBER REPEATER 78
4.5 IBM's 8218/8219 TEST CONNECTOR 79
4.6 IBM's 8220 OPTICAL FIBER CONVERTER 80
4.7 IBM's 8230 CONTROLLED ACCESS UNIT 81
4.8 IBM's TOKEN-RING NETWORK BRIDGE PROGRAM 83
4.9 IBM's 8209 LAN BRIDGE 86
4.10 IBM's 8232 LAN CHANNEL STATION 87
4.11 IBM's 3172 INTERCONNECT CONTROLLER 88
4.12 IBM's 3174 ESTABLISHMENT CONTROLLER 89
4.13 IBM's COMMUNICATIONS CONTROLLER 90
4.14 SUMMARY 91

Chapter 5. LAN Planning 93

5.1 THE SERVER CONCEPT 94
5.2 PLANNING THE LOCAL AREA NETWORK 96
5.2.1 Collecting Information 97
5.2.2 End-user and Backbone Ring Design Considerations 98
5.2.3 Connectivity to the SNA Mainframe 99
5.2.4 Backup and Recovery 100
5.2.5 Network Resource Naming Standards 101
5.2.6 Traffic Flow and Control 102
5.2.7 Network Management 102
5.2.8 Organizational Structure and Systems Management 103
5.2.9 Migration and Future Growth 103

5.3 SUMMARY 104

Chapter 6. LAN Design 105

6.1 PHYSICAL TOPOLOGY DESIGN 105
6.1.1 Multiple Floor Ring Configurations 105
6.1.2 Backbone Design 106
6.2 LOGICAL TOPOLOGY DESIGN 111
6.2.1 User Segment Logical Design 111
6.2.2 Multisegment LAN Design 112
6.3 SNA GATEWAY CONNECTIVITY 118
6.3.1 IBM Communication Controllers 118
6.3.2 Establishment Controller 121
6.3.3 Interconnect Controller 122
6.3.4 OS/2 SNA Gateway 125
6.4 SUMMARY 126

Chapter 7. IBM's Network Management Architectures 127

7.1 OPEN NETWORK MANAGEMENT ARCHITECTURE 128
7.1.1 Focal Point 128
7.1.2 Entry Point 129
7.1.3 Service Point 130
7.2 SNA NETWORK SERVICES FLOW 131
7.3 NETVIEW OVERVIEW 132
7.3.1 Network Command Control Facility (NCCF) 133
7.3.2 NetView Hardware Monitor 134
7.3.3 LAN Support 135
7.4 SYSTEMVIEW 135
7.4.1 End-Use Dimension 136
7.4.2 Application Dimension 137
7.4.3 Data Dimension 139
7.5 SUMMARY 140

Chapter 8. Token-Ring Network Management 141

8.1 LAN NETWORK MANAGER 141
8.1.1 Standards Implemented by LAN Network Manager 142
8.1.2 LAN Network Manager and NetView Connectivity 143
8.1.3 Controlled Access Unit Management 144
8.2 LAN STATION MANAGER 146
8.3 MANAGING THE TOKEN-RING NETWORK FROM NETVIEW 148
8.3.1 LAN Generic Command 148
8.3.2 LAN ADAPTER Command List 149
8.3.3 LAN BRIDGE Command List 150
8.3.4 LAND QNETWORK Command List 150
8.3.5 LAN RESETLAN Command List 152
8.3.6 LAN SEGMENT Command List 152
8.3.7 Using NetView for Problem Determination 153
8.4 SUMMARY 157

Chapter 9. IBM's OS/2 Server and Requester 159

9.1 TERMINOLOGY 160
9.1.1 Domain and Domain Controller 160
9.1.2 Additional Servers 161
9.1.3 Requester Workstations and DOS LAN Requester 162
9.1.4 DOS Remote Initial Program Load (RIPL) 162
9.1.5 User, User ID, Passwords and Guest Account 162
9.1.6 Shared Network Resources and Aliases 163
9.1.7 Domain and External Resources 163
9.1.8 System Administrator 165
9.2 PLANNING THE SERVER/REQUESTER ENVIRONMENT 165
9.3 DEFINING THE NETWORK ENVIRONMENT 166
9.4 OS/2 LAN SERVER 168
9.4.1 Resource Sharing 169
9.4.2 Print Spooling 169
9.4.3 Access Control Function 170
9.4.4 Remote IPL Server 173
9.4.5 Alerter Service 174
9.4.6 Net Logon Service 175
9.4.7 Replicator Service 177
9.4.8 Hardware Requirements 181
9.4.9 Software Requirements 181
9.5 OS/2 LAN REQUESTER 182
9.6 DOS LAN REQUESTER 183
9.6.1 LAN Support Program V1 184
9.7 IMPLEMENTING SERVER/REQUESTER 186
9.7.1 Defining OS/2 Communications Manager LAN Profiles 186
9.7.2 OS/2 EE LAN Server to OS/2 EE LAN Requester 189
9.7.3 OS/2 LAN Server to DOS LAN Requester 190
9.7.4 DOS Remote IPL Service from OS/2 LAN Server 192
9.8 SUMMARY 194

Chapter 10. IBM's Token-Ring Network Bridge Program 195

10.1 LOCAL BRIDGE CONFIGURATION 195
10.2 REMOTE BRIDGE CONFIGURATION 202
10.3 REMOTE DIAL SUPPORT 208
10.4 FILTERING PROGRAMS 209
10.5 SUMMARY 213

Chapter 11. Mainframe Connectivity with the IBM 3172 Interconnect Controller 215

11.1 OPERATING SYSTEM DEFINITIONS AND CONSIDERATIONS 216
11.1.1 IOCP Definitions for VM and MVS 219
11.1.2 Device Definitions for VM and MVS 220
11.2 DEFINING THE IBM 3172 ICP 221
11.2.1 The IBM 3172 Operator Facility/2 222
11.2.2 Defining the IBM 3172 Device to ICP 224
11.2.3 Defining Channel-Attachments to ICP 226
11.2.4 Defining Token-Ring Adapters to ICP 228
11.2.5 Defining the LAN Gateway Function 231

11.2.6 Creating the IBM 3172 ICP Working Diskettes
11.3 LOADING THE IBM 3172 ICP 235
11.3.1 Attached ICP Loading 238
11.4 MVS TCP/IP TO TOKEN-RING 239
11.5 VTAM DEFINITIONS FOR IBM 3172 242
11.5.1 Defining the External Communication Adapter 243
11.5.2 Defining SNA Node Type 2.0/2.1 in the XCA Major Node 244
11.5.3 Defining SNA Node Type 4 in the XCA Major Node 247
11.5.4 Defining SNA Node Type 5 in the XCA Major Node 250
11.5.5 Defining a Shared Token-Ring Adapter 251
11.5.6 Defining Dual Ring Backup 252
11.6 NETWORK MANAGEMENT SUPPORT WITH THE XCA MAJOR NODE 253
11.7 SUMMARY 255

Chapter 12. Mainframe Connectivity with IBM Gateways 257

12.1 IBM's 37X5 LAN GATEWAY WITH NCP 257
12.1.1 NCP OPTIONS and BUILD Definition Statements 258
12.1.2 Defining the Physical GROUP Definition Statement 259
12.1.3 Defining the Physical LINE Definition Statement 261
12.1.4 Defining the Physical NTRI PU 251
12.1.5 Defining a Downstream Physical Unit 262
12.1.6 Defining a Token-Ring Subarea Configuration 263
12.1.7 Defining a Duplicate TIC Configuration 263
12.2 VTAM DEFINITIONS FOR IBM 37X5 GATEWAY DSPU SUPPORT 266
12.2.1 Switched VBUILD Definition Statement 267
12.2.2 Switched PU Definition Statement 267
12.2.3 Switched PATH Definitions Statement 267
12.2.4 Switched LU Definitions Statement 268
12.3 IBM's 3174 ESTABLISHMENT CONTROLLER GATEWAY CONFIGURATION 268
12.3.1 Local 3174 Establishment Controller Gateway 269
12.3.2 Local Establishment Controller Gateway Support on the IBM 3174 DSPU 273
12.3.3 Local Establishment Controller Gateway Support for DSPU Workstations 274
12.3.4 VTAM Local Establishment Controller Gateway Definition 274
12.3.5 Remote 3174 EC Gateway 275
12.3.6 NCP Remote Establishment Controller Gateway Definition 277
12.4 IBM's OS/2 SNA GATEWAY CONFIGURATION 278
12.4.1 OS/2 SNA Gateway through a Local 3174 278
12.4.2 OS/2 SNA Gateway through an IBM 37X5 Gateway 280
12.4.3 Remote OS/2 SNA Gateway 281
12.5 SUMMARY 281

Appendix A. Control Field State Variables 283

Appendix B. SNA to Token-Ring Communications Protocol 287

Appendix C. The Differential Manchester Code 289

Appendix D. MAC Major Vectors 291

Appendix E. Standardized Group and Functional Addresses 295

Appendix F. IBM's Suggested MAC Addressing Guidelines 296

Appendix G. Cable, Closet and Ring Segment Drive Distance and Guidelines 301

Appendix H. LAN Network Manager Commands Supported by NetView 313

Appendix I. IBM's Token-Ring Network Bridge Program Parameters 319

Appendix J. Acronyms and Abbreviations 323

Glossary 327
Bibliography 345
Index 347

Preface

In today's fast paced "give it to me now" society, information has become almost as valuable as gold. Nations that once lead in industrialization may now lead the world into the age of information. Knowledge acquired through information can lead to power if used wisely, but this knowledge cannot be found without communication. Communication throughout man's history has provided the means for sharing information. The resources used have been pictures, speech and the written word. It is communication of information that has brought modern man to his current perch, ready to strike at the next opportunity.

Sharing information on shared resources efficiently and economically is the objective of a *local area network* (LAN). This premise does not preclude the previous paragraph. Looking at local area networks is, in a way, based on man's needs to stay atop that perch by making it easier to share information. This sharing of information can be small in some matters and grand in others. In the business world, sharing of information can mean tighter control on assets while providing better service to customers. In the scientific world, sharing of information can excite the imagination of the great thinkers of our time much faster than before, leading to theories and discoveries never thought possible.

It is the intent of this book to provide accurate and timely information on local area networking using IBM's Token-Ring Network. The book is organized in a manner so anyone with some computer networking experience can design, install and implement a token-ring network. It is not the intent of this book to be the defacto standard on token ring. The book was conceived entirely with the idea of being a handbook for understanding, assisting, and implementing token-ring networking.

Acknowledgment

I would like to extend my thanks to the following people for their support and belief in me. I would like to thank Jay Ranade for introducing me to the world of publishing as a means of expanding my knowledge in my areas of interest, and for his professional support. My thanks also to Gary Accardi and Walt Barlow for providing me with information that was pertinent, comprehensive data in the completion of this book. Books of this nature require not only editorial reviews but also technical reviews. Thanks go to Alex Berson for his encouraging review and suggestions, and to Dave Levine. Without Dave's technical input, sections of this book would not have been complete. Thank you Dave for your diligence. Finally, I would like to thank my wife Peg and our daughter Chelsea. With their support, encouragement, and unfounded understanding, I have been able to rise to the occasion time and time again.

I hope the information provided here helps you in your endeavors on implementing a local area network with IBM's Token-Ring Network. Good luck and remember to keep sharing information.

George C. Sackett

IBM's Token-Ring Networking Handbook

Chapter

1

Introduction to Local Area Networking

The computer as we know it today did not become a staple for doing business until the mid-1970's. The thrust behind the importance of the computer at that time was the ability to network computers. This networking of computers allowed people remote to the computer to access the information available to that computer. This networking marked the beginning of the information age.

Today the power of the mainframe computer resides on the desk of the end user. This capability has given rise to distributed processing. Local area networks can be used in distributed processing environments to improve the flow of information and the availability of this information through interconnecting mainframes, minicomputers, workstations and personal computers. As we move further into the 1990's, we will see the complete migration of mainframe applications to workstations. The mainframe will be the centralized data base server for the corporate network. The computing power that utilizes the information will reside on the workstation. This technology is leading many corporations to take advantage of the reduced price and increased performance in the workplace.

This chapter will introduce some of the basic concepts of networking and local area networking.

1.1 WHAT IS THE NETWORK?

We have all heard the term network or networking but just what is a network. A network is a means of transmitting or receiving information from one source to another. For instance, people network. As an example, car salesmen, after years in the business, have developed a network of associates. When the car salesman needs to locate a car to make a sale, the car salesman calls out to his network to retrieve information on the location of the car. Employment agents also develop a network. Their customers, people like you and me, become their network. Employment agents will frequently keep in touch with their clientele for possible openings or to locate a candidate for an opening. Without the capability of networking, these two careerists would have a difficult time. It's the same in computing. Networks provide the means for locating and transporting information.

In computing networks, the origin of the information request utilizes the services of a network to locate and return the information. This is done with addresses. In the two previous examples of the car salesman and the employment agent, a telephone number can be considered the address of their associate or client. Addresses in computer networking are used in the same manner. These addresses identify the network resource. In Figure 1.1 there are two popular architectures for networking: hierarchical and peer.

Hierarchical addressing is defined in a master-slave relationship. In a hierarchical network, the master controls the network and therefore assigns addresses to the network resources. A typical example of a hierarchical network is IBM's *systems network architecture* (SNA). This architecture has the mainframe as the master and all network resources as slaves. The basis of this is that if the master does not know beforehand of a network resources existence through a pre-defined address, then that resource cannot participate in the SNA network.

Peer networking does not need pre-defined network addressing. Instead, each resource on the network is seen as a peer. As an example, when you walk into a room of strangers one of the first things you do is introduce yourself to a few of the people. Your name is your address. Once introductions have been made you can then communicate more freely with your peers. The same concept is applied to peer networking. Each network resource is a peer to the other network resources. When a new network resource joins the network it introduces itself and notifies its peers of any other network resources that it knows about. Peer networks are open and share network information.

1.2 LOCAL AREA NETWORKS

Around the same time as the introduction of the IBM personal computer, local area networks were introduced. Local area networks are comprised of personal computers and workstations interconnected with a single cabling scheme allowing sharing of resources. Local area networks provide a single shared medium for mainframe host connectivity for these local area network resources. This is in contrast to the one-terminal-one-cable scheme of earlier mainframe host connectivity. Local area networks are quickly becoming the choice for connecting personal computers and workstations.

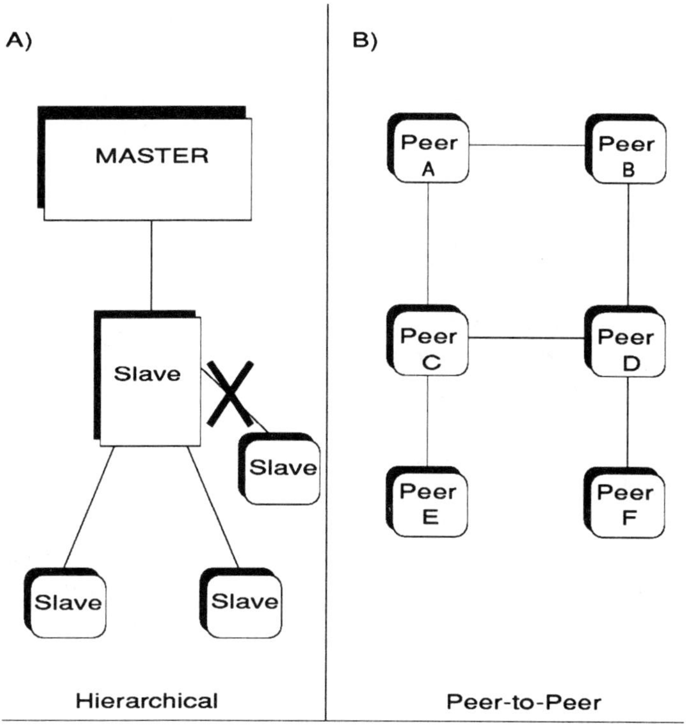

Figure 1.1 In diagram A, a master-slave relationship is depicted. New resources cannot enter the network until the master defines their address. In diagram B, a peer network is depicted. As new peers connect to the network, information about the connecting peers is exchanged. Peer D notifies Peer F of connecting routes to peers A, B, C and E and the network resources found on each. Likewise, if Peer F had peers attached to it, it would notify Peer D in the same fashion.

Link Layer	IEEE 802.2 Logical Link Control		
Physical Layer	IEEE 802.3 CSMA/CD Bus	IEEE 802.4 Token Bus	IEEE 802.5 Token Ring

Figure 1.2 The IEEE 802 local area network standards.

There are two primary contenders to wear the LAN crown. These are *Ethernet* from Xerox and *Token Ring* from IBM. Ethernet was developed by Xerox Corporation at their *Palo Alto Research Center* (PARC). The Ethernet in use today is based on standards developed by *Digital Equipment Corporation* (DEC), Intel and Xerox. This specification received great acceptance by industry users. The reason for its acceptance is its open standard. Any corporation or vendor could develop or write applications to use Ethernet. Currently the data rate for Ethernet is 10Mbps. Ethernet standards were incorporated into IEEE 802 local area network standards. In Figure 1.2 the IEEE 802 local area network standards family of standards are shown. IBM adopted IEEE 802.5 Token-Passing Ring. Due to token-rings architecture it provides for speeds and bandwidths at 4Mbps or 16Mbps with the future promise of 100Mbps using *fiber distributed data interface* (FDDI). Initially these LANs were implemented over standard telephone lines that exist in corporate office complexes.

The first usage of LANs was for connection purposes. Today data bases on LAN workstations provide vasts amount of information for the users on the LAN. LAN applications are being written that query the local data base or a remote data base that resides on the mainframe. Suddenly, information used by several different areas of a company can be distributed throughout the corporate enterprise. The wave we are about to see is cooperative processing with distributed power. We are just beginning to see the tip of the iceberg when it comes to using LANs and the way business exchanges information.

1.3 COMPARING LAN AND PBX

In corporate offices the phone system is the main means of communicating within the office and to the company's clients. These phone systems are managed by *private branch exchange* (PBX) systems. The PBX is in essence a local telephone exchange on the companies premise. Digital PBXs are capable of switching both voice and data.

For voice communications over a telephone a voice-grade line is needed. This line called a *telephone twisted pair* (TTP) or just twisted pair before the advent of the PBX had a direct connection to the telephone companies central office. This meant that an office with 100 telephones had 100 twisted pairs connecting them to the central office. These twisted pairs were bundled into a large cable commonly called a trunk. The trunk would actually have more than 100 twisted pairs because of backup and other telephone customers that may be using the same trunk. Figure 1.3 illustrates the usage of a PBX.

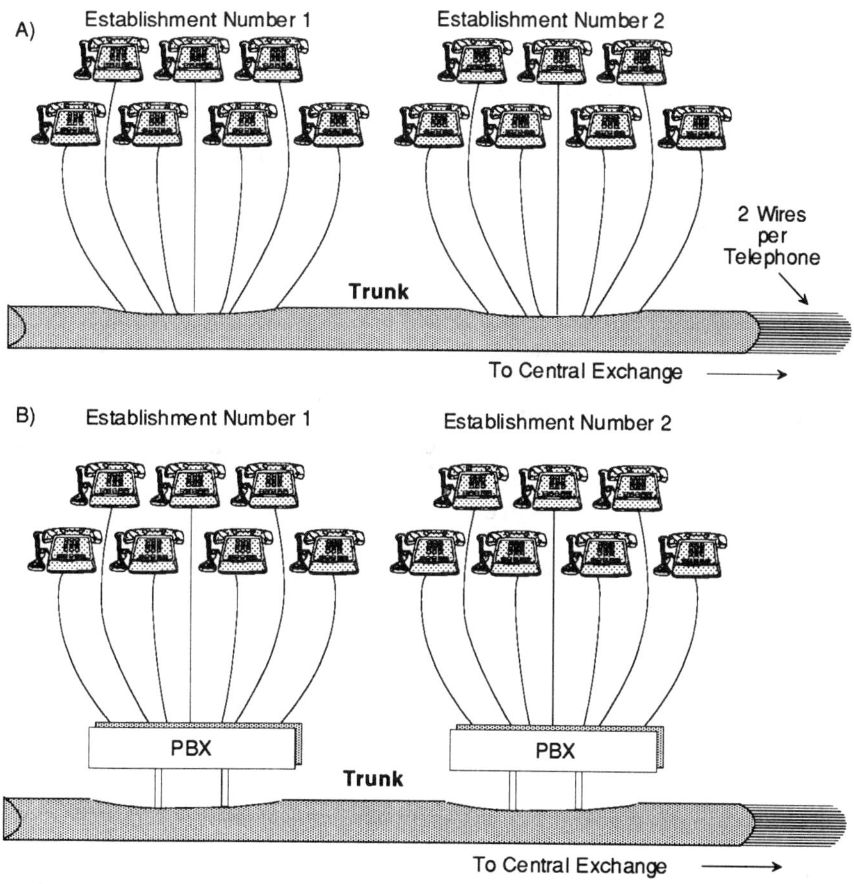

Figure 1.3 Diagram A illustrates telephone connectivity before the use of PBXs. Diagram B illustrates the use of PBXs.

When your boss called you on the phone to request your presence in her office, the call was routed from her telephone to the central office and then back to your telephone. Studies were done to see the actual usage of telephones within the corporate environment and found that the majority of calls were within the office complex. This lead to the development of the PBX.

In the early days of the PBX each telephone in the office was connected to a PBX with a twisted pair as shown in Figure 1.3. The older PBXs were connected to the central office via the trunk but with fewer twisted pairs. These trunk twisted pairs were shared by the entire office. The number of wires in the trunk were determined by the volume of incoming and outgoing calls giving each telephone reasonable access to outside lines. Today's PBXs use state-of-the-art digital technology but the function remains the same, connecting pairs of wires between two telephones.

A PBX uses circuit switching to provide connection rather than packet switching as found in LANs. This limits the user through a PBX to communicate with only one device at a time. LANs differ from a PBX in that devices attached to the LAN share the transmission media. Recall in the previous discussion that voice lines through a PBX use dedicated twisted pairs. LANs are designed for high-speed data transfer while supporting multiple concurrent sessions with other devices.

While the PBX had been designed primarily for voice communications, it can with digital technology provide effective LAN capabilities. Digital PBXs can communicate at rates of up to 64 *thousand bits per second* (Kbps) and accommodate thousands of terminals. This type of scenario is typical of casual connections requiring short connection times. LAN environments with high data requirements and a greater need of resource sharing amongst the LAN workstations offers greater flexibility for connection and performance over a PBX.

1.4 LAN AND WAN

SNA networks dominate the networks of business. These networks however can only operate at fairly low speeds. At first inception, SNA networks were running with 9600bps communication lines. Today SNA can handle direct connection of communications lines at speeds of up to 1 *megabit per second* (Mbps). Compared to local area networks this rate is slow. Local area networks are communicating at speeds of 4Mbps, 16Mbps and soon 100Mbps. LANs, through their high throughput and distributed application proc-

processing, are proving themselves to be more cost effective than the SNA networks of today.

In Figure 1.4 we can see a typical LAN-to-SNA configuration. Together these network configurations create a *wide area network* (WAN). A goal of wide area networking is to provide any-to-any connectivity between a LAN and an SNA network. In this figure, a typical office LAN is connected to an SNA communications controller. The LAN stations are connected to a *multistation access unit* (MAU). The MAU is in turn connected to the SNA communications controller through the controllers *token-ring interface coupler* (TIC). Data can then flow over the SNA backbone network.

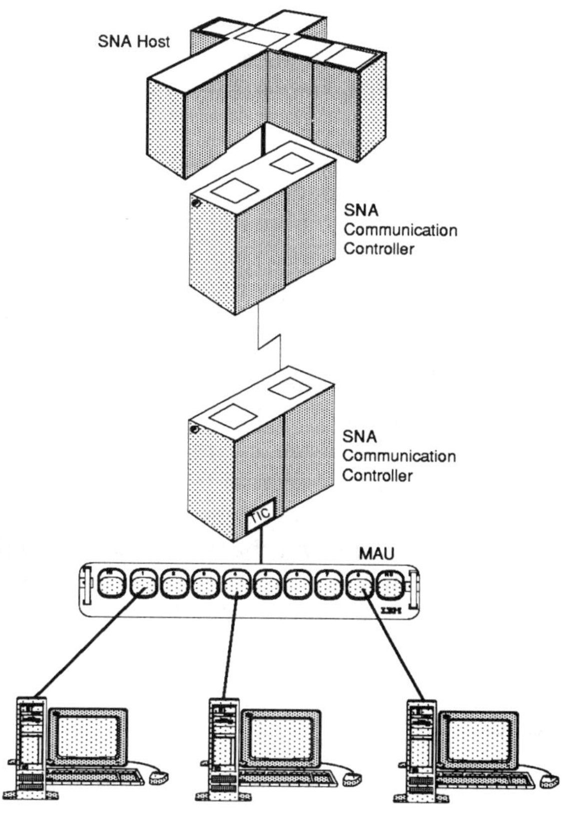

Figure 1.4 The local area network connectivity to an SNA network using a token-ring architecture to create a Wide Area Network (WAN). The token-ring is comprised of the workstations and their connectivity to the MAU and the SNA communications controller and its connection to the MAU.

1.5 CAPABILITIES AND BENEFITS OF A LAN

The main focus for using LANs is the sharing of network resources. As an example, not every workstation requires its own printer or hard disk. In fact many corporate LANs are instituted with diskless workstations. These workstations not only cut the cost of the workstation but inherently prohibit illegal duplication of software and the copying of vital corporate data to diskettes. LANs can also provide better reliability and availability over centrally controlled networks like SNA. Failure of a workstation on the LAN does not disrupt other users on the LAN. LAN workstations provide a robust productive environment. LAN users can use their workstations as stand-alone workstations, share resources on the LAN and be in session with external systems outside of the LAN like an SNA host application all at the same time. The flexibility and functionality of a LAN along with its ease of implementation furnish a dynamic cost-effective and efficient corporate networking environment.

Local area networks utilize a privately owned communications medium. This medium can be twisted-pair, coax or fiber-optic cables, as well as, the possibility of using radio frequencies providing for cabless LANs. These privately owned networks are ideal for single building, multiple building and/or campus situations. LANs needing connection to other LANs over long distances can utilize public communications lines.

Management and problem analysis fall within the scope of the corporate LAN provider. The LAN workstations and attachments themselves must have a degree of intelligence to support LAN protocols and therefore can also provide management and problem determination support using these protocols.

The capabilities, functions and characteristics of LANs provide a full set of features commonly known on an SNA network but with the advantage of improved flexibility, lower cost and increased end-user efficiency.

1.6 PLANNING A LAN

It is not uncommon for corporations to dive head first into implementing LANs without some forethought. When considering using LANs take into account the following:

- Corporate objectives
- Requirements of the end-user community

- An educated estimate on the number and location of workstations and the potential for growth
- Special functions
- Security issues
- Network management including inventory, configuration, problem and change management

Corporate objectives: Many corporations are feeling the squeeze on mainframe processing power. It may be a corporate objective to relieve the mainframe of processing thereby decreasing the cost to expand the mainframe simply for processing power. LANs can provide the answer through distributed and cooperative processing.

Requirements of the end user community: Functions of the LAN user must be determined. What is the objective for providing this end user with a LAN? Is it for interoffice mail? Word processing? Where is the data that this end user needs to perform their daily work activities? Does it reside on their workstation or is it on a LAN server or perhaps at the SNA host system or all three? These and other questions must be answered before implementing the LAN.

Number and location of workstations: The number of workstations, peripherals and their locations greatly affects the topology of the LAN. A large number of resources can dictate the type of cabling system required or influence the size of the LAN. The workload and type of processing needed by the end users influences performance and security and will indicate the need for servers and gateways. To satisfy the end user with good performance it may benefit the end-user community to be divided into work groups or location groups having their own LAN with connectivity to other LANs using bridges or gateways.

Special functions: Based on the end-user requirements, access to various network resources may be needed. These include public switched networks, external data bases residing on inter-LAN servers and/or the host system. If cooperative processing is used then application-to-application communication needs to be considered. If nothing else, plan for backup and recovery of LAN data.

Security issues: This issue can affect the topology and type of LAN implemented. Some corporations divide their large end user groups into small LANs with limited connection to other

LANs in the network. Another possible consideration is the type of protocol and media chosen for the LAN. Security problems may appear on LANs implemented using *carrier sense multiple access/collision detection* (CSMA/CD). In this protocol, data is broadcast simultaneously to all stations on the LAN creating the possibility of unauthorized access to data. This can occur if address uniqueness and acceptance of only frames addressed to this device is not enforced. In token ring the frame is passed serially from one station to another. The receiving station checks the destination address on the frame. If the address matches the stations address, the frame is accepted. If the destination address does not match, then the frame is sent back out over the ring. Duplicate addressing on a token-ring is prohibited by the adapter initialization process instituted by the IEEE 802.5 Token-Ring LAN standards.

Network management: Managing a growing LAN is a rigorous task. Once end-user groups see the advantage of having a LAN, the requests for LAN implementation in new areas will be nonstop. Managing the growth through careful planning in accordance with end-user needs will ease implementation. Tools to monitor the LAN are important in not only problem analysis and resolution but in preventon. Select a monitoring system that enables you to view utilizations of servers, bridges and gateways.

Chapter 2

Token-Ring Network Architecture

In order to understand the underlying architecture that defines a token-ring network we have to understand its origins. The networking architectures that have had the most influence on token-ring are IBM's *systems network architecture* (SNA) and the *international standards organization's* (ISO), *open systems interconnection* (OSI) and finally the IEEE 802 LAN Standards that define the Logical Link Control and Medium Access Control sublayers of the OSI data link layer.

2.1 SYSTEMS NETWORK ARCHITECTURE

SNA laid the ground work for wide area networking since its beginnings in 1974. The corner stone for implementing an SNA network is the *virtual telecommunications access method* (VTAM). VTAM provides communication access for applications that execute on the SNA mainframe. The users of earlier applications resided in close proximity to the mainframe computer. As corporations grew, corporate personnel required access to corporate information from locations remote to the mainframe computer. This lead to the development of a *network control program* (NCP) that executes in a front-end processor such as the IBM 3745 Communications Controller. The NCP offloads the chores of polling, activation and inactivation of networked resources from VTAM.

Corporations became dependent on computing as a means of storing and retrieving vital corporate information. This lead to the requirement of more than one mainframe computer providing the processing power necessary for processing corporate information. This corporate need forged a feature in SNA called multi-system networking fa*cility* (MSNF). This facility was made available to IBM users around 1978. MSNF was incorporated into VTAM V2. MSNF allows for the networking of mainframe computers. Corporate users can access data on any mainframe computer just as long as the mainframe computers are networked.

The expansion of corporate SNA networks outgrew the architected resource limits of SNA itself. This lead to SNA Network Interconnecti*on* (SNI). SNI was incorporated into VTAM V2.2 and NCP V3. This feature provides for the connection of two or more independent SNA networks. Large SNA networks that push the limits of SNA's addressing architecture can be broken into smaller independent networks, while still providing corporate information to the end users, relieving the address constraints.

The SNA address constraints were basically put to rest with VTAM V3 and the introduction of exten*ded network addressing* (ENA). ENA increased the number of addressable SNA resources to a theoretical point where every person on Earth could be provided with an SNA address. This however does not put SNI into retirement. Today SNI is being used by corporations as a means of communicating with other corporate subsidiaries while maintaining security and autonomy for each SNA network.

Throughout the growth of SNA, VTAM maintained centralized control and management of all network resources it activated. Activated resources are said to be owned by VTAM. This activation of network resources describes the boundaries of VTAM's domain. These resources are know as same-domain resources. Resources activated by another VTAM are known as cross-domain resources. Until VTAM V2, all network resources that were either activated or known to VTAM had to be hard coded. That is each resource, cluster controller, terminal, printer and application needed by end users of this VTAM had to be pre-defined to this VTAM, whether they were same-domain or cross-domain resources. For the most part, the latest version of VTAM is still quite static when it comes to recognizing resources within its domain. However, this is the nature of a master-slave relationship. No resource can participate in

VTAM's domain unless VTAM is aware of that resource's existence. The charcteristics of SNA are:

- Hierarchical – no resource can participate until it is pre-defined.
- Static – the network is interrupted when adding or removing resources.
- Routing mechanism is fixed – the routes for destination resources must be defined.

2.1.1 The Seven Layers of SNA

SNA is a proprietary seven-layer networking architecture developed by IBM. Figure 2.1 diagrams the SNA layers . From top to bottom they are:

Transaction Services: This top layer of SNA is where applications reside. Applications are programs that execute on the mainframe computer providing services to the end user. These services entail the receipt and delivery of data to and from the data's origin.

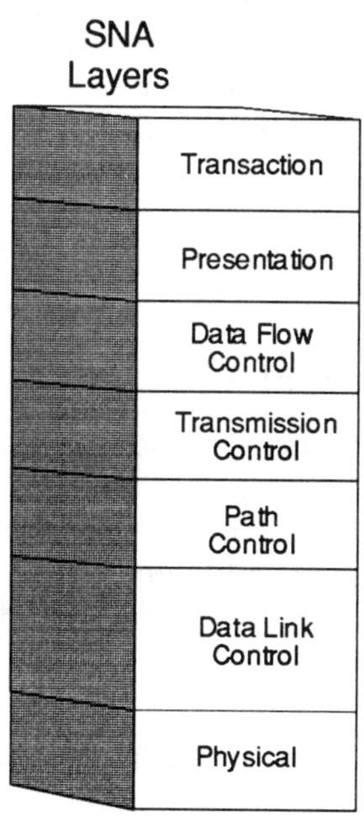

Figure 2.1 The seven layers of IBM's SNA.

Presentation Services: This layer presents the data delivered or received by the application layer. Its main concern is the representation of the data to another application or an end user. The services provided in this layer are 3270 data stream support, intelligent printer data stream support, and program-to-program communications protocols. It also provides the controlling mechanism for conversational communications between transaction programs.

Data Flow Control: This layer assigns sequence numbers, correlates requests and responses, enforces session request and session response mode protocols and coordinates session send and receive modes between SNA logical units (LU). SNA LUs are applications and logical representations for terminals and printers.

Transmission Control: The verification of sequence numbers and managing session level pacing set forth by the Data Flow Control is provided by the transmission control layer.

Path Control: The path control layer provides the protocols needed for routing SNA *path information units* (PIU) through an SNA network and SNA networks utilizing SNI.

Data Link Control: This layer controls the transfer of PIUs between two SNA nodes over a physical link. It also provides link-level flow control and error recovery. This layer supports System/370 and System/390 data channel, X.25, IEEE 802.2 and IEEE 802.5 protocols.

Physical Control: This last layer defines the physical interfaces used over the transmission medium. These definitions include the physical signaling attributes to establish, maintain and terminate physical connectivity.

Throughout SNA's evolution updates have been orchestrated with international standards. IBM's implementation of the IEEE 802.2 and IEEE 802.5 LAN standards allowed IBM to develop the IBM Token-Ring Network augmenting SNA. The international standard that fostered the IEEE LAN standards is Open Systems Interconnection.

2.2 UNDERSTANDING OPEN SYSTEMS INTERCONNECTION

In 1977 ISO established a working group with the charter of developing the Open Systems Interconnection Reference Model. ISO identified a worldwide requirement for computer systems from all vendors to connect, exchange data and communicate intelligently. The result is a set of international standards that are public domain and not specific to any vendor's hardware or software operating systems. In short, non-proprietary. The reference model is defined to have seven layers, protocols and basic commands. It is this set of standards that is known as *open systems interconnection* (OSI).

The layered concept deals with the constantly changing nature of standards and the products they employ. Systems that adhere to the OSI standards are said to be open to one another and thus are called Open Systems. Figure 2.2 identifies the seven laayers of the OSI reference model and the services each layer provides and receives from adjacent layers. Each layer in an open system communicates with its equal in another open system by using protocols defined in OSI. It is OSI's modularity and flexibility to changes based on non-proprietary standards that will thrust it into the mainstream in the mid-1990s.

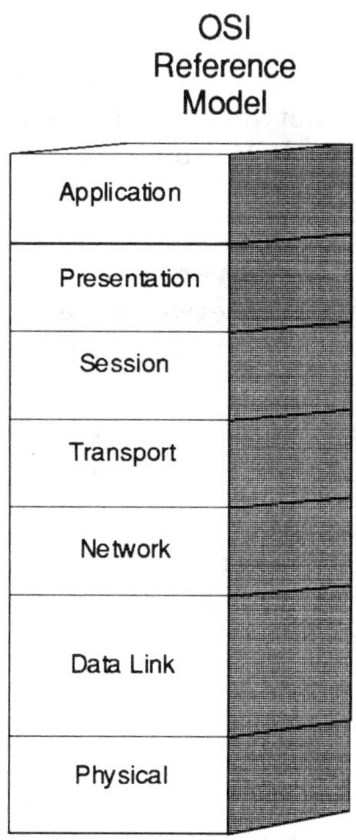

Figure 2.2 The seven layers of the OSI Reference Model.

2.2.1 The Seven Layers of OSI

The OSI Reference Model was accepted by ISO as an international standard in 1983. Again, as in SNA, the architectutre is described from top to bottom. The seven layers provide the following functions and services:

Application Layer: This layer supports semantic exchanges between applications existing in open systems. This layer also provides access to the lower OSI functions and services.

Presentation Layer: Just as in SNA, this layer concerns itself with the representation of the data to the end user or application. This includes data conversions and code translations (e.g., ASCII to EBCDIC).

Session Layer: This layer provides the mechanism for organizing and structuring interaction between applications and/or devices.

Transport Layer: This layer is responsible for transparent and reliable transfer of data. The lower layers handle the attributes of the transfer medium.

Network Layer: This layer is the agent for establishing connections between networks. The standards also include operational control procedures for inter-network communications as well as routing information through multiple networks.

Data Link Layer: This layer provides the functions and protocols to transfer data between network resources and to detect errors that may occur in the physical layer.

Physical Layer: This layer defines the mechanical, electrical, functional and procedural standards for the physical transmission of data over the communications medium.

The key to OSI is the adherence to the standard interfaces between the layers. As long as these standards are met different implementations can satisfy the OSI Reference Model.

2.2.2 The Importance of Open Systems and Standards

Today's information systems are based on networking architectures that are proprietary in nature. The reason for this is quite obvious. Once a network architecture is chosen, the selected vendor's customer is virtually locked into buying products from that vendor or vendors that have developed products to meet the selected vendor's networking architecture. This severely limits the users selection of hardware, operating systems and applications, including communications, networking equipment and services.

The OSI model provides a means for corporations to breakaway from the proprietary constraints that they have lived with for so long. The selection process for users is now wide open. Vendors must compete on equal ground for income. A standard networking platform that all vendors can develop to will inspire them to come up with software and hardware that will provide solutions to the business need rather than the business need being fit to the vendors solution. A case in point is the plethora of products adhering to the IEEE 802 LAN standards.

The *institute of electrical and electronic engineers* (IEEE) Computer Society established in the winter of 1980 the data link and physical standards for local area networks. Figure 2.3 shows the IEEE 802 standard that implements local area networking into the two lower layers of SNA and OSI as shown in . The data link layer

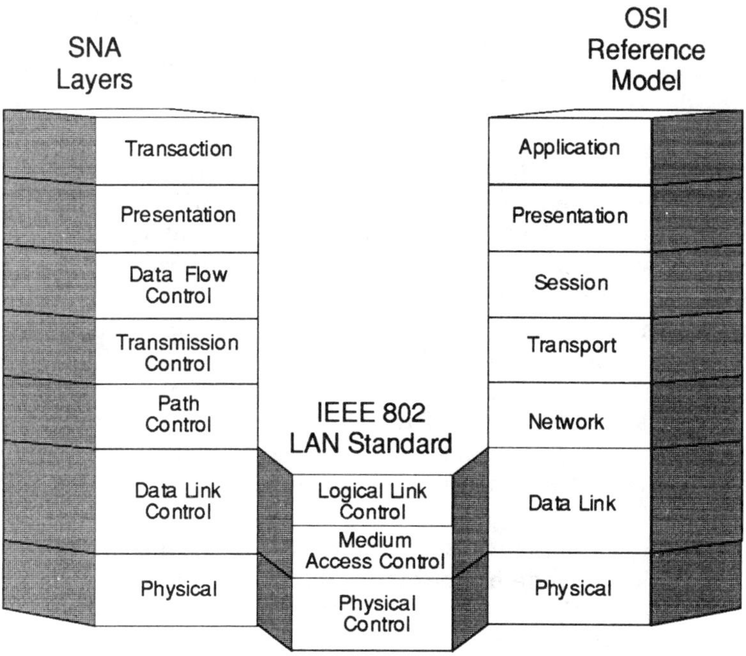

Figure 2.3 The IEEE 802 LAN Standard and the relationship to SNA and OSI.

for the IEEE 802 LAN standard is subdivided into two sublayers. These are the IEEE 802.2 standard for *logical link control* (LLC) and the IEEE 802.5 standard for token-ring *medium access control* (MAC).

2.3 LOGICAL LINK CONTROL SUBLAYER

The logical link control sublayer is IEEE 802.2. The LLC has two accepted types of operational procedures and a proposed third:

- Type 1 — connectionless
- Type 2 — connection oriented
- Type 3 — acknowledged connectionless

Together these three types of operations provide link-level services for applications.

Connectionless Operation. In this mode of operation a logical data link connection is not established between the LAN stations before transmitting information frames. The LLC does not guarantee delivery of the information unit. Using this mode of operation there is no flow control, correlation between frames, error recovery or acknowledgement of receipt of the information frame. These services must be provided by upper-layer services.

Connection Oriented. In this mode of operation a logical data link is established prior to transmitting an information unit. This operation creates a LLC type 2 control block. The control block in association with delivery and error recovery services constitute a link station. The LLC type 2 service provides sequence numbering of information frames at the data link layer, error detection and basic recovery and flow control including acknowledgement. The LLC type 2 acknowledgement allows for a window size of up to 127 outstanding frames sent before expecting an acknowledgement from the receiving station. This is also known as modulus 128.

Acknowledged Connectionless. This is the proposed method of operation. This mode of operation does not require a connection before transmitting information units. However, it does expect link-level acknowledgements from the destination station. This type of operation is particularly useful in LANs that may have high bursts of traffic like those used with file servers and backbone connectivity.

There are two classes of LLC operations defined in the IEEE 802.2 standard:

1. Class I — connectionless only
2. Class II — connectionless and connection oriented

All stations support connectionless operations. Only class II stations support type 1, type 2 and type 3 modes of operation.

The logical link control sublayer has three main functions:

1. A specification to interfacing with the network layer above.
2. Logical link control procedures.
3. A specification to interface with the medium access control sublayer below.

The interface specification to the network layer defines the calls for unacknowledged connectionless service. This type of service allows stations to exchange information units without establishing a connection or acknowledgements. This is also known as a datagram. The LLC sublayer also provides a connected service as an option to the network layer.

Service access points (SAP) provide the interface between the application and the logical link control. Each SAP is uniquely architected for an application existing on a specific device type. A main function of the SAP is to allow multiple applications executing on a device to access the token-ring network through a single connection or adapter. Service access points support connectionless and connection oriented transmission. Figure 2.4 contains a table of assigned SAPs by IEEE and IBM.

2.3.1 LLC Protocol Data Unit

The logical link control frame, shown in Figure 2.5, is comprised of four fields. These fields together are called the *logical link control protocol data unit* (LPDU).

The first field of the LPDU is the *destination service access point* (DSAP) address. This field is one byte in length and identifies the value of the service access point this LPDU is destined. The DSAP is broken down where the first six bits represent the SAP address. The seventh bit indicates whether this address is user-defined or defined by the IEEE LAN standards. The final bit indicates to the receiving station whether this SAP address is an individual address or a group address.

The next field in the LPDU is the *source service access point* (SSAP) address field. This field identifies the SAP address of the originating SAP. This field is also one byte in length and is used in much the same manner as the DSAP. The first six bits specify the SSAP address and the seventh indicates if the address was assigned by the IEEE LAN standard or the by the user. The final bit identifies this LPDU as either being a command frame or a response frame.

I/G U	IBM HEX	DEFINITION
IEEE SAPs	U bit = 1	
0 0 00 0000	X'00'	Null SAP
0 1 00 0000	X'02'	LLC Sublayer Management
0 1 00 bbbb	X'x2'	Network Management Function
1 1 00 0000	X'03'	Group LLC Sublayer Management
0 1 10 0000	X'06'	D.O.D. Internet
0 1 10 bbbb	X'x6'	National Standards Bodies
0 1 11 0000	X'0E'	Proway Network Management — Maintenance and Initialization
0 1 11 0010	X'4E'	Manufacturing Message Service (MMS)
0 1 11 1110	X'7E'	ISO 8208 (X.25 PLP)
0 1 11 0001	X'8E'	Proway Active Station List Maintenance
0 1 11 1111	X'FE'	OSI Network Layer Protocols
0 1 01 0101	X'AA'	Subnetwork Access Protocol (SNAP)
0 1 00 0010	X'42'	Bridge Spanning Tree Protocol
1 1 11 1111	X'FF'	Global SAP
bbbb can be anything except B'0000'		
IBM defined SAP values U bit = 1		
0 0 10 0000	X'04'	SNA Path Control Individual
1 0 10 0000	X'05'	SNA Path Control Group
0 0 00 1111	X'F0'	NETBIOS
0 0 10 1111	X'F4'	LAN Management Individual
1 0 10 1111	X'F5'	LAN Management Group
0 0 01 1111	X'F8'	IMPL
0 0 11 1111	X'FC'	Discovery
0 0 11 1011	X'DC'	Dynamic Address Resolution (Name Mngmt)
0 0 10 1011	X'D4'	Resource Management

Figure 2.4 The table of Service Access Point code points defined by IEEE and IBM.

The third field of the LPDU is the control field. This field has three formats: the *information format* (I-format), the *supervisory format* (S-format) and the *unnumbered format* (U-format). Figure 2.6 outlines these formats.

The information format (I-format) contains application level data. Each LPDU is sequentially numbered for the next send and receive LPDU. Each I-format LPDU is sequentially numbered from 0–127. The maximum number of unacknowledged I-formats at any given time cannot exceed 127. The POLL/FINAL bit is set to poll (B'0') in a command LPDU and to final (B'1') in a response LPDU. The poll/final bit is set to poll when requesting the remote link station to send a response with the final bit set. Before a link station can issue a second poll I-format to the remote link station the first poll must be answered. Normally the link station sends an I-format with the poll bit set to B'0'.

The supervisory *format* (S-format) LPDUs are used to acknowledge I-format LPDUs, request re-transmissions and temporarily suspend transmission of I-format LPDUs. The S-format LPDUs do not have an information field since they are really denoting the status of the link station. The S-format of the LPDU control field is two bytes in length. The first byte identifies this LPDU as a supervisory frame. The second byte indicates the transmitter receive sequence number and the value of the POLL/FINAL bit.

The supervisory frame has three command and response types. The first is the *receiver-ready* (RR) command and response. The supervisory bits are set to binary zero (B'00'). This RR command

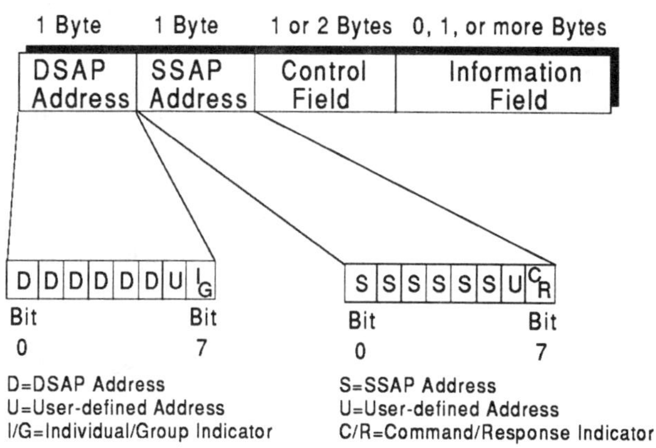

Figure 2.5 The format of the LPDU and a break out of the destination and Source Access Point fields.

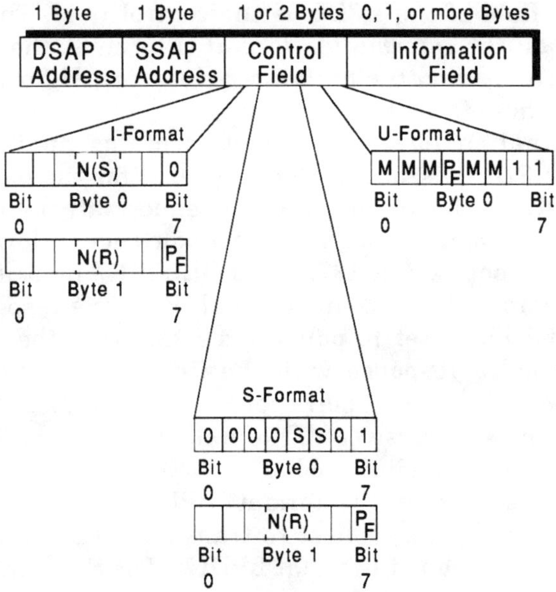

Figure 2.6 The three formats of the LPDU control field.

and response is used to notify other link stations that this link station is ready to receive another I-format LPDU. The transmitter receive sequence number indicates that all I-format LPDUs up to this sequence number have been successfully received by the link station. Another function of the RR command and response S-format LPDU is to indicate that a busy link station is now available to accept I-format LPDUs.

The link station indicates that it cannot receive I-format LPDUs by issuing the *receiver-not-ready* (RNR) command and response S-format LPDU. The supervisory bits are set to B'01' and the transmitter receive sequence number indicates that I-format LPDUs up to this sequence number have been successfully received prior to the busy or slow-down condition that forced the RNR S-format LPDU to be transmitted by this link station. LPDUs sent to the busy link station are not considered to have been sent successfully and will have to be retransmitted by the sending link station.

A busy sending link station can indicate that the busy condition has cleared by issuing the third command and response type of the S-format LPDU. This is the *reject* (REJ) command and response. A link station uses the REJ S-format LPDU to request retransmissions of I-format LPDUs starting with the sequence number indicated by the transmitter receive sequence number bits. I-format LPDUs transmitted up to but not including this value are considered to have been received successfully by the link station. The link station sending the I-format LPDU requested can send any additional I-format LPDUs that have been queued after sending the requested I-format LPDU. The architecture allows for only one sent RJE to be outstanding in any direction. The REJ condition is cleared when the link station receives an I-format LPDU with a send sequence number equal to the next receive sequence number.

The final LPDU control field format is the unnumbered format (U-format). This format is used to send additional control functions and data transfer functions. The control field is one byte in length and contains five bits that indicate the function. These are called modifier bits. The POLL/FINAL bit is found at bit 4. Bits 6 and 7 are always set to B'1'. Figure 2.7 contains a table identifying the various values for the modifier bits and the command or response.

Disconnect mode (DM) response is used by a link station to indicate that it is logically disconnected from the link. There is no information field in a DM response LPDU.

Disconnect (DISC) command is used to terminate asynchronous balanced mode operations set by a SABME command. This command is issued by a link station to a remote link station that this link station is suspending operation of the link and that the remote link station should begin asynchronous disconnected

M Bit Values		Command or Response
0 0 0	1 1	DM Response
0 1 0	0 0	DISC Command
0 1 1	0 0	UA Response
0 1 1	1 1	SABME Command
1 0 0	0 1	FRMR Response
1 0 1	1 1	XID Command or Response
1 1 1	0 0	TEST Command or Response

Figure 2.7 The list of unnumbered format commands and responses in an LPDU.

mode. The remote link station will then issue an unnumbered acknowledgement (UA) response if it is in asynchronous balanced mode or a DM response if it is in asynchronous disconnected mode of operation.

Unnumbered acknowledgement (UA) response is issued to acknowledge a SABME or DISC command LPDU. This UA response does not contain an information field.

Set asynchronous balanced mode extended (SABME) command is used to start data transfer in the extended asynchronous balanced mode of operation with the remote link station. The remote link station receiving the SABME command must issue an UA response. The remote link station then sets the send and receive variables to hexadecimal zero (X'00') and assumes the asynchronous balanced mode extended operation. Once the link station that issued the SABME receives a UA response from the remote link station it also sets its send and receive variables to X'00' and assumes asynchronous balanced mode extended operations. The remote link station can however reject the SABME command with a DM response LPDU. The SABME does not contain an information field.

Frame reject (FRMR) response is used by link stations to notify the sending link station that an LPDU was received in error. The error is detailed in a five-byte information field found in this FRMR response. Figure 2.8 outlines the format of the information

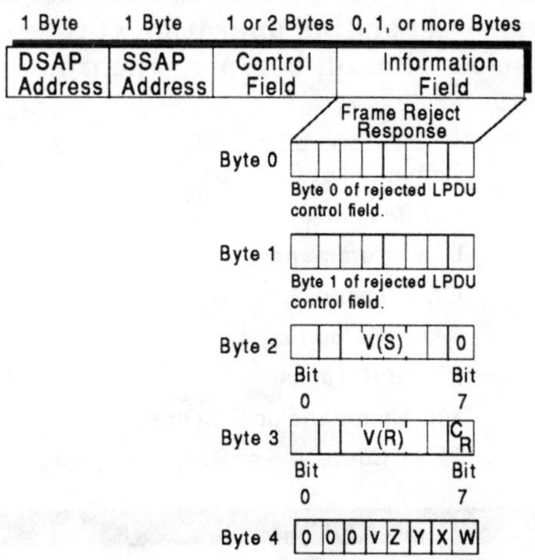

Figure 2.8 The frame reject information field format in an LPDU.

field. Byte 0 and byte 1 are copies of the control field that was received in the LPDU that was found to be in error. If the rejected LPDU control field was a U-format, byte 1 will be set to all X'00'. The third byte (byte 2) contains the *send-state variable* (V(S)) value for this link as set by the rejecting link station. The V(S) value is the next-in-sequence number for an I-format LPDU that is to be transmitted. The fourth byte (byte 3) is the *receive-state variable* (V(R)) value as known by the rejecting link station. The V(R) value is the next-in-sequence number for an I-format LPDU that is to be received on the link. Appendix A contains a list and description of control-state variables. The *command / response* (C/R) bit is set to B'0' if the reject LPDU was a command and B'1' if the rejected LPDU was a response. The remaining fifth byte (byte 4) of the FRMR response information field contains the reason for the rejection in the last five bits. Bit 3 of byte 4 identifies the reason for the reject is an invalid send sequence number. Bit 4 of byte 4 indicates the reject was caused by an invalid receive sequence number. Bit 5 of byte 4 identifies the length of the information field in the received I-format LPDU to be greater than the available buffer capacity causing the link station to reject the I-format LPDU. Bit 6 of byte 4 may have two reasons. The first being that the rejected LPDU had an information field and the control field indicated that it should not have or that the rejected LPDU was itself a FRMR response but its information field was not 5 bytes long. Bit 7 of byte 4 indicates that the rejected LPDU was invalid or unsupported. Unsupported LPDUs are: *Set Normal Response Mode* (SNRM) and *Set Asynchronous Response Mode* (SARM). Invalid LPDUs are: S-format or U-format LPDUs that have an information field and a UA response LPDU received without a corresponding SABME or DISC LPDU being sent.

Exchange identification (XID) command is used to carry identification and characteristics of the sending link station causing the remote link station to respond with an XID response LPDU. This command was included in the IBM Token-Ring Network implementation of the IEEE 802.2 standards to support SNA. Figure 2.9 details the IBM XID format utilized by the IBM Token-Ring Network implementation. Byte 0 of the XID is always set to a X'81' indicating that this XID follows the IEEE 802.2 Basic Format for an XID information field. Byte 1 bits 0 through 2 are reserved for future use by IEEE and are currently transmitted as B'000'. The remaining bits, 3 through 7, of byte 1 identify the class of service supported by the XID sender. A value of B'00001' indicates that the sender supports

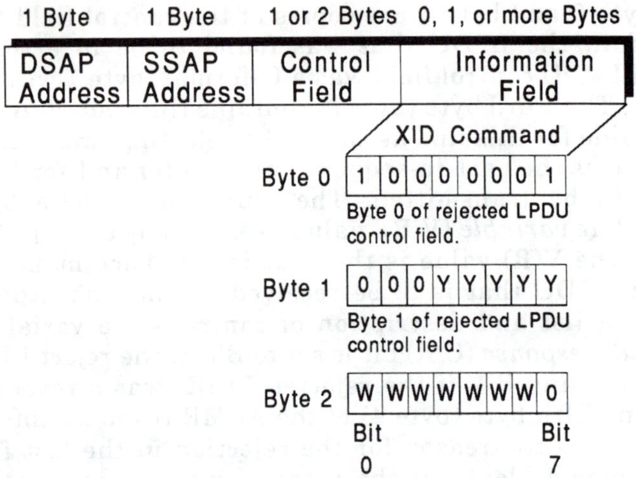

Figure 2.9 The format of the exchange identification command in an LPDU.

connectionless service only. A value of B'00011' indicates that the sender supports both connectionless and connection-oriented services. Byte 2 (bits 0–6) specify the maximum receive window size value of the XID sender. Bit 7 of byte 2 is reserved for future IEEE use and is currently transmitted as a B'0'. The remote link stations response to this XID command must always be an IEEE 802.2 XID response containing the above information.

Test com*mand* is used by the link station to perform a basic test of link station-to-link station connectivity. The test command can contain an optional information field of test characters that are returned by the remote link station to determine connection solidity in a test response. This command was also included by IBM in their implementation of the IEEE 802.2 standards to support SNA.

The final field of the LPDU is the information field. This field found on the I-format will contain, if present, higher layer protocols and user data. For example, an SNA pa*th information unit* (PIU) is inserted into the information field when token ring is being used as the transmission architecture over an SNA WAN. For a detailed chart on LAN-based communication protocols see Appendix B.

The above discussion covered connection-oriented service. Connectionless service however is quite different and is considerably streamlined as compared to connection-oriented service. Recall that connectionless service does not require data-link connection, hence there are no link stations in connectionless service. Communications are established using three unnumbered LPDU formats. These are XID, test and *unnumbered information* (UI) command or response. Connectionless uses XID and test in the same manner as described for connection-oriented. The UI command is used to transmit unsequenced data. This puts the responsibility of resequencing of data, error recovery and re-transmission of data on the application.

In summary, logical link control (LLC) is concerned with the delivery of information. LLC in conjunction with connection-oriented service uses *service access points* (SAP) to enable multiple applications to share a single connection to the LAN. Connection-oriented service utilizes link stations to manage the logical connections providing an extensive error recovery mechanism for maintaining data integrity. Connectionless service on the other hand provides no error recovery or guarantee of successful data transport.

2.4 MEDIUM ACCESS CONTROL SUBLAYER

Communications between stations on a token ring requires an addressing mechanism that will guarantee that each station address on a token ring is unique. This is needed to ensure receipt and delivery of information to and from the source and destination stations on a token ring. The *medium access control* (MAC) sublayer provides this addressing mechanism to control the transmission of data so that only one station is transmitting at any given time. The MAC determines whether a station on the token ring is in transmit, repeats to receive state and controls the routing of data over the LAN. The main functions of the MAC are:

Addressing. The MAC address is the physical address of the station's device adapter on a LAN. Recognition of the stations address found in the physical header of a MAC frame. Each station on a token ring must be able to recognize its own MAC address and an all-stations (broadcast) address or a null address for frames which are not to be received by the station. The MAC address identifies the physical destination and source of any frame transmitted over the token ring.

Frame copying. After MAC has recognized its own address, meaning that the frame received has this device's MAC address as the destination address, MAC uses this function to copy the frame from the token ring into the device adapter buffers.

Frame recognition. This function determines the type of frame received and the frames format. For instance, a system or user frame.

Frame deliminating. The MAC must determine the beginning and ending of a frame. This is performed during transmission or receipt of a frame.

Frame status generation and verification. This provides the checking and verification of frame check sequence bits and the frame status field in each frame to determine if transmission errors have occurred.

Priority management. This function warrants fairness of access to the token-ring medium based on priority by issuing priority level tokens for all participating stations on a token ring.

Routing. This determines which function in a node should process the frame.

Timing. This keeps track of timers utilized by the MAC management protocols.

Token (LAN) management. This is used to monitor the LAN using management protocols to handle error conditions at the access control level.

2.4.1 MAC Frame Format

A frame is the *basic transmission unit* (BTU) for the IBM Token-Ring Network. These frames are composed of several fields each 1 byte or more in length. Figure 2.10 details the MAC frame format. The high-order byte (byte 0) is transmitted first and the high-order bit within each byte is transmitted first. In other words, from left to right as indicated in Figure 2.10. The frame is composed of two sections with an optional section for information. The first section, the physical header, contains the *starting delimiter* (SD), the *access control field* (AC), the *frame control field* (FC), the destination and source address field and an optional routing information field. The second section of the MAC frame, the physical trailer, contains the *frame check sequence* (FCS), the *ending delimiter* (ED) and the

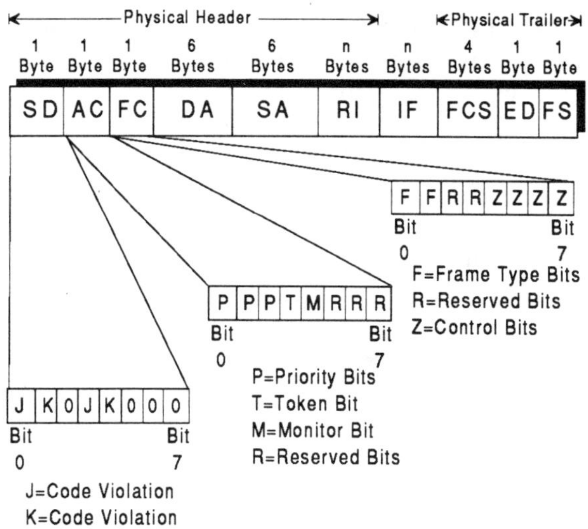

Figure 2.10 The medium access control frame format.

frame status field (FS).

Starting Delimiter (SD). Figure 2.10 depicts the format for the single byte SD field of the MAC frame. Token-ring frames and the tokens themselves are valid only when they are found with the combination of bits as shown in Figure 2.10. The J and K values in the figure identify code violation bits that define the byte as the starting delimiter of a frame. These code violation bits are determined using the differential Manchester code technique. Details on this are found in Appendix C.

Access Control (AC) Field. This one-byte field (Figure 2.10) utilizes all of its 8 bits to denote the access required by the frame on the LAN. The first three bits define the priority of a token or a frame. There are a total of eight priority levels ranging from the lowest (B'000') to the highest (B'111'). For more information on how these access priority bits are used, see Chapter 3 (IBM Token-Ring Concepts).

The fourth bit (bit 3) of the access priority field indicates whether the BTU is a token or a frame. If the BTU is a token then this bit is set to B'0'. If the BTU is a token-ring frame then this bit is set to B'1'.

The next bit, (bit 4) in Figure 2.10, is the monitor bit. A value of B'0' is always found in every transmitted frame or token. When a station claims the token it becomes the active monitor. The active monitor sets the monitor bit to a B'1'. The active monitor does this when it repeats the frame or the token priority is greater than B'000'. The active monitor sends the frame to the destination station. If the frame is returned with the monitor bit set to B'1' the active monitor purges the token or frame from the ring and issues a new token. This process prevents tokens with a non-zero priority and frames from being continuously transmitted around the ring.

The final three bits (bits 5–7) are used to reserve high-access priority for a token. There are eight reservation levels defined by these reservation bits. The lowest (B'000') to the highest (B'111'). More information on the reservation bits use can be found in the following chapter.

Frame Con*trol Field*: Figure 2.10 details this single byte field. The frame control field identifies the type of frame, including specific MAC and information frame functions. There are three categories of bits found in this field. These categories are: frame type, reserved and control.

The first two bits (bits 0–1) are designated as frame type bits.There are currently two types of frames that can be identified with these bits. They are the MAC and LLC frames. The bit values B'00' indicate that this frame is a MAC frame. Bit values of B'01' identify this frame as being a LLC frame. Bit values of B'10' and B'11' are presently undefined frame types and reserved for future use.

The next two bits (bits 2–3) are reserved bits and are not currently used. Their values are transmitted as B'00' and ignored by receiving stations.

The last four bits (bits 4–7) are the control bits of the frame control field. If a MAC frame is indicated then all stations that have an individual or group address that matches the destination address of the frame will copy the MAC frame into the adapter's buffers in accordance with the control bit values. If LLC frames are indicated then the control bits are not used and have a value of X'0'. Receiving stations do not interrogate the control bits of an LLC frame.

Destination Address (DA): The destination address field is always six bytes in length and is formatted as shown in Figure 2.11. Each byte is 8 bits in length. The first bit of the first byte (bit 0 of byte 0) indicates whether this destination address is an individual or group address. An individual address is denoted by the bit value of B'0'. A group address is identified when this bit, also referred to as the I/G bit, is set to B'1'. The second bit of

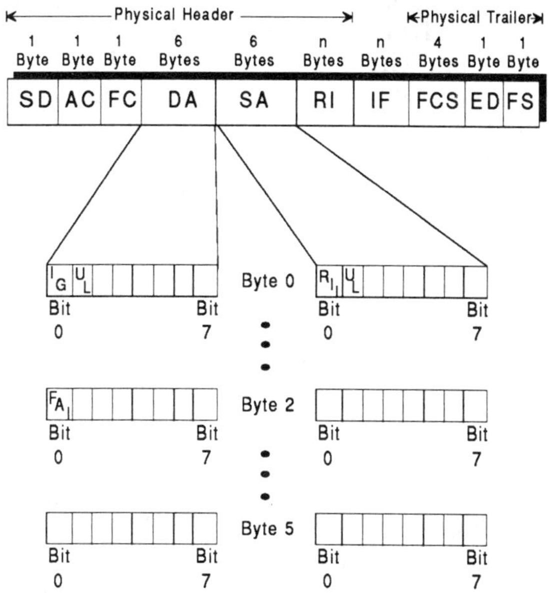

Figure 2.11 The destination and source address field formats of the MAC frame.

byte 0 (bit 1) is called the U/L bit. A B'0' value for this bit indicates that the address was defined by the manufacturer. A value of B'1' identifies the address as being defined by the end user or LAN administrator and is referred to as locally administered. A destination address of all B'1' is called an all-stations broadcast. This means that every station on the network in accordance with the routing information field will make a copy of the frame.

The first bit of the third byte (bit 0 of byte 2) specifies whether this locally administered group address is a functional (B'0') or group (B'1') address. This bit is also referred to as the functional address indicator.

Source Address (SA): Source addresses, like destination addresses, are always six bytes in length with each byte being 8 bits in length. Bit 0 of byte 0 in the source address field is called the *routing information indicator* (RII) bit. This bit is set to a B'1' if the routing information field is present and B'0' if the routing information field is not present. Bit 1 of byte 0 in the source addressing field is also the *universal/locally* (U/L) administered bit indicator. Its function is the same as that found in the destination address field.

Routing Information (RI) Field: This is an optional field and is used only when the frame is going to leave the originating token ring or source ring. There are two fields that comprise the RI field. These are the route control field and the route designator. Each is two bytes in length. The route control field is followed by up to eight route designator fields. Routing performed in this fashion is also called source routing. The format of the RI field is detailed in Figure 2.12.

The routing control field has five categories assigned to the bit values. These are: broadcast indicators, length, direction, largest frame and reserved.

Broadcast indicators originate at bit 0 of byte 0 for three bits (bits 0–2). There are three types of broadcast. The first is a non-broadcast indication (B'0??'). This value specifies that the route designator field contains a specific path for the frame to follow to reach its destination. The second type of broadcast is the all-routes broadcast. All-routes broadcast is identified with the values B'10?'. This indicates that all known routes in the network be used to transmit this frame to the destination address. The destination station will receive a copy of the frame for every successful route traversed to the destination station. For instance, if there are four different possible routes to a destination station and all routes are operative,

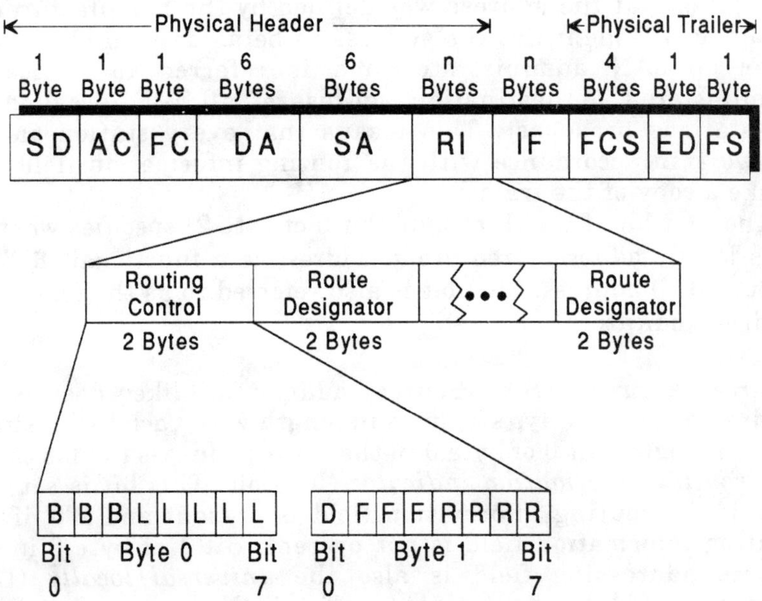

Figure 2.12 The routing information field and the routing control subfield.

then the destination station will receive four copies of the frame. An all-routes broadcast indicates that every bridge in the network will copy and forward the frame to the adjoining LAN segment or to the next route designator found in the routing information field. The third and final type of broadcast indicator is the single-route broadcast (B'11?'). This field specifies that the frame will be routed to specific bridges and then relayed from one segment to another with the intent that the frame will have traveled on every segment in the network one time. The '?' indicates that these bits can have any value since they are not interrogated.

The broadcast indicator bits are followed by five length bits. When a station receives a frame it must know how to parse the frame into its fields. The length bits in the routing control field indicate the length in bytes of the routing information field. The maximum length of the routing information field is 18 bytes (2 bytes routing control + (2 bytes routing designator * 8)).

All-routes and single-route broadcast frames have an initial value of hexadecimal 2 (X'2'). This is to indicate the length of the routing control field itself. As the frame crosses bridges the length bits are modified by the bridge to reflect the added route designator field(s). The first bridge to forward an all-routes broadcast adds a X'4' to the length bits. This is to reflect the source segment number and the segment number of the next ring. After this, every bridge appends a single route designator and updates the length field by X'2'. Since the total number of route designators in the route information field is eight, a frame cannot traverse more than seven LAN segments before reaching the destination address. If the length bits indicate that the length is an odd number of bytes, or less that 2 bytes or greater than 18 bytes the bridge will not forward the frame.

Non-broadcast frames already have a completed routing information field and therefore the length bits remain constant as the frame travels through the network.

The direction bit of the routing control field indicates to the bridge the order in which to interpret the route designator fields. A value of B'0' tells the bridge to interpret the route designator fields from left to right. This indicates that the frame is being transmitted from the originating station. A value of B'1' for this bit indicates that the bridge should interpret the route designator fields from right to left indicating that the frame is being transmitted from the target station.

Largest frame bits specifies the largest-size information field that can be transmitted between stations on a specific route. Stations originate a broadcast frame with the largest frame bits set to all ones B'111'. Bridges examine these bits. If the B'111' value is larger than the capability of the route at that bridge, the bridge will modify the largest frame bits to a suitable value that will allow a large information field along the with physical header and trailer to traverse the network. Figure 2.13 contains a table on the largest frame code points and their values.

The remaining four bits of the route control field of the routing information field are reserved for future use by IBM.

The second field of the RI field is the route designator field. This field is made up of two bytes. The first 12 bits of the two bytes indicate the ring number and the last 4 bits indicate the bridge number. Each ring is assigned a network wide unique number. Any bridge attached to the same ring can have the same ring number. Bridges attached to different rings have different ring numbers. Each bridge is assigned a number. The bridge number can be the same for bridges attached to the same ring. However, bridges attached to the same two rings must have unique bridge numbers. Bridging in this manner is called parallel bridging. It is the ring number that guarantees a unique route designator.

When a bridge receives a frame from the ring it interprets the route designator fields. The bridge compares the route designator field values with its attached ring number and its own bridge number. The following occurs:

- A bridge throws away a non-broadcast frame if no match is found.

BYTE 1 BITS 1- 3	DESCRIPTION
000	As many as 516 bytes in the information field.
001	As many as 1500 bytes in the information field.
010	As many as 2052 bytes in the information field.
011	As many as 4472 bytes in the information field.
100	As many as 8144 bytes in the information field.
101	As many as 11407 bytes in the information field.
110	As many as 17800 bytes in the information field.
111	Used in all-routes broadcast frames.

Figure 2.13 List of the largest valid frame code points for bits 1-3 of byte 1 in the routing control field.

- A bridge adds its route designator information when no ring number match is found on an all-route and single-route broadcast and forwards the frame.
- A bridge will discard an all-route or single-route frame if a target ring number match is found because the frame has completed a trip around the target ring.
- A bridge will forward a non-broadcast frame to the target ring after finding a match on the ring number and bridge number.

The last route designator field in the routing information field will not contain a bridge number. This is because the end of a route is the target ring number.

Information Field: The information field follows the route designator field. The information field for a MAC frame will contain MAC control information. The MAC control information contains a major vector length followed by the major vector identifier. Appendix D lists the MAC major vectors and a brief description of each. If this frame had been denoted as a LLC frame, then the information field would contain end user data. The LLC information is also called a logical link control protocol data unit (LPDU). See the previous discussion on LPDU.

Frame Check Sequence: This four-byte value is created using an algorithm that covers the frame control field, destination and source addresses, the optional routing information field and information field, and the frame check sequence itself. The algorithm results in the four byte cyclic redundancy check value placed in the frame check sequence field by the originating station. The frame check sequence is accumulated with the first bit of the frame control field through the last bit of the frame check sequence field. The frame type determines the position of the frame check sequence field and therefore the protection guaranteed by cyclic redundancy checking.

End Delimiter: The one byte end delimiter field will indicate code violations, errors or that this fame is one of many associated frames being transmitted. The first six bits must be found as depicted in Figure 2.15 to denote this as the ending delimiter. The values for these six bits is determined by using the differential Manchester Code as described in Appendix C.

The intermediate bit indicates whether this frame is the first or one of many intermediate frames of a multiple-frame transmission

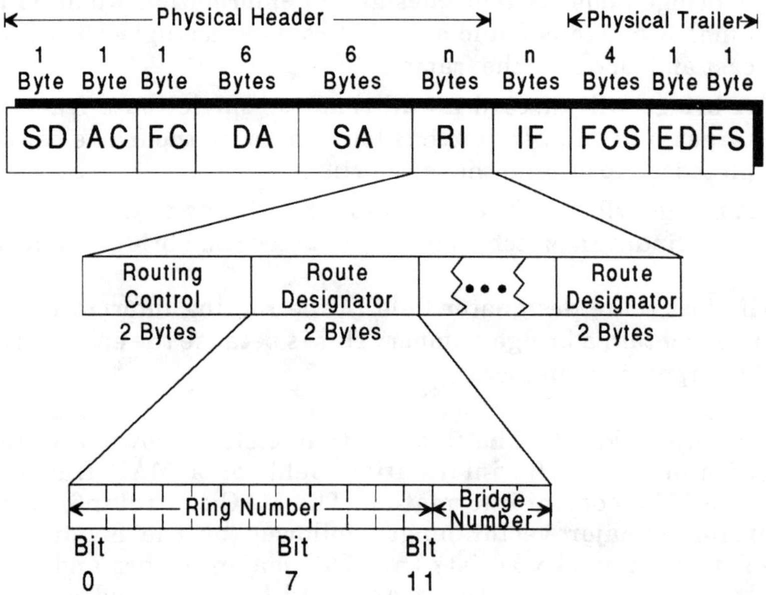

Figure 2.14 The route designator field of the routing information field of the MAC frame.

using a single token. If the frame is the first or an intermediate frame the value is set to a B'1'. If the frame is a single-frame or the last of the multiple-frame transmission the value is set to a B'0'. A bridge performing frame copying of a frame for an off-ring destination will not propagate the value of the intermediate bit.

The error-detected bit is set to a B'0' when a ring station originates a token, frame or an abort sequence. Other stations on the ring repeat the error-detected bit value unless a ring station detects either:

- A code violation found between the starting and ending delimiters of the frame
- A non-integral number of bytes in the frame
- A cyclic redundancy check error

A ring station that detects one of these errors checks the value of the error-detected bit. If the value is set to a B'0' the ring station is the first to detect one of the above errors and changes the error-detected bit value to a B'1'. If the value is already a B'1' then the station is not the first to detect the error and repeats the frame with the bit set to B'1'. However, bridges set this value to a B'0' when copying a frame destined for another ring.

Frame Status Field: The first two bits of this one-byte field and bits 4-5 are divided into two different indicators. The format of the frame status field is shown in Figure 2.15. The left bit of each pair represents an address-recognized indicator bit and the right bit of each pair is a frame-copied bit indicator. Two pairs of these bits are used because the frame status field is not included in frame check sequence. This is done to minimize errors. A ring station validates these bits only when the two pairs match. These bits are used during neighbor notification, duplicate address test and assured delivery.

These bits are set to B'0' when originating a frame. The address-recognized bits are set to a B'1' when a ring station matches its address with the destination address or an applicable group address, or when a bridge recognizes a frame to copy due to a routing information field match. The frame-copied bits are set to B'1' when the receiving ring station copies the frame into its receive buffer. These bit values indicate to the originating ring station whether the receiving ring station is non-existent or inactive, or the receiving station exists but for some reason did not copy the frame or whether the frame was copied.

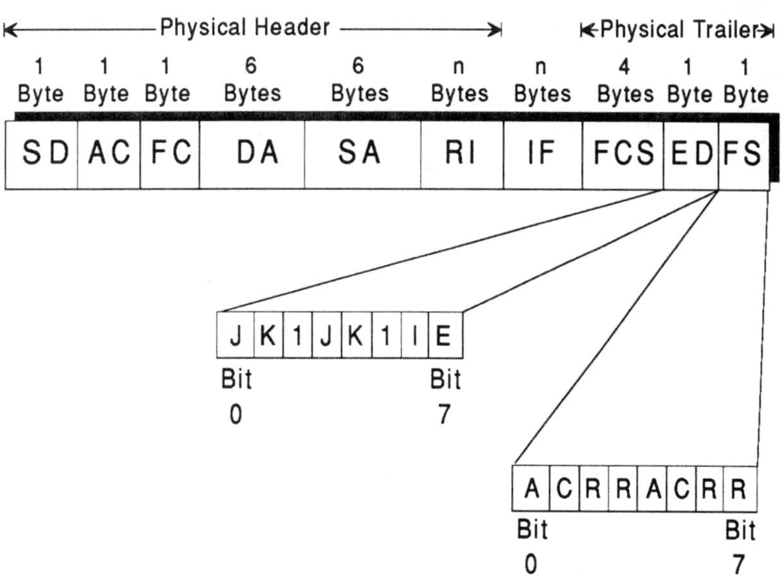

Figure 2.15 The end delimiter and the frame status field formats of the MAC frame.

The following details the valid values for the address-recognized and frame-copied bit pairs:

- B'00': The destination address ring was not recognized and the frame was not copied. If the routing information field is present the bridge did not recognize any route designator field.
- B'11': A ring station recognized its address as that of the destination address into the MAC frame and copied the frame to its receive buffer. The bridge on the ring recognized the appropriate route designator field to copy and forward the frame to an adjoining ring.
- B'10': The destination address was recognized by a ring station but the frame was not copied. A bridge recognized the need to copy and forward a frame to an adjoining ring but could not copy the frame. The receiving station logs this occurrence each time it is received.

A combination of B'01' is invalid because it indicates that the frame was copied but there was no ring station address recognized.

A duplicate address exists when the receiving station finds that the address-recognized bit is already set to B'1' and the destination address is not a group address. The ring station increments the frame-copied error counter of the non-isolating error count subvector for the MAC frame.

If routing information is available a bridge will copy the frame and transmit it on the source ring with the address-recognized and frame-copied bits set to B'11'. This indicates to the originating ring station that the bridge is forwarding the frame to an adjoining ring as designated in the route designator field of the routing information field. The bits are set to B'00' by the bridge when transmitting the frame to the adjoining ring.

Reserved Bits: The remaining bits not discussed in the frame status field are reserved by IBM for future use.

2.5 SUMMARY

In this chapter we reviewed the major influences on the IBM Token-Ring Network architecture. IBM's Systems Network Architecture (SNA) and the ISO Open Systems Interconnection (OSI) roles in designing the token-ring architecture were elaborated on identifying the need for token-ring to support both. The bits and bytes that make up the Logical Link Control and Medium Access

Control frames of the token-ring architecture were reviewed extensively to provide you with a foundation for the next chapter which discusses token-ring concepts.

Chapter

3

IBM's Token-Ring Network Concepts

A token-ring network simplifies network resource connectivity by providing a standardized architecture. Peer-to-peer communications between network resources and the ability to share these resources between attached devices enhances end user productivity while providing system availability.

The ring itself is described as having ring stations and the transmission medium attaching them. The ring station is the combined functions of the token-ring adapter, the logical link control and medium access control, service access point functions and the access protocols that allow a device attached to the ring to participate in token-ring communications.

In a ring there are two paths of unidirectional communications. Ring stations transmit on one physical path and receive data on the other. As the name indicates a ring is a continuous closed path. Traffic on the ring flows through each station adapter. A ring station transfers data to the ring. The data flows sequentially in one direction from one station to another. Each station receives the data. Upon receiving the data the station checks it for errors and inspects the destination address field against its own address. If there is a match, the station copies the data into its receive buffers and then regenerates the data back onto the ring to forward the

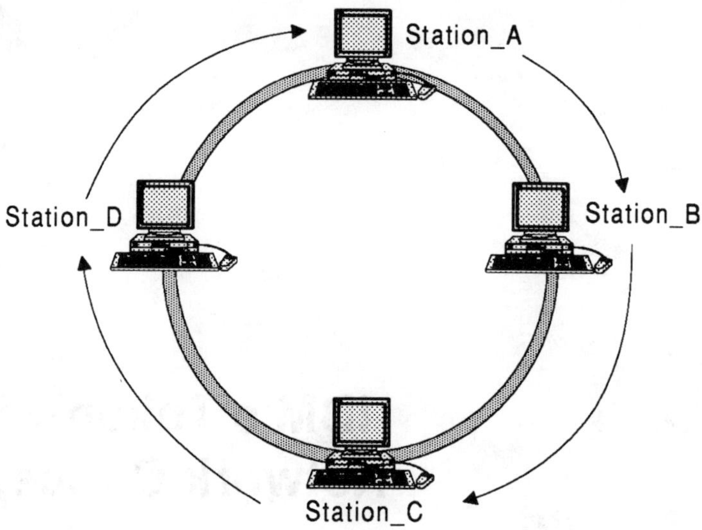

Figure 3.1 A sample Token-Ring Network and the flow of data around the ring.

data back to the originating station. The originating station then removes the data from the ring. Figure 3.1 outlines a sample token ring and the flow of data on the ring.

3.1 LAN TOPOLOGIES

Topography of a network describes the physical layout of the network. This includes all the hardware that makes up the network, for example: modems, communications lines, multiplexers. The points of connection to the network by the stations are called nodes or link stations.

There are several types of topographical designs and strategies used to implement local area networks. The majority of these are based on three types of topologies: star, bus and ring. Each topography has its advantages and disadvantages.

3.1.1 Mesh Topography

A topography where each station on the network is connected to the other stations on the network is called a mesh topography as shown in Figure 3.2. This type of topography has excessive wiring overhead since each station is connected directly to each other station. Each station requires *N*-1 communications ports where *N*

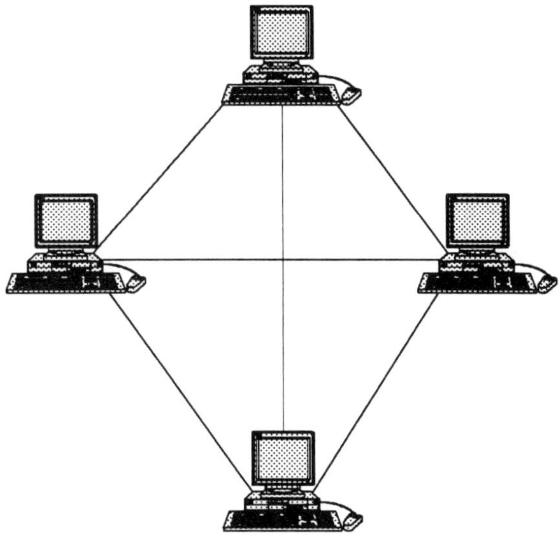

Figure 3.2 An example of a mesh network.

is the number of stations in the network. Each station on the network can act as an intermediate station for transmitting information frames between origin and destination stations. Though a mesh topography can become quite complex and overwhelming it provides a high degree of network availability since failure of a link or a station does not inhibit the routing of an information frame through an intermediate node. All nodes in a mesh network are considered adjacent to each other.

3.1.2 Star Topography

A star topography has a number of stations connected directly to a central controller as shown in Figure 3.3. The central controller is also referred to as a switch. Communications on the connecting links between the station and the switch of a star topography can be bidirectional and are point-to-point. A station on this type of network passes an information frame to the central controller which then forwards the information to the destination station.

The central controller manages and controls all communications between stations on the network. When a station uses connection-oriented data transmission the originating station sends a connection request to the central controller or switch. The switch then sets up the connection on behalf of the originating station. Trans-

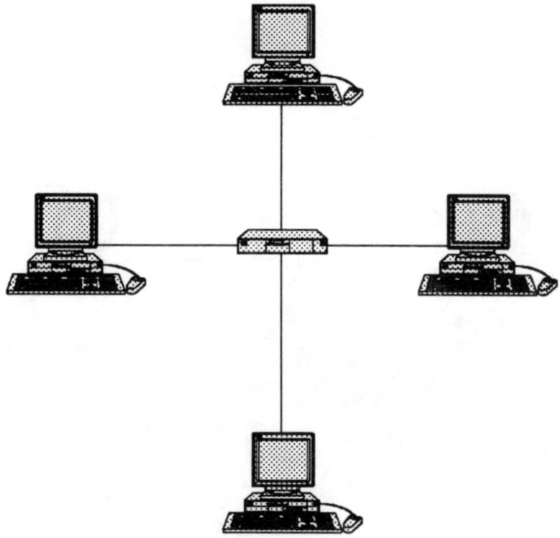

Figure 3.3 An example of a star network.

fer of information frames between the two stations can begin after the switch establishes the requested connection.

Failure of a station on a star network is easy to detect and remove from the network. However, failure of the central controller will disable communications throughout the whole network. This single point of failure is a great disadvantage in a star topography. The central controller must be made of very reliable components and some form of redundancy to overcome this disadvantage. The telephone systems in office buildings use a star topography. The telephones are the stations and the PBX is the central controller.

3.1.3 Bus Topography

A bus topography also supports bidirectional communications. All stations are connected to a single communications line as diagrammed in Figure 3.4. This single communications line is referred to as a bus. Information frames originating at a station are propagated away from the station in both directions on the bus in a broadcast fashion. Each station on the bus interrogates the information frame destination address field for its own address. If the destination field does not match the stations address the station discards the information frame rather than forwarding the frame

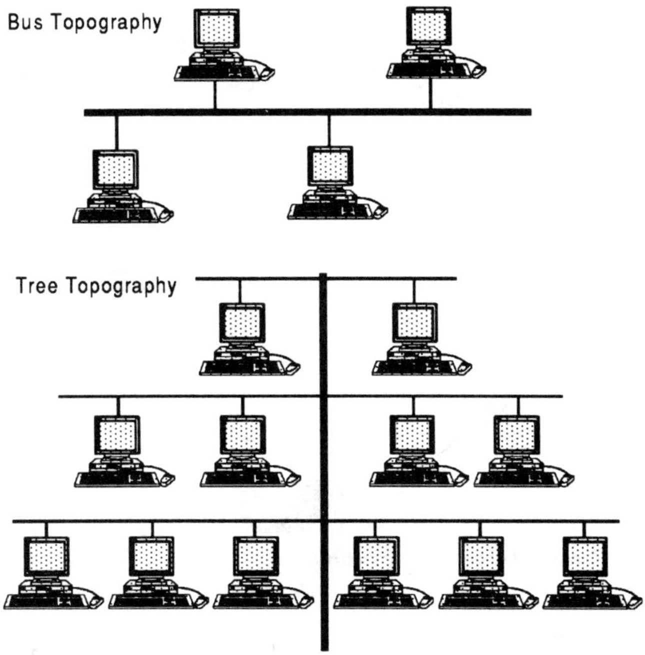

Figure 3.4 An example of a bus and a tree network.

back on to the bus. If the destination address matches the station address it accepts the information frame and processes the frame.

An extension to the bus topography is tree topography. Tree topology extends the branches of the bus topography allowing more stations to access the bus. Cable television networks are examples of a tree network.

On a bus or tree network there is no central point for management and control. These functions are distributed to each station on the bus. Each station must have the intelligence for error detection. A break in the bus can be difficult to locate but limits the outage to communications between stations that traverse the broken point.

3.1.4 Ring Topography

Local area networks that have each station attached to an adjacent station using point-to-point links form a physical ring. This type of configuration, depicted in Figure 3.5, is known as a ring topography. Each station attached and active to the ring regenerates the information frame then retransmits the information frame on the

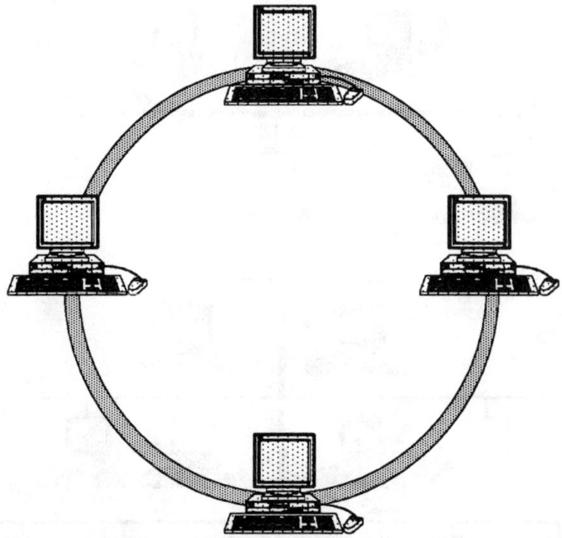

Figure 3.5 Ring network topography.

ring. The ring itself is logically circular and information travels in one direction.

Failure of a station in a ring topology disrupts the ring because the information frame is not regenerated. A break can also be caused by an outage in one of the point-to-point links. A loss of signal on the link will also cause a disruption on the ring. Though a fault in a ring can cause a complete outage the exact location of the fault can be determined through timing or by determining the status of each station on the ring. Additions or deletions of stations to the ring can also be disruptive if the change is not managed properly.

These short comings of a ring topography are overcome by a star-wired ring topography, sometimes called radial hierarchical wiring. A star-wired ring topology is a combination of a star and ring topography. This star-wired ring topography utilizes a relay center. Within the relay center the transmit path of one station is connected to the receive path of the next active station bypassing inactive stations. The connection between the relay center and the ring station is called a lobe.

The relay center is implemented as a wiring concentrator. The use of a wiring concentrator enables fault detection capabilities of a ring topography while providing the flexibility of installing, maintaining and reconfiguring a star topography.

The IBM Token-Ring Network is implemented using the star-

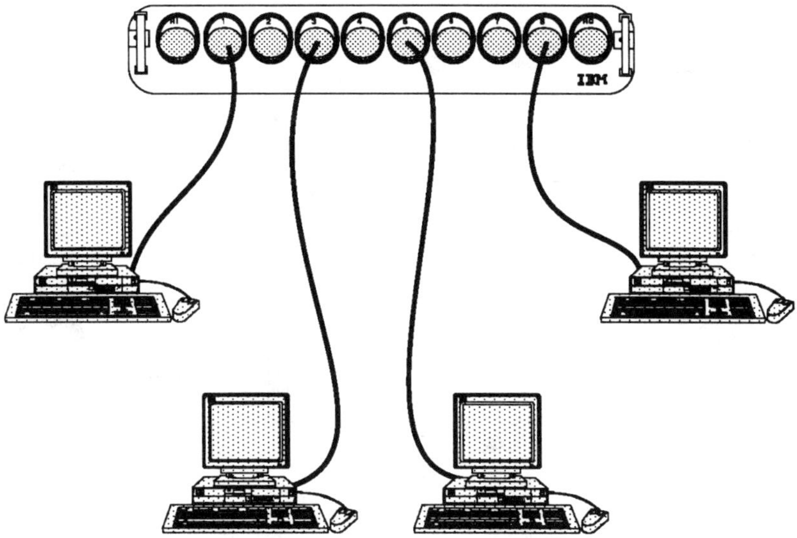

Figure 3.6 A star-wired ring network.

wired ring topography as diagrammed in Figure 3.6. Stations are physically attached to the wiring concentrator with a point-to-point link. The wiring concentrator under the IBM Token-Ring Network can be passive or active. A passive wiring concentrator uses the electrical current on the lobe wire to power the relay mechanism in the passive wiring concentrator. An example of a passive wiring concentrator from IBM is the IBM 8228 *multistation access unit* (MAU). Active wiring concentrators provide their own power and thus can contain some intelligence to provide error recovery, error message processing and, to a degree, management of the ring. The IBM 8230 *controlled access unit* (CAU) can control physical access to the ring and provide a bypass methodology when faulty or inactive stations are detected. Star-wired ring topologies allow stations to be added or removed from the network while the network is in use without affecting other stations on the network.

3.1.5 Multisegment

A ring in the IBM Token-Ring Network is called a LAN segment. In most corporations token-ring networks have demonstrated their worth and have been proliferated throughout the corporation. These large local area networks are made up of several rings or LAN segments. Interconnecting these LAN segments expands networking capability.

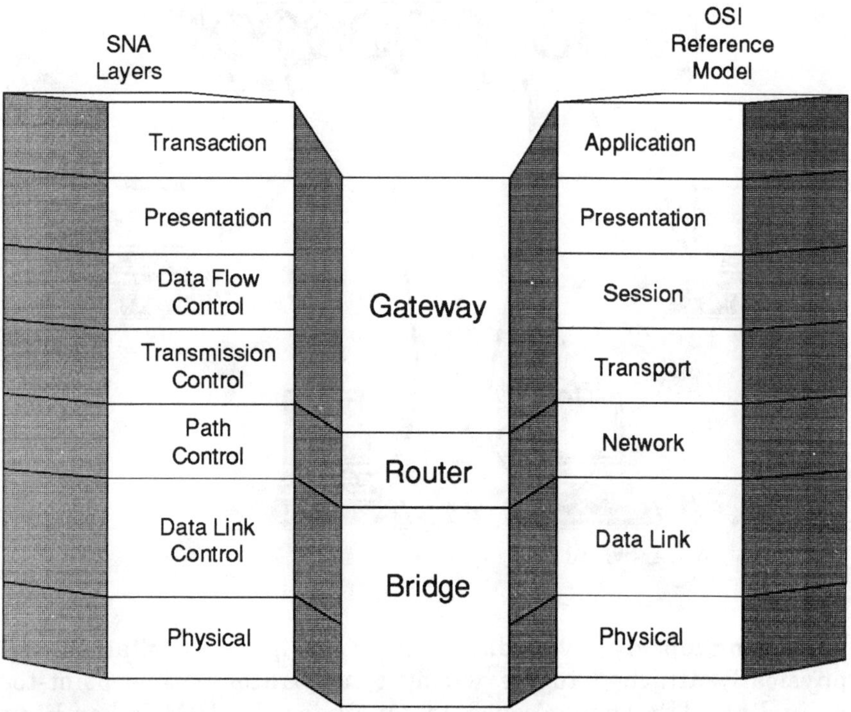

Figure 3.7 The relationship of bridge, router and gateway functions to the services provided by the OSI Reference Model and the SNA architecture.

LAN segments are interconnected through the use of bridges, routers and gateways. Figure 3.7 relates the differences of these interconnection techniques as compared to the OSI Reference Model and the SNA architecture. Bridges provide interconnection services at the data link layer of SNA and OSI. Bridges, for the most part, connect LANs that use the same Logical Link Control protocol. Routers on the other hand go one step above that and interconnect LANs over the network layer of SNA and OSI. Routers connect LAN segments that use the same transport protocols but different LLC protocols. Gateways are used to convert specific protocols from one type of network to another using layers three through seven of either SNA or OSI. An example for using an interconnection gateway is conversion of SNA 3270 protocols on a S/370 or S/390 data channel to DECnet protocols on a LAN.

Interconnection of LAN segments creates a multisegment local area network. A multisegment LAN increases the size of a LAN over the size supported by a single segment LAN as shown in

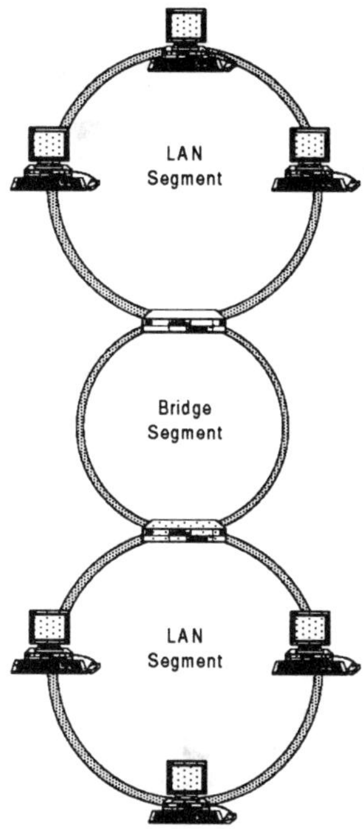

Figure 3.8 A multisegment LAN configuration.

Figure 3.8. A large single segment LAN can be split into smaller LANs thereby increasing the available bandwidth for each station providing a higher data throughput. Multisegment LANs interconnected via bridges reduce the impact of wiring changes and media errors because the bridge isolates the errors and changes to a single LAN segment. The bridges that separate the LAN segments can control traffic through the various segments by using a filtering mechanism further reducing unwanted traffic over specific LAN segments. Multisegment LANs increase the geographic area and provide a connectivity solution for segment interconnection.

3.2 TOKEN-RING ADDRESSING

Communications between any two stations on a token ring is established using an address mechanism. Each station or a group of stations is assigned a unique address in the MAC sublayer of the Data Link Layer of OSI and the Data Link Control of SNA. These unique addresses enable the attachment of any ring station to the IBM Token-Ring Network.

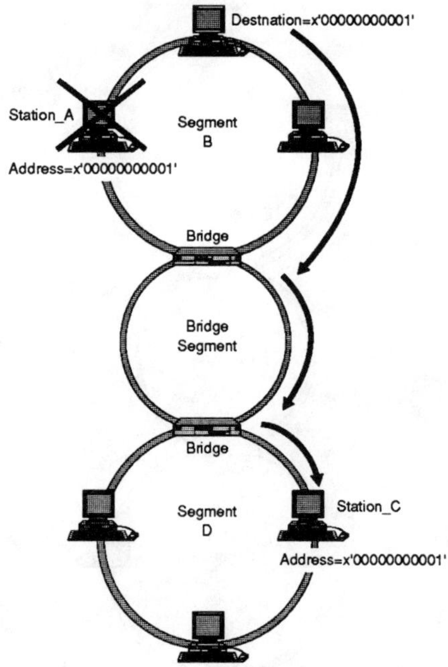

Figure 3.9 A diagram depicting duplicate station addresses on LAN segments.

3.2.1 Individual and Group Addressing

Ring stations are identified by a unique individual ring station address. A group address identifies a group of ring stations that will acknowledge the group address found in the MAC destination address field. Appendix E lists the standardized group addresses.

Each six byte address field must be unique within the LAN segment. Ring station addresses can be duplicated on different LAN segments. As shown in Figure 3.9, Station_A on segment_B has an address of x'000000000001' and Station_C has an address on x'000000000001' on segment_D. If Station_A becomes inoperative then stations on segment_B will access Station_C on segment_D. The reverse is true for stations on segment_D. To avoid inadvertent duplication of addresses the stations can be assigned universal or locally administered addresses.

3.2.2 Universal and Locally Administered Addresses

The universal address is assigned by IEEE. This address is found on all token-ring adapter cards. The address is unique for each token-ring adapter manufacturer. The IBM assigned address is x'10005A'. This address is set in the token-ring adapter card's *read only memory* (ROM) and is also commonly referred to as the burned-in address. Using the universal address eliminates the need for end-user involvement and thus less room for error on configuring the ring station for an individual address.

The universal address can be over-ridden by a *locally administered address* (LAA). A carefully orchestrated addressing scheme must be implemented to ensure unique addresses for each individual ring station using LAAs. Appendix F outlines an IBM suggested addressing scheme. The token-ring adapter sets the address at adapter-open time. LAA station addressing however, requires someone to administer the LAA station addresses for each LAN segment.

3.2.3 Null Address

In a token-ring network address scheme a special individual destination address can be sent with a value of x'000000000000'. This address is known as a null address. Frames carrying a null address are not addressed to any station on the LAN. Stations can send a null address but not receive a frame with a null address. When the sending station recognizes the null address frame the station strips the frame of its data and issues a new token.

3.2.4 All-Stations Broadcast Addresses

An all-stations broadcast address is received by all stations. The destination address values for all-stations broadcast address is x'FFFFFFFFFFFF' and x'C000FFFFFFFF'. All stations on the ring must be able to receive at least x'C000FFFFFFFF'.

3.2.5 Functional Addresses

The token-ring architecture calls for bit-specific functional addresses. There are currently 14 functional areas of the token-ring network architecture that have been assigned specific functional addresses. Ring stations use these functional addresses as a mask to identify these functions. These functions are defined at the access protocol level. There are a total of 31 possible functional addresses. Appendix E contains a list of the 14 functional addresses that have been assigned.

3.3 BRIDGING AND ROUTING

Interconnection of LAN segments is accomplished in an IBM Token-Ring Network mainly through bridges. Routers are more commonly used in a TCP/IP based LAN environment. These routers are called *internet protocol* (IP) routers. There are five types of bridge functions that are used for interconnecting LANs.

3.3.1 Source Routing Bridge

Source routing is an IBM bridge architecture defined for the IBM Token-Ring Network architecture. The source routing architecture has since been accepted into the IEEE 802.5 Standard.

Ring numbers and a bridge number are defined during the configuration of a bridge. Ring numbers are assigned to each segment that a bridge connects. This ring number does not have to be unique in the network. The bridge itself is characterized by the set of ring numbers. Each bridge in a network must have a unique bridge number. Together, these two numbers form the route designator field of the routing segment of the routing information field in the MAC frame format.

The originating station (i.e., the source station) issues a TEST or XID LPDU command on its ring with the destination address set to the null service access point address. If the destination station responds with a TEST or XID LPDU response then the source station does not set the route information indicator bit to a B'1' since the destination station is on the same ring or LAN segment. However, if the source station does not receive the TEST or XID LPDU response it determines that the destination station is off the ring. Off-ring determination is found in the IBM Token-Ring Network using all-routes broadcast route determination and single-route broadcast route determination.

In all-routes broadcast route determination the source station issues a TEST or XID LPDU command to all rings as seen in Figure 3.10. Copies of the TEST or XID LPDU command are forwarded by the bridges unless:

1. The frame has been on the next segment.
2. The hop-count limit would be exceeded in that direction. The hop count is set at bridge configuration time.
3. The bridge is set to filter this frame from being forwarded.

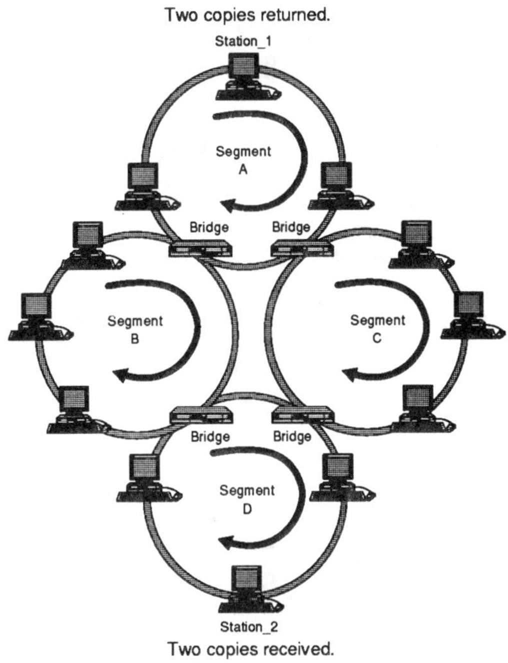

Figure 3.10 An all-routes broadcast route determination scenario.

As the frame is sent to the bridge the source sets the all-routes indicator. The first bridge then adds a route designator field identifying the source station ring number and bridge number and then a route designator field identifying the ring number and bridge number of the next ring followed by a null bridge entry. Any bridges that may be crossed after the initial bridge off of the ring will then add their bridge number and another two-byte designator field. In Figure 3.10, there are two possible routes between station 1 and station 2. Station 2 will respond to as many frames as there are available routes. In this example there will be two frames. Station 2 responds with a non-broadcast frame flipping the direction bit and containing a completed route information field. The frames are returned over the route received in the reverse order of the route information field. The route chosen is usually the first non-broadcast reply frame to arrive at the source station. However, variables such as the number of hops or the supported frame size can be used to determine the most efficient route.

Single-source routing reduces the overhead of the destination station during the routing discovery process. Using this mecha-

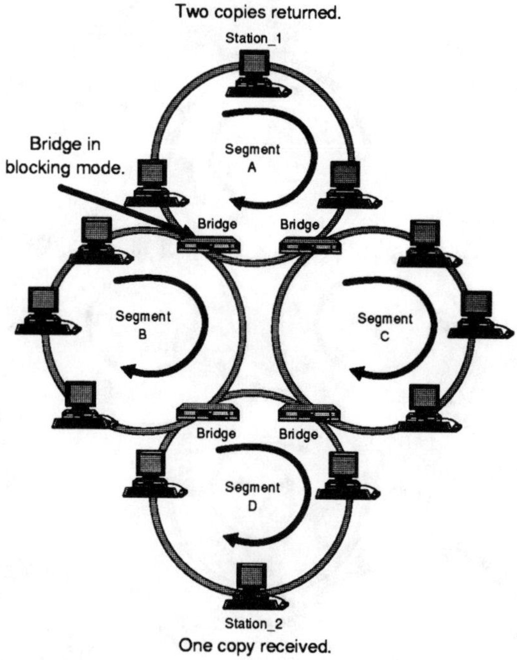

Figure 3.11 A single-route broadcast route determination scenario.

nism the source station again issues a TEST or XID LPDU command but sets the single-route broadcast indicator in the route control field of the routing information field. The single-route broadcast allows only one copy of the frame on each segment. The single-route broadcast frame is propagated according to the following:

- The bridge configuration allows the bridge to forward a single-route broadcast frame.
- The route designator field indicates that this frame has already been on the next segment.
- The bridge filters this frame.

The destination station after receiving the single-route broadcast route command responds with an all-routes broadcast frame, as shown in Figure 3.11, with the destination being the source station. The source station then receives as many all-routes broadcast responses as there are routes in the network. The source station chooses the preferred route.

Single-route broadcast is the chosen favorite of the two source routing techniques. The bridge options program determines if a single-route broadcast is to be forwarded. This can be set manually (local or remote) or automatically when using parallel bridges. The main advantage of single-route broadcast is the elimination of redundant frames in networks with parallel paths.

3.3.2 Transparent Bridge

The concept of transparent bridging is based on the fact that stations view all LAN stations as being on the same segment. Transparent bridges do not use routing information fields like that found in source routing. Instead transparent bridges inspect the source address of each frame on a segment. The transparent bridge builds a routing table called the filtering data base. This routing table contains the source address of stations that communicate with the bridge over a specific interface. In this way, the transparent bridge can determine if a frame is destined for a station on the source ring or off the source ring. A timer value is also placed with the entry. The entry will be removed from the routing table if the station has not sent a frame in a specified amount of time.

As diagrammed in Figure 3.12, Bridge_1 receives a frame from

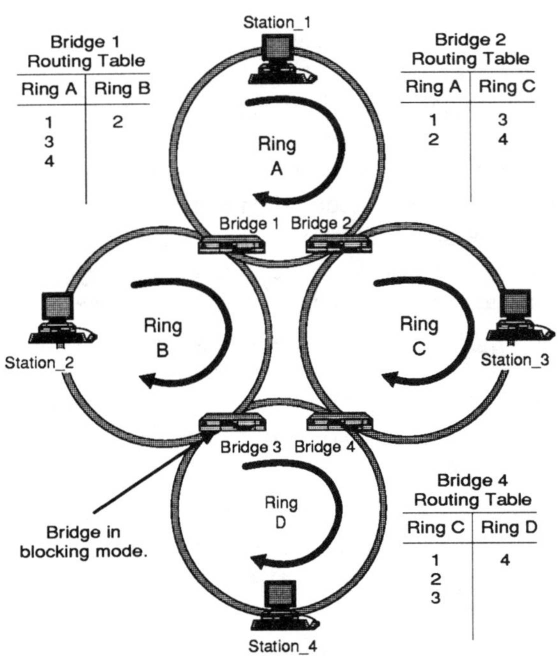

Figure 3.12 Transparent bridging and the use of the filtering database.

Ring_A. Bridge_1 inspects the source address field against the routing table for Ring_A. If the source address matches an entry in the Ring_A routing table then the bridge knows that the source station is on Ring_A. The destination address field is inspected but the address is analyzed for both Ring_A and Ring_B. If the destination address is found on Ring_A then the bridge ignores the frame. If however, the destination address is found to be on Ring_B then the bridge forwards the frame. An intermediate transparent bridge places the source address of a frame whose source and destination address are not in the routing table into the on-ring routing table and the destination address into the off-ring routing table.

Transparent bridging requires a single route between stations. There can only be one active route through a LAN when using transparent bridging. This is due to the fact that parallel bridges will always assume that all source and destination stations are on the originating ring therefore looping a frame endlessly. To minimize the impact of this an automatic single route selection process is required for transparent bridging. This single route selection process is known as the spanning tree algorithm.

3.3.3 Spanning Tree Algorithm

Multisegment LANs configured with transparent bridges use a spanning tree algorithm to always ensure a single active route. IBM has incorporated this algorithm for use with its source-routing bridges ensuring a single route for single-route broadcast frames. The difference between the two implementations is that the functional addresses used by transparent and source-routing bridges is not the same. The result of this is that a single-route broadcast configuration will be performed by all transparent bridges and separately by each source-routing bridge in a network that utilizes both transparent and source-routing bridges. The algorithm is called a spanning tree because there is no closed loop between LAN segments; the tree connects the subnetworks.

In a spanning tree algorithm there are four possible states that may be considered by the bridge:

1. *Blocking:* This state prohibits the forwarding of frames, address learning and does not participate in the spanning tree algorithm except to ensure that another bridge is forwarding frames onto the segment.

2. *Listening:* This state provides no frame forwarding or ad-

dress learning but does allow the bridge to participate in the spanning tree algorithm.

3. *Learning:* This state allows the bridge to build address tables from passing frames and participates in the spanning tree algorithm. It does not however provide for frame forwarding.

4. *Forwarding:* As you might assume this enables all three functions of the bridge: frame forwarding, address table building and spanning tree algorithm participation.

To fully understand spanning tree algorithm there are eight terms that must be defined. These are unique bridge identifier, port identifier, root bridge, path cost, root port, root path cost, designated bridge and designated port. These terms are described below:

Unique bridge identifier: The bridge identifier is made up of the MAC address on the bridges lowest port number and a two-byte priority level that is defined during bridge customization.

Port identifier: Each port on a bridge has a unique two-byte port identifier. This value is unique only within the bridge itself.

Root bridge: The bridge assigned the lowest bridge identifier becomes the root bridge. This bridge may carry the bulk of the traffic since it connects the two halves of the network.

Path cost: Preferred routes in an interconnected LAN. These routes have the least amount of impact on LAN performance. Fast bridges are preferred over slow bridges. LAN segments with minimal traffic are preferred over heavy traffic segments. These preferences lead to the cost of a bridge port. The higher the cost the less preferred route. Each bridge adds the cost of transmission through each port of the bridge to come up with the total cost of transmission for a path to any LAN segment through the root bridge.

Root port: This is the bridge port with the least cost for a path to the root bridge.

Root path cost: This is the path with the minimum cost to the root bridge from each bridge.

Designated bridge: The only bridge on a LAN segment that forwards frames is the designated bridge. All other bridges on the LAN segment are in the blocking state.

Designated port: The minimum cost path for all traffic from this bridge and subordinate LANs will travel through this port. This is the port that connects the LAN to the designated bridge.

Bridges broadcast frames called *bridge protocol data units* (BPDU) to determine a single loop-free topology. Figure 3.13 details a BPDU. The BPDU frame is exchanged quickly reducing the time in which LAN service is unavailable between stations.

In a LAN using spanning tree algorithms the tree itself is learned after the passing of BPDUs. Each bridge in the network assumes one of three roles. The bridge with the lowest bridge identifier becomes the root bridge. The root bridge forwards frames and periodically issues a 'HELLO' BPDU to all LAN segments connected to the root bridge. Each bridge based on information from the exchange of BPDUs will then select its root port. The bridge that provides the lowest path cost to the root bridge becomes the designated bridge for that LAN segment. The designated bridge is responsible for recognizing and receiving the 'HELLO' BPDU over the root port and updating the path cost and timing information and the forwarding of the BPDU across the bridge. The port on the designated bridge that connects the designated bridge to the LAN becomes the designated port. The designated port transmits BPDUs. Bridges that are parallel to the root or a designated bridge will not have a designated port assigned. These bridges are called stand-by bridges and will not forward frames. Stand-by bridges monitor the 'HELLO' BPDU but do not update the fields or forward them. During network reconfiguration the stand-by bridge may be needed to assume the role of the root or designated bridge. This is determined by the BPDUs monitored by

Bytes

2	1	1	1	8	4	8	2	2	2	2	2
Prot. ID	Prot. Ver ID	BPDU Type	Flags	Root ID	Root Path Cost	Bridge ID	Port ID	Msg. Age	Max Age	Hello Time	Fwd. Delay

Figure 3.13 The format of the bridge protocol data unit (BPDU).

the stand-by bridge. It is through the use of BPDUs that the topography of the LAN is maintained when using the spanning tree algorithm.

While spanning tree algorithm provides the automation necessary for transparent bridging it has its draw backs. For one, the single path between two stations is only as fast as the slowest link. Secondly, all inter-segment traffic is directed to a single root bridge whose processor speed and capacity may degrade network performance. Source-routing bridges overcome these draw backs by supporting parallel routes.

3.3.4 Parallel Routes

Parallel routes between two stations provides active redundancy for availability and load balancing when used with source-routing bridges. The implementation of parallel routes leads to a high availability duplexed-backbone topography. The ability to have parallel routes lends well with a mesh topography.

The advantages of parallel routes are seen clearly when parallel bridges are used between LAN segments. For instance if a single bridge is currently being used but the bridge itself processes rather slowly a second bridge between the LAN segments will increase bridge throughput thereby increasing end user productivity. Connection of remote LANs utilize communications lines. Perhaps the line speed for the connection between LAN segments is too slow to support the LAN traffic. A second bridge and a second line would reduce the load on the first bridge thereby opening up both bridges to handle more LAN traffic. Load balancing and throughput between LAN segments is enhanced when parallel routes are used.

The use of parallel routing provides for a way to explicitly route traffic over a specific path. This lends itself to routing servers that can perform active load balancing based on route characteristics such as: Number of hops, maximum frame size, timers based on route length and security. Used in this manner parallel routes can aid in providing better problem determination in cases of bridge or LAN failures.

3.3.5 Source Routing Transparent Bridge

In March 1990 IBM proposed to the IEEE 802.1 (inter-networking) committee a bridging concept called *source routing transparent* (SRT) bridge. SRT was proposed by IBM to answer the committees requirement that source-routing bridges and stations must have the capability to interoperate with transparent bridges and stations on the same network.

A problem with interoperability is the instance where two stations, one understanding source-routing route information fields and the other depending on transparent bridging therefore does not understand route information fields, attempt to establish communications with each other. The goal of SRT is to provide for this inter-operability by having source-routing stations interpret and understand the functions of the transparent bridge station.

The SRT bridge concept is based on the transparent bridge but will also include a tower on top of the base function to support source routing. The transparent function of the SRT bridge will forward frames based on the transparent routing table. The tower comes into play when a frame contains a routing information field. The SRT bridge will interpret the routing information frame and then base its decision on forwarding the frame from the information found in the routing information field.

SRT bridges form a single spanning tree with other SRT and transparent bridges in the same method as that used under a pure transparent bridging network. SRT stations will use the source-routing path if one exists or fall back to the spanning tree path. SRT stations use a single on segment route explorer frame. This route explorer mechanism results in one single route broadcast frame at the destination station.

The destination frame responds with one single route broadcast message containing no routing information. The originating SRT station will choose the route or use the spanning tree path. Transparent bridging stations do not respond to frames that contain routing information.

The concept of source routing transparent bridging is still in the proposal phases at the time of this writing. Changes will be mandatory as the IEEE 802.1 (internetworking) committee works on standardizing source routing transparent bridging.

3.3.6 Routers

Routers can also be used to interconnect local area networks. The router has the intelligence to provide switching and routing of information within the network layer. The information can reach its destination without the use of a common data link protocol.

Routers offer sophisticated and complex services over those provided by bridges. The interconnection of LANs via routers is dependent on the use of identical protocols. There are however, vendors that supply routers with a variety of protocols lessening the dependence on identical protocols but not removing it. The sole purpose of a router is to interconnect LAN segments that use the same transport protocols but different data-link, MAC-layer, or physical protocols.

A table of destinations is maintained by a router in much the same fashion as that found in transparent bridges. Thus, a router has knowledge of a destination station after the first attempt at routing to it. Routers utilize a router-to-router protocol to dynamically exchange the routing table when it is updated. The router will actively select a path based on parameters like cost, transit delay, congestion and hop counts. The router will process only those frames that are specifically addressed to it thereby requesting routing services.

Functions of bridges and routers are combined by some vendors creating a hybrid called a brouter. Brouters provide routing functions when it recognizes the frames request for routing services and acts like a bridge if routing services are not requested.

3.4 TOKEN PASSING RING PROTOCOL AND TOKEN CLAIMING

Token passing ring LAN protocols define the length of a token to be 24 bits and the shortest possible MAC frame to be 200 bits in length. The transmission of data on a token-ring LAN is accomplished by a station capturing the token. The station sets the token bit in the access control field to indicate that the data is a frame and not a free token. The header of this frame is updated with destination and source MAC addresses, data, a new frame check sequence value and the end delimiter and frame status field.

As the frame makes its way around the ring each station will receive the frame, inspect the frame for its station address in the destination field and perform *cyclic redundancy checking* (CRC). If the stations address is not in the destination field the station retransmits the frame. Stations that receive frames perform CRC checking and then retransmit the frame are in normal repeat mode. Stations operating in normal repeat mode perform data checking on the tokens and frames they receive. Each station will set the error-detected bit in the end delimiter and the address recognized and frame copied bits in the frame status field accordingly. The destination station copies the information field from the frame, processes the end delimiter and frame status field to denote that the frames address was recognized and that the frame was copied before sending the frame back out on the ring to the source station.

Once the source station receives the frame it removes the frame from the ring. The source station checks the frame with CRC checking and then interrogates the address recognized and frame copied bits of the frame status field for verification of successful delivery of the frame to the destination station. After receiving the frame header the source station releases a new free token on to the network for another station to capture for data transmission. This process of capturing and releasing a token is called single token protocol since only one token can exist on the ring at any given time.

The release of a free token by the source station after receiving a returned frame header underutilizes the higher speed mediums. On a typical 4Mbps token ring the length of 1 bit has been determined to be approximately 50 meters, a 24-bit token is approximately 1,200 meters and a 200-bit MAC frame is measured at 10,000 meters. Therefore, on a 4Mbps token ring high-bandwidth utilization is maintained at high traffic levels. At 16Mbps, however, 1 bit is measured at 12.5 meters, a token at 300 meters and the 200-bit MAC frame at 2,500 meters. The concept of early token release was implemented to provide better utilization of the 16Mbps token ring .

Early token release allows the source station to release a free token after transmitting the information frame but before the receipt of the transmitted header. After releasing the free token, an adapter indicator is set to stop the adapter from releasing a second free token after receiving the returned transmission header. The implementation of early token release allows multiple information frames to circulate on the network while still only using one token. Each station on a 16Mbps token-ring network can be optioned to use early token release but it is not required on all stations. The early token release option is implemented by default on an IBM 16Mbps Token-Ring Network.

A token-claiming process is the method used in determining the active monitor on the LAN. This process is also called the monitor-contention process. Token claiming begins under several different conditions. A loss of signal, expiration of the active monitors Receive_Notification Timer or the expiration of the Ring Purge Timer, all detected by the current active monitor, will initiate the token claiming process.

The expiration of the Receive_Notification Timer occurs when the active monitor does not receive the Active Monitor Present

MAC frame it just transmitted in the Receive_Notification Timer time limit. The Ring Purge Timer expiration occurs when the active monitor does not completely receive Ring_Purge MAC frames it just transmitted in the time limit specified by the Ring Purge Timer.

Any ring station that is not acting as the active monitor is a standby monitor. The standby monitor will initiate the token claiming process when its Good_Token Timer expires. This timer is started each time a token or frame is repeated by the station. If a token or frame is not received again over the course of the Good_Token Timer value, then the standby monitor will begin the token claiming process. The expiration of the Receive_Notification Timer indicates that the standby monitor has not received an Active Monitor Present MAC frame during the length of this timer. Again, the standby monitor will begin the token claiming process.

A third factor in determining the initiation of the token claiming process occurs when a ring station attaches to the ring. The attaching ring station will start token claiming when it does not detect an active monitor. This occurs when the station enters the ring with one of the above conditions true and when the station is the first station on the ring.

Ring stations detecting one of the conditions above enters into claim-token-transmit mode by broadcasting a Claim_Token MAC frame and repeating it at a specific time interval. All ring stations can be optioned to participate in the token claiming process. The default for each station is not to participate. However, a ring station must initiate the token claiming process if it detects one of the conditions above. Each ring station participating in the token claiming process analyzes the source address field of the Claim_Token MAC frame for its own address. If the source address is greater than the ring station's address it enters claim-token-repeat mode. If the source address is less than the ring station's address it transmits its own Claim_Token MAC frames. If the source address matches the ring station's address it broadcasts the Claim Token MAC frame until three of these frames have been received by the ring station. This indicates to the ring station that the ring is sound and that it has won the token claiming process. The ring station then completes the process by adding the token delay to the ring, purges the ring, starts its activate monitors and issues a new token. At this point the ring station has become the new active monitor.

3.5 ACTIVE MONITOR

The active monitor performs detection and recovery functions for each LAN segment on a token-ring network. Only one station per LAN segment can perform the functions of the active monitor. All other stations function as stand-by monitors.

The active monitor sets the monitor bit of the access control field to a B'1' as it repeats the frame. If this bit was already set to a B'1' it is assumed the frame or token has circled the ring once. The active monitor removes the frame, purges the ring and issues a new free token. The active monitor delays the issue of the token by a 24-bit ring delay to ensure that a token can circle the ring before returning to the originating station.

The active monitor keeps a Good_Token Timer. This timer time-out value is greater than the time it takes for the longest frame to circle the ring. Expiration of this timer indicates that a token or frame has been lost. The timer is started every time the active monitor transmits a start delimiter.

At specified times the active monitor broadcasts the Active Monitor Present MAC frame. The receipt of this frame by ring stations forces them to initiate timers and obtain their *nearest active upstream neighbor* (NAUN) address.

3.6 NEIGHBOR NOTIFICATION

The Active Monitor Present MAC frame is transmitted to the first ring station downstream from the active monitor. This first ring station begins the neighbor notification process by recognizing the Active Monitor Present MAC frame and sets the address-recognized bit and the frame-copied bit of the frame status field to B'1'. The first ring station then saves the source address of the copied frame as its NAUN address. In this case the address is that of the active monitor. This station then starts the Notification_Response Timer and transmits the frame.

Ring stations active on the ring repeat the Active Monitor Present MAC frame but do not process it since the address-recognized bit and the frame-copied bit of the frame status field have already been set.

The Notification_Response Timer of the first active station downstream to the current active monitor expires during the passing of the Active Monitor Present MAC frame along the ring. This expiration initiates the transmission of the Standby_Monitor Present MAC frame to its next active downstream ring station. The ring station downstream from the standby monitor then copies the source address of the Standby Monitor Present MAC frame into its NAUN address, sets the address-recognized and frame-copied bits of the access control field to B'1' and starts its own Notification_Response Timer. At the expiration of this timer the ring station transmits a Standby_Present Monitor MAC frame to its next active downstream station.

The Standby_Monitor Present process is repeated around the ring until the active monitor copies the source address field from a Standby Monitor Present MAC frame as its NAUN address. The active monitor sets the Neighbor_Notification Complete flag to B'1' signifying that the neighbor notification process is complete.

The neighbor notification as demonstrated enables ring stations on a token-ring network to learn its NAUN address and to give its address to its active downstream neighbor.

3.7 ACCESS PRIORITY

Access priority of a token or frame is determined by the values of the first three bits of the access control field. Figure 3.14 lists the access priorities currently available on the IBM Token-Ring Network. A station that requires a higher priority will set the last three reservation bits of the access control field. Ring stations select a priority and can transmit a token or frame at that priority if the available token priority is less than or equal to the priority assigned to the frame to be transmitted.

B'000'	Normal User Priority MAC frames that need no token Response type MAC frames
B'001'	Normal User Priority
B'010'	Normal User Priority
B'011'	Normal User Priority MAC frames that need token
B'100'	Bridge
B'101'	Reserved for IBM
B'110'	Reserved for IBM
B'111'	Specialized Station Management

Figure 3.14 Access priority bit settings for the IBM Token-Ring Network.

A ring station can reserve a priority to transmit frame by setting the reservation bits of the access control field in a passing frame or token. If the reservation bits have a value larger than what is requested then the bits remain unchanged and the station waits for the next token or frame. However, if the reservation bit values are lower than what is being requested, then the station sets the reservation bits to the required priority.

Interrogation of these bits by the originating ring station determines if the ring station will release a token with a higher priority than the frame it just transmitted. If the reservation bits are non-zero the ring station must release a token of non-zero bits. Ring stations originating a token of higher priority are said to be in priority-hold state.

3.8 RING ATTACHMENT PROCESS

Attachment of a station to the ring occurs in a five-phase insertion process. This process executes each time a station attaches to the token-ring network.

Phase 0: Lobe Testing — The station sends multiple Lobe_Media_Test MAC frames on the lobe wire to the multistation access unit (MAU). The MAU wraps the frames back to the sending station. The station's receive logic is tested. A successful test causes a phantom current of 5-volts DC to be sent to open the relay in the MAU creating a closed circuit between the stations adapter and the MAU.

Phase 1: Monitor Check — The now attached station starts its insert timer looking for Active_Monitor Present, Standby_Monitor Present or Ring Purge MAC frames before expiration of the insert timer. Expiration of the timer will initiate the token claiming process. If this is the first active station on the ring it will become the active monitor.

Phase 2: Duplicate Address Check — The station sends a Duplicate Address Test MAC frame where the destination address, source address and the stations address are all equal. If a duplicate address is found the address-recognized bit will be set to B'1'. Upon receiving the Duplicate Address Test MAC frame the station inspects the address-recognized bit. If it is set to B'1' the station will then detach from the ring.

Phase 3: Participation in Neighbor Notification — The station participates in learning its NAUN address and sends its own address to it next active downstream neighbor.

Phase 4: Request Initialization — This is the final phase of attachment to a ring. The bridge program on a ring may have a *ring parameter server* (RPS) function. During this phase the station issues a Request Initialization MAC frame to the RPS. If an RPS is not present, default values are used. The Request Initialization MAC frame may contain registration information for the LAN manager. This information may be the address of the ring station's NAUN, the product identifier for this station and the ring station's micro-code level. If an RPS is present it responds with an Initialize Ring Station MAC frame response. The information in this frame is used by the ring station to set physical location, soft error report timer, ring number and ring authorization level values. The last three values ensure that all stations on the ring will have the same values.

3.9 SUMMARY

In this chapter the overall architectural concept of the IBM Token-Ring Network was discussed. In a ring there are two paths of unidirectional communications. Ring stations transmit on one physical path and receive data on the other. The IBM Token-Ring Network is implemented using the star-wired ring topology. A ring in the IBM Token-Ring Network is called a LAN segment. LAN segments are interconnected through the use of bridges, routers and gateways. An addressing scheme and a routing approach have been implemented in the IBM Token-Ring Network that ensure address uniqueness within a segment and dynamic determination of routes. The concepts of token passing ring protocol, token claiming, active monitor, neighbor notification, access priority and ring attachment lend evidence to the fact that the IBM Token-Ring Network is simplistic in form yet allows for complex network configurations.

Chapter

4

Token-Ring Components

The IBM Token-Ring Network is implemented with the IBM Cabling System. This cabling system is a specification of components in a structured prewired office building. The specification includes the use of cables, connectors, wall faceplates and distribution panels. This wiring concept minimizes the impact of replacing or relocating equipment on the LAN.

The IBM Token-Ring Network utilizes the star-wired ring topology. The star-wired ring network configuration uses a wiring concentrator. This wiring concentrator provides for the attachment of multiple LAN devices to the ring at a central location. One or more wiring concentrators connected together form a star-wired ring.

The wiring concentrators are usually located in a room near the users of the ring. The wiring concentrators are installed on distribution panels. For example, these distribution panels are located in a room on each floor of a building. These rooms are commonly referred to as wiring closets. Wiring closets are used to simplify ring configuration changes. Instead of running new wire or cable to a new location to support a workstation, a jumper is used on the wiring closet that connects the prewired line from the workstation location to its new position on the wiring concentrator via the distribution panel. This structured wire approach and the use of wiring concentrators leads to high availability, an effective approach to problem determination and short recovery periods.

4.1 TOKEN-RING MEDIA

The media used to connect workstations to the wiring concentrators and connection between the wiring concentrators themselves is defined in the physical layer of the OSI Reference Model and SNA. This physical connection is implemented with mechanical, electrical, functional and procedural specifications that are understood by both end-points of the connection. In other words the type of connectors used, the voltage on the wire and the meaning of the voltage, and events initiated by the voltage. There are four major types of media used in LAN networking: coaxial cable, telephone twisted pair, shielded twisted pair and fiber optic.

Coaxial cable: This type of cable media has a low attenuation characteristic and drives signals at high-data rates over fairly long distances. Attenuation is the decrease in magnitude of an electrical or optical power between two points. The drive distance is the length a signal can be propagated over the cable before requiring a regeneration of the signal using, for example, a repeater. Your cable television connection is made with coaxial cable.

Telephone twisted pair (TTP): This is also referred to as *unshielded twisted pair* (UTP). Unshielded means that the wires do not have a metal shield around them. A metal shield reduces the interference of unwanted radio frequencies from having a negative effect on the cable.Therefore, UTP is very susceptible to unwanted radio frequencies and emit radio frequencies themselves when used for high-speed data transmission. Filters can be put in place to reduce or eliminate the unwanted radio frequencies but the filters reduce the signal strength. UTP also suffers from crosstalk, a signal generated from one pair affecting the signal on the other pair. UTP can be used in the IBM Token-Ring Network at 4Mbps and 16Mbps.

Data-grade media (DGM), *shielded twisted pair*: As the name implies, this type of cable contains a shield. Within each shield there can be one or more twisted pairs. The pairs are twisted in such a way that they themselves help to alleviate radio frequency interference within the shielded cable. Shielded twisted pair cable is suited to handle data rates over 20Mbps for most distances found in typical office buildings. Due to its low attenuation and high data rates over long distances DGM can be used for both 4Mbps and 16Mbps token-ring segments in the IBM Token-Ring Network.

Fiber optic: The previous cables all use copper wiring. Fiber optic utilizes glass and light pulses. A fiber-optic cable can contain thousands of fibers. Each fiber is thinner than the thickness of human hair. Because fiber optic uses light as the transmission signal, it is basically impervious to radio frequency interference. The rate of transmission in fiber-optic media is literally the speed of light. With minor signal attenuation fiber optic has data rates that can approach terabits per second. In other words 1 trillion bits per second! Fiber optic provides enhanced security over copper wire in that tapping into the fiber-optic signal will cause a loss of the signal and detection immediately noted. Copper wire on the other hand can allow the tapping of the signal without great loss to the delivery of data. Fiber optic is also suitable for IBM Token-Ring Networks.

Of the four cable types discussed, the last three are suitable for implementing the IBM Token-Ring Network. UTP, though suffering from high attenuation and radio frequency interference, is a well understood medium and inexpensive, yet undesirable for providing a stable token-ring network. Fiber optic possesses the highest throughput but is relatively new technology and hence expensive to implement. DGM shielded twisted pair cable is the most cost-effective solution available today for providing both high-speed data rates and immunity to radio frequency interference. Figure 4.1 contains a table outlining the pros and cons of each cable type.

4.1.1 Cable Types

There are seven classes of cables and currently eight cable types available for use with the IBM Cabling System. Each type is used for specific installation requirements. These requirements are location and environment. The installation requirements of cables is dictated by the local or state electrical codes in your area. Be sure to follow these codes as they have been implemented for your safety. Figure 4.2 contains a table outlining the characteristics of each cable class.

Type 1: Twisted Pair — This cable has a braided shield around two twisted pairs of #22 *american wire gauge* (AWG) solid wire for data communication. This cable type can support up to 16Mbps data transfer rates and is used strictly for data. As with all cable types listed here this cable can be installed in conduits. Type 1 can also come in two flavors: plenum and riser.

Plenum cable has an outer fire resistant covering, such as Tef-

Medium Type	Pros	Cons
Unshielded Copper Wire  Twisted pair	· Understood technology. · Knowledgeable technicians available. · Fast and simple installation. · Least expensive medium for LAN migration. · Can use existing telephone wiring found in building.	· Affected by electromagnetic interference. · Electrical and magnetic waves can be intercepted. · Cross talk between wires can cause transmission errors. · Exterior placement needs protection from lightning and corrosion. · Low data rate.
Shielded Copper Wire 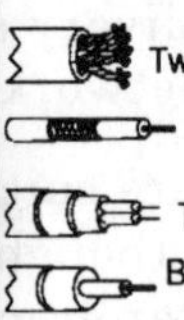 Twisted pair Coaxial Twinaxial Broadband (CATV)	· Understood technology. · Knowledgeable technicians available. · Fast and simple installation (except for CATV). · Minimal emanation of electromagnetic signals. · Shield provides some protection from interference, lightning, cross talk, corrosion.	· High-grade coaxial, twinaxial, and CATV cables are fairly expensive to use for migrating to LAN. · CATV cable is thick and ridgid requiring special tools to install around turns.
Fiber Optic  Fiber Optic Cable	· Useful for high-speed applications. · No electromagnetic signal emanation. · Not affected by cross talk, electromagnetic interference, lightning, corrosion. · Less expensive medium than coaxial or CATV cable. · Signal transmitted over greater distances than copper wire without boosting the signal.	· Knowledgeable technicians are scarce. · Device connection more expensive than copper wire. · Bi-directrional communication requires two fiber optic lines. · High cost for installation. · Cannot be split, use for point-to-point topologies.

Figure 4.1 A table outlining the pros and cons of each cable type.

lon, to reduce the fire hazard and emitted PVC fumes should a fire start. The resistance to fire and low hazardous vapor emissions gives this cable adequate protection to allow installation in air ducts (plenums) and other spaces within a building used for air passages without the use of conduits.

Riser cable also has the characteristics of fire protection without the use of conduit. Instead this cable is more suitable for use in a building riser. For example, building risers are elevator shafts and mail-drop chutes.

Type 1 cable can also be used outdoors. Used in this way the cable has a corrugated metallic cable shield around two twisted pair. Each wire of the twisted pair is made up of #22 AWG wire. This cable type can be used in an aerial installation or placed in conduit underground.

Type 2: Telephone Twisted Pair — This is the same as type 1 cable but has an additional four twisted pairs of #22 AWG solid copper telephone wires. The cable contains six twisted pair, two shielded and four unshielded pairs. This cable type has the added advantage of supporting two token-ring connections and one voice connection concurrently. The shielded pairs can carry data at speeds up to 16Mbps and data on the unshielded pairs (voice pairs) at 4Mbps.

Type 3: Telephone Twisted Pair — This is the recommended cable type for implementing token-ring networks over unshielded telephone twisted pair. This cable type has three or more twisted pairs at #22 or #24 AWG solid copper wire and support either voice or data. The solid copper wire must have a minimum of two twisted pairs per foot. The IBM Cabling System recommends that a maximum of 72 devices can be attached to a token-ring using type 3 cable.

Type 5: Optical Fiber — Optical fiber itself is fairly inexpensive but costly to install. It is not provided for plenum specifications and therefore must be installed in some kind of protective conduit. The non-plenum optical fiber type 5 cable contains two optical fiber strands. One for transmit and one for receive. This non-plenum type 5 can be used indoors, aerial or underground, as long as it installed using a conduit.

Fiber-optic cables can also be used in building risers also known as Type 5 R. These cables will contain multiple fiber strands. These can be useful when making connections over long distances within a building. The cable may be laid horizontally and vertically. This cable does not require conduit but cannot be run through a plenum.

Outdoor fiber-optic cables also contain multiple fibers and are used primarily as backbone or campus connections between buildings. The use of this cable requires installation in a conduit.

Fiber optic can be used for both voice and data with speeds of 16Mbps or greater. Fiber-optic cables are measured in microns instead of AWG. There are four thicknesses to a fiber as shown in Figure 4.2. The IBM Cabling System recommends the use of a 62.5 micron size of the fiber core and 125 microns for the cladding.

Type 6: Twisted Pair — This shielded twisted pair cable uses #26 AWG solid copper wire and is for data communications. The

Cable	Conductor	Pairs	Shielding	Outdoor	Use
Type 1	Solid Copper	Two AWG 22 Twisted	Braided or Corrugated	Yes	Main Paths Work Area to Wiring Closet
Type 2	Solid Copper	Two AWG 22 Twisted + Four TTP (AWG 22)	Braided No	No	Work Area to Wiring Closet
Type 3	Solid Copper	Four TTP (AWG 22/24)	No	No	Work Area to Wiring Closet
Type 5	Fiber Optics	Two Fiber (100/140)	No	Yes	Main Paths (inter Bldg)
Type 5R	Fiber Optics	Two Fiber (50/125)	No	Yes	Main Paths (up to 500m)
Type 6	Stranded Copper	Two AWG 26 Twisted	Braided	No	Jumpers in Wiring Closet
Type 8	Solid Copper	Two AWG 26 Parallel	Braided (each pair)	No	Work Area Under carpet
Type 9	Solid Copper	Two AWG 26	Braided	No	Main Paths (plenum)

Figure 4.2 A table of cable types.

twisted pairs are surrounded by a braided shield. Type 6 cable is used only for patch or jumper cable.

Type 8: Parallel Pairs — This cable type consists of two parallel pairs of #26 AWG wires for data communications. This cable is used for under-carpet installation. The cable is used in situations where location of the end-points do not allow for connection through plenums, conduits or risers. Type 8 cables support data rates up to 16Mbps. Each wire is a solid piece of copper wire.

Type 9: Twisted Pair — This cable type has two twisted pairs with a braided shield. Each wire of the pairs is #26 AWG. The wires can be made up of strands as well as a solid piece of copper. This cable is used mainly through plenum for main connections between token-ring segments or MAUs. The cable can service data rates up to 16Mbps. This cable can also be used in building risers. Type 9 cable is a lower cost solution to implementing type 1 plenum cable.

4.1.2 Patch Cables

Patch cables in a token-ring network are used in the same manner as patch cables for a modem patch panel. Patch cables have the IBM Cabling System data connector attached on each side. Under the IBM Cabling System these cables are used to connect IBM 8230s, 8228s, faceplates and distribution panels. They can also be used as a extension cables to connect IBM 8228s, IBM 8218 Copper Repeaters, IBM 8219 Optical Fiber Repeaters and IBM 8220 Optical Fiber Converters.

Cross-over patch cables are also referred to as *yellow cross-over patch cables* (YCP) because the sheathing on the outside of the cable is yellow. A YCP cable is used to swap the data from the main ring to the backup ring or vice-a-versa. The connectors of a YCP cable cannot be repaired and have a universal open-end wrench symbol on each end. If a YCP cable is damaged it cannot be repaired and must be replaced. The YCP cable is used for IBM 8218s, IBM 8219s and IBM 8220s.

A third type of patch cable is the optical fiber BNC-to-biconic patch cable. This cable connects an IBM 8230, IBM 8219 or an IBM 8220 to a distribution panel or a dual socket clip when fiber optic cabling is used. On one end of the patch cable are two BNC connectors. One connector is attached to an orange conductor and the other to a black conductor. The other side of the cable has two biconic connectors. These are also color coded orange and black. Each fiber of the patch cable is 100/140 micrometers in width.

4.2 IBM's 8228 MULTISTATION ACCESS UNIT

The star-wired topology of the IBM Token-Ring Network has as its foundation the IBM 8228 *multistation access unit* (MAU). The MAU itself will form the ring through an internal relay wiring mechanism without external power and is sometimes called a *passive wiring concentrator* (PWC). Each MAU has ten ports. Eight of these are used to connect LAN stations. The remaining two are used for connection between MAUs, repeaters or converters to extend the size of the ring. One port is called *ring-out* (RO) and one is called *ring-in* (RI). The ring-out is the transmit port of the MAU. The ring-in is the receive port for the MAU. Multiple MAUs can be connected by attaching the RO of one MAU to the RI of the next MAU. In this way up to 33 MAUs can be interconnected allowing for up to 260 devices to be attached and operational.

Guidelines for using type 3 media allow for up to nine IBM 8228s providing for a maximum of 72 attached devices. When using type

6 cable a total of twelve IBM 8228s and up to 96 devices can be attached to the ring. Appendix F contains guidelines on cables, closets and drive distances. Figure 4.3 illustrates a small token-ring network using interconnected multistation access units.

4.3 IBM's 8218 COPPER REPEATER

This device extends the distance of the media by repeating the signal. The IBM 8218 is a copper-to-copper repeater operating at 4 Mbps. The repeater itself is counted as a device on the token-ring and has its own MAC address which is universally administered. Two pairs of the IBM 8218 are required to provide the proper symmetry and amplification on the media providing for a backup path. Each repeater pair uses four YCP cables to provide a backup path should the primary path go down. Using the YCP cable ensures network availability. Figure 4.4 illustrates the use of the IBM 8218. The first pair of the IBM 8218 should be placed at the closet wiring location with the greatest number of MAUs or at the end of the longest inter-closet cable run. The second set should be placed anywhere along the rest of the ring in accordance with the allowable limits of the segment drive distance.

The segment drive distance is dependent on two types of cable configurations. The first occurs when the longest lobe is greater

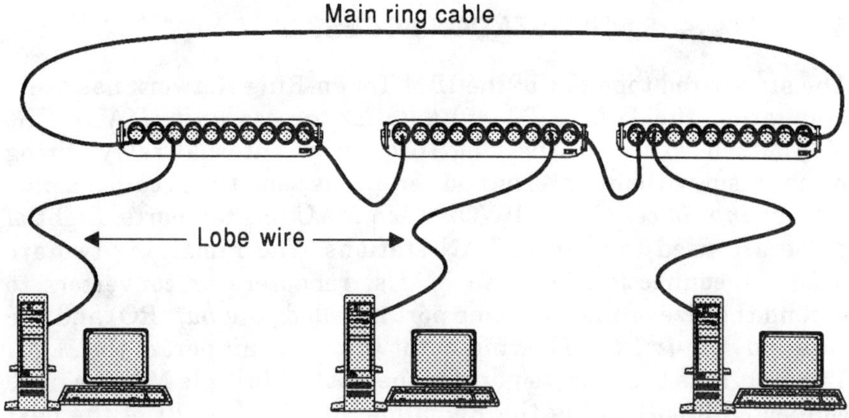

Figure 4.3 A small token-ring network using interconnected multistation access units.

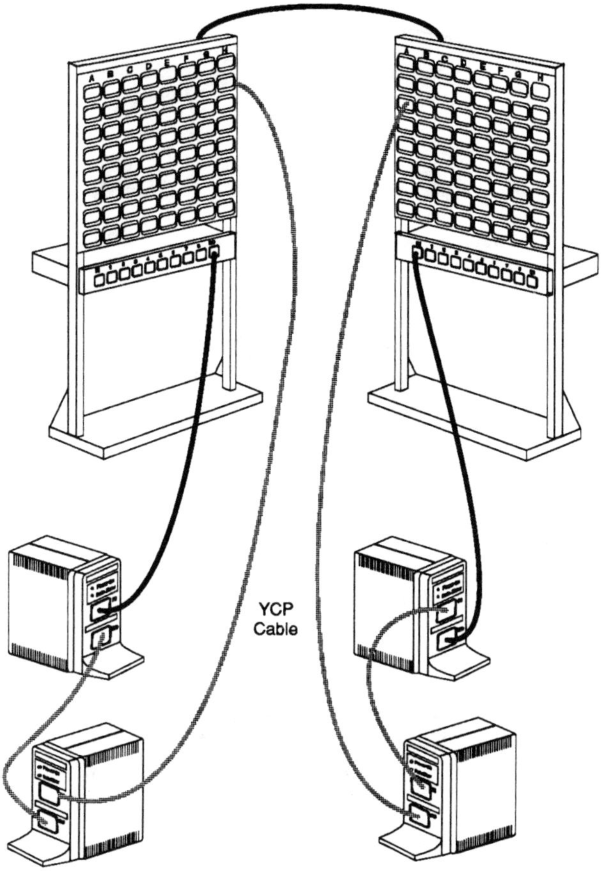

Figure 4.4 Illustrating the use of an IBM 8218.

than each cable that connects the repeaters to their nearest MAU in the ring segment. This calculation can be shown as:

```
Drive Distance = Longest lobe length + the cable length between
MAUs
```

The second scenario occurs when the longest lobe length is less than either of the cables connecting the repeaters to the nearest MAU in the ring segment. This equation is calculated as:

```
Drive Distance = Longest repeater-to-MAU length + length between
MAUs
```

The drive distances and the calculations discussed are illustrated in Figure 4.5.

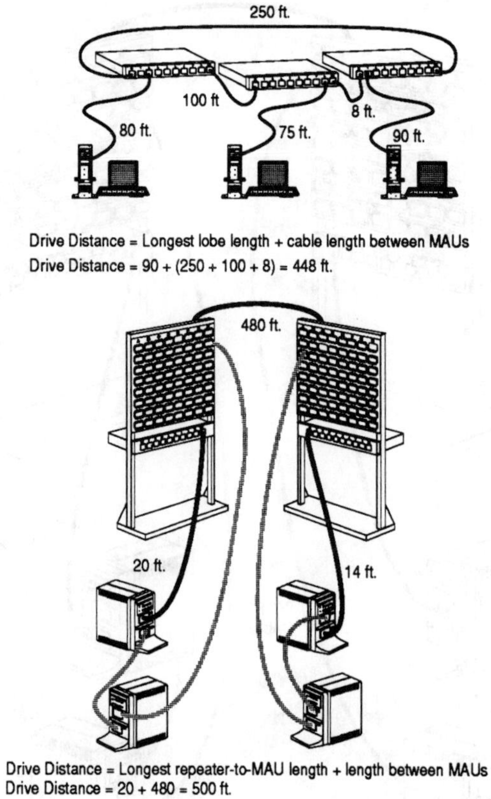

Figure 4.5 Drive distances and their calculations.

4.4 IBM's 8219 OPTICAL FIBER REPEATER

This repeater provides the same functions as the IBM 8218; however, it is used to repeat a signal between copper and optical fiber. The drive distance is calculated like that of the IBM 8218. The IBM 8219 effectively increases the distance between wiring closets to 2 kilometers using the IBM type 5 cable specification. Each type 5 cable contains two fibers each 100/140 microns. One is used to transmit and the other fiber to receive. The IBM 8219 has a standard 4-wire connector and two optical fiber connectors. The data rate at which the IBM 8219 can support traffic is 4Mbps, rather slow for optical media. The advantage to using IBM 8219 and optical fiber to connect wiring closets is the fact that optical fiber media is virtually unsusceptible to electrical interference. Fiber-optic cable is most advantageous when the cable must be laid outside or near electrically noisy areas.

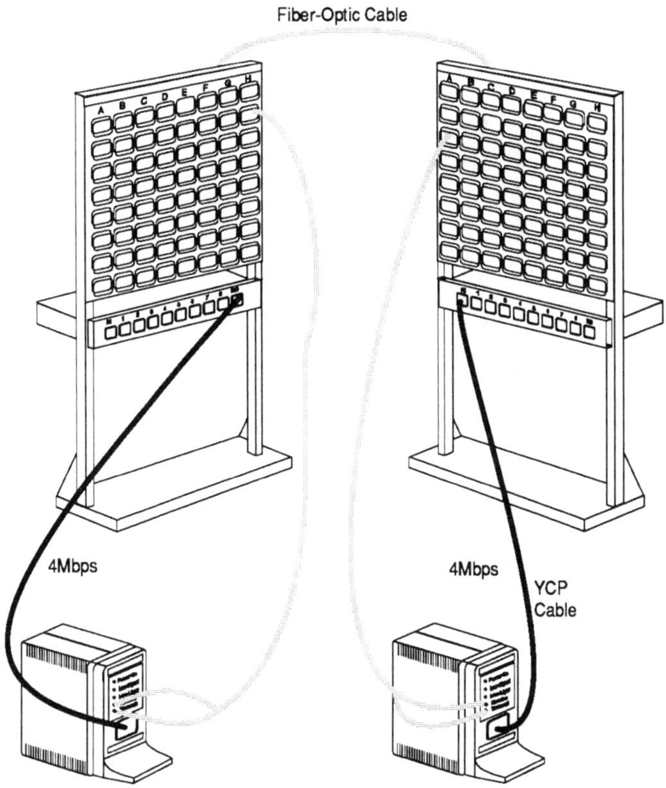

Figure 4.6 IBM 8219 repeaters connect two wiring closets.

In Figure 4.6, IBM 8219 repeaters are used to connect two wiring closets. Note that when using IBM 8219 repeaters only two YCP cables are needed to provide alternate path backup. Multistation access units cannot be placed between IBM 8219 repeaters since these components use copper connectors only. Just as in the IBM 8218 scenario the MAUs wrap the connection around when the inter-closet connection becomes unavailable.

4.5 IBM's 8218/8219 TEST CONNECTOR

This test connector tests the operation of the IBM 8218 or IBM 8219 during installation or for problem determination. The connector is inserted into the copper connector to verify signal continuity.

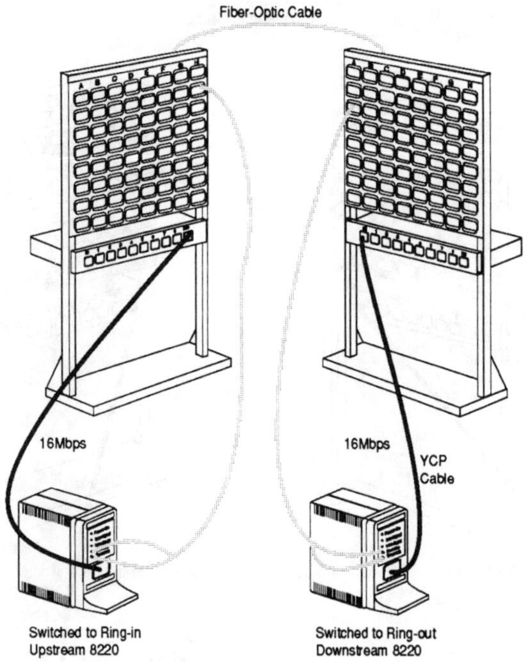

Figure 4.7 Two IBM 8220s are connected together to form the 8220 Fiber Optical Converter Subsystem.

4.6 IBM's 8220 OPTICAL FIBER CONVERTER

This converter extends the distance between MAUs or CAUs up to 2 kilometers (approximately 1.2 miles) at 4Mbps or 16Mbps and participates in token passing ring protocols. The converter provides copper-to-fiber media conversion. The IBM 8220's participation in token passing ring protocols enables it to provide error detection and automatic recovery as implied by the token passing ring protocols. Each IBM 8220 has two unique MAC addresses and therefore must be counted as two stations on the ring.

The IBM 8220 connects the token-ring to either the *ring-in* (RI) or *ring-out* (RO) on the MAU or CAU. The optical fiber pair is attached to the IBM 8220 using two optical connectors, one for receive and one for transmit. As diagrammed in Figure 4.7, two IBM 8220s are connected together to form the 8220 Fiber Optical Converter Subsystem. Each IBM 8220 is called a partner in this subsystem. The RI/RO switch of the IBM 8220 determines the operational mode as either upstream RI or downstream RO. The upstream converter ring-in is connected to the MAU ring-out and the downstream partner IBM 8220 ring-out is connected to the MAU ring-in. Loss of power or connectivity causes each IBM 8220 to go into a wrap mode forcing the main ring to the backup ring maintaining ring availability.

4.7 IBM's 8230 CONTROLLED ACCESS UNIT

Controlled access units (CAUs) have their own power and thus can have built in intelligence. The IBM 8230 Controlled Access Unit has two components. They are the base unit and the *lobe attachment module* (LAM). A maximum of four LAMs can be attached to the base unit. Each LAM can attach 20 ring stations. There are two types of LAMs that can be installed. LAMs with lobe interface ports supporting the IBM IEEE 802.5 connector ("ugly plug") or an RJ-45 connector to support type 3 media. These LAM types can be mixed on the IBM 8230. LAMs can be installed or deinstalled nondisruptively to the stations on the ring while the CAU is operational. If you configure the IBM 8230 without the use of LAMs it can be used as a repeater operating at either 4Mbps or 16Mbps. An IBM 8230 Controlled Access Unit can provide 80 ring stations with attachment to the ring.

The IBM 8230 can support either 4Mbps or 16Mbps data rates on the ring. However, if type 3 UTP media is used for the lobes, the CAU will only support a 4Mbps data rate with the use of the IBM

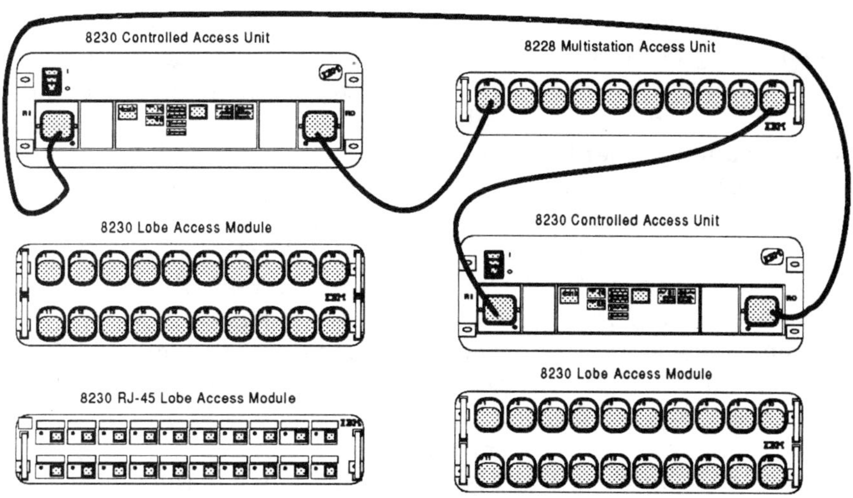

Figure 4.8 The CAU lobe port configuration.

8230 4Mbps Media Filter installed on the base unit. Both copper and fiber can be used for the ring-in and ring-out connections of the CAU. The connections can be both copper, both fiber or one of each. Using these connections, the IBM 8230 can be installed with the IBM 8218, 8219, 8220 and 8228. The IBM 8228 may be installed between connecting IBM 8230 CAUs but cannot be connected to the CAU lobe ports. This configuration can be seen in Figure 4.8. The connection to the IBM repeaters and converters does not allow the IBM 8230 to be half of the repeater/converter pair.

There are three MAC addresses assigned to the IBM 8230. This means that when counting the total number of stations attached to the ring, the total will be the number of lobes plus three for the IBM 8230. The first MAC address is assigned to the *primary-in* (PI) adapter. The PI adapter receives all token-ring data through the ring-in connector. The PI adapter will reclock and then retransmit the data just as if it were a station on the ring. The second MAC address is assigned to the *primary-out* (PO) adapter. This adapter reclocks and then retransmits all token-ring traffic just as if it were a station on the ring just before the data leaves the CAU through the ring-out port during normal operation. The final MAC address is assigned to the secondary (S) adapter of the CAU. This secondary adapter interfaces with the backup path just before ring-out, reclocking and retransmitting data when the backup path is in use. These three adapters are used during ring reconfiguration.

Automatic ring reconfiguration is provided by the IBM 8230 when a ring fault is detected. This automatic recovery is engaged when a fault or "hard error" has been detected. "Hard error" indicates that there is a physical problem with connectivity between stations and/or other CAUs and MAUs.

The automatic recovery is depicted in Figure 4.9. There is a disruption of signal between CAU_A and CAU_B. The PI port of CAU_B issues a beacon for its NAUN CAU_A. The S port of CAU_A also issues a beacon for its NAUN on the backup path which is the S port on CAU_B. The PO port on CAU_B changes the original beacon to one of recovery mode and puts the MAC address of the PO port on CAU_B into the source address field. CAU_C and CAU_D are in beacon repeat mode for the main and backup paths. CAU_A receives the recovery mode beacon and checks its S port. Seeing that the S port is also beaconing CAU_A then wraps its ring-out signal to the backup path. The S port on CAU_B recognizes the source address field as that of its own PO port MAC

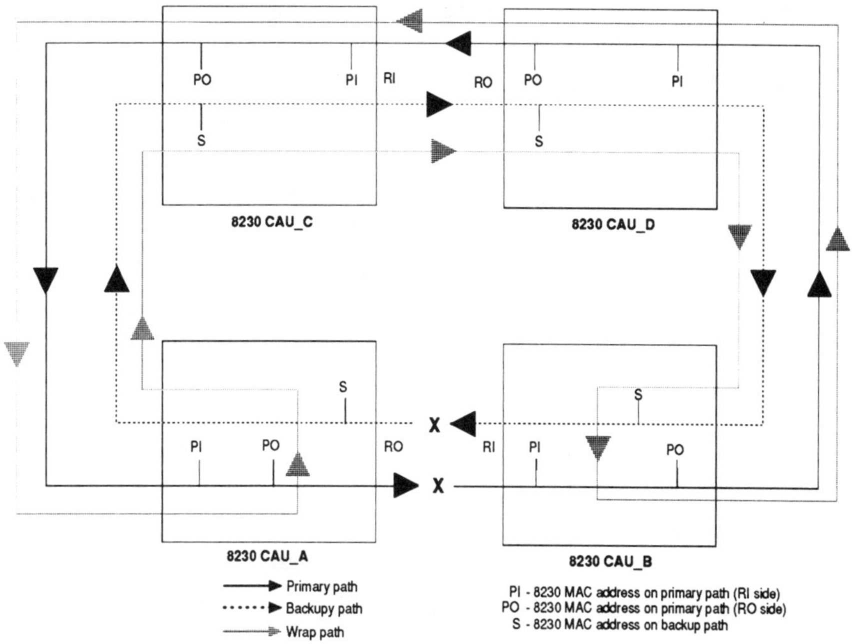

Figure 4.9 A CAU automatic recovery.

address. CAU_B then wraps the ring-in and ring-out into an internal ring within the CAU. The PO port on CAU_B recognizes its own beacon starts the active monitor contention process. The S port of CAU_B then checks the internal ring for faults. If no faults are found it will unwrap ring-out on CAU_B. The S port on CAU_A and the PI port on CAU_B continue to monitor the original fault. When a signal is reestablished between the two CAUs over this interface the IBM 8230s will unwrap CAU_A's ring-out and CAU_B's ring-in thus completing the ring.

4.8 IBM's TOKEN-RING NETWORK BRIDGE PROGRAM

The IBM Token-Ring Network Bridge Program is a personal computer based DOS 3.3 or higher application that provides token-ring bridging functions. The latest release of this program (Version 2.2) offers the following features:

- Interconnection of two token-ring segments operating at speeds of 4Mbps or 16Mbps.
- Supports the LAN Reporting Mechanism.
- Communicates with up to four LAN Managers using IBM LAN Manager.
- Provides interconnection of LAN segments locally or remotely.
- Forward frame filtering interface.
- Dial support between the two remote bridge halves.
- Remote bridge halves can be connected over an Integrated Services Digital Network using the IBM 7820 ISDN Terminal Adapter.

The IBM Token-Ring Network Bridge Program V2.2 operates on an IBM PC/AT, IBM Industrial Computer model, and IBM Per-

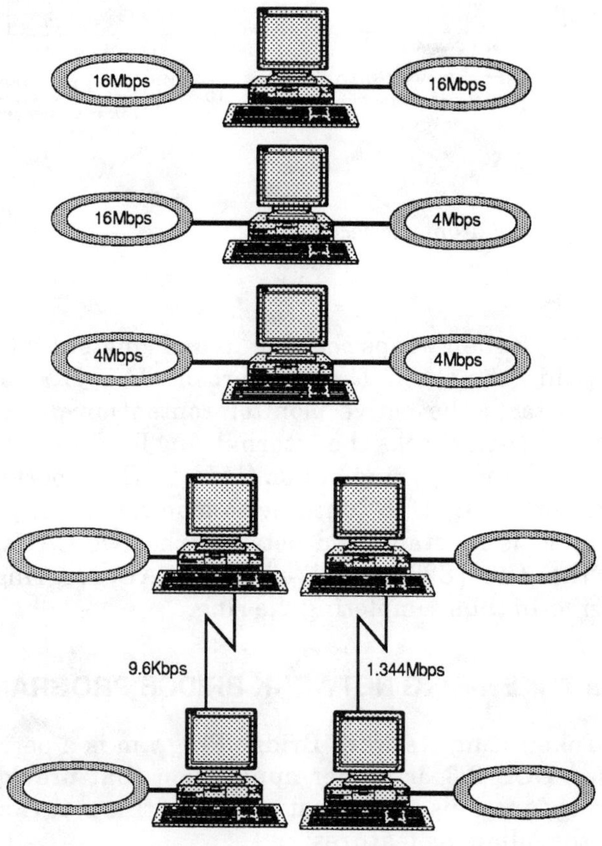

Figure 4.10 The IBM Token-Ring Network Bridge configurations.

sonal System/2 Model 30 or compatible personal computer. The size of the personal computer is dependent on the size of the ring segments attached by the bridge among other assorted factors such as ring speed, communications line speed, traffic and whether filtering is applied. For the most part, many installations utilize an IBM PS/2 Model 50Z with 640KB of memory, a 1.44MB diskette drive, a 40MB hard drive. For local bridging support there are two IBM Token-Ring Network 16/4 Adapter cards, one for each ring segment connected. In remote support, there are two matching *real time interface coprocessor* (RTIC) cards ,one in each remote bridge half. These cards can be either the IBM RTIC with 512KB of memory or the IBM X.25 Interface Coprocessor/2 card. Dial up support can be provided by the IBM 7855-10 V.32 modem or any V.25 bis mode. ISDN support is provided by the IBM 7820 ISDN Terminal Adapter which is an interface card that is installed on the personal computer.

There are four main functions of the IBM Token-Ring Network Bridge Program. First and foremost the bridge program connects multiple rings into a larger network by transferring frames between ring segments connected by the bridge. Secondly the bridge program displays ring and domain status for hard and soft errors. A third function is the ability to monitor performance by maintaining statistics. Lastly, the bridge program sends alert notifications and reports to a LAN manager. These functions are found in both the local and remote configurations of the IBM Token-Ring Network Bridge Program V 2.2.

Local bridge functionality of the bridge program can support three types of ring segment connection as depicted in Figure 4.10. The bridge program can connect a 16Mbps ring segment to a 16Mbps ring segment, a 16Mbps ring segment to a 4Mbps ring segment and a 4Mbps ring segment to a 4Mbps ring segment. This capability provides great flexibility during growth and migration of token-ring networks from 4Mbps to 16Mbps token-ring networks.

Remote bridge or split bridge configurations of the IBM Token-Ring Network Bridge Program consists of two bridge halves connected over telecommunications lines. A token-ring network adapter card is required by each half to attach itself to a LAN segment and a communications adapter to attach itself to the telecommunications line. As shown in Figure 4.10, the bridges can be connected at speeds from 9.6Kbps to 1.344Mbps (T1). Each bridge half must contain the same value for the common parameters of bridge number and ring segment number. Operational parameters need only be changed on one bridge. The IBM LAN Manager V 2.0 or the IBM LAN Network Manger V 1.0 will update the other half of the remote bridge pair if the change is made using one of these LAN managers.

Backup connection for remote bridges can be instituted using the dial support feature of the IBM Token-Ring Network Bridge Program V 2.2. This dial support can also be used for occasional connections between token-ring networks. Used in this fashion, a single token-ring network can access several different networks throughout the course of a day if needed without incurring the cost of dedicated communication lines to each remote site.

As you will see later on in the text, remote bridging plays a major role in enterprise wide networking. Through the use of currently owned telecommunication lines and IBM SNA equipment token-ring network resources can communicate to each other and the SNA host over existing corporate assets.

4.9 IBM's 8209 LAN BRIDGE

In contrast to the IBM Token-Ring Network Bridge Program, the IBM 8209 LAN Bridge is a dedicated dual Intel 80186 processor and does not require a keyboard, display, diskette or hard disk. Instead, the IBM 8209 is a standalone computer that uses non-volatile memory. Firmware within the IBM 8209 provides the command sets for the operation of the bridge and bridge management functions. Using the IBM 8209 frees the personal computer that was executing the IBM Token-Ring Network Bridge Program in local mode for use as an end-user LAN workstation.

The IBM 8209 has two possible configurations as shown in Figure 4.11. The bridge is used only for local bridging between two token-ring segments or between a token-ring segment and an Ethernet V2/IEEE 802.3 local area network. The main function of the IBM 8209 is to connect unlike multiple LAN types into a single logical network.

Each token-ring-to-token-ring attachment must have either 4Mbps or 16Mbps on both rings. Different ring speeds are not supported as in the bridge program. In this configuration the IBM 8209 implements source-routing only. It can be managed by the IBM LAN Manager V2.0 and the IBM LAN Network Manager V1.0 and has all the functions of the bridge program. The IBM 8209 improves performance over the bridge program since it does not require an operating system and peripheral devices such as hard disk drives and diskette drives to perform its functions.

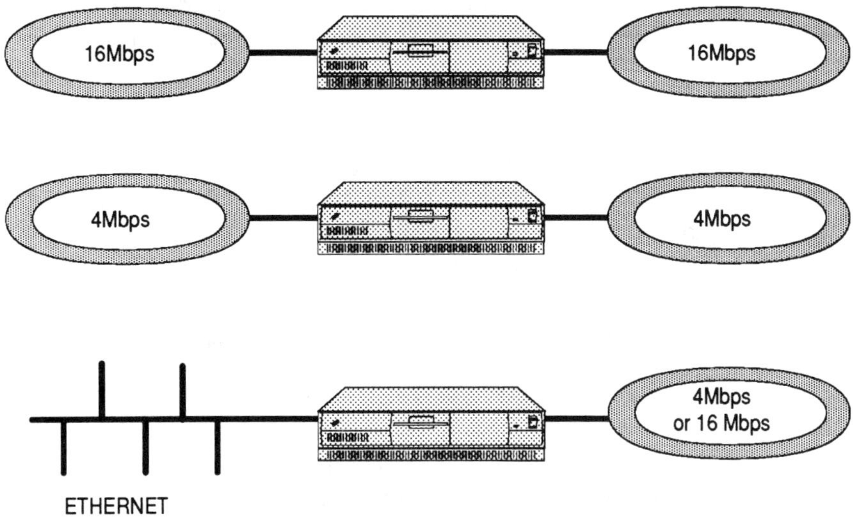

Figure 4.11 Three possible configurations for an IBM 8209.

In the Ethernet-to-token-ring attachment the IBM 8029 is seen as a source-routing bridge by token-ring stations and a transparent bridge using the spanning tree algorithm by Ethernet stations. The IBM 8209 provides for the conversion of frame formats between Ehternet and token-ring and vice versa. Ethernet is used widely in the engineering and scientific areas of corporations while token-ring has gained its popularity in the area of business applications. In this implementation token-ring can be used by the business groups, and Ethernet by the research and development areas of a corporation providing a single image local area network without incurring additional communications costs and utilizing existing corporate assets.

4.10 IBM's 8232 LAN CHANNEL STATION

IBM's commitment to non-SNA protocols has fostered the need for a channel-attached gateway to the SNA host computer. The IBM 8232 LAN Channel Station was IBM's first offering. This non-SNA gateway came in two models. Both models are based on the IBM 7532/266 Industrial PC/AT computer. Model 001 supported up to two LAN adapters and one System/370 channel adapter connection. The Model 002 increased this connection support to four LAN adapter connections and two System/370 channel adapter connections. The channel connections on the Model 002 can be to the same SNA host or different SNA hosts. The token-ring connection supported 4Mbps data rates.

The major impetus behind the IBM 8232 was to connect Ethernet LANs using *transmission control program / internet protocol* (TCP/IP) to TCP/IP executing on the IBM mainframe. The antiquated technology of the IBM 8232 gave way to a new product called the IBM 3172 Interconnect Controller.

4.11 IBM's 3172 INTERCONNECT CONTROLLER

Like the IBM 8232, the IBM 3172 Interconnect Controller connects the IBM SNA host to non-SNA hosts or workstations. The IBM 3172 uses the PS/2 Micro Channel architecture based Intel 80386 or 80486 microprocessor based computers. The Model 001 version comes with four LAN adapter slots and up to two channel adapter interfaces. The Model 002 increases the LAN adapter capabilities by one. The Model 003 is similar to the Model 001, but, adds another LAN adapter slot and offloads TCP/IP processing from the mainframe. It is called an interconnect controller because it connects dissimilar networks as opposed to connecting similar networks like bridges.

The IBM 3172 has extended the functions and features previously provided by the IBM 8232 LAN Channel Station. For one

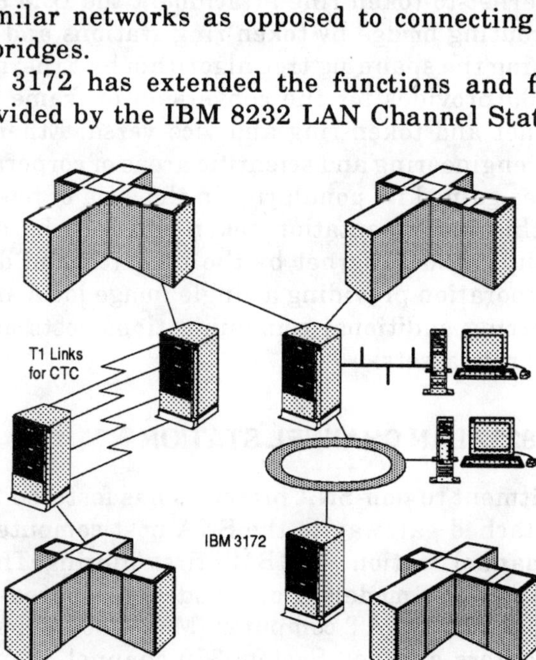

Figure 4.12 IBM's 3172 configurations.

the IBM 3172 can be used at token-ring data rates of 4Mbps or 16Mbps with a stated direction by IBM of supporting FDDI data rates of 100Mbps. Additionally the IBM 3172 can support SNA VTAM channel-to-channel connections using remote telecommunications lines as well as provide SNA *intermediate network node* (INN) traffic through the token-ring adapter. Figure 4.12 diagrams some of the possible configurations for the IBM 3172 Interconnect Controller.

Unlike the IBM 8232, the IBM 3172 can be remotely supported through its remote configuration support feature. The IBM 8232 needed someone physically located at the location to modify the IBM 8232 configuration. Using the *remote configuration support* (RCS) Program, on a token-ring attached OS/2 Extended Edition V1.2 of higher, the IBM 3172 can be configured, upgrades to the Interconnect Controller Program can be installed and the error log can be accessed by the OS/2 RCS workstation for analysis. A second feature provided by the IBM 3172 that was not available on the IBM 8232 is the ability to send alarm information to a communications network management application residing on the SNA host. This information can be useful in determining problems with stations off of the IBM 3172 or the IBM 3172 itself.

4.12 IBM's 3174 ESTABLISHMENT CONTROLLER

In the beginning of IBM SNA network computing, end-user terminals were connected to the mainframe computer using cluster controllers. These devices allowed for remote attachment of end-user terminals and printers either through mainframe channel connections or through communications controllers (i.e., front-end processors) using communications links. The cluster controllers were architected to allow a maximum of 32 physical terminal attachments and up to 255 logical attachments.

The IBM 3174 *establishment controllers* (EC) can be configured in a token-ring network using the Token-Ring Gateway feature. This feature allows the IBM 3174 Establishment Controller to connect to the SNA host computer via token-ring rather than SNA *synchronous data link control* (SDLC) communications lines or host channel connections. Figure 4.13 diagrams some of the token-ring configurations that can be used with the IBM 3174 Establishment Controller Token-Ring Gateway feature. In the figure the establishment controller can be either channel connected to the host SNA computer or remotely connected to the SNA host computer through a communications controller. The cluster controllers

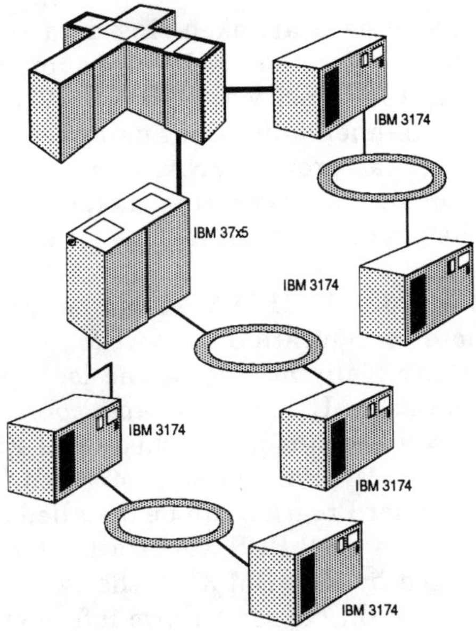

Figure 4.13 Some of the token-ring configurations that can be used with the IBM 3174.

attached to the token-ring are considered downstream physical units (DSPUs) from the EC. The advantage of providing connectivity with the EC is the reduction of channel connections and communications lines thus, saving resources and network communications costs.

4.13 IBM's COMMUNICATIONS CONTROLLER

Remote connectivity to the IBM SNA host computer is made possible through communications controllers. These communications controllers off-load the responsibility of communications protocols from the host computer. The IBM line has three well established lines of communications controllers. These are the IBM 3725, IBM 3720 and the IBM 3745 communications controllers. Currently the only line that is being marketed by IBM is the IBM 3745. The other two models can be purchased through third-party hardware suppliers if need be. Each line of communications controller supports IBM Token-Ring Networking.

Communications controllers can either be host connected through a channel or remotely connected using telecommunications lines. The communications controllers connected to a token-ring network through a token-ring adapter (TRA). Each TRA contains two token-ring interface couplers (TICs). Each TIC can be configured with a locally administered address (LAA). This address is defined by communications systems programmers in the *network control program* (NCP). The NCP is an executable module that is loaded into the communications controller from the SNA host computer. The NCP describes the characteristics and attributes of all network resources attached to the communications controller. The addition of token-ring connectivity greatly enhances the connectivity options available to IBM SNA networks.

Figure 4.14 illustrates some of the connectivity options available when using token-ring connections on communications controllers. The IBM Token-Ring Bridge Program can be used to provide for remote connectivity of communications controllers, establishment controllers and LANs over token-ring network providing for LAN-to-WAN connectivity.

4.14 SUMMARY

The IBM Token-Ring Network is implemented with the IBM Cabling System utilizing the star-wired ring topology. There are four major types of media used in LAN networking; coax cable, telephone twisted pair, shielded copper cable and fiber optic. The

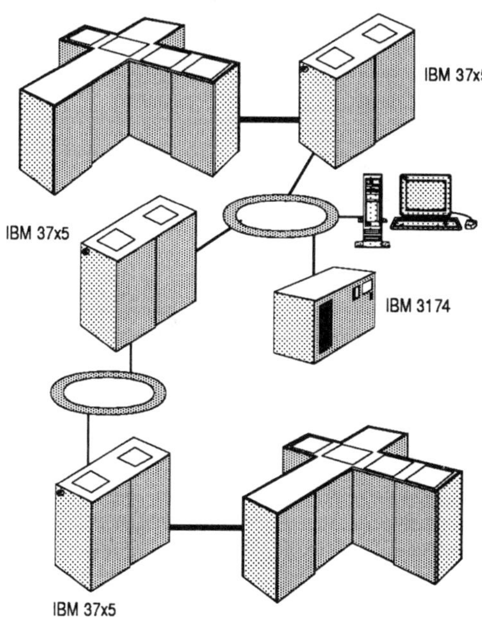

Figure 4.14 Some of the connectivity options available when using token-ring connections on communications controllers.

star-wired topology of the IBM Token-Ring Network has as its foundation the IBM 8228 *multistation access unit* (MAU). The MAU forms the ring through an internal relay wiring mechanism without external power and is sometimes called a *passive wiring concentrator* (PWC). *Controlled access units* (CAUs), like the IBM 8230, have their own power and thus can have built in intelligence. Token-ring networks can be interconnected through bridges. The IBM Token-Ring Network Bridge Program can perform both local bridging and remote bridging functions. Local bridging connects two or more token-ring networks directly. Remote bridging connects two or more token-ring networks over telecommunications lines. Connection of token-ring stations to the enterprise can be accomplished using the IBM 3172 Interconnect Controller, IBM 3174 Establishment Controller, IBM communications controllers or SNA physical unit emulators on token-ring workstations.

Chapter

5

LAN Planning

In the previous chapters, token-ring network architecture and the concepts and technology used to implement IBM's Token-Ring Network were discussed. In this chapter the planning and design of token- ring networking will be discussed.

The design of a token-ring network involves more than deciding on the type of technology to implement. Designing a token-ring network requires an understanding of the applications that will be in use on the LAN. The network designer must do some investigative work into the numbers of users and the type of traffic that will be generated over the network. For example, the explosion in imaging applications in corporate finance departments and customer service divisions of corporations will require large bandwidths to transfer these images. The end-user application requirements will dictate the immediate design of the local area network, but the final design criteria will be based on the following:

- The physical location of the network and its resources
- The logical connectivity requirements
- High availability
- Resource accessibility
- Control of application traffic flows
- LAN and WAN connectivity requirements

- Anticipated growth of the network
- The ability to migrate to and coexist with new emerging technologies
- Effectively managing the physical and logical entities of the LAN

The design alternatives available to satisfy these criteria can be exhaustive. Trying to meet all the requirements 100 percent will result in an unneeded complex design plan. A thorough understanding of the network topology, the capabilities of the technologies used and design trade-offs will greatly reduce the complexity.

The design of a token-ring network requires careful consideration to the question, "What are the corporations business requirements and how can token-ring networking provide a cost effective, yet robust solution to meet these requirements now and into the future?" The answer to this question lies in the understanding of the functions used on the LAN, the logical and physical topology design and the connectivity of LAN resources to the enterprise network, (e.g., mainframe connectivity).

5.1 THE SERVER CONCEPT

Recall that one of the purposes of a token-ring network is to share network resources. In a local area network this is often accomplished using a server. Servers can be categorized as being central or local. Central servers in an enterprise network are accessible by all LAN users. In the enterprise-wide network this server is usually the mainframe computer. The mainframe in today's computing environment is becoming more and more the centralized repository for corporate wide information. Local servers are viewed as being a powerful workstation on a LAN connected to a single LAN segment. Usually, only the users on that LAN segment access the local server. This group of related users performing related processes and functions on the LAN is called an affinity group. These local or departmental servers usually provide information that is specific to the departments use. The end-user applications on the token-ring stations can access either data on the central server or on the local server. The sharing of resources and the ability to access vital corporate data from servers by all LAN users has lead us into distributed cooperative processing environments.

Servers on a token-ring network usually provide two main functions. The first is to provide printer sharing. These "print servers" are often placed in the vicinity of the affinity group. In this type of

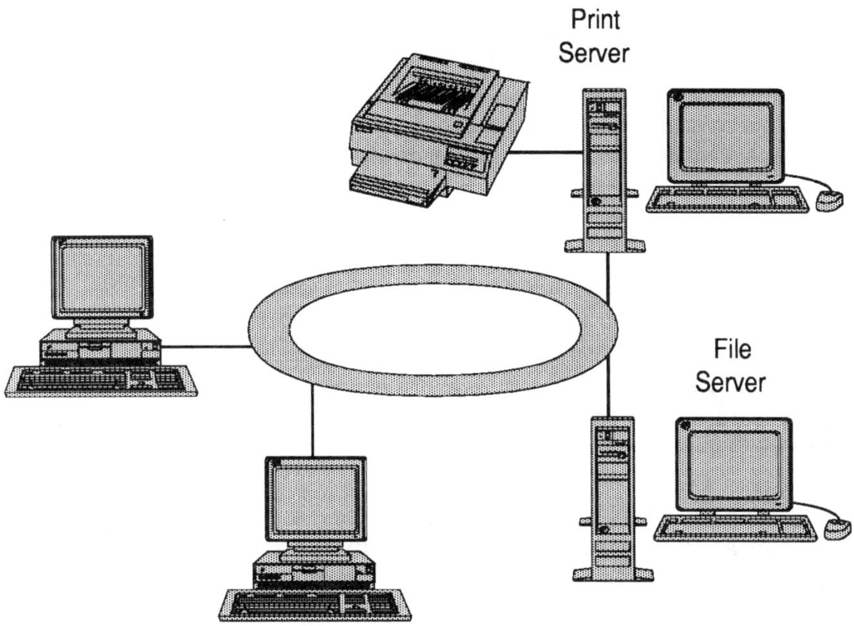

Figure 5.1 An illustration of a LAN server configuration.

configuration the affinity group will share a printer attached to the server as shown in Figure 5.1. This shared printing is cost effective by eliminating print delays and/or distribution of printed material from the mainframe. Not only does this reduce the cost of mainframe printing it also reduces the mainframe resources involved in the print process.

The second type of server found on local area networks is the file server. These file servers may also be referred to as disk servers. File servers can be powerful workstations residing on the LAN or even the mainframe computer. As the name implies, file servers provide shared access to files for the affinity group. The file server can be used for the departmental data base and/or as the distributor of networked applications. For example, popular personal computer applications like LOTUS 1-2-3 and Microsoft's EXCEL can be placed on the file server. The end-user station accesses the application program from the file server. Data specific to the end-user resides on the end-users workstation and not on the file server. Data specific to the department resides on the file server. The use of file servers reduces application license fees by allowing multiple LAN users access the same application program on the server and provides for the sharing of corporate data over the enterprise-wide network. The use of file servers reduces corporate data duplication, hence, reduces the requirements for disk storage enterprise wide resulting in a cost savings to the corporation.

A process known as client/server has grown out of the original server concept. A client is any entity on the network that requests information from a server. The server in this process is also known as an agent. In this process the client using cooperative processing techniques contacts an agent requesting information. The agent, on behalf of the client, processes, the request and returns the information back to the client. However, the roles of the entities can be reversed in the following process. The agent is now the client and the client is now the agent. The peer-to-peer relationship between client and server in an IBM environment utilizes *Advanced Peer-to-Peer Communications* (APPC).

Location of the servers is of vital importance to the design methodology as is the number of servers in the network. Determining the physical and logical relationships between LAN resources and the business needs requires a plan that encompasses the logical and physical design of the local area network.

5.2 PLANNING THE LOCAL AREA NETWORK

The planning of a token-ring local area network can be approached in many different ways. But, there are some basic steps that are necessary for planning any type of network, though the scope of each step may be different. These steps can be broken down into nine categories:

- The collection of information to assess requirements
- LAN segment and backbone design considerations
- Connectivity to the backbone
- Backup and recovery
- Network resource naming standards
- Traffic flow and control
- Management of the network and its resources
- Organizational structure and systems management
- Migration and future growth

5.2.1 Collecting Information

This process is sometimes the most tedious of all the steps in planning a network. It is, however, probably the most important step in the overall planning process.

The information collected should provide the designer with the physical layout of each installation and the relationships between the installations. The following physical requirements must be known for all locations:

- Cable location and their outlets
- The size and location of the wiring closets
- The required cable lengths between wiring closets
- The maximum lobe lengths for LAN attached devices using the cable types
- The number of stations that must be supported on the LAN segments

The information provided from this study is used to calculate adjusted ring length and the physical design of the local area network as well as the location of end-user workstations. Appendix G provides guidelines to cable, closet and ring segment drive distances.

This phase of the planning process identifies the application types and the access requirements of the end users. The LAN topology can take on different configurations depending on the types of applications and their locations. For example, end-user requirements to share files will require file servers in the network. The location of the end-users that need access to these files will also assist in determining inter-office communications to allow access to the file server. The end-user community will most likely need access to an SNA mainframe requiring a channel-attached gateway of some type. The frequency of accessing the mainframe and file servers must be assessed along with the duration of the access and the predicted traffic load over the network. These requirements will provide valuable input into selecting the key functions available on the network and the selection of products to provide this support.

As always, performance is an issue when designing networks. A basic rule of thumb when determining performance objectives is to design the network to meet these objectives during the peak periods of transmission. By designing the network based on the peak periods, you are guaranteeing that the performance objectives will be met during high volume transmissions. The selection of servers, gateways, cable types, and communications lines will be influenced by the amount of mainframe and server traffic; frequency, size of file transfers and the number and type of interactive transactions per mainframe and server connection.

Another factor in determining the design of a local area network is the number, size and location of affinity groups. Affinity groups will influence the topology through the use of bridging the various affinity group LAN segments. The locations and size of these groups will help determine the number of LAN segments, placement of servers and connectivity to the enterprise-wide network.

High availability of a token-ring network is always a main objective of the network design. Maintaining high availability is accomplished through the use of alternate paths, dual backbones and backup gateways. These will be described in greater detail in following sections.

5.2.2 End-user and Backbone Ring Design Considerations

The topology of the LAN is most commonly designed around a hierarchical multisegment structure with end-user rings and backbone rings. Figure 5.2 depicts end-user and backbone ring topology. The design of the end-user ring is performed after the

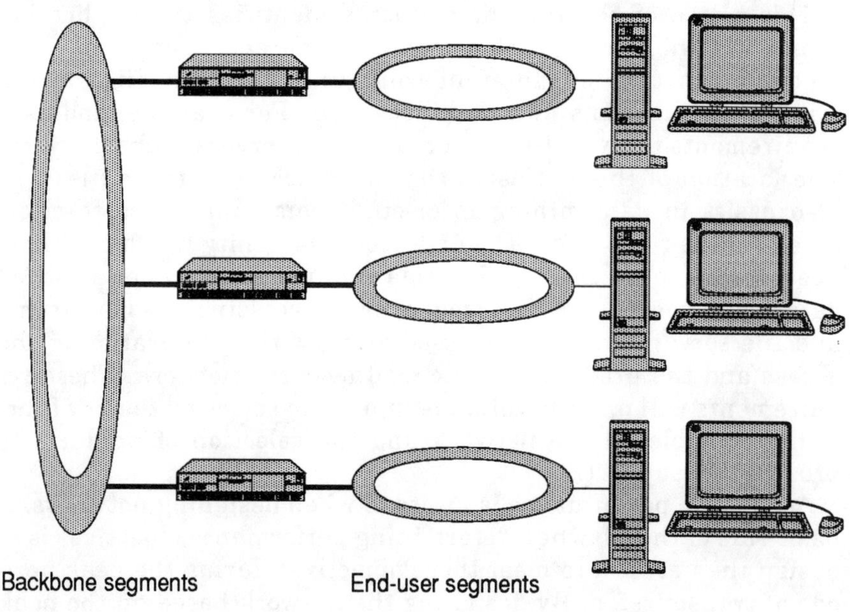

Figure 5.2 A sample end-user and backbone ring configuration.

collection of information. The information should be used as criteria in designing each end-user ring. It is typical to design the end-user ring based on the location of the end-user community. For instance, the ring segments are commonly divided up based on floors in a building or departments within the same building. End-user segments rarely , if at all, span buildings.

The backbone ring and its segments can be defined once the criteria has been applied to the end-user ring. The criteria will dictate the necessary connections needed by the end-user ring to the backbone and hence determine the backbone topology. Some of the end-user segments of the end-user ring may not need connectivity to the backbone at all, while for other end-user segments backbone connectivity may be a main requirement. The overall design of interconnecting the end-user and backbone rings must account for requirements that exists today and those that may appear in the future.

5.2.3 Connectivity to the SNA Mainframe

LAN stations connect to the SNA mainframe through gateways. In an IBM token-ring environment there are three types of gateways to choose from. These are shown in Figure 5.3.

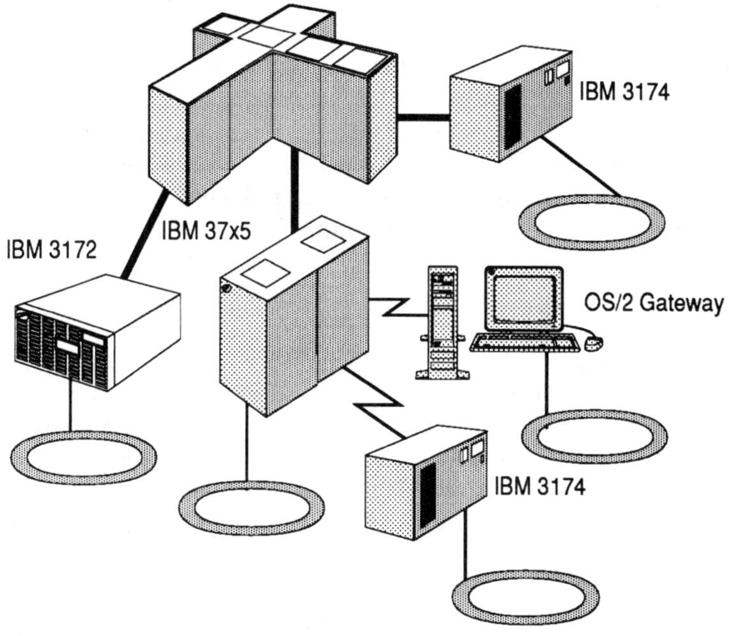

Figure 5.3 Token ring to mainframe connectivity.

The first is the communications controller. These gateways provide not only token-ring gateway functions but also standard SNA connectivity functions as well. A token-ring adapter is required on the communications controller gateway for token-ring connectivity to the SNA mainframe computer. This type of gateway is commonly used because of existing SNA backbone connectivity.

Establishment controllers like IBM's 3174 Establishment Controller can also provide a gateway function or token-ring devices. This controller is commonly used in an IBM SNA network by "dumb" terminals (e.g., IBM 3270 type terminals). The IBM 3174 acts as gateway for each station "downstream" to the IBM 3174. Each token-ring device using the IBM 3174 as a gateway to the SNA mainframe will be seen by the SNA mainframe as switched devices. The configuration and definitions required by the various SNA resources involved will be discussed in a later chapter. Token-ring resources can access the SNA mainframe through this gateway either remotely using a communications controller as the connection to the SNA mainframe or through local channel-attachment.

IBM's 3172 Interconnect Controller is the newest entry into IBM's gateway offerings. This device is channel-attached to the SNA mainframe. This direct connection to the SNA mainframe removes the necessity for a communications controller or an establishment controller. An added advantage of the interconnect controller is its ability to also provide bridging functions between Ethernet LANs and token-ring LANs.

The type and gateways used in the connectivity design should be selected based on the amount and type of traffic, performance objectives, availability requirements, the cost for implementing the gateway and the ability to manage the gateway equipment.

5.2.4 Backup and Recovery

There are many factors and considerations in designing backup and recovery into the network topology. Failure of any component in the network may affect availability. For example, a workstation that is beaconing will disrupt the entire ring segment. Use of a bridge will limit the effect of the beaconing workstation to the end-user segment rather than the entire token-ring network. The topology should be flexible in its ability to overcome bridge and router outages. Alternative routing will provide immediate recovery for these type of failures. Besides alternative routing techniques, a backbone failure can be recovered using dial-up digital lines. Today's technology can provide for a switched 56Kbps and 384Kbps speed lines. It must be understood by the end-user that these switched digital lines are for backup purposes and are only temporary. The impact of component failure must be weighed and recovery built into the network design.

5.2.5 Network Resource Naming Standards

Names on local area networks using token-ring are actually station addresses. Management of these addresses up to now has been difficult. The reason being that the end user has the ability to change his/her MAC address without notifying the LAN administrator. This could cause duplicate addresses on the same LAN segment which is prohibited. Deciding on an addressing standard revolves around the installations needs for control.

Universal addressing, sometimes called burned-in-address (BIA), eliminates the possibility of having duplicate addresses as long as the end-user does not administer their own address. Arguments, therefore, go in favor with locally administered addressing. Using a naming convention for LANs can provide meaning to a stations characteristics. As an example, the address can be based on the SNA exchange identification (XID) value of the resources physical unit, the end user's telephone number, or perhaps a room and building number.

Naming standards throughout the enterprise must be established to guarantee unique addresses and names. Some other resources that are LAN components that need naming uniqueness are:

- Bridges, routers and ring numbers
- SNA physical unit and logical unit names
- SNA XID
- LAN Network Manager symbolic resource names
- LAN Station Manager information
- TCP/IP names and addresses

Instituting a naming standard enterprise-wide will aid in problem determination, automation and operations. Appendix F provides IBM suggested addressing guidelines that may be used to forge a naming standard.

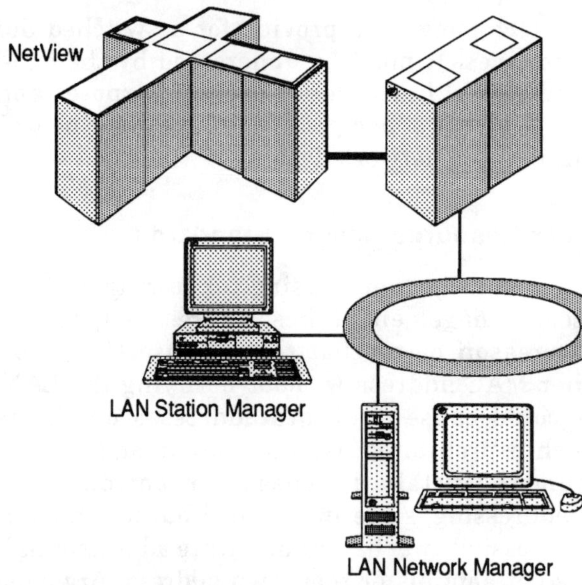

Figure 5.4 IBM's strategic LAN network management strategy.

5.2.6 Traffic Flow and Control

Multisegment LAN design requires a strategy for controlling the flow of data between interconnected segments. Application function and its usage of frames over the token-ring network are needed to determine the flow control strategy. There are a couple of ways to control the flow of data. One such way is to take advantage of bridge and router filtering mechanisms. Another way is to utilize the seven hop count limit on token-ring networks.

5.2.7 Network Management

LAN network management for token-ring networks has finally come of age with IBM's LAN Network Manager. This product offering along with IBM's mainframe network management system, NetView, offers a comprehensive solution to managing the token-ring network thorough automation, consolidation and integration of LAN management information. This network configuration is shown in Figure 5.4. An important aspect in implementing LAN management is the number and placement of the LAN managers. IBM's LAN Network Manager in conjunction with the IBM 8230 Controlled Access Unit (CAU) and the LAN Station Manger provides an extensive set of management functions. The relationships between these offerings and their usage are discussed in detail in the Chapter 8 Token-Ring Network Management.

5.2.8 Organizational Structure and Systems Management

Part of the planning process that goes into designing a token-ring local area network is the organizational structure. Many corporations began using token-ring LANs without creating an organization for managing the LAN or deciding where in the current organizational structure this responsibility should reside. Consequently, the roll-out of LANs through the corporate infrastructure is in disarray. A systems support structure must be in place in order to facilitate controlled management of the local area network.

Procedures must be put in place to manage this control. Daily operational tasks in concert with backup and recovery procedures must be well documented. Tools that support the management disciplines of change, problem, performance, configuration, operations and accounting must be used. The support structure and the LAN help desk rely on these management disciplines and proven procedures to provide a satisfactory level of service to the end-user community.

5.2.9 Migration and Future Growth

Implementation of the LAN design may possibly be the most difficult process in the planning stage. Migrating from current network configurations to a local area network can be quite difficult. The major objective during the migration phase is to minimize end-user outage. The impact on the end-user and ultimately the business must be assessed. Based on the assessment, scheduled outages, if any, must be agreed on by all parties involved. Through careful planning and public relations with the affected end-user communities the migration phase can be implemented smoothly.

The flexibility, ease of connectivity and the ability to share networked resources at a low cost is realized by all the various business groups in today's corporate environment. It goes without saying that the planning personnel must keep revising the growth plan for the LAN through constant communications with the end-user community. Failure to manage future growth will ultimately hinder the growth of the company.

5.3 SUMMARY

In this chapter, the criteria for planning a local area network was discussed. The importance of the end user's needs and the location of the end user in relation to the location of data were identified as a major criteria. The planning process requires a great deal of "up-front" research and discovery to implement a token-ring network. The issues of connectivity to other end-user segments and to the SNA mainframe were brought to the reader's attention to emphasize the importance of connectivity between future processing techniques in concert with existing processes on the SNA mainframe. The following chapter deals with the design of the token-ring local area network.

Chapter

6

LAN Design

The design of a token-ring local area network encompasses two areas — the physcial and logical design. The physcial design of the token-ring network is made up of the wiring, connectors, the multistation access units, controlled access units, the workstations, servers and bridges. The logical design of the token-ring network is comprised of the connectivity between rings and the logical design for high availability

6.1 PHYSICAL TOPOLOGY DESIGN

The design of the physical network for a LAN using token-ring network architecture is essential in the overall design process. Typically, high-rise office buildings and campus environments will require different physical configurations. These configurations may have a single token ring spanning several floors of an office building, multisegment LANs and backbone design.

6.1.1 Multiple Floor Ring Configurations

The simplest ring configuration for a multiple story building is depicted in Figure 6.1. Selecting this ring configuration provides for a simplistic network design and low cost. The simplistic design, however, lacks flexibility and resists change. A serial LAN configu-

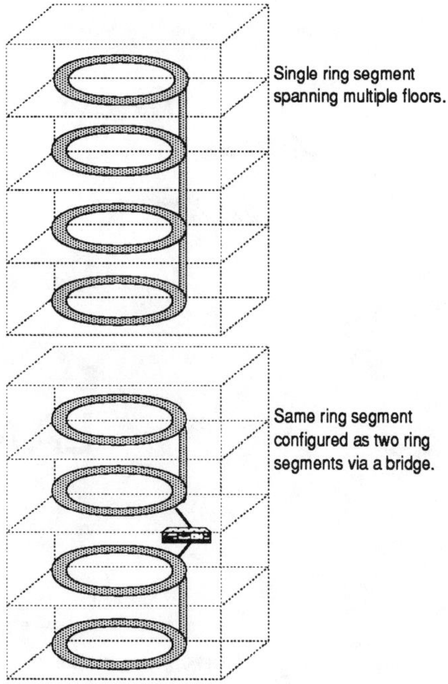

Figure 6.1 A simple multiple floor token-ring configuration.

ration typically cannot expand more than three segments due to segment length requirements. Token-ring LANs needing more than three segments require flexibility and ease of change. These criteria can be met implementing a backbone design. The following section will review a backbone design.

6.1.2 Backbone Design

Backbone configurations support multisegment LANs using several types of designs. Backbone designs are the favored approach when connecting between multiple ring segments is necessary. Each backbone design is specific to the needs of the LAN environment.

The simplest form of a backbone design is shown in Figure 6.2. Recall that a LAN segment is defined as a token-ring network up to the bridge. In Figure 6.2, the single ring configuration has been divided into four separate ring segments. Interconnection between the ring segments is accomplished by creating a backbone ring between the bridges. The bridge on each user ring segment isolates ring problems to the user ring.

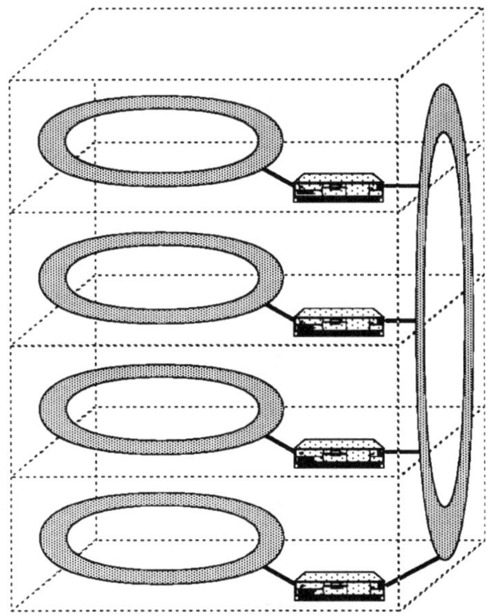

Figure 6.2 A single ring backbone configuration.

A backbone configuration that is very reliable with few cabling problems and minimum failures is the collapsed backbone configuration. As seen in Figure 6.3, the collapsed backbone ring is characterized by a centralized backbone ring and centralized bridges. Placing all the bridges in the same room eases the task of bridge maintenance. A spare bridge can also be configured to provide backup if a bridge should fail. The bridge itself, being that the backbone is consolidated into one room, can be the IBM 8209 bridge utilizing the token ring-to-token ring capabilities. This bridge is rack mountable and is self contained, and does not need a keyboard or display screen. This saves valuable space in the bridge room and reduces the load on the power supply.

The access units that connect the stations to the ring may consist of one access unit or multiple access units. This is dependent on the number of stations requiring token-ring access. In planning the physical connection to the access unit(s) in the bridge room, take into account the maximum distances between the bridges and the centralized backbone with the maximum lobe length for the user ring. This is approximately 100 meters for IBM 8228 Multistation Access Units. If the IBM 8230 Controlled Access Unit is used instead, the maximum lobe lengths may exceed 100 meters.

A collapsed backbone has minimal overhead costs to implement

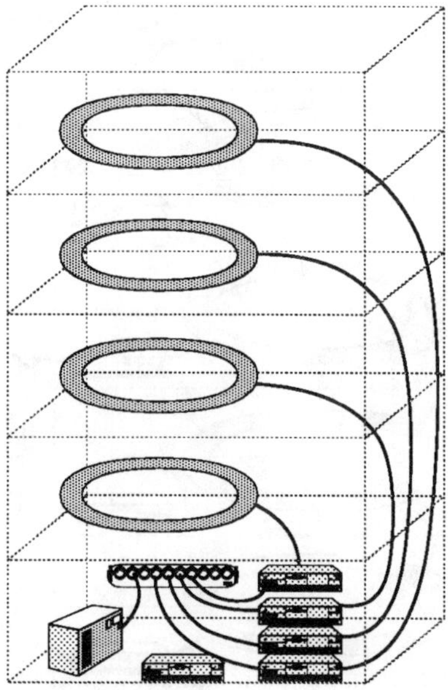

Figure 6.3 A collapsed backbone ring configuration.

the backbone since cables are installed in the same room there by eliminating the need for repeaters. Additionally, the short bridge lobe lengths enable an easy path to migrate from a 4Mbps ring to a 16Mbps.

In cases where there is not enough room to centralize the bridges, the bridges themselves can be distributed while maintaining a centralized backbone configuration. The centralized backbone varies from the collapsed backbone by virtue of placing the bridges close to the actual end-user ring. In a typical configuration, as diagrammed in Figure 6.4, the SNA host gateway and the access unit(s) remain centrally located, while the bridges may reside in wiring closets on each floor of the building. The maximum lobe lengths of a centralized backbone must be considered more carefully than with the collapsed backbone, specifically, with a single IBM 8228 Multistation Access Unit. A backbone speed of 4Mbps will allow for a maximum lobe length of approximately 350 meters using IBM Type 1 or Type 2 cables. At 16Mbps the maximum lobe length is approximately 160 meters.

A distributed backbone is considered when the physical make-up of the building will not permit a centralized backbone topology of either design discussed. Figure 6.5 depicts two types of distributed backbone configuration. A riser backbone is aptly named because

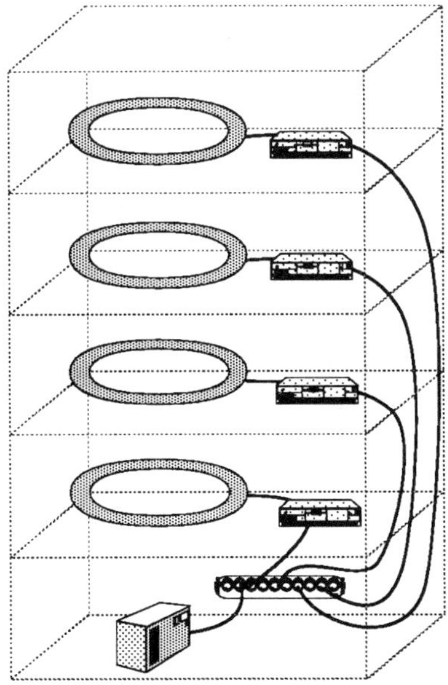

Figure 6.4 Centralized backbone configuration.

the cable actually runs up the building riser. In a riser backbone configuration each bridge is attached to the backbone through an access unit that, most likely, resides in the same wiring closet as the bridge. The backbone is routed through each wiring closet as shown in the riser configuration. A variation of this is the single backbone-dual riser configuration. The ring-in port of the bottom access unit is physically connected to a cable that returns from the top access unit through a different riser.

Access unit costs can be reduced by implementing the clustered bridge distributed backbone configuration. In a clustered bridge distributed backbone configuration the backbone is routed through more than one access unit that reside on different floors of the building. This clustered bridge distributed backbone configuration reduces costs by removing the need for access units on each floor and enhances maintenance by minimizing the number of access units that need servicing.

An alternative to the single-backbone dual-riser configuration is the dual backbone ring configuration. As depicted in Figure 6.6, each backbone ring is connected to the end-user rings through a bridge. This bridge configuration on the dual backbone ring can be physically configured in either or in combination with the collapsed and distributed bridge scenarios and distributed access

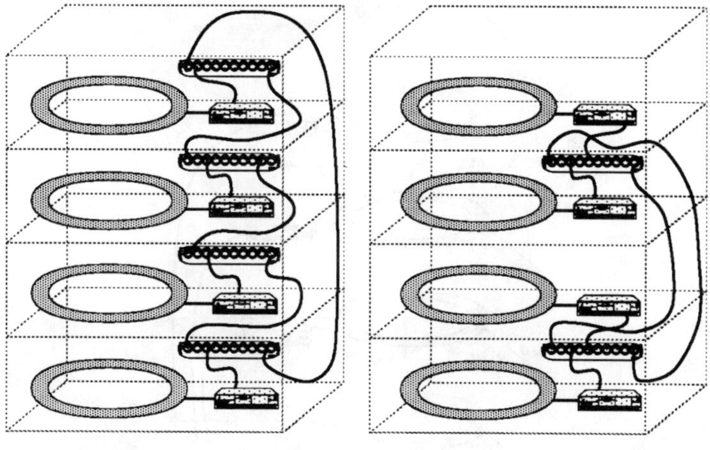

Figure 6.5 Distributed backbone configuration.

unit configurations.

The increased size of the physical backbone will require the usage of repeaters, in long or tall buildings and campus environments. For long distances, fiber-optic cable is used increasing the drive distance of the ring. Fiber-optic cabling is advantageous over copper wire because it has a longer drive distance, is unaffected by differential ground potentials and is less susceptible to lightning. Using multiple physical paths and the IBM 8220 converters and

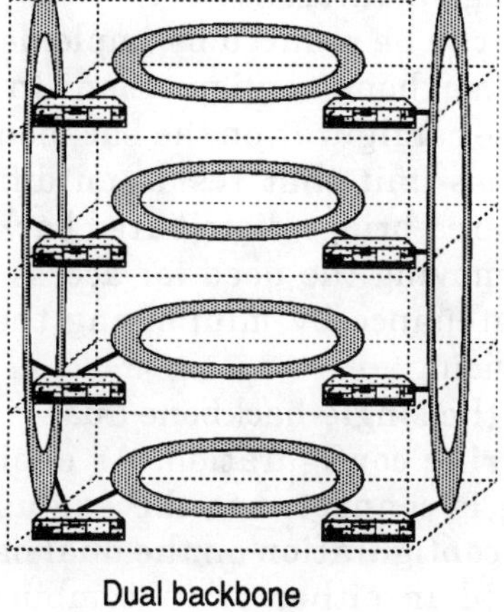

Figure 6.6 A dual ring backbone configuration.

the IBM 8230 Controlled Access Units in a large backbone is quite useful due to the automatic wrap feature of these devices. If one of the fiber-optic paths is cut, the other will be used by the IBM 8220 and the IBM 8230 automatically.

6.2 LOGICAL TOPOLOGY DESIGN

The design of the logical topology for a token-ring local area network has several dependencies. The logical design must provide solutions to the end-user requirements and physical restrictions. As an example, in small networks the placement of end-user workstations is largely dependent on the physical make-up of the building or floor. For the most part, a multisegement LAN implementation will provide the solutions to the following list of requirements for a bridged LAN topology:

- The number of workstations per segment or cable
- Balancing heavy traffic loads over interconnected LAN segments
- Consistent protocol use on each LAN segment
- Geographic assignment of LAN segments within a building, campus or over a Wide Area Network
- Defining affinity groups
- A provision for backup and recovery, enhanced availability and reliability
- Secured segments and workstations
- Access to SNA host gateways and LAN servers

Meeting these requirements results in a user segment logical design and a design for interconnecting the multiple LAN segments.

6.2.1 User Segment Logical Design

Typically, many network designers base the user segment design on the physical layout of the building. For instance, the user segments will be based on a per floor basis. One user segment for each floor or one user ring per two floors. Both of these and other design ideas are all feasible. In any case, the designer must consider all the physical specifications for the devices and cables used for the ring segment.

Designing user segments based on the physical layout of a building, however, does not take into consideration the application mix on the LAN segment. Defining affinity groups alleviates the application mix problem. Affinity groups are a group of users on the network with related tasks and require minimum access to other end users. An example of an affinity group is the financial department utilizing document imaging to keep track of company assets. The bandwidth required for imaging is greater than some other applications that may require little exchange of information between the file server and the workstation. In such a scenario, an affinity group of this type is warranted. Affinity groups that are not colocated can result in complex and inflexible designs. A balance between affinity groups and geographically based user segments must be attained for a working heterogeneous local area networking environment.

Departmental ring segments are often designed because the departments want ownership of the ring. These departments are then responsible for network management, controlled access, purchasing, installation, maintenance and change of the ring segment.

Mobility of the end-user community also plays a role in the design of the user segments. End user relocation inside a building or between buildings prohibits the use of affinity groups. In cases such as this, the best design possible is one based on geographic position.

Finally, there must be a coordinated effort to adhere to standards devised for the network. This will help avoid the duplication of names, addresses and ring numbers in the network.

6.2.2 Multisegment LAN Design

Interconnecting LAN segments can be accomplished using five different configurations. The topologies are based on bridging the LAN segments. The connectivity using bridges defines the type of topology selected. There are five main interconnecting topologies to choose from: serial, loop, parallel, mesh and backbone.

Serial configuration is typically used for small interconnected multisegment LANs. As the name indicates, the LAN segments are interconnected in a serial fashion as diagrammed in Figure 6.7. This simplistic configuration leads to low availability. Users accessing file and print servers on Segment B have only one way in and out. A bridge failure or a failure of some other component specific to the interconnection will stop intersegment communications. The inadequacy of alternate patching in a serial configura-

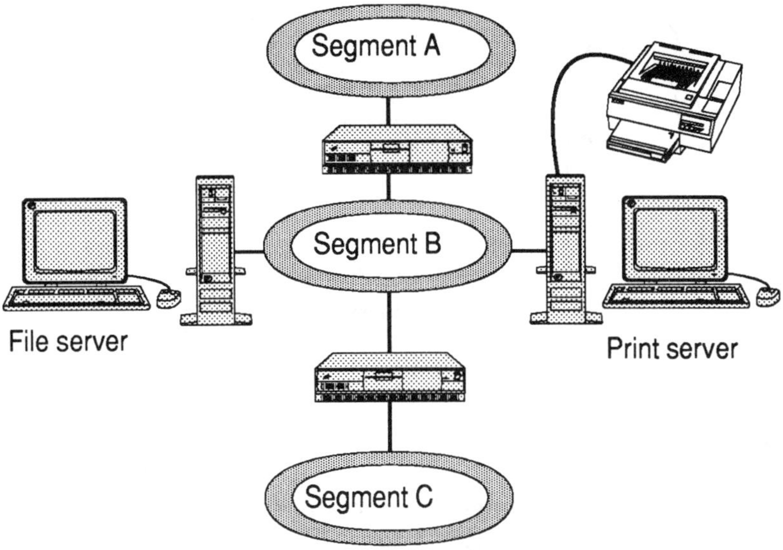

Figure 6.7 A serial LAN multisegment configuration.

tion is unacceptable for large multisegment LANs. Another draw back to the serial configuration is that the token-ring hop count of seven is reached after connecting only eight LAN segments. This not only affects expansion of the LAN, but also, the number of LAN managers and any-to-any communications.

A variation of the serial configuration is the loop configuration. As shown in Figure 6.8, a loop configuration is created when a

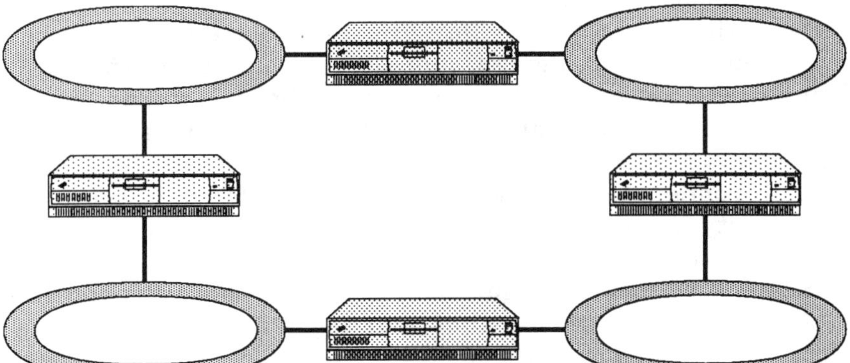

Figure 6.8 A loop configuration.

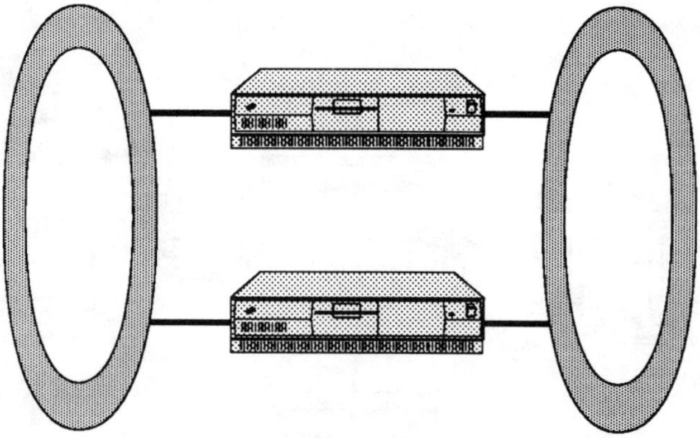

Figure 6.9 A simple parallel bridge configuration.

bridge connects the two end segments of the serial topology. Configuring the serial topology into a loop provides for alternate pathing should a bridge or path fail. The advantage to designing serial topology with the loop configuration is the increase in availability for intersegment communications. However, as the number of segments increase, the problem of hop count and the affects of any-to-any communication still exists.

Increased traffic between two LAN segments will be observed as bridge congestion. The congestion can be relieved by introducing a second bridge between the two LAN segments. This is called a parallel bridge configuration. Figure 6.9 depicts a simple parallel bridge configuration. In such a configuration, traffic between the two segments can flow through either bridge. If one bridge should fail, the connection between two stations can be reestablished through the second bridge. Both bridges can be active only when using source route bridging techniques. If transparent bridging is being used then one of the bridges must be in a standby mode. Parallel bridge configurations can address performance issues and availability requirements.

Mesh configurations pose an altogether different approach to availability and connectivity. Each segment in the network connects directly to the other segments in the network. As can be seen in Figure 6.10, mesh configurations can become quite complex in a LAN configuration greater than four segments. Mesh configurations, though producing the ultimate in availability, are impractical in the real world. The cost for bridges in this type of configuration are not justifiable. A major concern in a mesh configuration is the management of all-routes broadcast messages

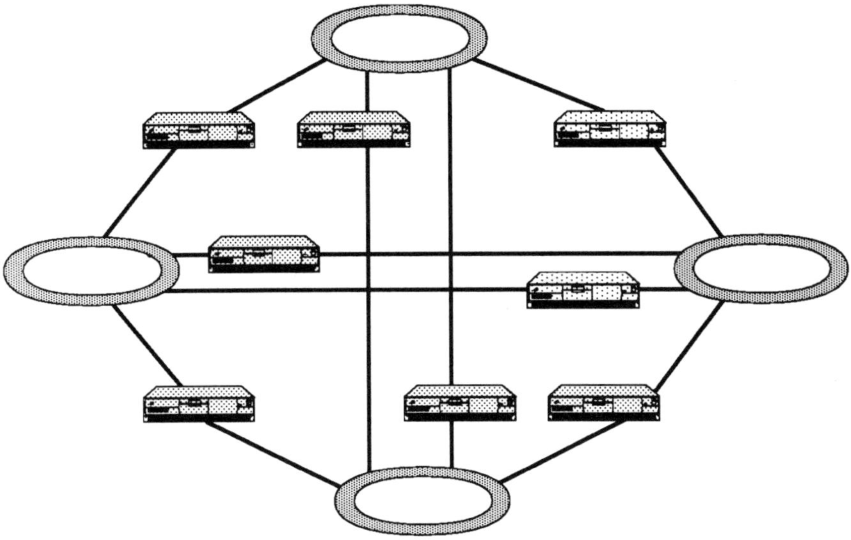

Figure 6.10 A token-ring mesh configuration.

and trouble shooting. The number of all-routes broadcast messages received by the destination station is unnecessary overhead and may not result in the shortest path even in a low use network. Another concern with mesh configurations is the ability to trouble shoot problems. Imagine sitting at the network help desk supporting a configuration like that in Figure 6.10 and trying to determine why two stations can no longer communicate with each other.

The most proven approach to multisegment network connectivity is the backbone ring configuration. A single backbone configuration, as shown in Figure 6.11, has several advantages over the previous topologies discussed. For one, each end-user segment is attached to the backbone through a bridge. This eliminates the hop count limit constraint since an any-to-any connection will not pass through more than two bridges. In general, backbone ring configurations are more desirable with large multiple segment LANs.

Backbone configurations simplify change. The addition or deletion of a segment to the multisegment LAN is a matter of removing the bridge connection from the backbone ring. The ability to adapt to newer technologies on the backbone ring will not affect the end user segment allowing for a smooth migration to newer technologies.

Centrally located resources can now be administered on the

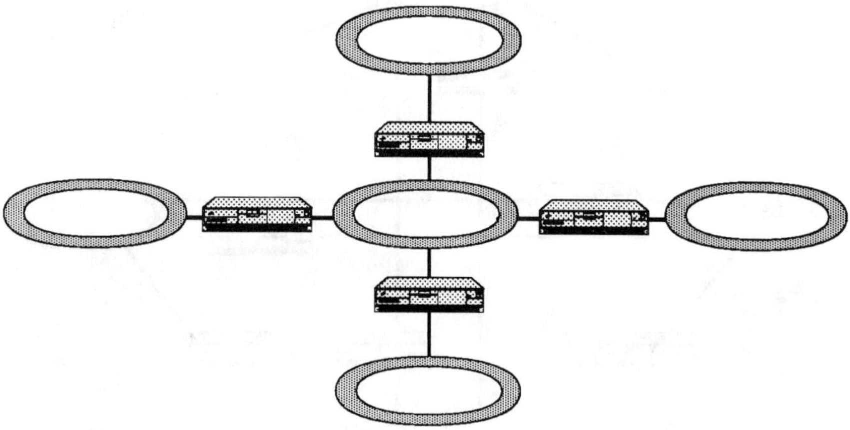

Figure 6.11 A single backbone configuration.

backbone ring. This will provide access to network wide file and print servers. This can help in reducing costs while at the same time providing end user access to high quality resources such as letter quality laser printers. Care should be taken if designing the backbone with heavily used servers. Traffic to these servers could begin to affect performance on the backbone, thereby, affecting end users not accessing the servers. It may be wiser to place the servers on the individual end user segments and or create a segment of servers off the end-user segment.

The single backbone configuration does have its draw backs. In a single backbone configuration, each user segment relies on a single bridge to access the other segments on the network through the backbone segment. Failure of this bridge or any of the components connecting to the bridge from the user segment would result in failed sessions without the ability to restart them through an alternate route. The backbone ring itself becomes a critical component and a possible performance bottleneck.

High availability is always a main requirement for network designers. From the network designer standpoint, if it is shown that the cost of a network outage will damage the corporations income, then configurations utilizing a single point of failure should not be considered. A dual or duplex backbone configuration can provide

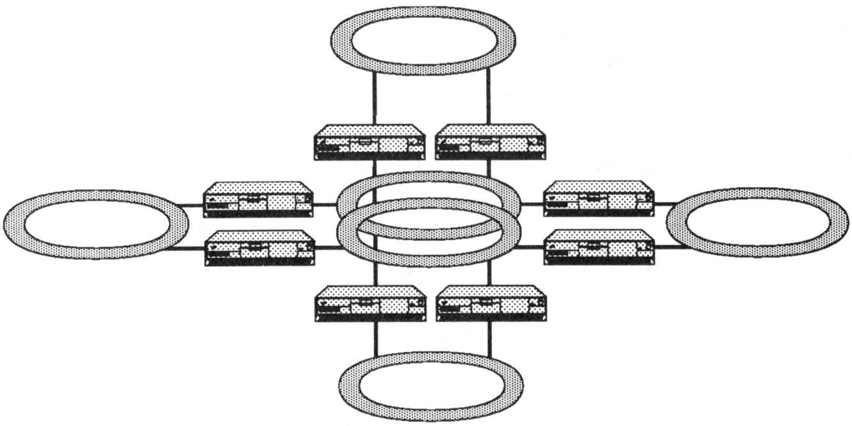

Figure 6.12 A dual ring backbone configuration.

high availability.

Component failures on the LAN can be bypassed using this dual backbone configuration. As seen in Figure 6.12, the cost of this is a second backbone ring and two bridges for each end-user ring. The extra cost for this must be weighed against the cost to do business should a failure occur on a single backbone configuration.

Duplex backbones eliminate single point of failure. Bridge failure may fail the existing session, but the session may be reestablished by the partners through the second bridge. Failure of a backbone will not be cause for alarm. Sessions can be reestablished over the second backbone using the secondary bridges from the end-user segments. Redundancy for end-user segment connectivity is achieved.

Another advantage to a duplex backbone configuration is performance on the backbone. Load balancing over the two backbones is balanced due to the source routing algorithm.

LAN server and SNA host gateway configuration are enhanced when using a duplex backbone configuration. LAN servers and SNA host gateway devices can be attached to either a backbone ring, to a second level server/gateway ring that is connected to both backbone rings or directly to end-user rings.

6.3 SNA GATEWAY CONNECTIVITY

Connectivity to an SNA host mainframe computer in today's corporate networking strategy is most important. SNA is the most widely used networking architecture in the corporate world. Corporate data, therefore, resides on the SNA host computer system. Access to corporate data from token-ring LANs is paramount to developing a plan and design for token-ring networks.

Token-ring devices attach to the SNA network through gateways. IBM provides four types of SNA gateways for token-ring. These are communications controllers, establishment controllers, interconnect controllers and OS/2 gateways.

6.3.1 IBM Communication Controllers

IBM communication controllers have historically been used to provide leased *Synchronous Data Link Control* (SDLC) line support for remote location access to the SNA mainframe. There have been four types of communication controllers offered by IBM. Each communication controller was geared for different markets. These are the IBM 3705, 3720, 3725, and 3745 Communication Controllers. The only model that IBM currently offers is the IBM 3745. The other models can be acquired through third-party suppliers. Of the four models, there are two that remain in force as SNA communications controllers. These are the IBM 3725 and the IBM 3745. The addition of token-ring support to these communication controllers allows the network designer to utilize a high-speed access token-ring network to the already established SNA backbone network. Figure 6.13 details the token-ring support provided by the most recent IBM communication controllers.

Each communication controller is attached to the token ring through a token-ring interface coupler (TIC) of a token-ring adapter (TRA). Information specific to a token-ring interface, such as the locally administered address (LAA), is defined in the communication controllers Network Control Program (NCP). The NCP defines the token-ring interface as a nonswitched (leased), full-duplex, point-to-point line. The token-ring interface is viewed by SNA as a physical unit type 1 (PU T1). Workstations on the token ring accessing the SNA host through the TIC of the communication controller are viewed as a PU T2 device. The line connection for these devices is defined on the SNA host software, Virtual Telecommunications Access Method (VTAM) as a switched, half-duplex, point-to-point line configuration.

Token-Ring Functions					
Communication Controller	**PU T2.0** w/ NCP	**PU T2.1 w/NCP**	**PU T4/5 w/NCP**	**4 Mbps w/NCP**	**16 Mbps w/NCP**
3720	V4Subset V4R2 V5 all rels	V5R2 V5R2.1 V5R3 +	 V5R2.1 V5R3 +	V4 Subset V4R2 V5 all rels	None
3725	V4R2 V4R3 V4R3.1	V4R3 V4R3.1	 V4R3.1	V4R2 V4R3 V4R3.1	None
3745 Models 210, 310, 410, 610	V5 all releases	V5R2 V5R2.1 V5R3 +	 V5R2.1 V5R3 +	V5 all releases	V5R3 +
3745 Models 130, 150, 170	V5R2.1 V5R3 +	V5R2.1 V5R3	V5R2.1 V5R3 +	V5R2.1 V5R3 +	V5R3 +

Figure 6.13 The communication controller support for token-ring networking.

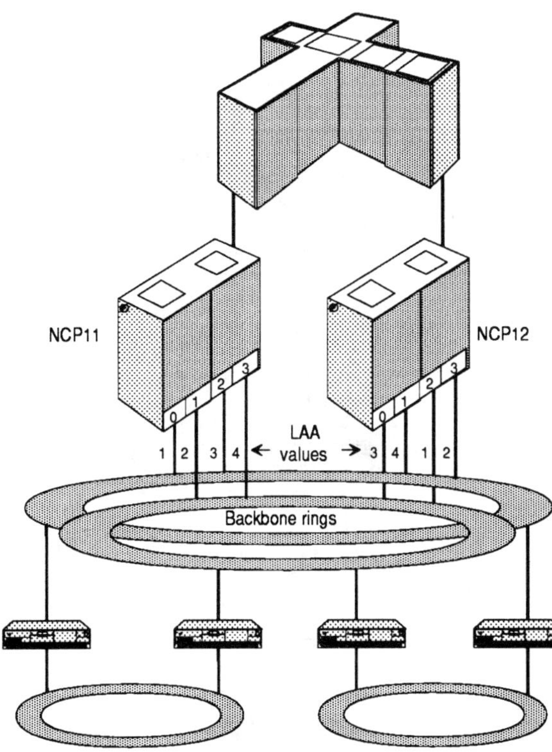

Figure 6.14 Duplicate TIC addressing using a dual ring backbone configuration.

There are two types of high-availability configurations that can be utilized for communication controllers. The first is the dual backbone ring configuration and the second is an isolated dual host-ring configuration. In the first scenario, high availability is achieved using the dual backbone approach as illustrated in Figure 6.14. This dual backbone configuration is enhanced through the duplication of TIC addresses (LAAs) on the two communication controllers. In the figure TIC positions 0 and 1 on NCP11 and TIC positions 2 and 3 on NCP12 have the same TIC addresses. Likewise, TIC postions 2 and 3 on NCP11 and TIC positions 0 and 1 on NCP12 have the same TIC addresses. Duplicate token-ring stations addresses on the communication controller is possible because the addresses are attached to different rings. The duplication of these TIC addresses in conjunction with the dual backbone rings provide multiple paths and provide implicit load balancing. Figure 6.15 illustrates the isolated host-ring configuration. The addition of the dual host-rings is used when the backbone ring exhibits high utilization.

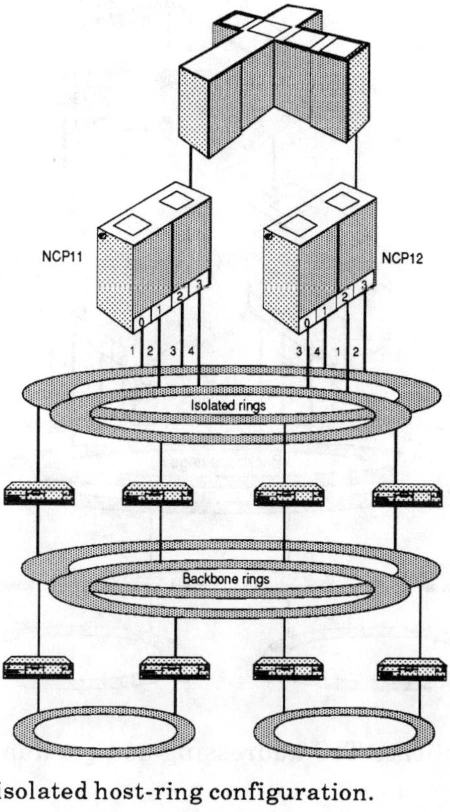

Figure 6.15 An isolated host-ring configuration.

6.3.2 Establishment Controller

End users in an SNA network have historically accessed the SNA host computer through cluster controllers. These devices provided for up to 32 physical connections to "dumb" terminals per cluster controller. These terminals are commonly referred to as IBM 3270 type terminals. Access to the SNA host computer therefore was limited to 32 physical terminals. The IBM 3174 Establishment Controller has increased this number dramatically by supporting up to 260 "downstream" physical units (DSPUs). Each of these downstream PUs, with proper software and hardware, support from 5 to 255 logical units (LUs). The IBM 3174 Establishment controllers emulate the functions of cluster controllers for attached logical units and provide token-ring gateway functions for downstream physical units.

The IBM 3174 token-ring gateway is available for both channel-attached and remote-attached establishment controllers. The establishment controllers can support both 4Mbps and 16Mbps rings and provide multiple SNA host support. A management feature of the establishment controller is the inclusion of a Ring Error Monitor Facility. This facility allows the establishment controller to capture token ring errors on the attached segment and forward these to a centralized management application like IBM's NetView.

High availability for establishment controllers is depicted in Figure 6.16. In this figure all the establishment controllers are active and participating in token-ring activity. Again, duplicate addressing is utilized to provide redundancy and hence high availability. The downstream physical units (DSPU), in this case the workstations, issue a route explorer frame to locate the shortest path to the establishment controller gateway. The DSPU receives routing information from both establishment controller gateways. The routing information found in the first response received will determine which of the establishment controller gateway to use for subsequent communications.

There are some issues that must be resolved before forging ahead with an establishment controller configuration. Congestion could occur within the establishment controller depending on the number of physical units it is supporting. Secondly, The same physical device on the end users desk may have different logical unit names depending on which establishment controller gateway is being used. This may cause definition problems for mainframe applications like IBM's CICS which rely on consistent logical unit names for the end-user terminals.

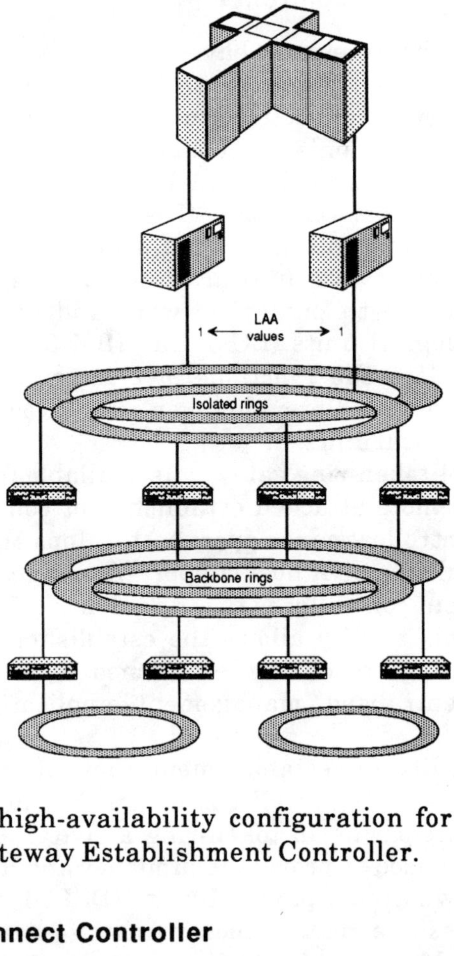

Figure 6.16 A high-availability configuration for the IBM 3174 Token-Ring Gateway Establishment Controller.

6.3.3 Interconnect Controller

The move towards interoperability between different physical computing platforms has necessitated the need for an interconnect controller. This type of controller "interconnects" two or more dissimilar computing platforms. IBM's 3172 Interconnect Controller offering provides connectivity between non-SNA resources with the SNA mainframe. The interoperability of a SUN SPARC workstation with an SNA mainframe database application can be accomplished using TCP/IP over token-ring, the IBM 3172 Interconnect Controller and IBM's TCP/IP for MVS. The ability to interconnect thees dissimilar networks has lead to the explosion in distributed processing.

The IBM 3172 attaches to the SNA mainframe with at least one mainframe channel connection. The IBM 3172 views the SNA mainframe as one of the networks begin interconnected. Any other

ICP Version		V1.0	V2.0	V2.1	V2.2	V2.X
Host program	TCP/IP	**Yes**	**Yes**	**Yes**	**Yes**	**Yes**
	MMS	**Yes**	**Yes**	**Yes**	**Yes**	**Yes**
	AIX	**Yes**	**Yes**	**Yes**	**Yes**	**Yes**
	VTAM/SNA		**Yes**	**Yes**	**Yes**	**Yes**
	VTAM/CTC			**Yes**	**Yes**	**Yes**
Channels	Parallel	**Yes**	**Yes**	**Yes**	**Yes**	**Yes**
	Serial VTAM/CTC			**Yes**	**Yes**	**Yes**
	High speed serial					**Yes**
	High speed serial					**Yes**
LANs	Token-ring	**Yes**	**Yes**	**Yes**	**Yes**	**Yes**
	ENET/802.3	**Yes**	**Yes**	**Yes**	**Yes**	**Yes**
	IEEE 802.4 MAP 3.0	**Yes**	**Yes**	**Yes**	**Yes**	**Yes**
	IEEE 802.4 SNA support		**Yes**	**Yes**	**Yes**	**Yes**
	PC Network			**Yes**	**Yes**	**Yes**
	FDDI			**Yes**	**Yes**	**Yes**
Links	T1 w/DS			**Yes**	**Yes**	**Yes**
	J1, E1 w/DS				**Yes**	**Yes**
	>T1					**Yes**
Models	Gateway	**Yes**	**Yes**	**Yes**	**Yes**	**Yes**
	CTC			**Yes**	**Yes**	**Yes**

Figure 6.17 The IBM 3172 Interconnect Controller functional support.

network that attaches to the interconnect controller is categorized as a LAN. Figure 6.17 contains a table identifying the functional levels of software support for the IBM 3172 Interconnect Controller.

The use of an interconnect controller brings to fruition the "cloud" concept for connectivity to an SNA mainframe. The advantage of using an IBM 3172 over an IBM 3745 or IBM 3174 as the gateway to the SNA mainframe is the increase in dynamism. After initial configuration, the IBM 3172 can be modified with minimal interruption if any to the network. Another advantage to using the IBM 3172 is the elimination of a front-end processor and the Net-

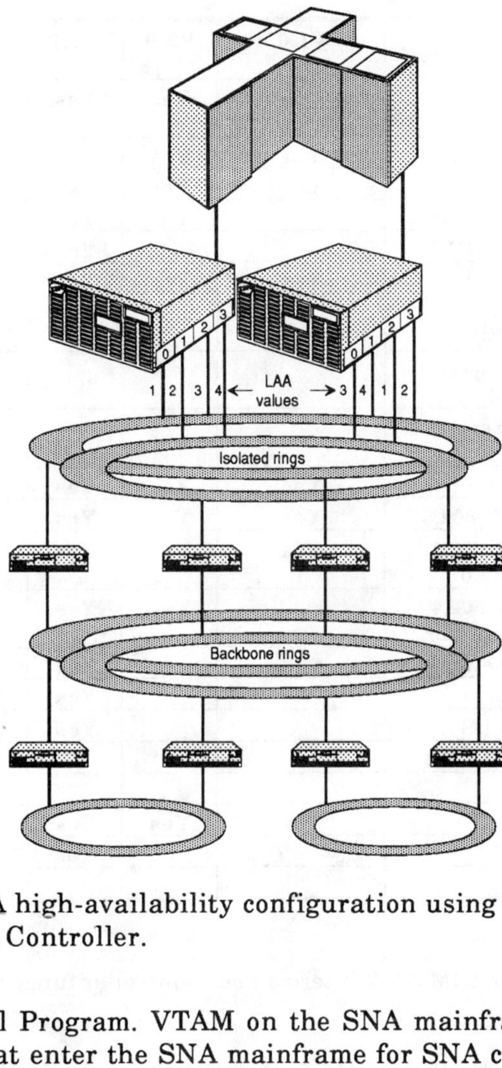

Figure 6.18 A high-availability configuration using the IBM 3172 Interconnect Controller.

work Control Program. VTAM on the SNA mainframe views all resources that enter the SNA mainframe for SNA connectivity as switched devices. Figure 6.18 diagrams a possible network configuration utilizing IBM 3172 Interconnect Controllers.

It can be seen from the figure that the IBM 3172 can replace the IBM 3745 for SNA connectivity and can still utilize the high-availability dual backbone ring configuration as was done with communications controllers and establishment controllers. Again, this enhances load balancing and availability to the SNA host computer.

The IBM 3172 is extremely flexible in design. It implements SNA host channel, SNA, MAP 3.0 and TCP/IP protocols over the most popular LAN standards Ethernet and Token-Ring Networks.

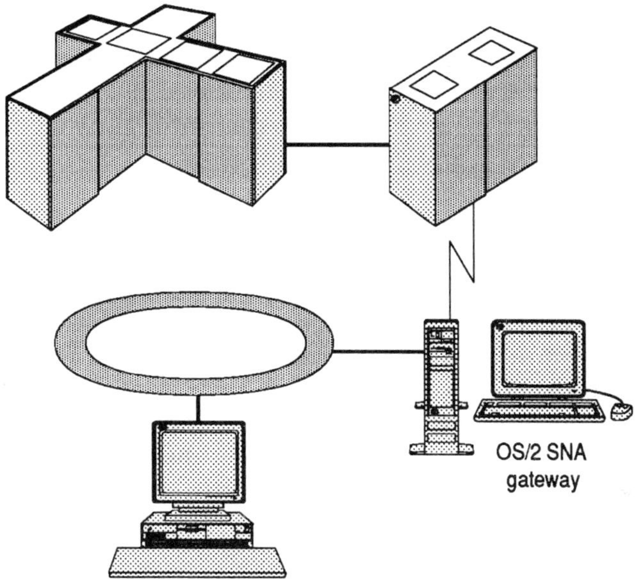

Figure 6.19 An OS/2 SNA Gateway configuration to support.

6.3.4 OS/2 SNA Gateway

The IBM multitasking operating system, OS/2, utilizes its Communications Manager feature to act as an SNA gateway for other stations attached to the same token-ring as the OS/2 SNA Gateway. The OS/2 SNA Gateway appears to the SNA host computer as a PU T2 device as shown in Figure 6.19. The workstations on the ring view the OS/2 SNA Gateway as a PU T4 node. Each workstation on the ring accessing the OS/2 SNA Gateway for SNA host connectivity acts like an LU T2 device.

The OS/2 SNA Gateway can support up to 254 SNA logical units. This is because of the SNA SDLC address field specifications for originating and destination fields. Since the gateway emulates a PU T2 device, the SNA host activates a single physical unit on a single SDLC line. The physical line however may be an SDLC link, a token-ring connection or an X.25 connection.

The logical units defined in the gateway can be either allocated to the workstation logical units using a pool or dedicating logical units in the gateway to each logical unit on the workstations. For instance, if there is only a limited number of workstation LUs that require SNA host access then a pooled environment is most advantageous. Pooling LUs is more efficient and reduces configuration and activation requirements on the SNA host. However, in many SNA host sessions a logical unit requires specific definitions on the SNA host. In these instances the dedicated LU environment is preferred. This will guarantee consistency for the end user, SNA system programmers and network designers.

6.4 SUMMARY

In this chapter, the criteria for designing a local area network was discussed. The criteria emphasized to a large degree high availability and minimum impact on the LAN for configuration changes. Functional requirements of LAN server placement was reviewed along with cost effectiveness of the servers use. Finally, SNA host connectivity using token-ring and gateway controllers was discussed with emphasis on availability and performance. The next chapter introduces the reader to IBM's network management strategy.

Chapter

7

IBM's Network Management Architectures

The importance of managing an SNA network became evident after IBM introduced the concept of multi-domain networks in the late 1970's with the Multi-System Networking Facility (MSNF). MSNF provided VTAM hosts with the ability to communicate and share resources between them. SNA networks have since migrated from single-domain to multiple domain, and in 1984 to multiple network configurations with SNA Network Interconnection (SNI). Now, the complexity of managing these networks has increased even further by with the advent of local area networks including the management of the network equipment. A comprehensive network management system is needed as the focal point to manage and control all of the variables that comprise today's complex networks.

NetView is IBM's strategic tool for managing these highly complex SNA networks. NetView resides under IBM's Open Network Management (ONM) architecture as the cornerstone for a full, comprehensive network management system that incorporates four major network management functions:

1. Configuration Management
2. Problem Management
3. Performance Management
4. Accounting and Availability Management

To support a local area network environment, non-SNA resources must be included into ONM for true end-to-end centralized network management. The service point provides this functionality under ONM. It allows non-SNA resources, such as controlled access units and LAN Network Manager, to generate architected network management alerts. These alerts can then be processed by NetView or a similar host-based *communication network management* (CNM) application.

7.1 OPEN NETWORK MANAGEMENT ARCHITECTURE

Introduced in 1986, Open Network Management (ONM) laid the ground work for what has become known as integrated network management. Open Network Management through published network management architectures allows users and vendors to incorporate non-IBM and non-SNA resource management under SNA. An Application Program Interface (API) is provided under ONM that allows users and vendors to access network management data and commands. This facilitates the notion of centralized network management which includes both voice and data. Using ONM with IBM and non-IBM resources, systems and network alarm data can be integrated, thus, reducing the time it takes to gather alarm information for analysis about a specific system or network incident. ONM accomplishes this using a three tiered structure: Focal point, Entry point and Service point (Figure 7.1).

7.1.1 Focal Point

The focal point in ONM is the central repository for the consolidation and integration of disparate IBM and non-IBM resources. A focal point provides centralized network management for the network. It resides in the SNA host and can be a product or a set of products that supply comprehensive support for managing the network. Some examples of a focal point application are IBM's NetView, Information/Management, and Systems Center's Net/Master and Info/Master. The focal point can take action on the receipt of alarms either through manual operation or automated operations. Alarms

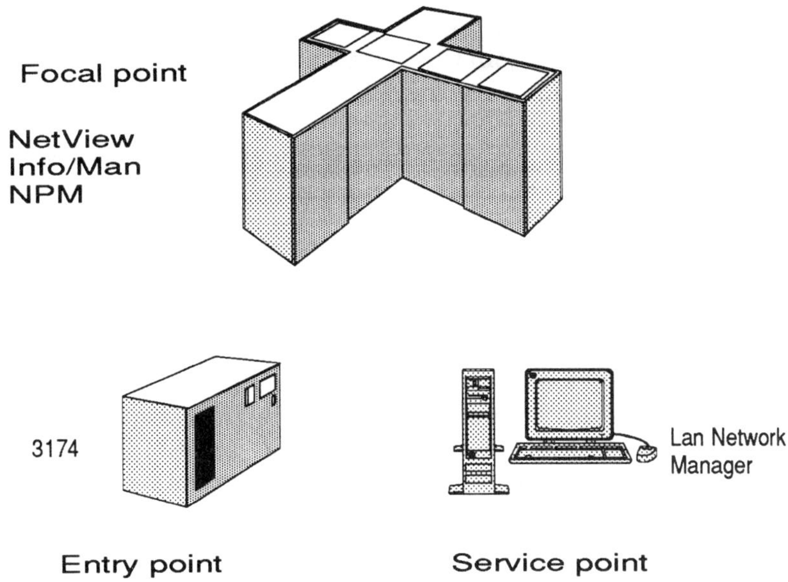

Figure 7.1 The three-tiered structure of ONM.

arrive at a focal point via an entry point or a service point. The network operator, along with the focal point, determines the actions necessary for managing the network. In Figure 7.1, a focal point is residing on an SNA host computer that is running VTAM. The figure indicates that NetView is the focal point for this network. However, any Communications Network Management (CNM) application that has the AUTH=CNM operand specified on the VTAM APPL definition statement possesses the ability to be a focal point. For more information on the VTAM APPL defintion statement consult Introduction to SNA Networking. More than one focal point application can reside on an SNA host.

7.1.2 Entry Point

An entry point provides access to mainframe computer information through the enterprise network. The typical example of an entry point is a cluster controller. Other types of entry points are S/36, S/38, AS/400, and intelligent workstations (e.g., personal computers, mini-computers). All of these entry points provide the management services for end-user display stations. These management services of entry points report alarms and, for some resources, even inventory information to the focal point. Entry points, for lack of a better term, speak SNA. They converse with SNA fluently, allowing them to join the hierarchical structure of SNA.

An entry point transports network management data and session data to a host over the same communications line. An SNA PU is an entry point. The PU performs the functions of network management as well as those functions concerned with transporting session data for its peripheral resources. The entry point is in the same SNA domain as the focal point. This is because the focal point works in conjunction with VTAM and VTAM owns any entry point that it activates. The entry point supports the SNA architected management formats and protocols to the focal point. An example of an entry point is the IBM 3174 Establishment Controllers.

Many vendors use emulation software for their non-IBM equipment that mimics an SNA resource such as an IBM 3X74 cluster controller. But, for other non-IBM resources vendors where emulation is not feasible, ONM provides the third tier called Service point.

7.1.3 Service Point

Until this tier, only IBM resources or emulators of IBM resources have been participating in ONM. This tier provides a way for non-IBM equipment and non-IBM resources to report alarm information to the focal point. The non-IBM management system sends information to the service point which will then map the non-IBM alert information into IBM alert information and send that information on to the focal point. The focal point can then interpret the alarm, record it in its alarm database and possibly take some action by sending a command to the non-IBM management system through the service point. In this fashion, the focal point application of ONM can manage non-IBM resources. As shown in Figure 7.1, IBM's LAN Network Manager is a service point.

The service point rounds out the ONM architecture roles by providing SNA network management for token-ring resources. Token-ring resources, for the most part, do not have SNA addressability and do not implement the SNA network management services formats and protocols. The service point converts native non-SNA network management protocols to SNA formats and then transmits them to the focal point. As with the entry point, the service point must be in the same domain as the focal point. The service point communicates with the focal point on an SSCP-PU session.

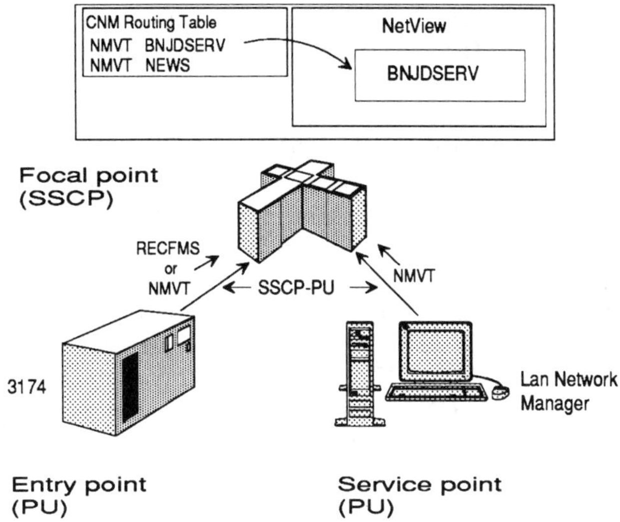

Figure 7.2 A typical ONM flow using SNA network management services.

7.2 SNA NETWORK SERVICES FLOW

Prior to Open Network Management, information pertaining to non-SNA resources (e.g., modems, multiplexers, matrix switches) were not consolidated by the SNA CNM application. A different management system outside of the main processor of the computer center handled the management of non-SNA resources. ONM now eliminates the need for two separate management systems to ascertain and diagnose network problems. The consolidation of network fault messages and control under one single application can greatly decrease the time needed to resolve network problems. However, ONM does not eliminate the need for the management system that passes the network fault to NetView. But it does impose a requirement to the network management staff that in order to manage a token-ring local area network from a centralized point, LAN Network Manager must be in communications with VTAM on the SNA host.

Take a look at the diagram in Figure 7.2. This figure provides a typical ONM flow using SNA network management services. In this diagram, a focal point CNM application resides on an SNA mainframe. The NetView application named NPDA, the Hardware Facility, receives all unsolicited and solicited Network Mangement Vector Transport (NMVT) alerts from the network.

Notice that we have two forms of network management service (NS) request units (RU) that can flow to the focal point. Prior to NMVTs, an NS RU named Record Formatted Maintenance Statistics (RECFMS) was used for unsolicited alerts. In fact, this format is still used by many devices for both unsolicited and solicited RUs. RECFMS is sent to the focal point as a solicited reply in response to the Request Maintenance Statistic (REQMS) NS RU.

Once the service point has received and translated the non-SNA alarms into an NMVT, both the service point and the entry point flows are the same. Each transmits the alarm to the focal point via the SSCP-PU session. The SSCP receives the NS RU and must determine the recipient CNM application for this NS RU. It does this by scanning the CNM Routing Table. Comparing the NS RU header received from the network with values defined in the CNM Routing Table, the SSCP can then deliver the NS RU to the associated CNM application.

In the example, the CNM application is NPDA, which has an Application Control Block (ACB) named BNJDSERV. The BNJDSERV ACB is defined to receive both RECFMSs and NMVTs. After determining the receiving application, the SSCP delivers the NS RU to the named ACB which will then process the alarms. A stipulation for SSCP routing of NS RUs, is that only one CNM application can receive an NS RU. In this case, the ACB for NPDA (BNJDSERV) was opened and participating in an SSCP-LU session with VTAM before the NEWS ACB was opened.

7.3 NETVIEW OVERVIEW

In May 1986, IBM launched their long-range plan for centralized network management. At the core of the plan is NetView. In this initial release, NetView is a conglomeration of previously independent communications network management (CNM) program products. This repackaging of CNM program products allowed IBM to deliver a comprehensive network management package at a reasonable price. There are five main functions provided with NetView: Network Command Control Facility (NCCF) was released in 1979 as a program product along with the Network Problem Determination Application (NPDA); Network Logical Data Manager (NLDM) was released in 1984; and the VTAM Node Control Application (VNCA) and Network Management Productivity Facility (NMPF) which were both originally offered as field-developed programs (FDP). All five applications were released as a supported CNM program product in 1986. This discussion will focus on the

```
NCCF      N E T V I E W        NETV01 OPER1      07/13/92 08:52:44
C NETV01  DISPLAY NET,ID=TRLINE01,SCOPE=ALL
' NETV01
IST075I NAME = TRLINE01, TYPE = LINK STATION
IST486I STATUS= ACTIV--E, DESIRED STATE= ACTIV
IST081I LINE NAME = TRLINE0, LINE GROUP = TRLINE , MAJNOD = NCP11
IST396I LNKSTA   STATUS   CTG GTG  ADJNODE    ADJSA   NETID
IST397I TRLINE01 ACTIV--E  1   1   NCP12       12
IST610I                  LINE TRLINE0 -STATUS ACTIV--E
IST314I END
C CNM40  DISPLAY NET,ID=TRLINE11,SCOPE=ALL
' CNM40
IST075I NAME = TRLINE11, TYPE = LINK STATION
IST486I STATUS= ACTIV--E, DESIRED STATE= ACTIV
IST081I LINE NAME = TRLINE1, LINE GROUP = TRLINE, MAJNOD = NCP12
IST396I LNKSTA   STATUS   CTG GTG  ADJNODE    ADJSA   NETID
IST397I TRLINE11 ACTIV--E  1   1   NCP11       11
IST610I                  LINE TRLINE1 -STATUS ACTIV--E
IST314I END
-----------------------------------------------------------


???
```

Figure 7.3 An example of the NetView Command Facility display.

two functions used to assist in managing a Token-Ring network NCCF and NPDA.

7.3.1 Network Command Control Facility (NCCF)

At the heart of the NetView CNM programs is the Network Command Control Facility, now known as the NetView Command Facility (Figure 7.3). This program encompasses the role of the VTAM Primary Program Operator (PPO). The PPO is allowed to issue VTAM operator commands and receive solicited and unsolicited VTAM operator messages. These messages are not the same as solicited and unsolicited NS RUs. The operator messages are of the VTAM IST message type found in the VTAM Messages and Codes manual. The Command Facility provides points of entry into the CNM interface for end-users to capture and modify network management data. These customizable points of entry are known as exits. The exit routines must be coded in IBM Assembler Language. The facility also provides an interpretive language called Command Lists (CLIST) and Restructured Executive Executable language (REXX). The CLIST and REXX languages provide a means of simplifying and automating the network operator's responsibilities.

```
NETVIEW         SESSION DOMAIN:  NETV01          OPER1   07/13/93  09:16:02
NPDA-31A                 * ALERTS-HISTORY *                       PAGE 1 of 1

SEL# DOMAIN RESNAME TYPE TIME  ALERT DESCRIPTION PROBABLE CAUSE
(1)  NETV01 LANMGR01 LAN 09:08 COMMUNICATIONS OVERRUN:TOKEN-RING ADPT INTF
(2)  NETV01 LANMGR01 LAN 09:08 COMMUNICATIONS OVERRUN:TOKEN-RING ADPT INTF
(3)  NETV01 LANMGR01 LAN 09:08 COMMUNICATIONS OVERRUN:TOKEN-RING ADPT INTF
(4)  NETV01 LANMGR01 LAN 09:08 COMMUNICATIONS OVERRUN:TOKEN-RING ADPT INTF








ENTER SEL# (ACTION), OR SEL# PLUS M (MOST RECENT), P (PROBLEM), DEL (DELETE)


???

CMD==>
```

Figure 7.4 An example of NetView Hardware Monitor display.

7.3.2 NetView Hardware Monitor

The NetView Hardware Monitor (previously known as Network Problem Determination Application, NPDA) receives SNA network management services data that concerns hardware faults for resources in an SNA network. In addition to SNA resources, token-ring resource alarms can be received by the Hardware Monitor from LAN Network Manager. The Hardware Monitor application notifies a network operator of resource outages and their probable cause, and recommends actions to rectify the problem (Figures 7.4 and 7.5).

The Hardware Monitor receives unsolicited and solicited network management services data from SNA resources (e.g., PUs, LUs) and LAN Network Manager. This data comprises a formatted request unit (RU) that contains code points and is known as the Network Management Vector Transport (NMVT) or Record Formatted Maintenance Statistics (RECFMS). The code points are used to display pre-defined alert display messages and accompanying recommended actions that reside in files on the SNA host processor's peripheral storage devices. These files can be customized by end users to suit their network management needs. The resulting alert errors are logged to the Hardware Monitor alert data base and to an external logging file, such as IBM's System Management Facility (SMF) for further processing and analysis at a later time.

```
NETVIEW        SESSION DOMAIN: NETV01   OPER1        07/13/92 09:27:26
NPDA-45A       * RECOMMENDED ACTION FOR SELECTED EVENT *   PAGE 1 OF 1
 NETV01    UA6R1NH    LANMGR    LANMGR01

 DOMAIN    | SP  | --- | TP  | --  (LAN)

USER  CAUSED - NONE

INSTALL CAUSED - NONE

FAILURE CAUSED - COMMUNICATIONS PROGRAM
                 TOKEN-RING ADAPTER
    ACTIONS - I120 - REVIEW LINK DETAILED DATA
              I132 - CONTACT TOKEN-RING ADMINISTRATOR RESPONSIBLE FOR THIS
                     LAN

ENTER ST (MOST RECENT STATISTICS), DM (DETAIL MENU), OR D (EVENT DETAIL)

???
CMD==>
```

Figure 7.5 The recommended action screen for NetView Hardware Monitor.

7.3.3 LAN Support

Faults detected on a LAN can now be forwarded to the NetView focal point using ONM services. In addition, the fault data has been enhanced to include fault domain alerts, LAN errors occurring on the adapter addresses and a filtering scheme based on the adapter addresses. The extended support for LANs is increasingly important for LANs positioned for distributed and cooperative processing. In NetView V2R2 and LAN Network Manager V1.1 there are over eighty functions that can be processed from NetView on LAN Network Manager. Appendix H lists the LAN Network Manager commands that can be executed from a NetView V2R2 focal point.

7.4 SYSTEMVIEW

ONM opened the doors for consolidating and integrating systems and network management data. In doing so, different vendors that adhered to ONM's focal point, entry point and service point functions implemented them using different user interfaces, data definitions, communications and application services. This leads to further confusion for operations personnel and longer training periods for new staff. A strategy was needed for defining all the various disciplines of systems and network management (i.e., Information Systems Management). Enter SystemView from IBM.

SystemView was announced September 5, 1990 and like its counter part for application standardization, Systems Application Architecture (SAA), SystemView identifies a clear structure for defining the standards for information systems management. SystemView is a strategy for managing information systems while providing a business solution that follows the standards set by SAA and Open Systems Interconnection (OSI). These include a consistent user interface, a common communications interface and a standardized definition of resources and data.

The SystemView structure addresses a set of guidelines, standards and interfaces that will create a seamless view for the integration of information management systems across the enterprise. These are:

- End-Use Dimension
- Application Dimension
- Data Dimension

Through the implementation of these three dimensions it is hoped that SystemView will provide a coherent information systems management solution across heterogeneous systems.

7.4.1 End-Use Dimension

The end-use dimension outlines the guidelines and standards for presentation of a SystemView application to an end user. These guidelines call for the presentation to be either graphic, textual or command language. Once the end user selects his/her interface, no matter which SystemView application the end user interfaces with, that is the presentation shown. The end user could be an operator, system administrator, business analyst or a systems programmer. The end user can switch from one SystemView application to another and not be aware of the application switch. This is accomplished by utilizing the Common User Access interface defined in SAA. The initial conformance to this is the announcement of NetView Version 2 Release 1 and the NetView Graphic Monitor Facility (GMF). These two offerings work in conjunction to provide the beginnings of a graphic user interface adhering to SystemView end use dimensions. The information systems enterprise network is depicted graphically on an OS/2 based personal computer. Each graphical object depicted is a "managed object." These display objects will have a defined appearance and characteristic. The appearance and characteristics of each display object follows them between SystemView applications. This reduces possible end user errors due to misinterpretation of the presentation. The display objects correspond to data objects defined in the SystemView data dimension.

The initial offering of NetView GMF is used for problem management by notifying the end user of resource status changes graphically. In the future, the graphic interface shall be used for configuration management. Modifications to the configuration of the network will be done with a simple "point-and-click." For instance, the network administrator will add, delete, move or modify network resources using the graphic display objects. Coding of VTAM and NCP definition statements for SNA resources will be a thing of the past. This method of system definition requires a comprehensive set of disciplines. These are defined by the application dimension.

7.4.2 Application Dimension

Management applications used today are inherently dedicated to a specific function, system or resource. This leaves information systems managers with the task of correlating data and events recorded by various information management systems. The objective of the application dimension is to provide a comprehensive set of management applications and tools that will not only facilitate the integration of different management data but will also automate various information systems management tasks.

It has become quite evident that the main purpose of MIS is to provide a product to the business end of a company. That product is information. The information is provided by means of a service. That service is information systems. The success of the MIS department in providing the product and service in a timely and consistent manner is through well orchestrated information systems management disciplines.

Under the Application Dimension there are six disciplines as shown in Figure 7.6.

Business management offers inventory management, registration, financial administration, business planning, and management services for computer related facilities that can effect the business (e.g., environmental management). Under this discipline pur-

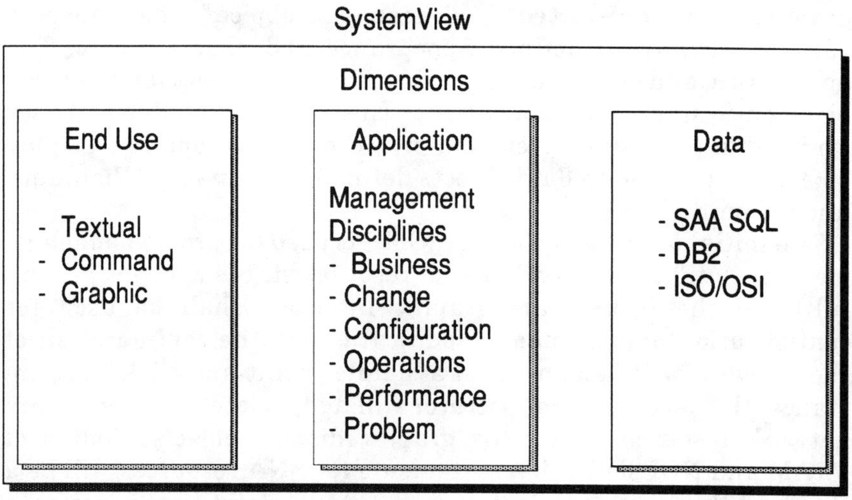

Figure 7.6 IBM's SystemView architecture, dimensions and disciplines.

chases, leasing and maintenance contracts of information systems hardware and software can be kept under tight control. As a business unit expands, plans for procurement of office space, furniture, voice and data facilities and equipment can be utilized by change management.

Change management can be viewed as the key SystemView application. Nothing effects the stability of an information system quite like an uncoordinated change. Under change management, information from the business management application can automatically be introduced into the planning and scheduling of enterprise-wide changes. Conflicts can be flagged that may or will cause problems if the changes are implemented as planned. This feature greatly enhances the MIS decree of providing product and service in a timely and consistent manner.

Configuration management can use information from business and change management to define the physical and logical connections and dependencies of enterprise-wide information system resources. Configuration templates provided by the data dimension can be used to generate configuration standard definitions for these resources.

Operations management is responsible for managing the use of the information systems resources and supporting the processing workloads. Through information from the previous management applications, the operations management application can dynamically create automated tasks for the new configuration implemented by the configuration management application. Automation of operations will play a major role in SystemView changing the status of operations personnel. By automating repetitive and mundane operational tasks, highly skilled operations personnel will be required to handle those instances where automation has not been or cannot be implemented. True, these highly skilled operations people will require a higher salary than many companies are used to paying, however, less personnel will be needed due to the enhanced use of automated techniques.

Performance management under the application dimension will still execute its normal functions of capacity planning and collection of performance data. However, under SystemView we will see the performance application make configuration changes and tuning suggestions through the change management application. This may be done directly or through the problem management application.

Problem management has the tasks of detecting, analyzing, correcting and tracking incidents and problems reported by information systems across the enterprise. It is possible that change, configuration and performance management applications can report change or configuration conflicts and performance thresholds exceeded, thus providing a type of checks-and-balances procedure.

The disciplines described here use generic definitions of resources and adhere to compatibility with open standards such as Open Systems Interconnection (OSI). The cooperative processing between the disciplines is made possible by the sharing of commonly defined data. This data is defined in the Data Dimension.

7.4.3 Data Dimension

The Data Dimension describes the long awaited data repository. The data base for the data dimension will initially be using the SAA Structured Query Language (SQL) data base interface. The Data Dimension defines the data models utilized by the End Use and Application Dimensions. This common repository will be consistent with the OSI standards (ISO/IEC 10165-4, Guidelines for the Definition of Managed Objects and ISO/IEC 10165-1, Management Information Model). The SystemView Data Model, as previously stated, will describe the characteristics and relationships among enterprise-wide resources. It is this standardization on resources characteristics and relationships that will facilitate the seamless switch between SystemView applications.

7.5 SUMMARY

In this chapter IBM's NetView and SystemView were reviewed. Their capabilities and their roles in IBM's network management strategy was discussed. NetView serves as a focal point and LAN Network Manager plays the role of a service point. Together they can assist you in managing an enterprise-wide network.

SystemView is not a product. It is not something tangible that can be touched. It is an information systems management strategy that utilizes SAA's CUA and SAA's communications interface guidelines for Logical Unit 6.2. Not only is SystemView using IBM standards but it is also complying with and supporting the ISO/IEC 9595 architected interface Common Management of Information Services (CMIS) and the ISO/IEC 9596 protocol Common Management Information Protocol (CMIP) for the exchange of management information with OSI networks. By using consistent user interfaces, a common repository definition of data, true integration and automation, SystemView can and will provide management functions across SNA and non-SNA networks.

Chapter

8

Token-Ring Network Management

Management of token-ring resources is accomplished under ONM and SystemView using IBM's LAN Network Manager, LAN Station Manager and NetView. The LAN Network Manager acts as a service point for forwarding network management information to NetView on the SNA mainframe. LAN Network Manager along with the IBM 8230 Controlled Access Unit and LAN Station Manager provide management data that can be used for all six disciplines described in the Application Dimension of SystemView. The integration of these network management offerings in conjunction with ONM and SystemView provides a comprehensive platform for increasing network availability, control and network operations productivity.

8.1 LAN NETWORK MANAGER

The IBM LAN Network Manager program replaces IBM's LAN Manager program for managing multisegment Token-Ring Networks. The program is an application under IBM's OS/2 Extended Services personal computer/workstation operating system. In con-

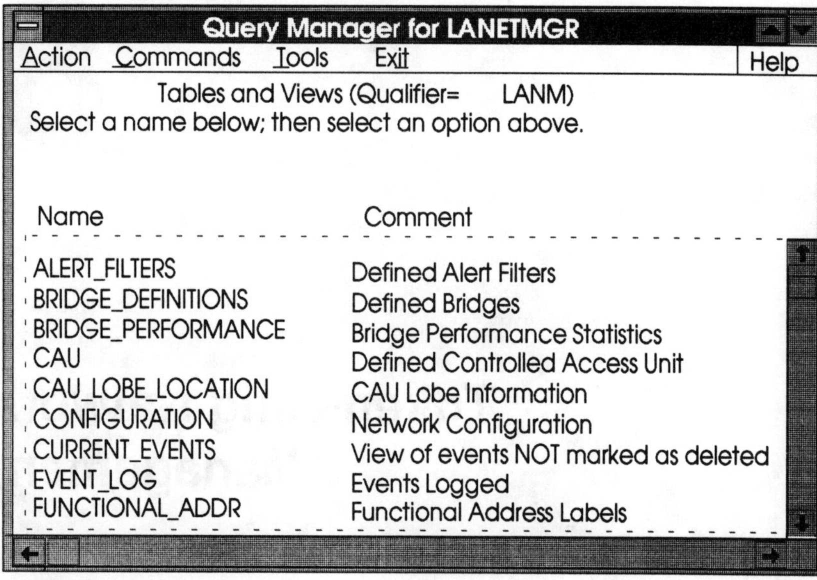

Figure 8.1 Sample display from LAN Network Manager using OS/2 Presentation Manager interface.

junction with the IBM 8230 Controlled Access Unit and LAN Station Manager, LAN Network Manager can provide security, configuration, problem, asset and performance data that can be used by a SystemView Manager (e.g., NetView). The LAN Network Manager program can manage up to 256 LAN segments with 255 bridges, surpassing IBM's LAN Manager support of up to 64 bridges.

8.1.1 Standards Implemented by LAN Network Manager

LAN Network Manager uses Systems Application Architecture (SAA) specifications for the operator interface and the data base system (Figure 8.1). The operator interface is based on OS/2 Presentation Manager meeting the SAA and SystemView End-Use Dimension Common User Access (CUA) requirements for a consistent end-user interface to the LAN Network Manager. The data base system is based on the IBM OS/2 Database Manager and the IBM OS/2 Query Manager Facility. Both of these applications are described under the SAA relational data base requirements and the SystemView Data Dimension specifications. The data base system utilizes Structured Query Language (SQL) allowing for customized applications to access the LAN Network Manager data bases. The information that can be accessed using SQL are:

1. Alert Causes Text Table
2. Alert Details Table
3. Alert Filters Table
4. Bridge Definition Table
5. Bridge Performance Table
6. CAU Lobe Location Table
7. CAU Table
8. Configuration Table
9. Event Log Table
10. Functional Address Labels Table
11. Location Definition Table
12. Message Text Table
13. Segment Type Table
14. Station Definition Table
15. System Parameters Table

LAN Network Manager allows the end user to customize these tables. However, it is recommended that only the following tables be customized due to internal dependencies of the other tables. The tables that may be customized without impact to the stability of LAN Network Manager are: Alert Causes Text Table, Segment Type Table, Message Text Table.

8.1.2 LAN Network Manager and NetView Connectivity

Connectivity to a focal point communications network management application, such as NetView, residing on the SNA host computer can be accomplished using the OS/2 Communications Manager. This is accomplished by establishing an SSCP-PU session between VTAM and the OS/2 Communications Manager as depicted in Figure 8.2. Network management information to and from the SNA host computer flows on this SNA session. NetView recognizes the LAN Network Manager by its service point name. This name must be the same on the VTAM PU definition statement

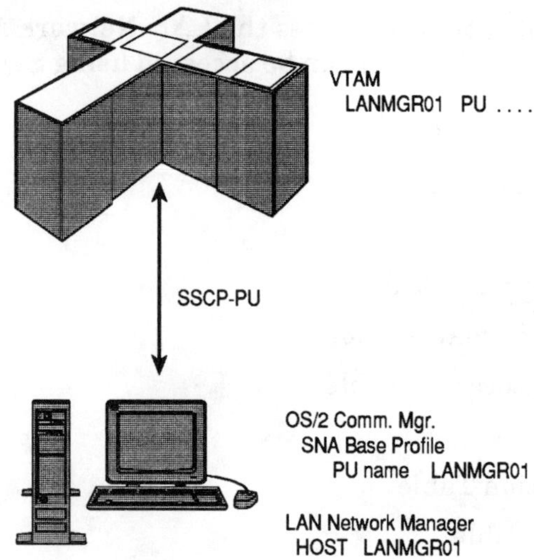

Figure 8.2 The network management flow requirements between VTAM and LAN Network Manager.

that describes the OS/2 Communications Manager physical unit, the service point name parameter of the Host Parameter Fields definition on LAN Network Manager and the PU name parameter in the Communications Manager SNA Base Profile definition. Appendix H lists all the possible LAN Network Manager commands that can be entered from NetView V2R2 with LAN Network Manager V1.1.

8.1.3 Controlled Access Unit Management

Management of the IBM 8230 Controlled Access Unit by LAN Network Manager is made possible by performing a registration procedure. A Registration_Request command is issued by LAN Network Manager at startup or upon a restart of the LAN Network Manager. This Registration_Request command is received by all active Controlled Access Units within LAN Network Manager's managed domain. A Controlled Access Unit can only be registered with one LAN Network Manager at a time. Registration is completed after LAN Network Manager successfully matches the returned password against the LAN Network Manager's definition file.

A Controlled Access Unit is unregistered or considered unregistered when one of the following occurs:

- LAN Network Manager shuts down
- LAN Network Manager is turned off
- LAN Network Manager loses the link to the bridge that connects the Controlled Access Unit
- The path between the Controlled Access Unit and the registered LAN Network Manager is down (e.g., the bridge is down or one of the segments along the path is inoperable)

The Controlled Access Unit sends events to the registered LAN Network Manager. If the Controlled Access Unit does not receive a confirmation response after six retries, the Controlled Access Unit assumes that it is no longer registered to the LAN Network Manger. It then sends out a Function_Present event to all LAN Network Managers in the network domain. The first LAN Network Manager to respond to the Function_Present event becomes the new registered LAN Network Manager for this Controlled Access Unit. Controlled Access Units do not send unsolicited events to the registered LAN Network Manager to ensure connectivity and registration.

Registered Controlled Access Units enable the LAN Network Manager to change and view various Controlled Access Unit parameters. Among these are:

- Microcode level
- Set password and Controlled Access Unit parameters
- Enable and disable lobe receptacles and attachment modules
- Controlled Access Unit adapter address
- Configuration parameters
- Lobe and lobe attachment module status
- Backup path status
- Wrap status
- Reset the Controlled Access Unit

LAN Network Managers not registered with a Controlled Access Unit can obtain information but cannot control the Controlled Access Unit. The following lists the queriable information available to an unregistered LAN Network Manager:

- Controlled Access Unit ID
- Lobe and lobe attachment module status
- Microcode level

- Controlled Access Unit adapter address
- Reconfiguration parameters
- Topology information

This same information is also given to workstations attached to the Controlled Access Unit that are executing IBM's LAN Station Manager V1.0.

Object Class	Attributes	Provided by			
		End User	LAN Station Manager	Controlled AccessUnit	LAN Network Manager
TRN Layer 1	Access Unit ID	Yes	-	Yes	-
	Segment data rate	-	Yes	-	-
	Lobe receptacle number	Yes	-	Yes	-
	Lobe attachment module number	-	-	Yes	-
	Wall faceplate label	Yes	-	-	Yes
TRN Layer 2	Adapter address	-	Yes	-	-
	UAA	-	Yes	-	-
	Functional address	-	Yes	-	-
	Group address	-	Yes	-	-
	NAUN	-	Yes	-	-
	LAN segment numbcr	-	Yes	-	-
	Adapter microcode level	-	Yes	-	-
	Adapter number	-	Yes	-	-
Environment	Physical location (40 characters)	Yes	-	-	Yes
	Machine type	Yes	-	-	-
	Serial number	Yes	-	-	-
	User defined (40 characters)	Yes	-	-	Yes
	Machine specific ROM date	-	Yes	-	-
Resource Management	Station primary name	-	Yes	-	-
	Registration information list	-	Yes	-	-

Figure 8.3 A table listing the source for LAN Station Manager fields.

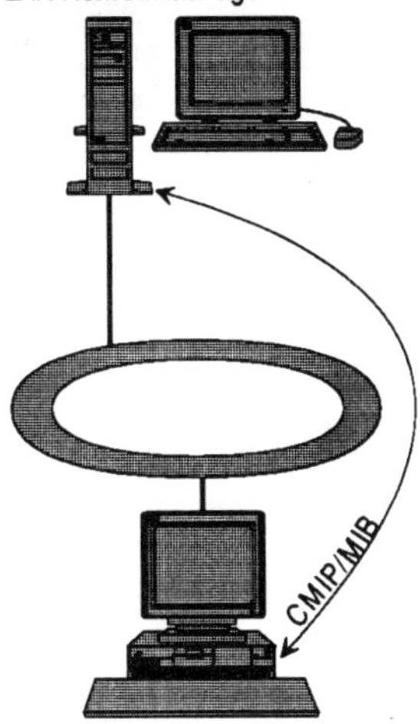

Figure 8.4 A LAN Station Manager V1.0 to LAN Network Manager V1.1 communication flow.

8.2 LAN STATION MANAGER

Management of corporate assets and access to these assets is critical in a LAN environment. The ease of mobility for the LAN workstations makes it imperative that a mechanism be put in place to manage these network resources. LAN Station Manager in concert with Controlled Access Units and LAN Network Manager V1.1 provide LAN asset control and access control.

LAN Station Manager contains informational fields that are maintained by the end user, LAN Station Manager, Controlled Access Unit and the LAN Network Manager. Figure 8.3 lists the provider of the various fields contained in LAN Station Manager.

Communications between LAN Station Manager and LAN Network Manager V1.1 is accomplished using Common Management Information Protocol (CMIP) as shown in Figure 8.4. CMIP is the International Standards Organization's (ISO) specification for the transmission and definition of management information. CMIP is also being defined as the management protocol for Open Systems Interconnection (OSI) network management. LAN Station Manager uses CMIP to forward a block of data called the Management Information Base (MIB) to LAN Network Manager V1.1.

The information provided by the MIB is kept in the LAN Network Manager station configuration database and can be used to

Command	Description
LAN	Generic LAN command
LAN ADAPTER	Monitor and control LAN adapter
LAN BRIDGE	Monitor and control LAN bridge
LAN QNETWORK	Get current network status
LAN RESETLAN	Reset LAN Network Manager
LAN SEGMENT	Test LAN ring or bus

Figure 8.5 The NetView LAN commands used with LAN Network Manager.

prohibit unauthorized ring access. Access control is accomplished through the LAN Network Manger and the Controlled Access Unit. The access authorization can limit a workstations ability to access the ring or a CAU to specific time intervals. This increases security on a LAN in an "open office" environment during non-business hours. Access control can also alert the LAN administrator to a workstation having been moved or that it is accessing the LAN from a different access unit adapter. LAN Station Manager information therefore is useful in tracking LAN asset changes and LAN topology.

8.3 MANAGING THE TOKEN-RING NETWORK FROM NETVIEW

The consolidation and integration of Token-Ring Network management data with SNA network management data occurs on NetView. NetView is a communications network management application residing on the SNA host computer. Under ONM NetView is a focal point and under SystemView NetView is a SystemView Manager. LAN Network Manager forwards network management data to NetView on the SSCP-PU session.

NetView V2R2 incorporates six command lists to manage a token-ring LAN controlled by LAN Network Manager. These commands are entered from the Command Facility of NetView. The response from the commands may be displayed on more than one screen. Figure 8.5 lists the commands and their usage.

8.3.1 LAN Generic Command

This command list is valid only with IBM LAN Network Manager V1.1. It is a generic interface to the LAN Network Manager from NetView V2R2. The command provides access to all LAN Network

Manager functions from a single NetView console. The format of the command is:

```
LAN SP=service_point_name,[APPL=application,]lan_network_man-
ager_command
```

The *service_point_name* is the SNA physical unit name assigned to the LAN Network Manager by VTAM on the SNA mainframe. An application residing on the LAN Network Manager can be the target for the command. The application is specified by the APPL parameter. If the APPL parameter is not specified the name of the application defaults to LANMGR. The value specified for *lan_network_manager_command* must be a valid command that can be executed on the LAN Network Manager. To obtain a list of supported commands through the NetView LAN command list enter the following command on the NetView Command Facility screen:

```
LAN SP=service_point_name,CMD HELP
```

The *service_point_name* is the physical unit name assigned by VTAM to the LAN Network Manager. The command sent to LAN Network Manager is CMD HELP. This will return a list of LAN Network Manager commands to NetView's Command Facility.

8.3.2 LAN ADAPTER Command List

The status of a LAN adapter can be retrieved using the LAN ADAPTER command list. This command also invokes the authority to remove an adapter and list the current configuration of the Token-Ring Network. The command format is:

```
[LAN] ADAPTER {PROFILE lanseg adpname spname|REMOVAL lanseg
adpname spname|LIST lanseg spname}
```

The LAN keyword of the command is optional and does not have to be used to invoke the command list. The PROFILE optional keyword retrieves the current status of a specific adapter or an asterisk can be used on the *lanseg* parameter instructing LAN Network Manager to find the adapter on all managed LAN segments. Using as asterisk for the *lanseg* parameter is valid only on the PROFILE option. The REMOVAL optional keyword instructs LAN Network Manager to inactivate an adapter on the managed ring segment. Once the adapter is removed it can only be reinserted into the ring by restarting the adapter's supporting tokenring code. The LIST optional keyword results in the LAN Network

Manager creating a list of all currently active adapters as they appear on the ring. The list is shows the adapters in their upstream order. The *lanseg* parameter value is the ring segment number. To obtain the *lanseg* value use the LAN QNETWORK command. The *adpname* parameter is the name of the adapter assigned by the LAN Network Manager or the LAA name as assigned by the LAN administrator. The *spname* is the SNA physical unit name assigned to the LAN Network Manager.

8.3.3 LAN BRIDGE Command List

NetView can obtain information about IBM Token-Ring Bridges and control these bridges using the LAN BRIDGE command. This command allows NetView to link and unlink bridges to the controlling LAN Network Manager as well configure these bridges. The format of the LAN BRIDGE command list is:

```
[LAN] BRIDGE {PROFILE brgname spname|LINK brgname spname|UNLINK
brgname spname|CONFIGURE brgname spname configdata}
```

The LAN keyword is optional and is not required to use this command list. The PROFILE keyword instructs the LAN Network Manager to query the specified bridge for its current configuration. This configuration is returned to NetView and displayed by NetView's Command Facility. The LAN Network Manager receiving the request is specified by the *spname* parameter. The *spname* is the SNA physical unit name given to the LAN Network Manager by VTAM on the SNA mainframe. The LAN Network Manager queries the bridge identified by the *brgname* parameter. The *brgname* parameter can be either the LAA name assigned to the token-ring adapter for the bridge or the actual symbolic name assigned to the bridge by LAN Network Manager. The LINK keyword instructs the LAN Network Manager to dynamically link to the specified bridge. This may be requested by the NetView operator because of a recent link failure or because the original controlling LAN Network Manager has disconnected from this bridge and a new LAN Network Manager is to take control of the bridge. The UNLINK keyword requests the LAN Network Manager to disconnect the currently active link it has to the specified bridge. The CONFIGURE keyword modifies the current configuration of a linked bridge. The *configdata* parameter of the CONFIGURE keyword indicates the bridge parameter to be changed. Figure 8.6 contains a table listing the configuration commands that can be issued using the CONFIGURE keyword and their descriptions.

configdata parameter	**Value**	**Description**
BDGNUM	n x'0' - x'F'	Changes the bridge number.
FORWARD	YES | NO	Activates or inactivates frame forwarding.
INTERVAL	nn	Changes the performance notification interval.
LOSTHRED nn.nn	Numeric 0 - 99.99	Changes the percent frame lost threshold.
LANSEG ***adapname***	nnnn Numeric x'1'- x'FFF'	Changes the LAN segment number.
HOPCNT ***adapname***	n Numeric 1 - 7	Changes the hop-count limit.
SGLROUTE ***adapname***	YES | NO	Changes the single-route broadcast .
LNKPASS0	new passowrd	Changes the link password 0.
LNKPASS1	new password	Changes the link password 1.
LNKPASS2	new password	Changes the link password 2.
LNKPASS3	new password	Changes the link password 3.

Figure 8.6 The configuration paramters used on the CONFIGURE keyword of the LAN BRIDGE command list.

8.3.4 LAN QNETWORK Command List

To obtain the status of the whole LAN the LAN QNETWORK command list can be issued from NetView. The command returns to the NetView Command Facility a list of all the managed LAN segments, their status and a list of all linked bridges controlled and managed by the specified LAN Network Manager. The format of the command is:

```
[LAN] QNETWORK STATUS spname
```

Again the LAN keyword is optional. The STATUS keyword indicates to the LAN Network Manager that the status of all token-ring segments, and bridges known to this LAN Network Manager be returned to NetView's Command Facility. The *spname* parameter is the SNA physical unit name assigned to the LAN Network Manager. For NetView to support the maximum configuration of 255 bridges, the LAN Network Manager does not send to NetView duplicate resource data received from the linked bridges. Duplicate resource information can occur, for example, in a parallel bridge configuration.

8.3.5 LAN RESETLAN Command List

This command is issued by a NetView operator to reinitialize the LAN Network Manager. This command list can be used to reinitialize the LAN Network Manager with a new configuration from NetView rather than requiring someone physically at the LAN Network Manager. Another use of the LAN RESETLAN command list is to reopen the LAN Network Manager token-ring adapter if it has been closed due to an error condition. The format of the LAN RESET command is:

```
[LAN] RESETLAN spname
```

The LAN keyword is optional. The name of the targeted LAN Network Manager is specified by the *spname* parameter. This is the SNA physical unit name assigned to the LAN Network Manager by VTAM.

8.3.6 LAN SEGMENT Command List

This command list is used by a NetView operator to determine the viability of a token-ring segment. LAN Network Manager tests the requested ring segment for continuity and its capability for transferring data. The format of the command is:

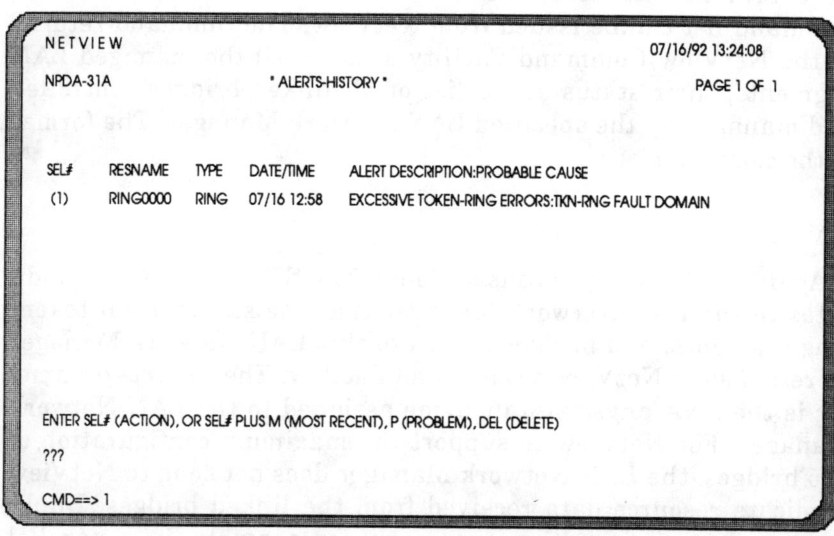

Figure 8.7 The Hardware Monitor display for a token-ring error.

```
[LAN] SEGMENT TEST lanseg spname
```

The LAN keyword is optional for this command list. The TEST keyword instructs the LAN Network Manager to verify the specified segments capability for transferring data. the *spname* parameter is the SNA physical unit name of the LAN Network Manager assigned by VTAM. The *lanseg* parameter value is the ring segment number. The range for this value is hexadecimal 0000 to 0FFFF. The ring segment number can be found using the LAN QNETWORK command list.

8.3.7 Using NetView for Problem Determination

In this scenario a token-ring adapter experiences an abnormal signal and issues a BEACON command on the token-ring. The BEACON command indicates a serious ring problem, perhaps a broken cable. The LAN Network Manager recognizes the BEACON command and forwards an NMVT to NetView's Hardware Monitor notifying the network operations staff of the failure.

The Hardware Monitor's Alerts Dynamic display (Figure 8.7) indicates that a token ring segment is experiencing a problem. The first alert displayed is the failing ring segment. The name of the

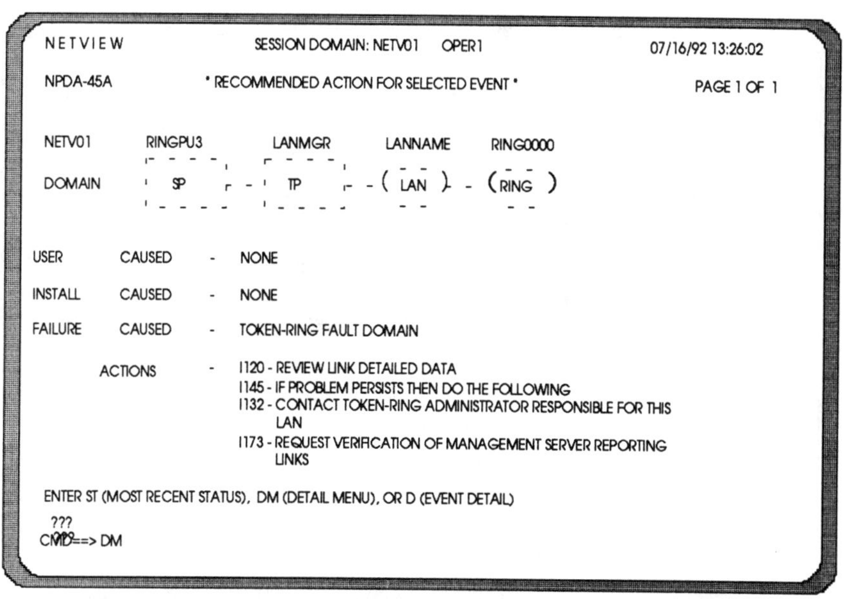

Figure 8.8 The Hardware Monitor display for recommended actions on a token-ring error.

failing ring is found in the RESNAM column and is identified by the name RING0000. Under the PROBABLE CAUSE column NetView identifies that the most likely reason for the alert is that a token-ring fault occurred in the LAN Network Manager domain. By pressing the "ENTER" key the Hardware Monitor displays the Alerts Static screen which assigns selection numbers to the alerts displayed on the Alerts Dynamic screen and freezes the screen from scrolling when new alerts enter the Hardware Monitor. Recommended actions to correct the ring segment failure are displayed by entering the associated number of the alert. In this case, as shown in Figure 8.7, the number 1 is entered on the command line and the "ENTER" key is pressed.

Figure 8.8 provides the network operator with a list of recommended actions to recover the failing resource. The actions listed indicate that the operator should review detailed data on the link, then contact the ring segments LAN administrator and verify the validity of the ring segment. To access detailed information on the link configuration the network operator enters DM on the command line and presses "ENTER." This results in the Hardware Monitor's EVENT DETAIL MENU display. At this point the operator enters the number 4 to obtain the link configuration for the failing ring segment.

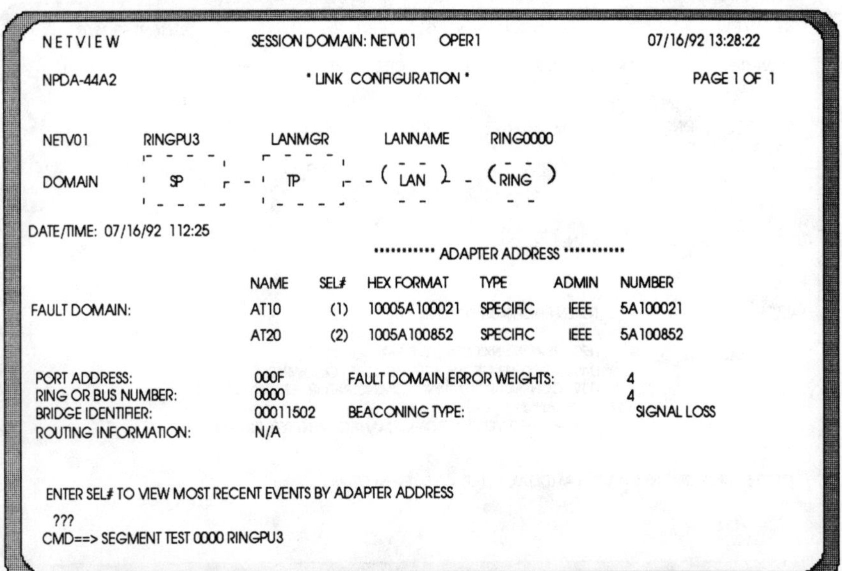

Figure 8.9 The Hardware Monitor detailed Link Configuration display for a token-ring error.

The LINK CONFIGURATION display, as shown in Figure 8.9, provides the network operator with pertinent information to the ring segment. This information includes the adapter address, the fault domain, the segment number and beaconing type. The beaconing adapter is the first adapter listed and identified by the selection number 1. The next active upstream neighbor to the beaconing adapter is the second adapter listed and identified by selection number 2. To verify that the ring segment is capable of transferring data the operator can enter the LAN SEGMENT command list. The segment number and the name of the LAN Network Manager values for the LAN SEGMENT command are shown on this screen. The response to the LAN SEGMENT command is displayed on NetView's Command Facility screen as seen in Figure 8.10. The CNM377I message indicates to the network operator that the LAN SEGMENT command list is being processed and that NetView is waiting for a response from LAN Network Manager. The response as displayed in the figure indicates that the ring segment is still experiencing a signal loss. The response also provides more detailed information on the names of the beaconing adapter and the nearest active upstream neighbor to the beaconing adapter. The characters following the adapter address identify the name assigned to the adapter by the LAN Network Manager. This

```
NCCF            NETVIEW                     NETV01  OPER1          07/16/92 13:29:42

* NETV01        SEGMENT TEST 0000 RINGPU3
C NETV01        CNM377I SEGMENT : INPUT ACCEPTED AND BEING PROCESSED . . PLEASE WAIT
LAN SEGMENT     NUMBER. . . . . RING0000
ERROR DATA :
                    BEACONING ADDRESS. . .  1005A100021/T47B02
                    NAUN ADDRESS. . . . . . . . . 1005A100852/T48B04
                    BEACON TYPE. . . . . . . . . . . SIGNAL LOSS
                    DFI998 OPERATION ENDED

??? ***
```

Figure 8.10 The NetView Command Facility messages resulting from the LAN SEGMENT command.

```
NETVIEW                    SESSION DOMAIN: NETV01    OPER1                  07/16/92 13:28:22
NPDA-44A2                          * LINK CONFIGURATION *                    PAGE 1 OF 1

NETV01        RINGPU3           LANMGR        LANNAME       RING0000

DOMAIN        |  SP  |- - |  TP  |- - ( LAN ) - - ( RING )

DATE/TIME: 07/16/92 112:25
                                    *********** ADAPTER ADDRESS ***********
                          NAME    SEL#   HEX FORMAT    TYPE       ADMIN    NUMBER
FAULT DOMAIN:             AT10    (1)    10005A100021  SPECIFIC   IEEE     5A100021
                          AT20    (2)    1005A100852   SPECIFIC   IEEE     5A100852

PORT ADDRESS:             000F        FAULT DOMAIN ERROR WEIGHTS:          4
RING OR BUS NUMBER:       0000                                              4
BRIDGE IDENTIFIER:        00011502    BEACONING TYPE:                      SIGNAL LOSS
ROUTING INFORMATION:      N/A

ENTER SEL# TO VIEW MOST RECENT EVENTS BY ADAPTER ADDRESS
 ???
CMD==> ADAPTER REMOVAL 0000 1005A100021 RINGPU3
```

Figure 8.11 The LAN ADAPTER command to remove the beaconing adapter from the token ring.

```
NCCF          NETVIEW                 NETV01  OPER1                         07/16/92 13:29:42
* NETV01      ADAPTER REMOVAL 0000 10005A100021 RINGPU3
C NETV01      ADAPTER ADDRESS/NAME............           10005A100021/T47B02
              LAN SEGMENT NUMBER.............            0000
              LAN SEGMENT TYPE................           TOKEN-RING 4MBPS
              NAUN ADDRESS/NAUN ADAPTER NAME.            10005A100852/T48B04
              MICROCODE LEVEL.................           000002342279A
              PRODUCT ID.......................          3531373030303030303030303030030202
              ADAPTER MONITORED...............           YES
              UNIVERSAL ADDRESS...............
              GROUP ADDRESS...................           00000000
              FUNCTIONAL ADDRESS..............           00002019

NETV01        CNM241I ARE YOU SURE YOU WANT TO REMOVE ADAPTER 10005A100021?
              PLEASE ENTER 'GO' TO CONFIRM THE ACTION OR ENTER 'CANCEL' TO
              TERMINATE IT.
NETV01        CNM377I SEGMENT : INPUT ACCEPTED AND BEING PROCESSED . . PLEASE WAIT
NETV01        DFI999 OPERATION COMPLETED SUCCESSFULLY

??? ***
GO
```

Figure 8.12 The Command Facility display with an adapter profile.

name is more symbolic and can assist in directing the ring segments LAN administrator to the correct ring station. The three asterisks at the bottom of the Command Facility display indicate that the "ENTER" key should be pressed to return to the LINK CONFIGURATION display screen.

Since the problem is still persisting the network operator will remove the adapter from the ring by issuing the LAN ADAPTER command list as depicted in Figure 8.11. Note that all the information needed for this command list is found on the LINK CONFIGURATION screen. The ring segment number (0000), the adapter name (10005A100021) and the service point name of the LAN Network Manager (RING0000). After entering the LAN ADAPTER command and pressing the "ENTER" key the network operator is presented with the Command Facility display which indicates that the command is being processed and then displays the adapter profile as shown in Figure 8.12. The command list first issues a LAN ADAPTER PROFILE command to verify that the adapter should be removed from the ring. The network operator can continue the procedure by entering "GO" on the command line or "CANCEL" to terminate the removal request. Entering "GO" and pressing the "ENTER" key dictates to the LAN ADAPTER command list to issue the actual removal command to the LAN Network Manager. The command facility indicates that the command is accepted and waiting for a response. The DFI999 message indicates to the network operator that the adapter has been removed from the ring. At this point the network operator can contact the local LAN administrator and direct him/her to the failing ring station to resolve the problem.

8.4 SUMMARY

In this chapter, LAN management was discussed. Management of token-ring resources is accomplished under ONM and SystemView using IBM's LAN Network Manager, LAN Station Manager, IBM 8230 Controlled Access Units and NetView. The LAN Network Manager acts as a service point for forwarding network management information to NetView on the SNA mainframe. LAN Network Manager can provide security, configuration, problem, asset and performance data that can be used by a SystemView Manager (e.g., NetView). LAN Network Manager utilizes the SAA guidelines Common User Access (CUA) under OS/2 Extended Edition, Presentation Manager, and the SAA guidelines for structured query language (SQL) under OS/2 Database Manager. Together, the IBM 8230 Controlled Access Unit and the IBM LAN Station Manager provide detailed configuration information on the topology of the Token-Ring Network managed by LAN Network Manager. Management of all token-ring resources can be accomplished through the ONM focal point, NetView, using six basic commands and some eighty commands available with NetView V2R2 and LAN Network Manager V1.1.

Chapter

9

IBM's OS/2 Server and Requester

The design objective of Token-Ring Networks is resource sharing. Resources such as printers, databases and programs can be shared on a Token-Ring Network using a LAN server and requester. IBM offers three products that provide for this shared environment: OS/2 LAN Server, OS/2 V1.2 and V1.3 Extended Edition (Extended Services in OS/2 V2.0) and DOS LAN Requester.

The OS/2 LAN Server provides file and print server functionality. OS/2 LAN Server allows requester workstations to use its own resources along with other workstations on the LAN as shown in Figure 9.1. OS/2 LAN Server runs as an application under IBM's OS/2 Extended Edition operating system. This operating system comes integrated with the OS/2 LAN Requester program. The combination of OS/2 EE workstations and OS/2 LAN Server under OS/2 EE V1.2 or V1.3 implement the goal of Token-Ring Networks, sharing of resources.

However, in many LAN environments there are also DOS workstations. These too need to be integrated into the shared resource environment of OS/2 LAN Server. The DOS LAN Requester (DLR) function is an embedded component of OS/2 LAN Server V1.2 and

V1.3. Once DLR is installed on the DOS workstation it can then use the resources of the LAN server.

9.1 TERMINOLOGY

The server/requester LAN environment introduces new concepts in local area networking. Definitions of these concepts may seem obvious but it is important to describe each to get a full understanding of the server/requester environment.

9.1.1 Domain and Domain Controller

Domains in a Token-Ring Network are logical and not physical entities. The domain is defined as a group of servers, applications and users on a LAN. A LAN can be divided into several affinity groups as depicted in Figure 9.2. Each affinity group is considered a domain. As an example, domains can be organized according to the different departments on the LAN.

Each domain is controlled by only one domain controller. The domain controller is the primary server for that domain. The domain controller must be the first server started in the domain to make available resource sharing on the other domain servers. Being the primary server within the domain, the domain controller

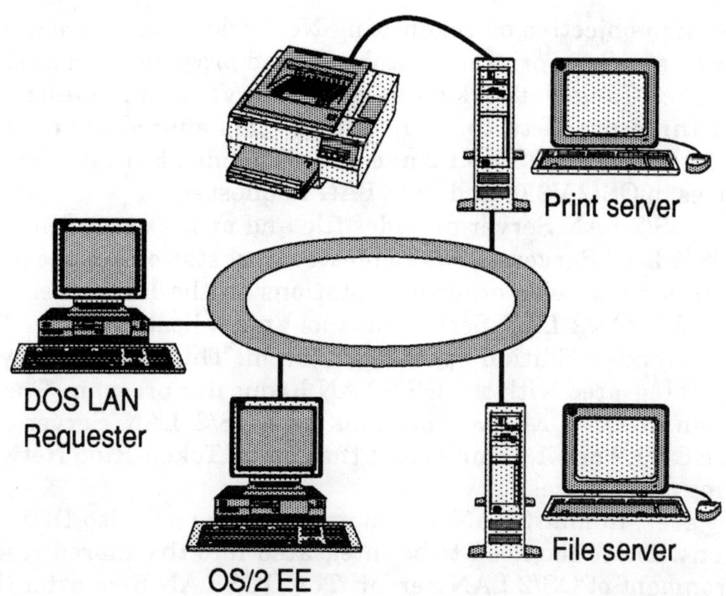

Figure 9.1 The IBM OS/2 LAN Server and Requester configuration.

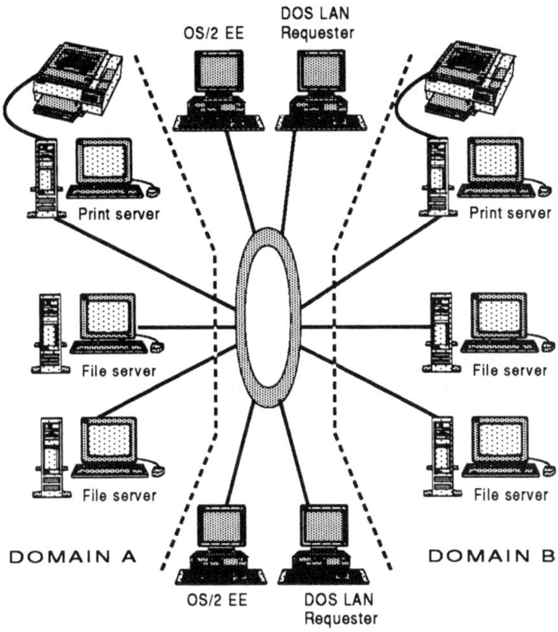

Figure 9.2 The Token-Ring Network defined with two domains.

is the repository for information on the domain's user, application and other resource definitions. Though a domain controller has added responsibilities it can still act as a LAN file and print server.

9.1.2 Additional Servers

The domain controller defines each server in the domain. The definitions for each server within the domain controller determine accessibility by the users on the token ring. The additional servers in the domain may be dedicated to specific resource sharing. For instance, one server may be dedicated to providing print services while another to providing application or database file services. The connection of users to the servers is always made by the domain controller. In this way the user is unaware of the physical location of his/her applications and directories. Access to information, no matter how many servers involved, is all that matters to the user. Servers can only belong to one domain controller, hence one domain.

9.1.3 Requester Workstations and DOS LAN Requester

End users log on to the domain from a requester workstation. This workstation can be either OS/2 EE using the OS/2 LAN Requester feature or a DOS workstation using the DOS LAN Requester function provided by OS/2 LAN Server V1.2 or V1.3. Logging on to the domain controller from a requester workstation requires the end user to specify a user ID an optional password and the name of the domain to which the end user is attempting to access. The domain controller validates the user ID and password. If the end user profile is defined with access to the specified domain and the end user is not already logged on to that domain from another workstation then access to the shared network resources is granted. Users can only be logged on from one workstation at a time with in the domain.

9.1.4 DOS Remote Initial Program Load (RIPL)

In many LAN environments cost and security are important. Diskless or medialess workstations may be used on a LAN in this type of environment. For these end users the workstation receives its initialization files and information from a server (Figure 9.3). This is accomplished by the DOS Remote Initial Program Load (RIPL). DOS workstations supporting RIPL must have a token-ring adapter with the RIPL feature installed. This feature requests RIPL at power on from the defined RIPL server for this workstation. This function supports only DOS workstations on a Token-Ring Network with OS/2 LAN Server V1.2 and higher.

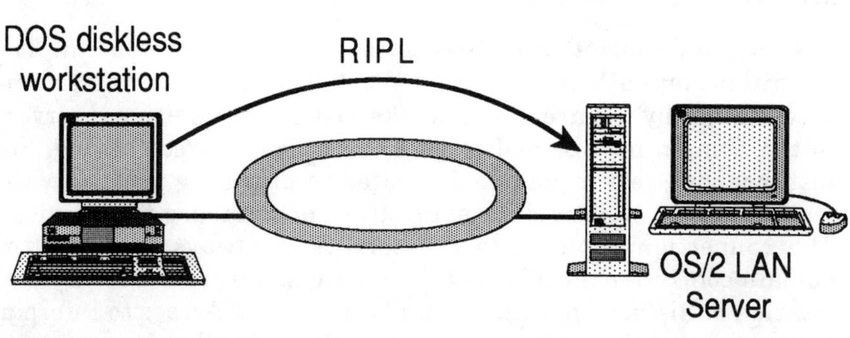

Figure 9.3 A DOS workstation issuing a RIPL request to the OS/2 LAN Server.

9.1.5 User, User ID, Passwords and Guest Account

Each end user on the LAN is defined as a user of the LAN resources and is assigned a user ID. The user ID is not related to a physical workstation on the token-ring network. This allows the end user to access the shared resources within the domain from any workstation acting as a requester. Users can be defined to multiple domains. User IDs are unique throughout the LAN and therefore impose a serial log on restriction to the domains.

Security on the LAN is provided by the use of passwords. A password can be assigned to a user ID. At log on time, the end user must provide the current password to gain access to network resources within the domain. Access to resources within the domain are specified in the access profile for the end user in the domain controller. Password access at the resource level may be used when the user is accessing network resources outside of his/her native domain.

Domain controllers can have defined to them a global profile for non-native domain users accessing resources in its domain. This "guest account" specifies the type of access allowed without defining all the non-native users to this domain. The most common use of "guest" is for connectivitiy to printers.

9.1.6 Shared Network Resources and Aliases

The sharing of networked resources is the design objective for a token-ring LAN. Files, applications, printers and serial devices are among these shared resources. Accessing shared network resources requires a device assignment. When accessing files, a drive is assigned as the device. For printer or serial device shared resources a port is assigned.

Shared resources are given an alias name on the domain. The alias name allows the end user to access the resource without them having prior knowledge on which server the resource can be found. Figure 9.4 shows a listing from an end users DOS BAT file for establishing shared resource connections. The server establishes knowledge of these resources by defining the Universal Naming Convention (UNC) name. This name is composed of the server name and the full path to the resource. Note the relationships between the UNC names and the aliases listed in the figure. Using alias "logical names" requires no knowledge on the end users part for locating the requested shared resource.

```
NET USE LPT1: \\SRVR01DC\LPT1Q
NET USE LPT2: \\SRVR02DC\LPT1Q
NET USE LPT3: \\SRVR02DC\COM1Q
NET USE F: \\SRVR01DC\MISC
NET USE N: \\MAILSRVR\WINMAILP
NET USE M: \\MAILSRVR\WINMAILD
NET USE O: \\SRVR02DC\LOTUS
NET USE X: \\SRVR02DC\EXCEL30
NET USE W: \\SRVR02DC\WINWORD
```

Figure 9.4 Defining shared resource alias names.

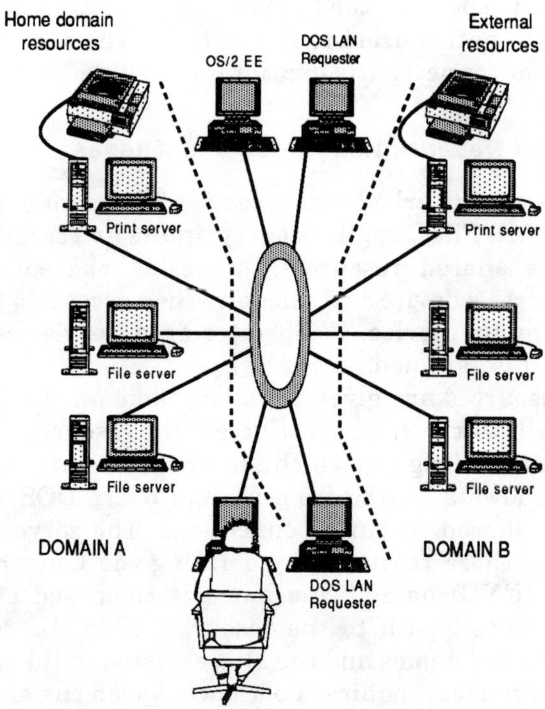

Figure 9.5 A diagram depicting home domain and external domain resources to the end-user.

9.1.7 Domain and External Resources

There are two types of LAN resources from a LAN system administrators perspective. These are domain and external resources. In both instances the resource may be a program, a data base, directories, printers or serial devices. The system administrator defines the resources in the domain controller. The resources are defined as being within the scope of control of a domain controller or external to the domain controller. Each user on a domain is assigned to each resource and granted access privileges.

Domain resources are those that are defined and controlled within a domain as shown in Figure 9.5. These resources are considered to be in the home domain of a end user. External resources are therefore not in an end users domain. External resources are defined and controlled in another domain.

End users can access external resources using two methods. End users can issue a NET USE to the alias name of the resource in the external domain as ong as they are defined in that domain. As long as the end users user ID and password are defined in the external domain's domain controller the end user can access the external resources. The second method is to use a "guest account." The guest account is used to allow users not defined in the external domain access to that external domain's resoruces.. This guest account is used to allow any end user of this domain to access the external resources with the defined access privileges assigned to the guest account. The guest account is used by the system administrator as a generic user for all end users accessing external resources from their home domain. This reduces the system administrator's duties of constantly adding end user profiles on the domain controller for access to the domains resources.

9.1.8 System Administrator

It is the responsibility of the system administrator to monitor the domain. Each domain requires careful management of domain resources and their definitions. The system administrators responsibilities include defining end users to the domain, the sharing of networked resources, and access privileges for each user allowed to log on to the domain. The system administrator has a special user ID that grants him/her administrative status. This allows the system administrator to log on the domain controller from any workstation or server in the domain. One system administrator is recommended for each domain. However, while more than one is allowed, only one can be logged on to the domain controller performing administrator services at any time.

9.2 PLANNING THE SERVER/REQUESTER ENVIRONMENT

The planning stage for creating your server/requester environment may end up being the most crucial. It is easy to under estimate the amount of thought that must go into planning a LAN environment. The establishment of naming standards and access controls in the beginning will provide valuable management controls later on as the LAN expands. In creating a plan for the server/requester environment several questions must be answered.

First and foremost is the type and number of workstations on the LAN. In many LAN installations today diskless workstations are being seen as a means of securing corporate data. In these LANs it is a requirement to determine which machines need the DOS RIPL function along with the DOS LAN Requester versus OS/2 workstations using OS/2 LAN Requester. Another important aspect of planning a server/requester LAN is the accessibility given to each machine. Not all workstations may be provided access to every server and shared disk/directory, printers and serial devices in the network. This access is determined by the NET USE command once the requester has started NETBIOS on their workstation.

The application mix needed by the end users over the LAN must be analyzed. This analysis must provide which applications are shared and on which servers they will reside. Once this is done the system administrator must determine which end users will need access and the type of access to these shared applications. Another concern is the initial load of shared printing. The number of print servers may be determined by the volume of printing as well as the number of users requiring print server access privileges. The type of applications can affect the print volume.

Finally a naming convention must be established for user IDs, machines, files, printers, serial devices, server names, domain names and alias names. A naming convention for these resources may be as follows: three characters for the type of resource, three characters for its location and two characters uniquely identify the resource within a domain and specific location.

A carefully laid out plan will prove to have fewer inconsistencies and minimal interruptions during the definition process and network operations.

9.3 DEFINING THE NETWORK ENVIRONMENT

The system administrator may also wear another hat, that of the network administrator. In this role, the system administrator is responsible for ensuring network access for the end users, defining access privileges to vital data and administering the usage of shared resources. In the role of network administrator he/she defines unique names for the resources within the domain. These are:

- Users and group of users
- Network applications
- Aliases
- Shared resources
- Access permission to resources
- Spooler queues
- Serially attached device queues

The complexity of defining the network environment is minimized by following a logical step-by-step process that takes into consideration experience and inter-dependencies of defining the network environment. These are:

1. A comprehensive study for all servers, resources, users, groups of users and access control. This may be accomplished by a well thought out implementation plan.
2. Use the default administrator ID (e.g., USERID) and password (e.g., PASSWORD) created during the installation of OS/2 LAN Server to log on to the OS/2 LAN Server.
3. Create a new administrator user ID and password. Log off with the default administrator ID and log on with the new administrator ID.
4. Disable or delete the default administrator ID and password.
5. Stop the NET LOGON service at the domain controller during resource definitions. This will stop any pre-defined users from using an unconfigured domain controller. NOTE: Reset this service after successfully defining the domain controllers resources.
6. Define the machines in the domain. These include all servers and DOS Remote IPL machines. This step actually defines the

boundary of the domain to the domain controller.

7. Create and assign the resources on every machine in the domain. These include shared directories, files, applications, printers, and serial devices.
8. Define aliases to the defined resources. Aliases can be used to address directories, printers, serial devices and external resources.
9. Define all users that are allowed to log on to this domain. An alternate or backup administrator user ID should be defined in this step.
10. Define groups of users as determined by the planning process.
11. Assign users and groups of users access privileges to the aliases and the defined domain and external resources.
12. Define the shared applications as public applications. These applications should also be set up as being available to the OS/2 Program Starter for those users that apply for them. If an OS/2 user applies for these applications a Public Applications group is added to their Desktop Manager application when the user logs on to the domain. For DOS users, a group called Shared Applications is presented on the DOS LAN Requester full-screen interface.
13. Define a LOGON profile for each user. This is a command file that will be executed in the users workstation once logged on to the domain. This file usually contains a number of NET USE commands to assign domain resources to the end users operating system.
14. Define all Remote IPL images and NET RUN applications.
15. Restart the NET LOGON service.

Using these steps as a guideline in defining a server/requester network environment will ease the definition process and lessen later complications during network growth.

9.4 OS/2 LAN SERVER

The IBM OS/2 LAN Server is an installed software product that executes under IBM's OS/2 V1.3 and higher. This software should be installed on a high-performance machine with ample memory and disk storage. Typically this machine would be a Compaq SystemPro series or an IBM PS/2 Model 95. In order for end users to access this LAN server they must be using IBM's OS/2 LAN Requester V1.2 and higher for OS/2 users and for IBM DOS users the IBM DOS LAN Requester along with the IBM LAN Support Program V1.1 or higher is required. The server includes all requester functions plus the following additional functions:

- Resource sharing
- Print spooling
- Access control function
- Remote IPL server
- Alerter
- Net logon
- Replicator

These services and functions provided by OS/2 LAN Server execute in a non-dedicated mode. Meaning, other programs can be executing at the same time as OS/2 LAN Server on the server machine. The IBMLAN.INI initialization file defines these services.

9.4.1 Resource Sharing

Resource sharing is a function that runs in OS/2 LAN server that allows sharing of the following resources:

- Disks
- Print queues
- Serial/parallel devices
- Processor
- Memory

The last two shared resources are realized when and end user issues the network utility command NET RUN. This command can be issued, by an OS/2 requester only, to execute a program in the server's memory. The only requirement behind doing this is that the program must not request interaction with a user and that it is not dependent on video mode displays. In other words, the program must be able to run in a "batch" mode in the background on the server using standard input/output processes allowing for file redirection.

9.4.2 Print Spooling

The OS/2 LAN Server provides full function printing services. These services include print requests from a requester, the print spooler function of OS/2 Presentation Manager, user and administrator interface to manage the spooler queue along with local and remote control of the spooler queues. OS/2 workstations can access these print servers through the OS/2 Presentation Manager spooler queue name. For DOS LAN Requester stations the print sharing facility supports the Presentation Manager spooler. Both requesters can control and manage printing on the print server by having full remote control of the print spooler, automate print schedules and receive printing notification messages.

9.4.3 Access Control Function

Access privileges to the shared resources in a LAN environment offer a security level. In an OS/2 LAN Server access control is separated into two functional categories: System access control and resource protection.

System access control is governed by a central component in OS/2 LAN Server called User Profile Management (UPM). The UPM defines three types of users: user, local administrator and network administrator. Each type of user is provided with a profile. The profile defines the subsystems available to the user and their access privileges. These subsystems include OS/2 Database Manger, OS/2 Communications Manager and OS/2 LAN Requester. The category of user has the following privileges:

- Log on and off to/from the server
- View their user profile
- Change their password
- Add or change their user ID's comments

Local administrator users have the capabilities of a *user* but can also use the OS/2 Database Manager to access locally based databases. The network administrator includes all the functional capabilities of the previous two plus:

- Add or delete users (including administrators)
- Specify user privileges
- Change the password option for users and network resources
- Change access levels

- Create, modify or delete groups of users
- Possesses administrator authority for all subsystems that use UPM

The second category of access control is resource protection. Resource protection is invoked each time an end user requests access to a resource or an application opening a file on the server. The end user is granted access according to the access authority level granted the end user in their profile. Resource protection can be applied to the following resources:

- File resources including directories and subdirectories
- Spooler queues
- Serial devices
- Named pipes

Each resource has a resource access control profile. Information in the resource access profile contains end user access authority. This information includes: *user access list*, *group access list*, *universal access permissions* and *audit trail of access attempts*. During an attempt by an end user to access a resource the OS/2 LAN Server searches the access control profile of that resource in the following manner:

OS/2 LAN Server first determines if the end users ID is present in the *user access list* for the resource. If the end user ID is found OS/2 LAN Server determines the access privileges based on the requested action. If the profile indicates that the end user ID is present and has authority for the requested operation then the end user is granted access to the resource. However, if the end user ID is present but the profile indicates that the end user does not have authority to proceed with the requested operation then access is denied and the end user is informed through a notification message. If during the search process OS/2 LAN Server did not discover the end user ID in the *user access list* then OS/2 LAN Server searches the group access and universal access permissions.

Failing to find the end user ID in the *user access list* OS/2 LAN Server searches the *group access list* for the resource. If the end user ID belongs to a *group access list* OS/2 LAN Server then determines the access authority granted to that group and applies them to the end user. The access authority granted here in the *group access list* is combined with those granted to all end users by *universal access permissions*. At this point OS/2 LAN Server can determine whether this end user has sufficient access privileges to

Permission	Description
NONE	User is denied access to resource.
READ	User is allowed to read files and execute programs. Files can not be modified by user in a shared directory.
WRITE	User can modify existing files in a shared directory. Does not include create or delete permissions.
CREATE	User can create files and sub directories in a shared directory. The user can not modify the file once it is created.
EXECUTE	User can run a command or program.
DELETE	User can delete files and sub directories.
ATTRIBUTES	User can change OS/2 file attributes.
PERMISSIONS	User can change resource access permissions.

Figure 9.6 Permissions that may be assigned by the NET ACCESS command.

perform the requested operation. Based on the combined permissions the end user is either granted the requested access or denied access and informed through notification messages. If the end user ID is not found in a *group access list* OS/2 LAN Server grants permission for a requested operation based on *universal access permissions* defined for the resource.

Universal access permissions apply to any end user ID not explicitly defined to a resource through the user access list or group access list created for the resource. The default permission denies all access privileges. This default forces a system administrator to determine access requirements of the end user community enforcing some type of security mechanism for shared resources. Figures 9.6 and 9.7 list the permissions that may be assigned to end user

Permission	Files	Printers	Serial Devices	Named Pipes
NONE (N)	Y	Y	Y	Y
READ (R)	Y		Y	Y
WRITE (W)	Y		Y	Y
CREATE (C)	Y	Y	Y	Y
EXECUTE (X)	Y			
DELETE (D)	Y			
ATTRIBUTES (A)	Y			
PERMISSIONS (P)	Y	Y	Y	Y

Figure 9.7 The applicable access permissions for resource types.

IDs and which are applicable to resources.

A feature available with the access control function of OS/2 LAN Server is audit trail. The audit trail, as previously described, resides in the resource's control profile. Information in the audit trail can be used for accounting, security, configuration and problem determination. The size of the audit trail can be changed by the network administrator. The network administrator specifies what categories of access are to be recorded. The following lists these areas:

- Start and stop status of the server
- Log on with user type indicated
- Log off with a reason for the disconnection
- Start and stop of resource access with reason
- Resource access with resource name and operation
- Access permission violations
- Changes to the user and group definition file
- Changes to resource access permissions

The information provided by the audit trail can be displayed, printed or cleared by the network administrator. The audit trail print out can be directed to a file where it can be manipulated to create management reports and archived for historical reporting and trend analysis.

9.4.4 Remote IPL Server

The remote initial program load (IPL) function is only available to DOS diskless or medialess workstations. Medialess workstations are used for three reasons. The first is to provide consistent levels of system software across the LAN and the second is to provide enhanced security for the removal of vital corporate data and illegal copying of software programs and the third is a lower cost for implementing a LAN. The choice for a medialess workstation would be one without a diskette but with a hard drive. A medialess workstation without a hard drive but with a diskette would defeat the second reason stated above. The remote IPL service provides the following functions:

- IPL of a DOS based workstation from an OS/2 LAN Server
- IPL of a remote DOS workstation using diagnostic diskettes from an IBM OS/2 LAN Server

- Support for multiple concurrent remote IPLs
- Support for multiple remote IPL servers on a LAN
- User selectable IPL images in an authorized list
- Image-build function

The network administrator defines the stations on the LAN that this OS/2 LAN Server will remotely IPL. The DOS workstations network adapter number (MAC address) is defined in an authorization profile. This file also defines the IPL image that will be used by the DOS workstation. An IPL image is a binary file created by the network administrator. This image can be used by all remote IPL DOS workstations. Each workstation can have only one active Remote IPL Server supporting it. However, an alternate server can be used to remotely IPL a DOS workstation should its original Remote IPL Server become inoperable. One remote IPL workstation definition is required for each remote IPL requester workstation on the LAN.

An OS/2 LAN Server requires the following to support remote IPL for DOS workstations:

- DOS V3.3 and higher
- DOS LAN Requester feature of OS/2 LAN Server V1.2 and higher installed
- LAN Support Program V1.1 and higher

9.4.5 Alerter Service

The alerter service in OS/2 LAN Server sends alert notifications to users logged on to the server. The alerts can be directed to specific user IDs or machine IDs on the LAN. This is done using the *alertnames* parameter in the Server section of the IBMLAN.INI file. Alert conditions can be monitored in minute intervals from 0 to 65535 minutes. Once an alert is encountered it can be directed to the user IDs and machine IDs defined by the *alertnames* parameter. Error conditions can be threshold set to send an alert only after an error has occurred several times. The *erroralert* parameter in the Service section of the IBMLAN.INI file can be set from 0 to 65535 errors before an alert is sent. The default of 5 should be ample warning of impending problems that could affect all users on the LAN. Figure 9.8 lists the error events that can be set to a threshold for the *erroralert* parameter.

A prime concern for a LAN network administrator is the amount

IBMLAN.INI parameters	Description
maxchdevjob	Maximum number of shared serial devices requests the server can accept for all serial device queues. 0 - 65535
maxchdevq	Maximum shared serial device queues. 0 - 65535
maxchdevs	Maximum number of shared serial devices. 0 - 16
maxconnections	Maximum connections requester can have to the server. Must be at least as big as maxusers/ 1 - 1024
maxlocks	Maximum number of file locks . Applies to lock requests issued by DOS requesters only. 1 - 8000
maxopens	Maximum number of open files, pipes and devices the server can have at one time. 40 - 8000
maxsessopens	Maximum number of files, pipes and devies one requester can have open at the server. 1 - 8000
numbigbuf	Number of 64KB buffers the server uses for moving large files or amounts of data. 0 - 128
maxsessreqs	Maximum number of resource requests one requester can have pending at the server. 0 - 65535
maxshares	Maximum number of resources the server can share with the network. 2 - 500
maxusers	Maximum number of users that can use the server at one time. 1 - 254
maxsearches	Maximum directory searches the server can perform simultaneously. 1 - 1927

Figure 9.8 The IBMLAN.INI parameters that are counted in the erroralert parameter.

of disk space available on the LAN server's drives. The *diskalert* parameter in the Server section of the IBMLAN.INI file determines at what amount of free disk space, in kilobytes (KB), on all of the LAN server drives is allowed before sending an alert. The default of 500 KB should be sufficient, but, if space is of a concern increasing this number will provide the network administrator with enough warning to clean up the disk drives on the server.

The number of log on attempts by end users can be monitored using the *logonalert* parameter in concert with the *alertsched* parameter to determine when an alert should be sent for log on violations. This parameter only affects the domain controller.

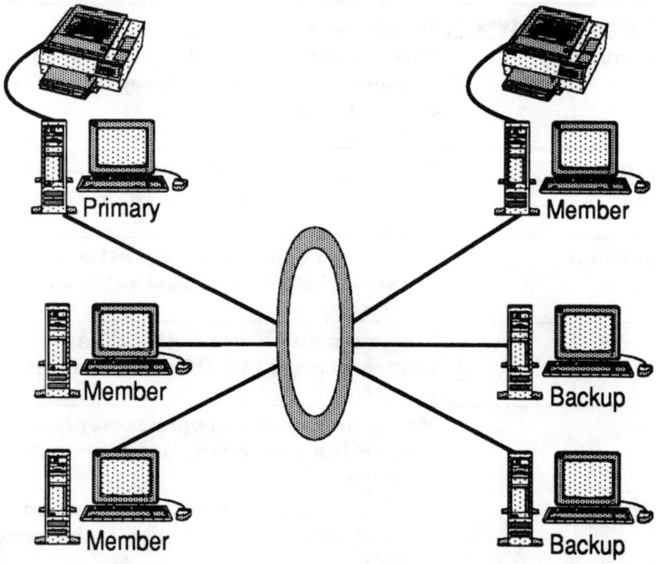

Figure 9.9 The Net Logon servers and their roles on a single Token-Ring Network.

The Alerter section in the IBMLAN.INI file contains the *sizalert-buf* parameter. This parameter determines the size, in bytes, of the alert buffer. The range is 512 to 16384 and the default is 3072.

The alerter program that actually issues the alerts is specified by the *alerter* parameter in the Services section of the IBMLAN.INI file. If you happen to be so inclined as to write your own alerter program function you would place the fully qualified name of your program here. The default value is the path and file name of SERVICES\ALERTER.EXE.

9.4.6 Net Logon Service

The Net Logon service provides two functions for OS/2 LAN Server. There are three types of Net Logon servers as depicted in Figure 9.9: primary, member and backup. The Net Logon service allows the user and group definition files, created through User Profile Management (UPM), to be centralized and provides access service to any server in the domain. The UPM file created is named NET.ACC and is master user and group definition file found on the domain controller. When this file is altered by the network administrator it is copied to all servers within the domain controllers domain. Each server must be executing the Net Logon service to receive a copy of the NET.ACC file. The time frame for the copy to take place is determined by the *pulse* parameter in the Net Logon section of the IBMLAN.INI file. The default time frame is 60 seconds.

The server defined as the domain controller is considered the primary server. Only one server in a domain can be the primary server. The role of primary server is set by entering the following command on the server:

```
NET ACCOUNTS /ROLE:PRIMARY
```

Network log on requests are also handled by the primary domain controller. Log on requests are validated by the primary domain controller. The primary domain controller also provides log on assignments, access to home directories and applications.

As a member server, OS/2 LAN Server can receive a copy of NET.ACC from the primary domain controller. A server is defined as a member server by entering the following network command:

```
NET ACCOUNTS /ROLE:MEMBER
```

A domain can have multiple member servers. Member servers do not perform log on requests but do provide users with the resources for log on assignments and applications.

The final role for a server is backup. A server can only become a backup domain controller after the primary domain controller fails. Servers are defined as backup domain controllers by issuing the following command:

```
NET ACCOUNTS /ROLE:BACKUP
```

Just as with member servers, there can be multiple backup servers. Each receives a copy of the NET.ACC file. The backup domain controller does not take on the primary domain controller role automatically. Only log on requests through the application program interface (API) are possible. Log on requests from the full-screen interface or the command line are not accepted because the backup domain controller does not have a copy of the domain control database (DCDB). This problem can be overcome by using the Replicator service.

The role of the backup domain controller must be changed manually by issuing NET ACCOUNTS command as described above for the primary domain controller role after Net Logon service has been stopped at the backup domain controller. The sequence of commands on the backup domain controller needed to take on the role of primary domain controller are:

```
NET STOP NET LOGON

NET ACCOUNTS /ROLE:PRIMARY

NET STOP SERVER

NET START SERVER
```

Prior to issuing these commands the appropriate levels of administrative and application software must be available from the backup server. This can be accomplished by using the Replicator service.

9.4.7 Replicator Service

Important files, such as DCDB, and levels of software (e.g., applications) can be replicated throughout the LAN from one server to several other servers or requesters on the LAN. The server sending the files is called the exporter. The server or requester receiving the files is called the importer. The Replicator service provides the following benefits:

- Replication of one or more directories from a server to any server or requester
- Selective replication of appropriate directories for the importer
- Dynamically add or delete from the set of directories being replicated
- Replicate an entire directory or individual files within a directory
- Replication integrity ensuring that partial replication never occurs
- Local replication providing a mirrored image of the files

The Replicator service eases the management of files across the LAN. Replication of common files can be distributed to other servers from the master copy on the exporter server. Administrative files, such as DCDB and DOS remote IPL images, can be copied to backup domain controllers for recovery purposes should the primary controller fail. The Replicator service is invoked at server startup or when it is explicitly requested on the domain controller and the importer server or requester by issuing the following command:

```
NET START REPLICATOR
```

Before issuing this command there are some definitions that are

Parameter	Workstationacting as
exportlist	exporter
exportpath	exporter
guardtime	exporter
importlist	importer
importpath	importer
interval	exporter
logon	importe
password	importer
pulse	exporter
random	exporter
replicate	both
tryuser	importer

Figure 9.10 The IBM OS/2 LAN Server replicator parameters.

required to specify how and what files are to be replicated. These definitions are found in the IBMLAN.INI file and specify the export path to be used by exporters and the import path to be used by importers. Figure 9.10 contains a table of the replicator parameters used in the IBMLAN.INI file.

The *replicate* parameter is used to determine if this workstation is an exporter, importer or can act as both. Figure 9.11 illustrates a typical configuration of a workstation acting as an importer for exporters. The server workstation labeled TRSRVR1 is defined as an exporter to TRWRK1. TRSRVR1 specifies TRWRK1 as a workstation that it can export to by defining it on the *exportlist* parameter of the IBMLAN.INI file. The data and information that TRSRVR1 is to export is defined by the *exportpath* parameter. The export path on TRSRVR1 defines the directory named APPL.DAT on drive C as the source for the export the TRWRK1. The second server workstation, TRSRVR2, also defines TRWRK1 as the receiver of exported data from its directory named ADMIN.DAT on drive D as the source for export to TRWRK1. The importer workstation, TRWRK1, has defined itself as import capabilities only through the *replicate* parameter. Since TRWRK1 has been defined as an importer it uses the *importlist* parameter to define which export servers it can import from. The *importlist* parameter, therefore, for TRWRK1 denotes both TRSRVR1 and TRSRVR2 as the exporters it can receive data from. The *importpath* parameter on TRWRK1 defines the directory and drive that will receive the

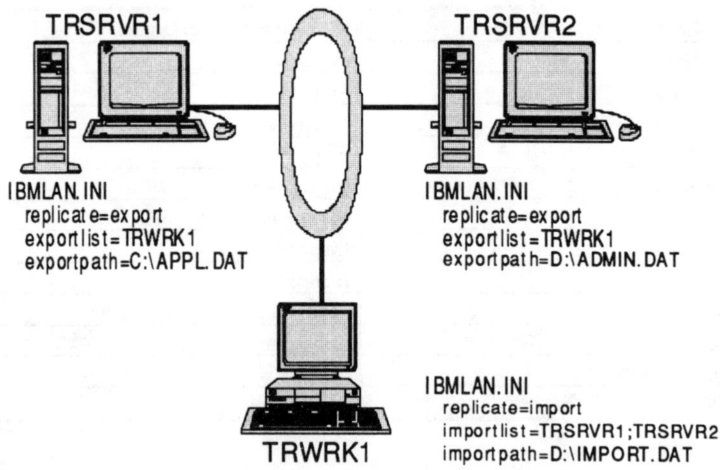

Figure 9.11 The defintions in the OS/2 LAN Server and OS/2 workstation to support the replicate feature.

imported data. In this example the import path is the directory named IMPORT.DAT on drive D. The RIPL and INFO first-level sub-directories of IMPORT.DAT must be manually defined or already present before beginning replication. The sub-directories of RIPL and INFO will be created dynamically if they are not already present.

The exporter workstation determines how files and subdirectories of the first-level subdirectory are to be exported using the REPL.INI file. Placement of this file will determine which subdirectory levels will be replicated. This file contains only two parameters: extent and integrity. The *extent* parameter determines whether all files and subdirectories of this first-level subdirectory are to be replicated. The value of *tree* for the *extent* parameter indicates that all files and subdirectories in the first-level directories will be replicated. The value of *files* for the *extent* parameter indicates that only files from these directories will be replicated. Stability of the files is determined by two parameters that affect the integrity parameter of the REPL.INI file. The values specified for the integrity parameter are governed by the *guardtime* and *interval* parameters of the IBMLAN.INI file for the definition of the Replicator service. These two IBMLAN.INI parameters define the number of minutes the Replicator service must wait before an importer can copy the data. *Guardtime* is only valid when the REPL.INI integrity parameter is set to *tree*. The default for *guardtime* is two minutes. The *interval* parameter of the

IBMLAN.INI file determines how many minutes are to pass before the exporter checks the export path for changes. The value of tree for the integrity parameter in the REPL.INI file indicates that all files and subdirectories of the first-level directory must be stable for the time period specified by the guardtime parameter of the IBMLAN.INI file. The value of *files* for the *integrity* parameter in the REPL.INI file indicates that updates are exported immediately, consequently, the *guardtime* parameter of the IBMLAN.INI file has no effect.

The first-level subdirectories are used by the Replicator service in two ways. One usage is to prohibit replication and the other is to indicate the status of replication for this first-level subdirectory and those that follow it. In the sample configuration shown in Figure 9.12, IMAGES is the first-level subdirectory of the subdirectory RIPL. RIPL is a first-level subdirectory of ADMIN.DAT. Placing the REPL.INI file in the RIPL subdirectory indicates to the Replicator service that only files in the first-level subdirectories of RIPL are to be replicated.

First-level subdirectories under the export path can include a file named USERLOCK.xxx. The *xxx* can be valid combination of characters. The prefix name of *USERLOCK* indicates to the Replicator service that files in this subdirectory are not to be exported. This file can be used to control data is to be replicated. During replication from the exporter the Replicator service creates a *signal file* in each first-level subdirectory it is authorized to replicate. These two functions provide management control and status by the Replicator service.

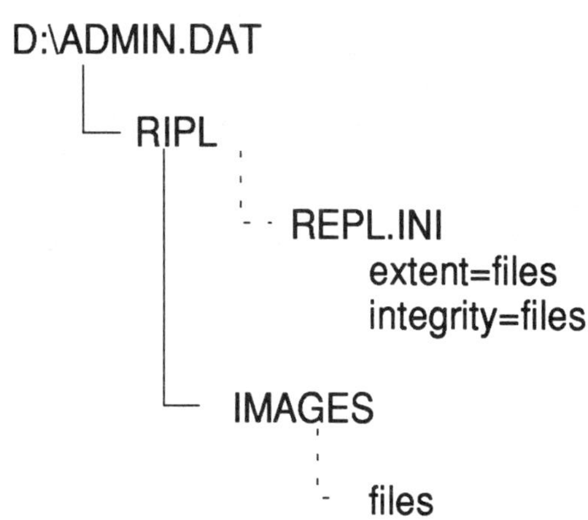

Figure 9.12 The subdirectory configuration for the replicator feature.

9.4.8 Hardware Requirements

The IBM OS/2 LAN Server is a workstation on the token-ring network that supports IBM OS/2 Extended Edition V1.2 and higher. The workstation selected must have at least 6MB of memory, a 1.44MB diskette drive, a hard drive (i.e., fixed disk) of at least 40MB and the LAN adapter and cable necessary to connect to the token-ring network. Each server can optionally have printers, more fixed disks and serial devices attached. At least one workstation on the token-ring LAN must be a server to institute a server/requester environment. Multiple servers may be defined on the network but at least one must be defined as a domain controller.

9.4.9 Software Requirements

The implementation of IBM OS/2 LAN Server requires IBM's operating system OS/2 Extended Edition V1.2 for OS/2 LAN Server V1.2, IBM OS/2 Extended Edition V1.3 for OS/2 LAN Server V1.3 and IBM OS/2 Extended Edition V2.0 for OS/2 LAN Server V3.0. The OS/2 Communications Manager of OS/2 Extended Edition must be configured with LAN communications support. The operating system must also have installed OS/2 LAN Requester. If DOS workstations are on the LAN and require DOS Remote IPL then the OS/2 LAN Server must also have DOS 3.3 or higher installed and the IBM LAN Support Program V1.1 or higher installed.

9.5 OS/2 LAN REQUESTER

Workstations executing IBM's OS/2 Extended Edition V1.2 and higher have the capability of acting as an OS/2 LAN Requester. This function must be selected during installation of OS/2. As a requester, the workstation can access applications, files and directories on a server via a local drive name (e.g., letter D through Z). This makes the files, applications and directories appear to be locally accessed. There are four major functions of the OS/2 LAN Requester:

- Routing Services
- File Requester
- Printer Requester
- Message Requester

The redirection of input/output operations from the workstation to a server on the LAN is a function of routing services. This service, transparently to the end user, allows remote access to resources residing on a server across the LAN. Remote files are accessed through the file requester of OS/2 LAN requester. This function is called when input/output operations to a file on a remote resource (e.g., server) is requested. These remote files are managed by the requester as if they were local files. This function is also called when a workstation requires execution of a remote program in the server. Print outs of files or as the result of a program can be directed to print server using routing services and managed by the printer requester function of OS/2 LAN Requester. The printing services allow an end user to redirect the print to a different printer, list print jobs in the remote spooler queues, and also to hold, cancel release and delete their own print jobs in these queues. End users can send messages to each other using the message requester function of OS/2 LAN Requester. The message requester is used for simple exchange of messages and not as an electronic mail system. The messages can be typed on the command or they can be retrieved and sent from an ASCII file.

Each end user can be assigned a *home directory* on the server for his/her personal use. The network administrator must assign the home directory. During the assignment of a home directory an alias is automatically created and is given the same value as the end user's user ID. Access to this directory is determined by an access control profile that is automatically created which grants the end user all permissions to the home directory. The home directory is not deleted when the user's user ID is removed from the system. It is manually deleted by the network administrator.

9.5.1 Hardware Requirements

An OS/2 LAN Requester can be any workstation on a LAN that is executing IBM's OS/2 Extended Edition V1.2 and higher. The workstation must have a minimum of 4MB of memory, a 1.44MB diskette drive and at least a 40MB fixed disk. A LAN adapter with the appropriate cable must be installed for connection to the LAN. As with servers, an OS/2 LAN Requester may have optional printers, fixed disks and serial devices attached.

9.5.2 Software Requirements

OS/2 LAN Requester necessitates IBM OS/2 Extended Edition V1.2 and higher and the OS/2 Communications Manager configured for LAN communications.

9.6 DOS LAN REQUESTER

OS/2 LAN Server V1.2 and higher provides the DOS LAN Requester for DOS workstations on the LAN. DOS LAN Requester provides DOS based workstations and end users with similar functions as those described for OS/2 LAN Requester. During the installation of DOS LAN Requester there are two groups of applications defined in the full screen interface. These are: LAN Services and Served Applications. LAN Services provides management functions for the end user to manage the network services. Served Applications are used by the end user to start network shared applications. The end user has the option of defining up to eight extra groups of applications to the DOS LAN Requester. The end user has full control over the application groups.

The LAN Services group provides the end user with utilities to print one or more files from their workstation to a network or local printer. In so doing the end user can manage printer jobs and printers in the domain. LAN Services also allow the end user to allocate and change their directory on the server and print these files to a printer. An end-users log on password, user description assignments and screen colors can be modified by the end user using the LAN Services group functions.

The Served Applications group lists the applications that can be found by the DOS LAN Requester on a server workstation. The initial application found in the group at installation is the Messaging application. But, other applications can be added, such as, LOTUS 123, Microsoft Word for Windows and others.

9.6.1 Hardware Requirements

The DOS LAN Requester requires a workstation executing DOS V3.3 or higher with a minimum of 64KB of free memory for the redirector function. A diskette drive rated at a minimum of 720KB and a fixed disk with at least 20MB of disk storage. The LAN adapter and the associated cable necessary to connect to the LAN is also required. Optionally the DOS workstation may have printer, serial and extra fixed disk devices attached.

9.6.2 Software Requirements

In order for the DOS workstation to access the LAN it requires DOS V3.3 or higher along with the IBM LAN Support Program V1.1 or higher. If the workstation is medialess it will also require DOS RIPL DOS 3.3 or higher, and LAN Support Program V1.1 or higher in the OS/2 LAN Server.

Device driver name	Description
DXMA0MOD.SYS	Interrupt arbitrator required driver.
DXMC0MOD.SYS	Token-ring adapter type I, II, /A, 16/4 and 16/4/A suppppport.
DXMC1MOD.SYS	Used for 3270 Workstation Programinstead of C0.
DXME0MOD.SYS	Ethernet Network adapter support.
DXMG0MOD.SYS	New PC Network and PC Network BASEBAND adapter support.
DXMG1MOD.SYS	Instead of G0 for 3270 Workstation Program use.
DXMG2MOD.SYS	Origional PC Network adapter.

Figure 9.13 The LAN Support Program device drivers.

9.6.3 LAN Support Program V1

The LAN Support Program V1 has several releases. Each release has kept its parameter list consistent with the previous release. The program itself is actually a group of files called device drivers. Device drivers provide a software interface to a device. In this case the device is actually the token ring adapter card. There are eight drivers provided with LAN Support Program but for token-ring attached devices only three are needed. These device drivers are loaded during initialization by specifying them in the DOS CONFIG.SYS file. Figure 9.13 lists the device driver file names and describes each.

Token-ring adapter support is provided by using the DXMA0MOD.SYS, DXMC0MOD.SYS and DXMT0MOD.SYS files. The format of the DXMC0MOD.SYS statement in the CONFIG.SYS file is:

```
DEVICE=DXMC0MOD.SYS addr0,mem0,etr0,addr1,mem1,etr1
```

The *addr0* parameter if coded indicates that a locally administered address is to be used versus the universal address. The *mem0* parameter defines the shared memory address in the DOS memory where the adapter is to use storage. The *etr0* parameter specifies whether early token release is to be used over the primary token ring adapter. A value of 0 indicates that early token release will be used. A value of 1 indicates that early token release is not to be used. The value of 0 is only applicable if the adapter is using a data rate of 16 Mbps. The *addr1, mem1* and *etr1* have the same meanings but are used to define the variables for the alternate token ring adapter card in the workstation if one is present. As an example the CONFIG.SYS file with the LAN Support Program device driver would look like:

```
DEVICE=DXMCOMOD.SYS 400022010900,C200,0
```

In this example the device driver statement defines a Token-Ring Adapter type I, II, /A, 16/4 or 16/4/A adapter because we are using the DXMC0MOD.SYS driver. The locally administered address for this workstation is 400022010900 and the driver is to used the DOS memory segment at address C200. The last variable indicates that the adapter is on a 16Mbps token-ring and that early token release is enforced by this workstation.

The DOS LAN Requester utilizes network basic input/output services (NETBIOS). Support for NETBIOS is offered by the LAN Support Program through the device driver named DXMT0MOD.SYS. Figure 9.14 lists the important NETBIOS device driver parameters and defaults. The *stations* parameter defines the number of link stations that NETBIOS will support on this workstation to establish sessions. The *sessions* parameter defines the number logical connections between two NETBIOS names. The *names* parameter defines a sub-address specific to the link station and is used to set up sessions. The *extra.saps* parameter refers to the number of data link control (DLC) service access points (SAP) available to this workstation for NETBIOS use. The SAP is a communications port between the DLC layer and the higher layer services of the token-ring adapter. A SAP value of X'F0' is the interface to NETBIOS services. SAP values of X'04', X'08' and X'0C' are used to interface to SNA Path Control Services.

Keyword	Abbrv.	Value range	Suggested Minimum	Default
STATIONS	ST	0 - 254	1	16
SESSIONS	S	0 - 254	1	16
COMMANDS	C	0 - 255	1	12
NAMES	N	0 - 254	2	17
OPEN.On.LOAD	O	Y | N	-	Y
EXTRA.SAPS	ES	0 - 99	0	0
EXTRA.STATIONS	EST	0 - 99	0	0

Figure 9.14 The NETBIOS device driver parameters.

9.7 IMPLEMENTING SERVER/REQUESTER

The implementation of server/requester is fairly basic. The most important part of implementation is the agreement of parameters between the various servers and requesters. This section will review the implementation of OS/2 LAN Server to OS/2 Extended Edition V1.3 LAN Requester and DOS LAN Requester. DOS Remote IPL will also be discussed. Prior to defining the server and requester workstations the OS/2 Communications Manager must be installed and have the LAN profiles properly defined.

9.7.1 Defining OS/2 Communications Manager LAN Profiles

After starting the Communications Manager select the Advanced item on the action bar with the mouse or use the F10 function key and move using cursor keys to the Advanced item and press enter. A list of items as shown in Figure 9.15 is presented. Item number

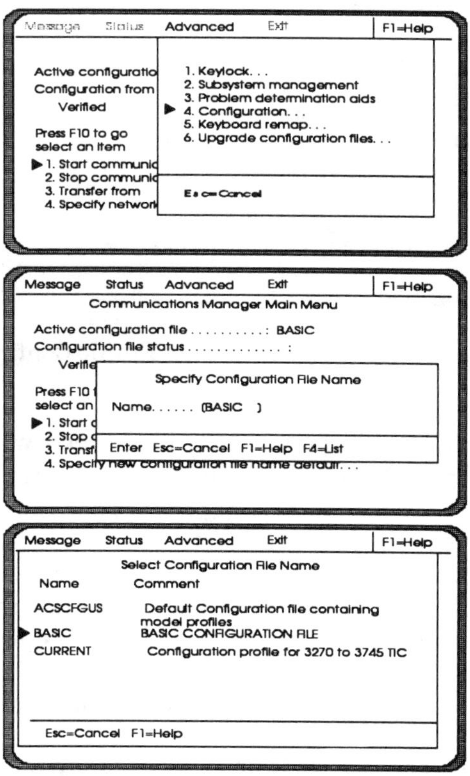

Figure 9.15 OS/2 Communication Manager screens for defining LAN communication configuration profiles.

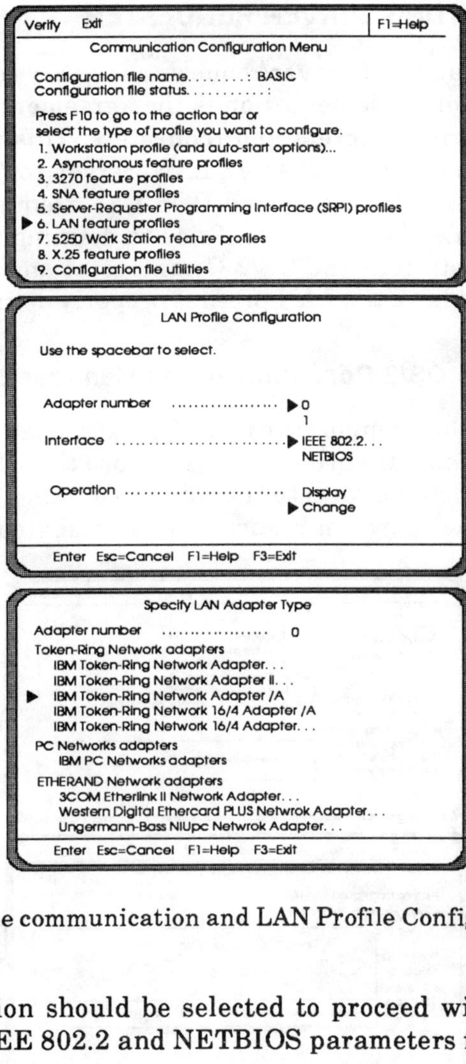

Figure 9.16 The communication and LAN Profile Configuration screens.

4, Configuration should be selected to proceed with defining the token-ring IEEE 802.2 and NETBIOS parameters for Communications Manager.

A pop-up window appears requesting the name of the configuration file you want to create or modify. The configuration file name BASIC appears. A list of other configuration files can be presented by pressing the function key F4 as shown in Figure 9.15. On this selection menu the BASIC configuration file can also be selected by positioning the selection arrow next to the item and pressing the ENTER key.

The next screen presented is the Communications Configuration Menu as shown in Figure 9.16. Note that the selected configuration file is displayed on the Configuration file name line. Selecting item number 6 LAN feature profiles the administrator is presented with the LAN Profile Configuration. This screen allows the administrator to select which adapter, interface and operation are to be used against the selected configuration file. In this example the primary adapter (i.e., adapter 0) and not the alternate adapter (i.e., adapter 1) panel. The IEEE 802.2 interface is also selected for the change operation. Pressing the ENTER key brings up the Specify LAN Adapter Type panel. It is here on this panel that the available LAN adapter types for Communication Manager are displayed. Selecting IBM Token-Ring Network 16/4 Adapter /A determines the requirements for the IEEE 802.2 and NETBIOS parameters. This same procedure is used to select the NETBIOS profile.

The IEEE 802.2 Token-Ring Profile panel is displayed as shown in Figure 9.17. This panel displays the current configuration as determined by the adapter type. The Use universally administered address (UAA) item defaults to Yes. Therefore, to use a locally administered address (LAA) this item should be set to No. The LAA is defined on the second panel of the IEEE 802.2 Token-Ring rofile description. The key parameters for servers and requesters in the IEEE 802.2 profile are the maximum number of SAPs, maximum number of link stations and maximum number of users and the transmit and receive buffer sizes. These buffer sizes must match the other workstations accessing the server in order for a connection to be successful.

The NETBIOS Profile panel also depicted in Figure 9.17 has similar parameters. The important ones to maintain are the maximum link stations, maximum sessions, maximum commands and maximum names parameters. After completing the NETBIOS and IEEE 802.2 profiles the VERIFY command is executed from the Communications Configuration Menu display. Successful verification of the parameters for Communications Manager displays the panel as shown in Figure 9.18. From this panel you would select option 4 to stop and restart the whole system to make the changes for Communications Manager effective.

9.7.2 OS/2 EE LAN Server to OS/2 EE LAN Requester

Figure 9.19 illustrates the OS/2 LAN Server to OS/2 LAN Requester configuration. The OS/2 LAN Server must have a systems administrator define LAN Requester users and their access profiles. The administrator selects LAN Requester from the GROUP MAIN window of the OS/2 workstation. From here the administra-

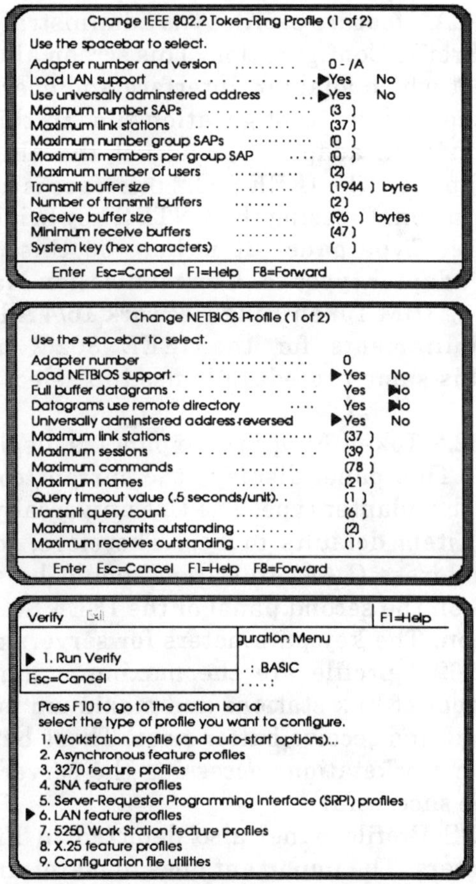

Figure 9.17 The IEE802.2 Token-Ring Profile and NETBIOS Profile screens.

tor selects the LOGON category and enters the system administrator user ID and password to define a new end user to the OS/2 LAN Server.

The administrator is presented with the User Profile Management option and selects MANAGE. From this option the administrator selects the MANAGE USERS category and then selects the function NEW. At this juncture the administrator selects ADD A NEW USER ID. It is at this point the administrator enters the end user's user ID, a description of the user on the User comment field, the end user's password. The profile associated with this new user is defined by the next three categories. The type of user being defined is specified on the Select user type. In this example the user is defined with the user type of USER. The enforcement of

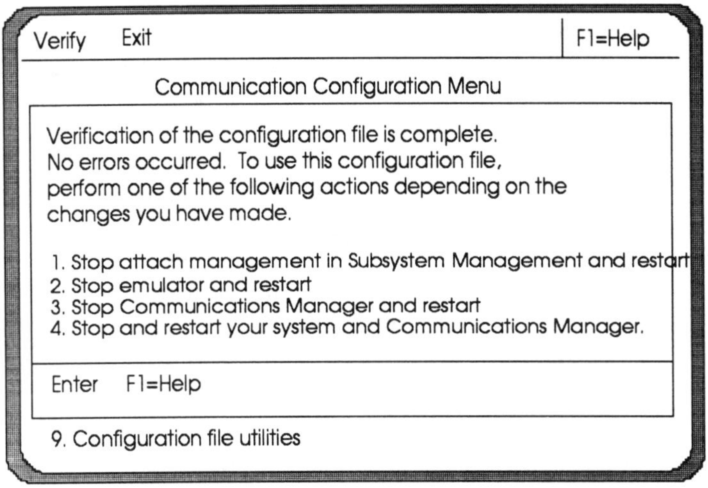

Figure 9.18 The final Communication Configuration screen for defining LAN communication profiles.

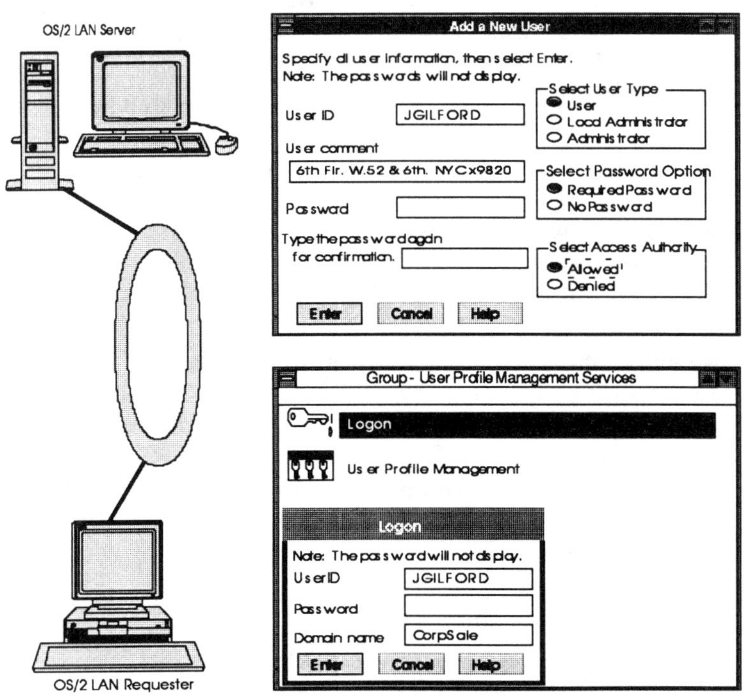

Figure 9.19 The OS/2 LAN Server Add User screen and OS/2 LAN Requester logon screen.

security through requiring a password during log on is specified through the Select password option. Access authority granted to the new user is determined by the value specified for the Select access authorization field. In this case access to the server is allowed.

The OS/2 LAN Requester workstation end user must select the LAN Requester program from the GROUP MAIN window of the OS/2 workstation. The LOGON option is presented and the user enters their user ID password and the domain to which the user is defined. All three variables must match to complete a successful connection between the OS/2 LAN Requester and the OS/2 LAN Server.

9.7.3 OS/2 LAN Server to DOS LAN Requester

The procedures described for OS/2 LAN Server to OS/2 LAN Requester still hold true for defining a DOS end user to the OS/2 LAN Server. The difference is on the DOS LAN Requester. The difference is actually in the presentation of the log on request. Instead of the log on request occurring through OS/2's Presentation Manager interface it is performed through the DOS textual interface. However, the user ID, password and domain name to which the user is defined must still all match for successful connection to the server.

9.7.4 DOS Remote IPL Service from OS/2 LAN Server

A paramount requirement for the DOS Remote IPL service is that the token-ring adapter card in the DOS workstation must have the remote IPL feature installed. This feature, at boot time of the workstation, issues a remote IPL request to the LAN. Non-server workstations discard the request but servers analyze the request. The server determines the requesting workstation via the UAA number imbedded in the request. The server searches its remote IPL workstation database for the UAA number. If it is found the server then performs the remote IPL service for the DOS workstation. If the UAA is not found then the remote IPL request is discarded. LAA addresses are not permissible for remote IPL, only UAA addresses can be used.

As you can see from the diagram in Figure 9.20, the image used to load the requesting DOS workstation is defined in three areas on the OS/2 LAN Server. From the bottom up the image is created by selecting an installed image that comes with the DOS Remote IPL Service of OS/2 LAN Server. A standard image with this is

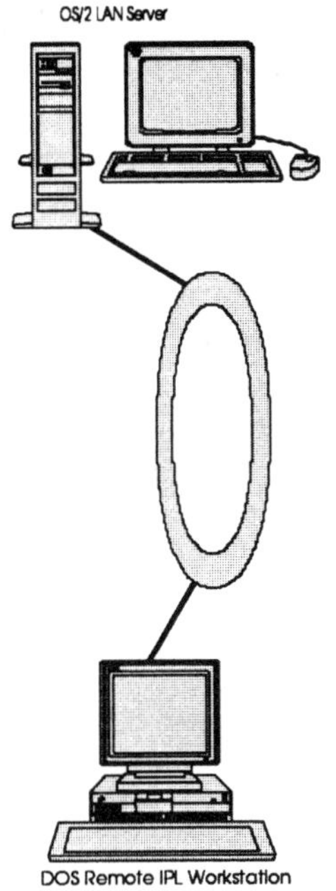


```
Main Panel
  Definitions
    Machine Parameters
      New
        Create
          Remote IPL Workstation
            Machine ID                 JGILFORD
            Description                DOS4.0 remote IPL
            Network adapter number     10005A28933B
            Remote IPL server          Corpsale
            Default IPL image          STD3H400
            Expanded memory support    No
Main Panel
  Definitions
    IPL Images
      Manage images
        STD3H400
          Create image profile
            Image ID        STD3H400
            Description     DOS4.0 for DOS LAN Requester
            Definition file Yes
Main Panel
  Definitions
    IPL Images
      Manage images
        STD3H400
          Make (PF10)
            To server
```

```
DOS disk IPL capability must be inhibited by enabling remote IPL

Insert the install diskette of PC LAN Program V1.3 in the A: drive
At the DOS prompt, key: A:PCLPSRPL /E
-OR-
Insert the Remote Program Load diskette in the A: drive
At the DOS prompt, key: A:RPLBOOT

After any of the options above, remove the dkt. from the A: drive
IPL the workstation by presseing ALT+CTRL+DEL
```

Figure 9.20 List of OS/2 LAN Server and DOS LANRequester screens and menus to define the DOS RIPL service.

STD3H400. This image is created using the Make action of the IPL Images selection. Under the Make action the destination of the binary IPL image is specified. Selecting To server from the Make pull-down menu opens a panel that allows the administrator to select which server(s) is to create and store the IPL image. This server name must also be defined on the Remote IPL server field of the Remote IPL workstation definition. To diskette can also be selected. In this case the IPL files are written to the A: diskette drive of the OS/2 Server.

Information determining what will be built in to the IPL image file is specified by the Create image profile definition panel. This panel allows the administrator to enter three fields defining the IPL image profile. The name of the image profile is assign in the Image ID field. The Description field provides a means for describing the programs included in the IPL image. The Definition file field indicates whether the image will be in a file on disk or on a bootable diskette. The STD3H400 image includes DOS V4.0, CONFIG.SYS, AUTOEXEC.BAT and DOS LAN Requester files that are loaded into the DOS workstation. The CONFIG.SYS and AUTO-EXEC.BAT files can be customized by the administrator for use by the remote DOS workstation to start and operate.

The Remote IPL workstation definition under Machine parameters defines the various fields specific to a DOS Remote IPL workstation. The important fields for defining the remote IPL workstation are the Network adapter number, Remote IPL server name and the Default IPL image fields. The Network adapter number must be the UAA number assigned by the manufacturer of the token-ring adapter that resides in the DOS workstation. The Remote IPL server name is the name of the server that contains the IPL binary file that is to be loaded into the DOS workstation. This name must be the same as the name selected in the To server selection under IPL images. Finally the name of the default IPL image used by the DOS workstation is defined on the Default IPL image field.

9.8 SUMMARY

The objective of Token-Ring Networks is the sharing of printers, databases and programs. IBM offers three products that provide for this shared environment: OS/2 LAN Server, OS/2 Extended Edition LAN Requester and DOS LAN Requester. The terminology and concepts applicable to the server/requester environment implemented by these products was discussed. Server/requester environments are managed by system and network administrators. Their role is management of the domain resources and their definitions. It is part of the administrators responsibilities to plan the LAN environment by establishing standards and access controls.

The functions and features of OS/2 LAN Server, OS/2 LAN Requester and DOS LAN Requester were discussed in detail. The relationships between each were described and their hardware and software requirements were reviewed. Configuration, connection and implementation of the server/requester LAN environment were detailed to give the reader a working knowledge of requirements and interdependencies between the three different server/requester entities for a token-ring network environment only. The next chapters will discuss token-ring network device access to the SNA mainframe.

Chapter

10

IBM's Token-Ring Network Bridge Program

Token-ring networks may be interconnected using bridges. Bridges by definition connect two LANs using the same logical link control (LLC) protocols but different medium access control (MAC) protocols. The IBM Token-Ring Network Bridge Program provides this bridging capability between two IBM token-ring networks. The IBM Token-Ring Bridge Program V2.2 connects token-ring network segments running 4Mbps or 16Mbps either locally or remotely. Local bridging requires one bridge computer (i.e., PC or PS/2) and remote bridging requires two bridge computers connected through communication lines operating at 9.6Kbps to 1.344Mbps (i.e., T1). Appendix I lists the various hardware, software and planning requirements to implement IBM Token-Ring Network Bridge Program. Figure 10.1 illustrates the two possible IBM Token-Ring Network Bridge Program configurations.

10.1 LOCAL BRIDGE CONFIGURATION

The IBM Token-Ring Network Bridge Program executes under the DOS operating system on a personal computer. The local bridge

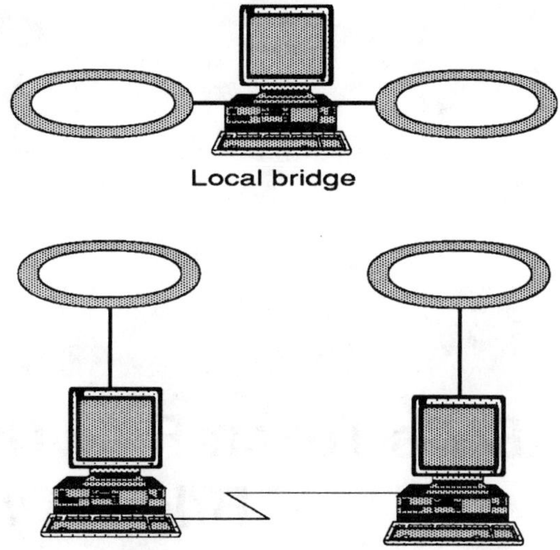

Figure 10.1 The local and remote IBM Token-Ring Network Bridge Program configurations.

configuration program has 22 configuration parameters that must be entered or confirmed. Appendix I contains a list of the parameters with their defaults and range of possible values. The first configuration panel displayed is shown in Figure 10.2.

The first fields on this panel are the bridge number and LAN segment number fields. Recall that the routing information field of the MAC frame contains a bridge number and LAN segment number. The values coded here are inserted into the routing information field of the MAC when an explorer frame is received for a destination station. The bridge number must be unique especially if the bridge being defined is part of a parallel bridge configuration. The next parameters identify the LAN segment numbers. The primary token-ring adapter is referred to as adapter 0. The alternate token-ring adapter is referred to as adapter 1. The primary and alternate adapters are determined at installation time. The parameter value for LAN segment number is 3-digits long. The number assigned to the LAN segment by this bridge must be referenced by all other bridges attached to the same LAN segment.

The main function of a bridge is to forward frames to the adjoining LAN segment. This function can be turned on automatically at the bridge program initialization or by the IBM LAN Network Manager. The value for this field should be set to NO if LAN

```
ECCPCG10        IBM TOKEN-RING NETWORK BRIDGE PROGRAM                Page 1 of 4
                       Configuration Program                            13:47:48
- - - - - - - - - - - - - - - - - - - - - - - - - - - - - - - - - - - - - - - -
Type the desired values in the fields below.
Press F6 (Save) to save the configuration parameters to the file ECCPARMS.BIN.
Press F3 (Exit) to exit to DOS.

Bridge number                                         ( 1 )   (0-9, A-F)
LAN segement number connected to primary adapter      ( 001 ) (001-FFF Hexadecimal)
LAN segment number connected to alterntte adapter     ( 002 ) (001-FFF Hexadecimal)
Frame forwarding active                               ( Y )   (Y=Yes, N=No)
Bridge performance threshold                          ( 10  ) (0-9999 Decimal)
Restart on error                                      ( Y )   (Y=Yes, N=No)
Drive for memory dump on error                        ( 0 )   (0=Default, A,B,C,)
Drive for error log                                   ( 0 )   (0=Default, A,B,C,D))

<--Any message occuring while this panel is active will be displayed here-->

F1=Help          F3=Exit                                         PgDn
F6=Save
```

Figure 10.2 Screen 1 of the configuration program for the IBM Token-Ring Network Bridge Program local bridge configuration.

Network Manager is to have control of the forwarding function. LAN segments can be isolated by specifying NO on this field. An example of isolating a LAN segment could be to stop the broadcast of a beaconing adapter.

Beaconing adapters can cause congestion on a bridge. The bridge performance threshold field allows the network administrator to set a threshold for the number of frames that have not been forwarded for every 10,000 frames. Each time the threshold is met the bridge sends an alarm to all linked LAN Network Managers. A bridge can be linked with up to four LAN Network Managers. The value coded here should be adjusted after analysis of the bridge performance. A happy medium should be met to provide the highest throughput on the bridge with satisfactory end user response time.

At times a bridge may need to reinitialize itself due to an adapter check or reduced critical resources such as workspace on the hard disk. A new feature in IBM Token-Ring Network Bridge Program V2.2 provides for automatic restart without operator intervention. This feature actually "reboots" the bridge computer, re-loading DOS and the bridge program. This function is vital in locations where a lack of knowledgeable personnel or minimal access to the computer is provided. The restart on error field defines whether automatic restart is to be used. If the restart on error field is coded as YES then be sure that the DOS AUTOEXEC.BAT file does not contain commands that require an operator's response (e.g., time and date).

The remaining two fields on this first configuration screen are self explanatory. The first of these two fields identifies the computer drive that will contain a file on which the computers memory contents and buffers can be written to (i.e., memory dump). The drive selected must have at a minimum of 210KB of space to dump memory. The name of the file that contains the memory dump is ECCDUMP.DAT. This file is overwritten with each memory dump. The drive for error log field identifies the computer drive on which the bridge error log is written. This error log is used to record errors that cause the bridge program to stop. The name of the error log file is ECCLOG.DAT. This file is appended to each time the bridge program writes to the file. This file can be viewed by any DOS text editor to determine the cause for the bridge outage. Both these files must exist on the system drive which is usually drive C or another drive allocation that follows drive C (e.g., drive D, drive E).

The second screen presented in the bridge configuration is shown in Figure 10.3. The hop count limit field specifies the number of hops (i.e., bridges) a broadcast frame may traverse including this bridge. This field may be used to direct and control traffic through the bridged network. A bridge interrogates the routing information field of a frame as it enters the bridge to determine the number of hops already traversed. If this value plus 1 (for this bridge) is equal to or greater than the hop count limit the broadcast frame is not forwarded.

The parameter server function on the bridge identifies the LAN segment number to an adapter when the adapter inserts into the ring. This process then allows the bridge to notify LAN Network Manager of the new adapter attachment. This function is enabled by specifying a Y in the Parameter Server field of this screen.

Statistical errors, analysis and reporting of these errors is accomplished through the implementation of the Error Monitor function. The error monitor function collects error statistics reported by adapters on each LAN segment attached to the bridge. A probable cause for these errors is determined by the error monitor function through analysis and reports on these errors to LAN Network Manager.

```
ECCPCG20          IBM TOKEN-RING NETWORK BRIDGE PROGRAM                    Page 2 of 4
                          Configuration Program                               13:53:08
- - - - - - - - - - - - - - - - - - - - - - - - - - - - - - - - - - - - - - - - - - -
Type the desired values in the fields below.
Press F6 (Save) to save the configuration parameters to the file ECCPARMS.BIN.
Press F3 (Exit) to exit to DOS.

                                  LAN SEGMENT 001        LAN SEGMENT 002

Hop count limit                   ( 7 )                  ( 7 )  (1-7)

ENABLED FUNCTIONAL ADDRESSES

    Parameter server              ( Y )                  ( Y )  (Y=Yes, N=No)
    Error monitor                 ( Y )                  ( Y )  (Y=Yes, N=No)
    Configuration report server   ( Y )                  ( Y )  (Y=Yes, N=No)


F1=Help        F3=Exit                                               Pg•p
F6=Save                                                              PgDn
```

Figure 10.3 Screen 2 of the configuration program for local bridge configuration.

The final field on the second configuration screen determines whether the Configuration Report Server function is enabled. This function notifies the linked LAN Network Managers of current active configurations for each attached LAN segment and reports changes in nearest active upstream neighbor addresses and which station on the segment is the current active monitor.

The third screen presented during local bridge configuration specifies the use of single-route broadcast functionality in the bridge. Recall that single-route broadcast insures that only one copy of the broadcast frame will traverse a LAN segment at any one time specifically in parallel bridge configurations. The screen presented is in Figure 10.4. The single-route broadcast field specifies to the bridge program whether the bridge will pass single-route broadcast frames from one LAN segment to the other. The mode of operation for handling single-route broadcast frames in the local bridge computer may be manual or automatic. It is best when choosing a value for the mode of operation to keep it consistent through out the network. In manual mode the single-route broadcast selection mode field is specified with an M. The single-route broadcast field is set for both LAN segments attached to the bridge computer. A value of Y indicates that single-route broadcast

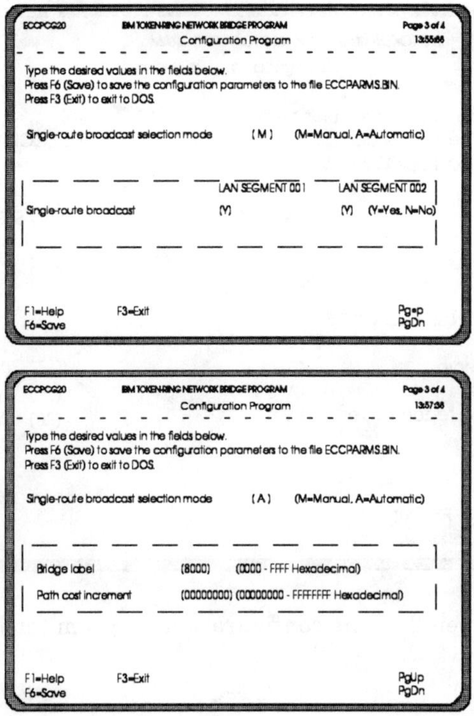

Figure 10.4 Screens 3 and 4 of the IBM Token-Ring Network Bridge Program for local bridge configuration.

frames are passed from one LAN segment to the other. A value of N (NO) tells the bridge program to throw away all single-route broadcast frames received from the LAN segment. Under automatic mode of operation the bridge program communicates with other bridge programs on the LAN segment. This communication allows each bridge to determine the setting for the single-route broadcast field. Automatic mode of operation uses a path cost and bridge label to determine the single-route broadcast field.

As shown in Figure 10.4 the bridge label is a four hexadecimal character value that is unique through the network. The value coded for the bridge label combined with the adapter address of the token-ring adapter that attached the bridge to the LAN segment creates a network-wide unique bridge identifier. The automatic mode of operation uses the bridge identifier to determine which bridge in a parallel bridge configuration will forward single-route broadcasts. The path cost field is used by the automatic mode of operation to determine which bridge in a parallel bridge configura-

	Adapter II & Adapter/A (4 Mbps)	16/4 Adapter & 16/4 Adapter/Aa (4 Mbps)	16/4 Adapter & 16/4 Adapter/A (16 Mbps)
Adapter II & Adapter/A (4 Mbps)	16	40	34
16/4 Adapter & 16/4 Adapter/A (4 Mbps)	40	64	40
16/4 Aapter & 16/4 Adapter/A (16 Mbps)	34	40	16

Figure 10.5 The path cost values for a local bridge configuration.

tion will be used as the path between the two LAN segments. It is recommended that the default value of hexadecimal '00000000' be used to allow the bridge program to determine the path cost value automatically based on the type of token-ring adapter sued, the data rates of the token-ring adapter used and the combinations of these token-ring adapters in the bridge computer.

The path cost value combinations used for the bridge are shown in Figure 10.5. The path cost value is defined in each bridge. The path cost is the relative length of the path between this bridge and a centrally located bridge. The centrally located bridge is also called the root bridge. This is the bridge program in the network that send the "HELLO" message every two seconds. The "HELLO" message is used by the root bridge to determine when other bridges enter and leave the network. The change in configuration affects the relative length of the path between bridges and therefore the path cost value. The actual path cost value of a bridge is the sum of path cost increments in the bridges between the originating bridge and the root bridge plus the path cost increment value of the origin bridge.

The final configuration screen shown in Figure 10.6 provides the list of passwords that LAN Network Managers may use to link to the bridge program. The LAN Network Manager that links to the bridge program using the link password defined in the Link password 0 field becomes the controlling LAN Network Manager. LAN Network Managers linking to the bridge program using the passwords in the other link password fields are monitoring the bridge. These link passwords must be defined in the LAN Network Manager definition for the bridge. The default for the old password

```
ECCPCG20          IBM TOKEN-RING NETWORK BRIDGE PROGRAM           Page 2 of 4
                          Configuration Program                     13:53:08
- - - - - - - - - - - - - - - - - - - - - - - - - - - - - - - - - - - - - - -
Type the desired values in the fields below.
Press F6 (Save) to save the configuration parameters to the file ECCPARMS.BIN.
Press F3 (Exit) to exit to DOS.
Press F5 (Clear Fields) to clear all the fields if any errors have been made.

Passwords must be 6-8 alphanumeric characters.
New password must be typed twice to confirm.
                          OLD              NEW           NEW
Link password 0         (        )       (        )    (        )

Link password 1         (        )       (        )    (        )

Link password 2         (        )       (        )    (        )

Link password 3         (        )       (        )    (        )

F1=Help         F3=Exit                  F5=Clear Fields            PgUp
F6=Save                                                             PgDn
```

Figure 10.6 The link password screen for the local bridge configuration definition.

field is 00000000. The value must be entered in the old password field when defining the new password for the first time. The passwords must be 6-8 alphanumeric characters including the symbols @, #, $, %.

10.2 REMOTE BRIDGE CONFIGURATION

IBM token-ring bridges can connect token-ring LANs over long distances using remote bridges. An example of a remote bridge configuration is shown in Figure 10.7. The two bridge segments are connected using a telecommunications line and two token-ring bridges. In this type of configuration the two remote bridges are called a remote bridge pair. Each bridge in the pair acts as a half-bridge and the two together provide the complete bridge function.

The first screen displayed for the remote bridge configuration has many of the same parameters as the local bridge configuration program. This section will discuss only those parameters that affect the remote bridge configuration. Figure 10.8 shows the first screen of the remote bridge configuration program. The *Bridge number* parameter denotes a unique bridge number to the bridge-

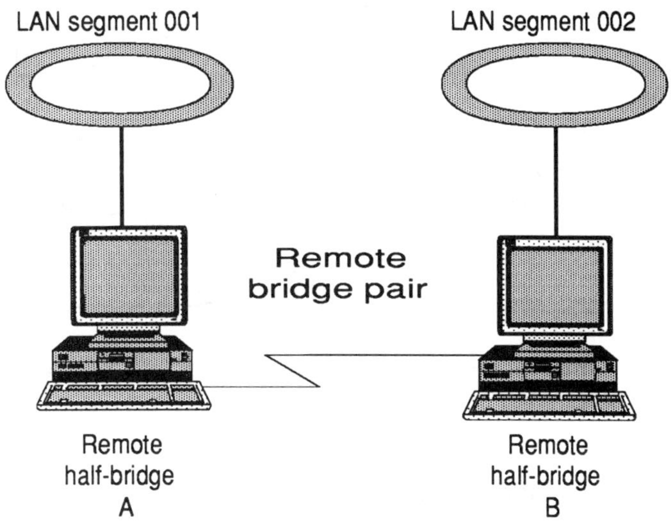

Figure 10.7 Diagram depicting the remote bridge configuration.

half. This value must be the same on both bridge-halves to be recognized as a remote bridge pair.

Each remote bridge-half defines the LAN segment number assigned to the local LAN segment and the remote LAN segment. In Figure 10.7, remote bridge-half A is local to LAN segment 001 and its remote LAN segment is 002. Likewise, remote bridge-half B is

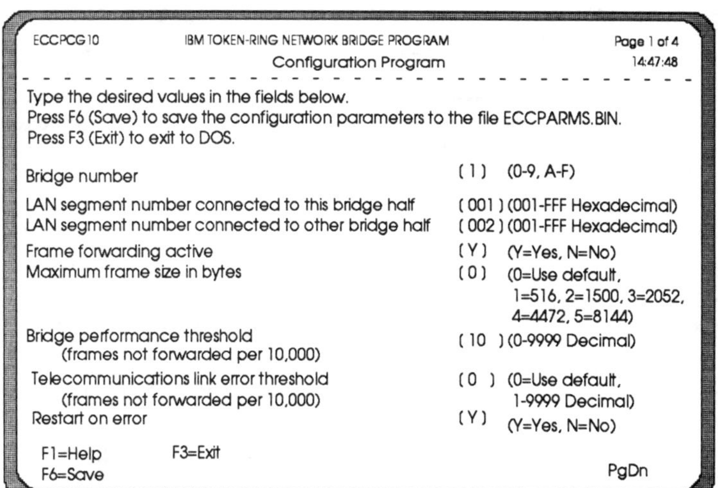

ECCPCG10 IBM TOKEN-RING NETWORK BRIDGE PROGRAM Page 1 of 4
Configuration Program 14:47:48

Type the desired values in the fields below.
Press F6 (Save) to save the configuration parameters to the file ECCPARMS.BIN.
Press F3 (Exit) to exit to DOS.

Bridge number	[1]	(0-9, A-F)
LAN segment number connected to this bridge half	[001]	(001-FFF Hexadecimal)
LAN segment number connected to other bridge half	[002]	(001-FFF Hexadecimal)
Frame forwarding active	[Y]	(Y=Yes, N=No)
Maximum frame size in bytes	[0]	(0=Use default, 1=516, 2=1500, 3=2052, 4=4472, 5=8144)
Bridge performance threshold (frames not forwarded per 10,000)	[10]	(0-9999 Decimal)
Telecommunications link error threshold (frames not forwarded per 10,000)	[0]	(0=Use default, 1-9999 Decimal)
Restart on error	[Y]	(Y=Yes, N=No)

F1=Help F3=Exit
F6=Save PgDn

Figure 10.8 Screen 1 of the IBM Token-Ring Bridge Program remote bridge configuration.

Line speed	Recommended Maximum frame size	Token-Ring Adapter & Adapter/A support	Memory	Value
9.6Kps <= S < 38.4Kps	516 bytes	4 or 16/4	16KB	1
38.4Kps <= S < 56Kps	1500 bytes	4 or 16/4	16KB	2
56Kps <= S < 1.344Mps	2052 bytes	4 or 16/4	16KB	3
S = 1.344Mps	4472 bytes	16/4	32KB	4
	8144 bytes	16/4 @ 16Mbps	64KB	5

Figure 10.9 The recommended maximum frame size for various line speeds and token-ring adapters.

local to LAN segment 002 and its remote LAN segment is 001. The LAN segment numbers are assigned accordingly in the *LAN segment number connected to this bridge half* and *LAN segment number connected to other bridge half* parameters.

The size of token-ring frame transmitted over the telecommunications line is dependent on the data rate of the line. Figure 10.9 contains a table outlining the various supported line speeds and their recommended maximum frame size. The table details the maximum frame size default values if a 0 has been entered on the configuration screen for the *Maximum frame size* parameter. The optional values that may be entered to define the actual maximum frame size are: 1 for 516 bytes, 2 for 1500 bytes, 3 for 2052 bytes, 4 for 4472 bytes and 5 for 8144 bytes. Applications that may send

Line speed	Recommended default threshold (frames/10,000)	Assumed maximum frame size	Approx. bit error rate
9.6Kbps	1581	516 bytes	4.17×10^{-5}
19.2Kbps	815	516 bytes	2.06×10^{-5}
38.4Kbps	1151	1470 bytes	1.04×10^{-5}
56Kbps	1085	2052 bytes	7×10^{-6}
64Kbps	972	2052 bytes	6.23×10^{-6}
256Kbps	253	2052 bytes	1.56×10^{-6}
512Kbps	127	2052 bytes	7.83×10^{-7}
1.344Mbps	49	2052 bytes	2.98×10^{-7}

Figure 10.10 The telecommunications link error threshold value defaults.

data over a remote bridge connection should have their outbound frame size adjusted to be equal to or less than the maximum frame size handled by the remote bridge programs.

The quality of the telecommunications line can affect successful transmission of token-ring frames between the remote bridge halves. The *Telecommunications link error threshold* parameter specifies the number of frames not received by the other bridge half. The number is specified in frames per 10,000. The bridge will send an alert notification to a LAN Network Manager when the threshold is reached. If a 0 is placed in this parameter then the default taken is listed in Figure 10.10.

Figure 10.11 diagrams the configuration screen requesting information on single-route broadcast and path costs. Selecting of automatic *(A)* for the *single-route broadcast selection mode* parameter

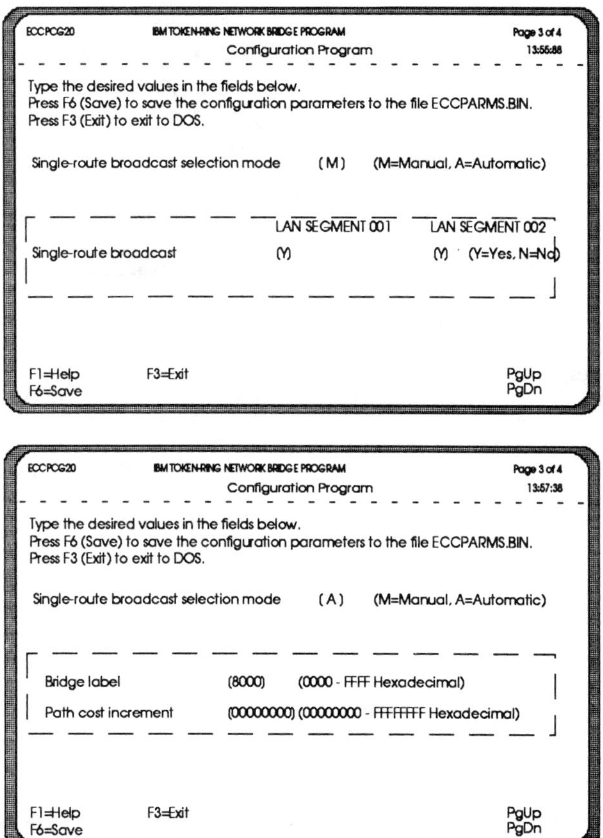

Figure 10.11 Defining a single-route broadcast to the IBM Token-Ring Bridge Program for a rettoe bridge configuration.

Line speed	Default value (milliseconds)
9.6Kbps	940
19.2Kbps	870
56Kbps	824
64Kbps	821
1.344Mbps	801

Figure 10.12 The default path cost increment values for remote bridge function.

is not recommended for remote bridge functions when the remote bridge-pair is the only bridge connection between two LAN segments. In this case the single-route broadcast parameter should be set to Y for YES and the single-route broadcast selection mode parameter should be set to M for Manual so as to not isolate the LAN segment from the network. Another caution to automatic mode is indicated when the data rate of the telecommunications line is running at low line speeds like 9.6Kbps and when the bridge pair are bridging large LANs separated over long distances. Setting these two parameters wrong for the illustrated bridge and line

```
ECCPCG20          IBM TOKEN-RING NETWORK BRIDGE PROGRAM                 Page 1 of 1
                  Communications Adapter Configuration Program             13:59:08
- - - - - - - - - - - - - - - - - - - - - - - - - - - - - - - - - - - - - - - - - -
Type the desired values in the fields below.
Press F6 (Save) to save the configuration parameters to the file ECCSBPARMS.BIN.
Press F3 (Exit) to exit to DOS.

Line data rate in bits per second _ _ _ _ _ _ (0      )   (9600-1344000 decimal)

Electrical interface _ _ _ _ _ _ _ _ _ _ _ _ (0)          (1=V.24, 2=V.35, 3=X.21)

Communications adapter transmit
buffer size in bytes _ _ _ _ _ _ _ _ _ _ _ _ (0   )       (0=Use Default,
                                                           1-65535 decimal)

Bridge Mode _ _ _ _ _ _ _ _ _ _ _ _ _ _ _ _ _ (0   )      (1=Leased, 2=Switched)


F1=Help            F3=Exit
F6=Save
```

Figure 10.13 The Communications Adapter Configuration screen for remote bridge configuration.

configurations causes excessive traffic over the telecommunications line due to messages generated by automatic mode of single-route broadcast.

As in local bridge configurations a remote bridge configuration can place a path cost on the relative length of the path between the bridge a a root bridge. By specifying automatic single-route broadcast the bridge used the path cost value to determine which parallel path between two LAN segments is to be used for single-route broadcast. A value of 0 in the Path cost increment parameter causes the bridge to select a default value based on telecommunication line data rates. Figure 10.12 contains a table with the appropriate default path cost values for each data rate.

Remote bridge configurations require information for the Communications Adapter Configuration Program. This single screen as shown in Figure 10.13 is used to provide the bridge program with configuration values for the communications adapter. The *Line data rate in bits per second* parameter defines the data rate of the telecommunication line between the two bridge halves. The value must be specified since the bridge program does not perform clocking. Instead data rate clocking is performed by the modem or DCE device. The value specified must match on both bridge halves.

The type of cable that connects the communications adapter to the DCE device is specified in the *Electrical interface* parameter. The various types of interfaces available are V.24, V.35 and X.21. This parameter does not default and must be the same value on both bridge halves.

The *Communications adapter transmit buffer size* parameter defines the maximum number of bytes that can be on the communications adapter transmit queue at any given time. The specification of 0 in this parameter indicates defaults will be taken. The defaults taken are based on the data rate of the telecommunication line. Figure 10.14 lists the defaults for the various line speeds.

The type of facility used for the telecommunication line is de-

Line speed	Default value
9.6Kbps	1,100
19.2Kbps	2,200
56Kbps	6,417
64Kbps	7,489
512Kbps	56,320
1.344Mbps	65,535

Figure 10.14 Default values for communications adapter transmit buffer size for specific line speeds.

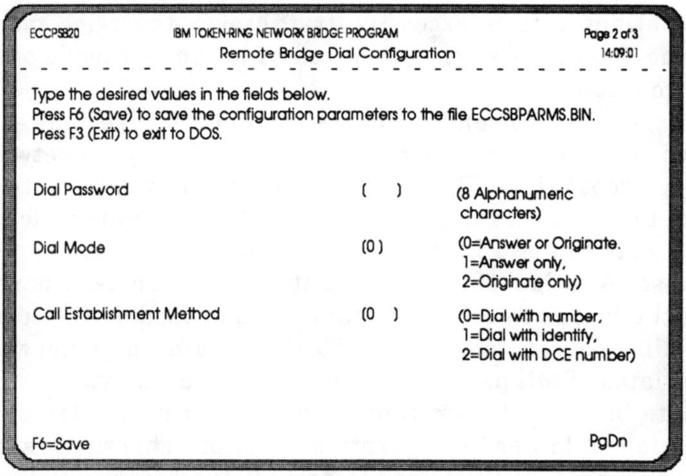

Figure 10.15 Remote dial configuration screen.

fined in the *Bridge mode* parameter. A value of 1 in this parameter indicates that the telecommunications line is a dedicated or leased line. A value of 2 indicates that the connection between the bridge halves is made by a switched or dial-up connection. In a switched connection a telephone number is needed to make the connection. This switched connection capability is called remote dial support.

10.3 REMOTE DIAL SUPPORT

Selecting a value of 2 in the *Bridge mode* parameter for the Communications adapter configuration program specifies to the bridge program that the remote dial feature must be configured. The remote dial application in conjunction with the supplied remote dial application allows the remote bridge to initiate or receive calls. The dial feature may be automatically started when the bridge half needs to send frames to the other bridge half or the dial procedure can be started manually through an operator command. Once the connection is made the switched line may remain connected or it can be automatically disconnected after the successful transmission of frames.

Setting the *bridge mode* parameter to switched on the first screen of the Communications Adapter Configuration Program will reveal the Remote Bridge Dial Configuration screen after pressing the Page Down key on the bridge computer keyboard. This screen will appear as shown in Figure 10.15. The *dial pass-*

word parameter contains eight alphanumeric characters that must match the password value passed by a dial frame received from the ring. If the passwords match the bridge proceeds to dial the phone number indicated in the dial frame. A blank value in the *dial password* parameter negates the password check and the bridge will dial the phone number found in the dial frame.

The mode of switched operation in a bridge is determined by the value specified in the *dial mode* parameter. The remote bridge may either originate or answer a switched connection or have the ability to do both. A value of 0 will allow the bridge to dial and answer switched connections. A value of 1 indicates the bridge may only answer a switched connection and not allow the dialing of phone numbers. The last value of 2 specifies that the bridge can only dial and not answer a switched connections.

The final parameter on the first screen for Remote Bridge Dial Configuration is *call establishment method*. This parameter value determines the method of switched establishment. A value of 0 indicates that the bridge will use the phone number provided in the call request frame. The *dial with identify* value of 1 indicates that the bridge is to verify the password embedded in the call request frame. The final value of 2 specifies that the bridge shall *dial with DCE number* preprogrammed in the modem attached to the communications adapter.

The remaining parameters determine the dial timing parameters that may be customized for the auto-dial and auto-answer operations. The details of each parameter can be found in Appendix I.

The parameters here must be in agreement on both bridge halves for successful remote dial procedures.

The supplied remote dial application that comes with the bridge program and executes under the DOS operating system. Figure 10.16 shows the Dial-Up Application screen provided when the DIALAPP program is executed. After entering the appropriate parameters for the needed switched request the request is initiated and processed.

In order to utilize a dial application, whether user written or the IBM provided dial application, the Bridge mode parameter must be reconfigured to indicate that switched mode will be used if the switched connection is being used to recover from a leased-line outage. In addition, the connection from the communication adapter to the leased-line modem must be moved to a switched modem is the leased-line modem does not support switched-network backup facility.

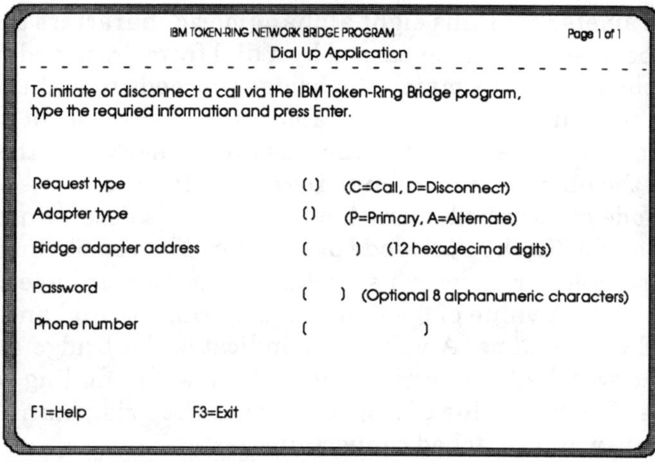

Figure 10.16 The Dial-Up Application parameter screen for remote dial support of the IBM Token-Ring Network Bridge Program.

10.4 FILTERING PROGRAMS

Performance and security on a LAN is of utmost importance due to the ease of connectivity to the ring. The performance and security management can be accomplished through the use of a filter. IBM Token-Ring Network Bridge Program allows for filters. These filters are implemented with filter programs. Filter programs inspect each frame that enters the bridge and can filter on any value found in the frame. The most favored filtering parameters are the MAC addresses found in the frame. The filtering mechanism allows the bridges to either forward or filter frames out of the bridge.

The bridge program allows for up to ten filter programs to be used with each bridge half in a remote bridge configuration or with each adapter of a bridge in a local bridge configuration. The filter programs implemented on each adapter and bridge half may be different from the other adapters and bridge halves. This capability will allow for refined filtering as frames cross several bridges. For instance bridges that connect to the backbone of a wide area network will forward all frames. But, as the frames reach corporate site bridges, these bridges may not forward the frames that are not known to the MAC address standards for the building, As the building frames pass through the floor bridges the floor bridges may filter on addresses not known in the standards for the floor. In this way, control of traffic through a bridge can enhance performance and impose access security to the ring segments.

The IBM Token-Ring Network Bridge Program comes with three different filter programs that can be implemented immediately. The first program limits the number of pairs of adapter addresses that can use the telecommunications line between two remote bridge halves at any given time. This program is called FILTER1.COM and is generically know as the Link Limiting Filter Program. The second program supplied filters on the NETBIOS names and frame types found in using the NETBIOS protocol. This program is named FILTER2.COM and is also referred to as the NETBIOS Filter Program. The third filter program supplied by IBM is known as the Address Filter Program and is named FILTER3.COM. This program filters frames based on MAC addresses found in the destination address field and source address field of a MAC frame.

The bridge program can also implement user written filter programs. These end-user filter programs allow you to inspect the entire MAC frame and base a filter on fields other than those used by the supplied filter programs or to enhance them. The user-written filter programs must be written in assembler language. The requirements, process and procedure of writing a user filter program are beyond the scope of this book. For information on how to write such a program consult the *IBM Token-Ring Network Bridge Program User's Guide.*

The Link Limiting Filter Program has three parameters these are the LINKS, TIME and CONT parameters. The LINKS parameter identifies the number of unique source and destination address pairs that can send frames over the telecommunications line between two bridge halves at any given time. This helps in reducing the amount of traffic between the remote bridge halves. The LINKS parameter can be any value from 1 to 255 and it is a required parameter with no default value. The TIME parameter is optional and indicates the amount of time in seconds that frames must pass over the telecommunication line in order for the line to be declared active. The value for the TIME parameter ranges from 1 to 3600 seconds with a default value of 60. The specification of the CONT parameter indicates to the bridge program that on start up if the FILTER1 program does not initialize properly to continue with the initialization of the bridge program. If the CONT parameter is not coded the bridge program will pause during initialization waiting for operator intervention. This is a critical feature of the FILTER1 program due to the fact that remote bridges are usually put in sites where no personnel are trained to handle the bridge. Should an error occur on loading the FILTER1 program the bridge may be in a suspended state without any network operator at the central site aware of the problem. It is highly recommended that the CONT parameter be used on the FILTER1 program. An example of using the FILTER1 program is as follows:

```
FILTER1 LINKS=2 TIME=25 CONT
```

This example indicates that only two pairs of source and destination address pairs can traverse the telecommunications line between remote bridge halves at any given time. The telecommunications line will be declared down if traffic has not be sent over the line after 25 seconds.

The NETBIOS Filter program is used to control the traffic of NETBIOS frames over bridges. NETBIOS was the first protocol implemented on IBM personal computers. It is used mainly to access LAN servers. The NETBIOS filter program, FILTER2, has five parameters. The format of the FILTER2 command is:

```
FILTER2 ADP=PRI|ALT ACTION=DISCARD|FORWARD|DISCARDDB|DISCARDALL
[NAME=name|FILE=file] [CONT]
```

The ADP parameter indicates to the bridge program which adapter on the bridge will be receiving the frames for filtering. A value of PRI indicates that filtering will be determined by frames received on the primary adapters. A value of ALT indicates that frames received on the alternate adapter will be filtered. The ACTION parameter value specifies what the bridge will do with the frame once it has gone through the filtering process. The DISCARD value indicates that a frame meeting the filtering criteria will not be forwarded. The FORWARD value indicates that the frame will be forwarded to its destination if the frame meets the filtering criteria. If a match is not found the opposite action is taken on the frames for these two values. NETBIOS DATAGRAM_BROADCAST frames can be discarded if the DISCARDDB value is used. Finally the DISCARDALL value indicates that all NETBIOS frames will not be forwarded. The NAME parameter allows you to specify a NETBIOS name. The full 16-character name can be specified or several names can be specified by using an asterisk or a question mark in place of a letter. NETBIOS names with a common prefix can be chosen by entering the common prefix of the name followed by an asterisk (e.g., LAN*). Common characters within names can be specified with the uncommon letter replaced by a question mark (e.g., SERV?1). The FILE parameter value is the name of a file that contains up to 50 NETBIOS names; one name on each line of the file. The names in this file can be entered as described for the NAME parameter. The CONT parameter is used as described for the link limiting filter program. The NETBIOS filter program can be implemented as in the following example:

```
FILTER2 ADP=PRI ACTION=DISCARD NAME=LANSRV1
```

The address filter program discards all frames that do not meet the filtering criteria. For this program the criteria is a match on the source and destination MAC addresses. The addresses may be specific or specified in a range. The format of the address filter program is:

```
FILTER3 ADP=PRI|ALT SA=addr1[-addr2] DA=addr3[-addr4] [CONT]
```

The ADP parameter is used in the same manner as the NETBIOS filter program. The SA parameter value identifies the MAC address to be checked in the frame. The addr1 value is required. The addr2 value is optional. If it is used it indicates a range inclusive of the addr1 and addr2 values that will be used to check the source field. The DA parameter is used in the same manner as the SA parameter but the values are compared against the destination address. If both the SA and DA parameters are specified both arguments must be satisfied to discard the frame. Again, the CONT parameter is used as in the previous filter programs. The following is an example of using the address filter program:

```
FILTER3 ADP=ALT SA=400023174001-400023174022 CONT
```

10.5 SUMMARY

IBM token-ring bridges use IBM's Token-Ring Network Bridge Program. The program executes in a dedicated personal computer with the DOS operating system. The program provides two functions. One function is called local the second is called remote. A local bridge function connects two local LAN segments by using two token-ring adapters. The remote bridge function uses two personal computers each executing the Token-Ring Network Bridge Program. In a remote bridge configuration the two bridge computers act as one logical bridge. Each bridge computer is called a remote bridge half. Each bridge half has a token-ring adapter and a communications adapter. Remote bridges are connected through telecommunications lines. These telecommunications lines can be leased or switched lines. The bridge program can control the traffic through the bridge using filter programs. Filter programs may be used to restrict access and manage performance on the bridge and telecommunication lines.

Chapter

11

Mainframe Connectivity with the IBM 3172 Interconnect Controller

The dominant method of having remote devices communicate with mainframe applications is through communication controllers like IBM's 3745. These devices require a network control program (NCP) for defining network resources and providing networking services on behalf of these resources. In this environment, new devices are defined to the NCP and the NCP is regenerated and loaded into the communication controller, interrupting resources attached to the communication controller. In a token-ring environment the NCP and communication controller can act as a token-ring gateway to the mainframe, however, token-ring connectivity to the mainframe may still be interrupted by the NCP loading process. Token-ring devices can now access the mainframe directly, by-passing the communication controller, and connecting to the mainframe through an IBM 3172 Interconnect Controller.

Token-ring devices can communicate with applications residing on an IBM mainframe that is executing the operating systems and access methods listed in Figure 11.1. This chapter will concentrate solely on VTAM and TCP/IP connectivity. The IBM 3172 Interconnect Controller also provides for a wide array of connectivity op-

ICP Version		V1.0	V2.0	V2.1	V2.2	V2.X
Host program	VM & MVS TCP/IP 2.0 +	Yes	Yes	Yes	Yes	Yes
	VMOSI/MMS OSI/CS 1.1	Yes	Yes	Yes	Yes	Yes
	VM AIX/370 1.2	Yes	Yes	Yes	Yes	Yes
	VM & MVS VTAM/SNA		Yes	Yes	Yes	Yes
	VM & MVS VTAM/CTC			Yes	Yes	Yes
Channels	Parallel	Yes	Yes	Yes	Yes	Yes
	Serial VTAM/CTC			Yes	Yes	Yes
	High speed serial					Yes
LANs	Token-ring	Yes	Yes	Yes	Yes	Yes
	ENET/802.3	Yes	Yes	Yes	Yes	Yes
	IEEE 802.4 MAP 3.0	Yes	Yes	Yes	Yes	Yes
	IEEE 802.4 SNA support		Yes	Yes	Yes	Yes
	PC Network			Yes	Yes	Yes
	FDDI			Yes	Yes	Yes

Figure 11.1 The operating systems and access methods supporting various ICP versions.

tions. Figure 11.2 lists the possible networking architectures that can be connected to the IBM 3172. The discussions that follow will concentrate on definitions of the IBM 3172 to mainframe operating systems and access methods, and management of the IBM 3172 Interconnect Controller over token-ring networks.

11.1 OPERATING SYSTEM DEFINITIONS AND CONSIDERATIONS

IBM mainframe computers offer two widely used operating systems. These are the Virtual Machine (VM) and Multiple Virtual Storage (MVS) operating systems. Each operating system is available with various features. For our purposes we will refer to all the various releases of the operating systems as VM and MVS.

Mainframe host computer	3081
	3083
	3084
	Enterprise System/3090 (ES/3090)
	4361(not Model 1 CTC)
	4381
	ES/9000
	ES/9370

Figure 11.2 The mainframe host computers that support the IBM 3172 Interconnect Controller.

Channel attachment of the IBM 3172 to the mainframe is provided by parallel and serial channels. Attachment to an IBM System/370 (S/370) mainframe is accomplished using a block multiplexor channel. This channel can transmit data at up to 4.5MBps. Channel attachment to an IBM Enterprise System/390 (ES/390) and Enterprise System/9000 (ES/9000) mainframe computers may be accomplished by utilizing IBM's Enterprise Systems Connection (ESCON), providing data rates up to 200MBps. In both channel configurations the IBM 3172 is defined to the operating system as an IBM 3088 Channel-to-channel (CTC) Control Unit.

The IBM 3172 is assigned a Unit Control Word (UCW) or Input/Output Configuration Program (IOCP) addresses by the VM or MVS systems programmer through a system generation (SYSGEN) or IOCP generation (IOCPGEN) process. The addresses assigned to the IBM 3172 are dependent on the use of the adapters within the IBM 3172. The assigned channel must be defined as non-shareable between operating systems. An address range of 32 or 64 must be defined in the VM operating system environment to compile an IOCP definition for an IBM 3088 control unit. The MVS operating system environment does not have this constraint. The addresses assigned to the channel can be used by the IBM 3172 to connect to access methods on the mainframe. Connecting to TCP/IP requires a contiguous even-odd pair of addresses. The even address is used by the IBM 3172 to send LAN traffic to the mainframe. The odd address is used to send data from the mainframe to the IBM 3172 and out to the LAN. SNA VTAM connectivity to the IBM 3172 requires only one address. The address used to connect to VTAM can be either odd or even. These channel configurations are shown in Figure 11.3.

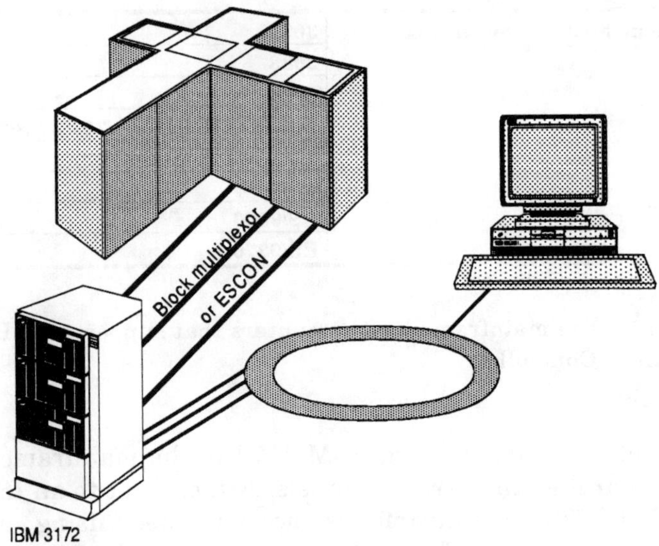

Figure 11.3 The VTAM channel configurations.

4.5MB data streaming channel

```
C3172     CNTLUNIT     CUNUMBR=040,PATH=(05),
                       PROTCL=S4,SHARED=N,UNIT=3088,
                       UNITADD=((04,8))

D3172     IODEVICE     UNIT=CTC,ADRESS=((040,8)),
                       STADET=N,CUNUMBR=040
```

Other data streaming channel

```
C3172     CNTLUNIT     CUNUMBR=040,PATH=(05),
                       PROTCL=S,SHARED=N,UNIT=3088,
                       UNITADD=((04,8))

D3172     IODEVICE     UNIT=CTC,ADRESS=((040,8)),
                       STADET=N,CUNUMBR=040
```

Data Channel Interlock channel

```
C3172     CNTLUNIT     CUNUMBR=040,PATH=(05),
                       PROTCL=D,SHARED=N,UNIT=3088,
                       UNITADD=((04,8))

D3172     IODEVICE     UNIT=CTC,ADRESS=((040,8)),
                       STADET=N,CUNUMBR=040
```

Figure 11.4 The IOCP defintion statements for block multiplexor channel attachment to an IBM 3172.

11.1.1 IOCP Definitions for VM and MVS

In a non-ESCON environment there are three types of channel configurations to choose and each type can be logically connected to only one channel adapter on the mainframe host operating system. The definitions for these are printed in Figure 11.4. The CNTLUNIT macro identifies the type of control being defined along with the channel and address requirements. The difference between the three definition specified in Figure 11.4 is the PROTOCL keyword. The value specified for PROTOCL defines the type of channel that will be attached to the device. A value of S4 indicates that the device is attached to a 4.5MBps data-streaming channel as shown in the first example. A value of S indicates that the control unit is attached to a data-streaming channel other than 4.5MBps. Usually this data-streaming channel data rate is up to 3MBps. Finally a value of D for the PROTOCL keyword defines a Data Channel Interlock (DCI) channel as the connection to the control unit. The SHARED keyword of the CNTLUNIT macro has a value of N, indicating that the channel is not to be shared by other operating systems. The CUNUMBR value is an internal number for the operating system control program representing the control unit being defined. This value is usually set to match the starting address for the device. The UNITADD keyword identifies the starting unit address and the range of addresses allowed on this channel for the device. The UNIT keyword specifies the type of device being defined. As discussed previously, the IBM 3172 is defined as a IBM 3088 Channel-to-channel control unit.

In an ESCON environment the ESCON adapter for the IBM 3172 can support up to 16 logical hosts by using an ESCON Director. The ESCON Director is basically an intelligent device that maps the connection from the IBM 3172 to other operating system channels. Since, the IBM 3172 can support up to two ESCON channel adapters a logical total of 32 host operating systems may be supported. A typical ESCON connection and definition is depicted in Figure 11.5. Note that in this configuration the IBM 3172 is not directly connected to the mainframe. Instead, the IBM 3172 is attached to an ESCON Director which is actually a channel I/O switch. The CHPID macro defines the channel path from the mainframe to the ESCON Director. It also defines the type of channel being defined. In this case the TYPE keyword with the value of S indicates that it is a serial channel. The SWITCH keyword defines the ESCON Director address the CHPID is connecting.

The CNTLUNIT macro points back to the CHPID definition

ESCON IOCP Definition

```
P3172    CHPID       PATH=((34)),TYPE=S,SWITCH=00

C3172    CNTLUNIT    CUNUMBR=100,PATH=(34),
                     LINK=(C1),CUADD=1,
                     UNITADD=((B0)),UNIT=3172

D3172    IODEVICE    ADDRESS=(040),CUUNUMBR=100,
                     UNITADD=B0,UNIT=CTC
```

Figure 11.5 The IOCP defintions for an IBM 3172 using an ESCON channel attachment.

through the PATH keyword. The LINK keyword assigns a link address to the channel. The UNITADD keyword defines the starting address of the device being defined. Note that when defined ESCON channel addresses a range of addresses is not specified. Finally, a major difference between non-ESCON and ESCON channel and control unit definitions is the UNIT keyword on the CNTLUNIT macro. Under ESCON the Interconnect Controller is actually defined to the CNTLUNIT macro as a 3172. This is in contrast to the non-ESCON definition just discussed where the UNIT keyword for an Interconnect Controller is specified as 3088. NOTE: The IBM 3172 Interconnect Controller must be defined as the last device on a channel for both non-ESCON and ESCON channel definitions.

11.1.2 Device Definitions for VM and MVS

The type of device being defined is referenced by VM in the RDEVICE macro. The VM operating system releases have different requirements and must be broken out. In a Virtual Machine/System Product (VM/SP) operating system environment the RDEVICE macro and RCTLUNIT macro must specify an address range of 32 or 64 for the 3088 and for CTC a minimum of 8 as the address range. The definition for the IBM 3172 on the RDEVICE macro for VM/SP looks like:

```
RDEVICE ADDRESS=(640,32),DEVTYPE=3088

RCTLUNIT ADDRESS=640,CUTYPE=3088,FEATURE=32-DEVICE
```

These macros are added to the real I/O configuration file DMKRIO in VM/SP operating system environments.

The first variable of the ADDRESS keyword on the RDEVICE macro specifies the base address of the IBM 3172 control unit base address. The second variable indicates the address range that was defined in the IOCP generation. The DEVTYPE keyword of the RDEVICE macro identifies the type of device associated with the address. For IBM 3172 devices this keyword value is 3088

The RCTLUNIT macro the base unit address for the control unit being defined on the ADDRESS keyword. The CUTYPE keyword the type of control unit begin defined in this case a 3088 and the FEATURE keyword indicates the number device addresses that area assigned to the control unit starting with the control unit base address. In VM/SP this value must be 32 or 64.

In a Virtual Machine/Extended Architecture (VM/XA) or Virtual Machine/Enterprise System Architecture (VM/ESA) operating system environment only the RDEVICE macro is required. The IBM 3172 in these environments is defined as a channel-to-channel adapter (CTCA) device. The RDEVICE macro for VM/XA and VM/ESA is defined in the real I/O configuration file named HCPRIO. The macro definition looks like:

```
RDEVICE ADDRESS=(640,8),DEVTYPE=CTCA
```

On this definition the second variable, denoting the address range, is valued at 8 since the device being defined is a channel-to-channel adapter.

The MVS environment defines the IBM 3172 as a channel-to-channel device on the IODEVICE macro in the MVS Control Program. The definition of the macro looks like:

```
IODEVICE UNIT=CTC,ADDRESS(640,8)
```

The UNIT keyword is defined with the value of CTC indicating the I/O device acts like a channel-to-channel device. The ADDRESS keyword indicates the base address of the IBM 3172 as 640 and up to 8 addresses (i.e., 640-647) starting with the base address are reserved for the device.

11.2 DEFINING THE IBM 3172 ICP

The Interconnect Control Program (ICP) V2.1 is a number of programs that are generated on a workstation utilizing IBM OS/2 Extended Edition V1.2 and higher. The ICP is generated and either transported to the IBM 3172 via diskette are loaded over the token-ring network from the IBM 3172 Operator Facility/2 (OF/2) workstation. The ICP provides the following support on the IBM 3172 Interconnect Controller:

- LAN Gateway support on both Model 1 and 2. This enables a workstation on a LAN to communicate with a mainframe computer.
- Channel-to-channel controller support enabling remote mainframe computers to communicate over telecommunications lines.
- VTAM V3.4 support using the Interconnect Enhancement Feature for SNA/VTAM application access from workstations on the LAN and Remote CTC feature allowing VTAM support for CTC connectivity between remote mainframes.
- Network management support using SNA management services, Asset Management and Central Site Control Facility (CSCF).
- TCP/IP connectivity and management.

Figure 11.6 contains a table listing the host application and operating system requirements in relation to the version and release level of ICP to provide LAN gateway functions.

11.2.1 The IBM 3172 Operator Facility/2

The Operator Facility/2 (OF/2) executes under IBM OS/2 Extended Edition V1.2 or higher and Presentation Manager and is installed using the standard OS/2 EE installation process. OF/2 defines the adapters (e.g., LAN and channel) and host access methods (e.g., VTAM and TCP/IP) that will be communicating through the IBM 3172. OF/2 can be used in two modes. The first mode is stand-alone. This mode indicates that the workstation is not attached to the token-ring. In stand-alone mode the OF/2 workstation can create and maintain up to 16 IBM 3172 profiles. The ICP generated from a stand-alone OF/2 workstation must create ICP diskettes which are then transported to the IBM 3172 and then manually loaded. This process is discussed in detail in section 11.3.

The second mode of operation for the OF/2 workstation is attached mode. This mode indicates that the OF/2 workstation is attached to the token-ring network and has connectivity to the Token-Ring Adapter installed on the IBM 3172. In this mode of operation the ICP can be loaded into the IBM 3172 remotely over

Host application	TCP/IP 2.0 +	AIX/370 1.2	OSI/MMS	OSI/CS 1.1	VTAM 3.4 +
Operating system	VM MVS	VM	VM	VM MVS	VM MVS
		Model 1			
LAN Gateway					
Token-Ring (IEEE 802.5)	1.0	1.0			2.0
Ethernet (Version 2.0)	1.0	1.0			
IEEE/802.3	1.0	1.0		1.0	2.0
Token-Bus Broadband (IEEE 802.4)					2.0
MAP 3.0 Broadband			1.0		
PC Network	2.1				
Interconnect Enhancement Feature					2.0
Parallel channel	1.0	1.0	1.0	1.0	2.0
Remote CTC Controller					
T1					2.1
Remote CTC Feature					2.1
ESCON					2.1
Parallel channel					2.1
		Model 2			
LAN Gateway					
FDDI	2.1				2.1
Interconnect Feature					2.1
Parallel Channel	2.1				2.1

Figure 11.6 The ICP version and feature support for various host applications and operating systems.

the token-ring network. This is accomplished using NETBIOS protocols over the token-ring interface between the OF/2 workstation and the ICP executing in the IBM 3172. An attached OF/2 workstation not only creates and maintains up to 16 IBM 3172s but it can also manage them. The attached OF/2 workstation can connect to the IBM 3172 using token ring, wide area network (WAN) or a bridge.

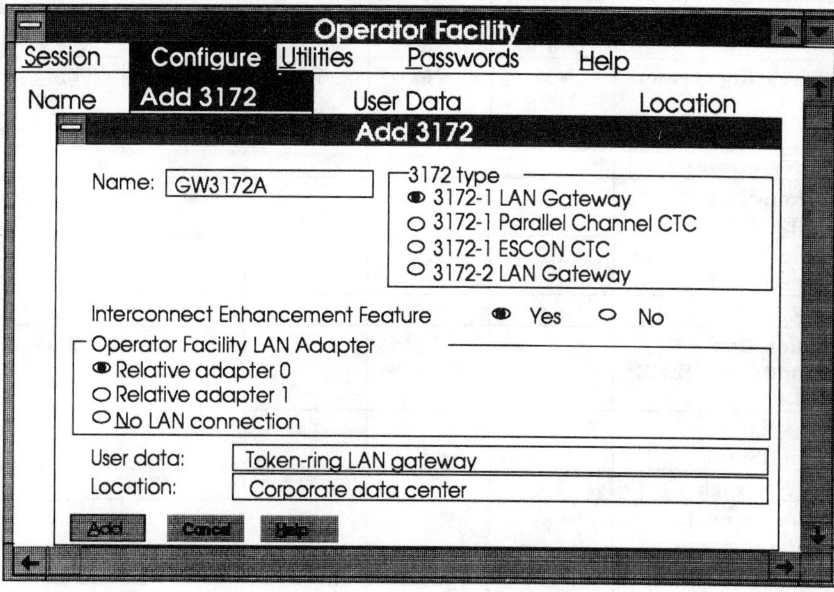

Figure 11.7 Selection menu for defining an IBM 3172.

OF/2 requires IBM OS/2 EE V1.2 and higher, OS/2 Communications Manager and OS/2 LAN Requester software to operate in attached mode. Resources utilized by these software requirements and NETBIOS must be ensured. The NETBIOS resource allocations for the Names parameter should be at a minimum of 30. The Link Stations parameter of NETBIOS must be at a minimum of 36.

11.2.2 Defining the IBM 3172 Device to ICP

The OF/2 must have an IBM 3172 defined to it. This is accomplished by using the Configure action and selecting Add from the selection menu presented as shown in Figure 11.7. The name associated with the IBM 3172 being defined is entered into the Name field of the Add 3172 window. The type of IBM 3172 being defined for our example is indicated by selecting 3172-1 LAN Gateway. In the example connectivity to VTAM V3.4 will be used, so the Yes field of the Interconnect Enhancement Feature option is selected. The OF/2 identifies which LAN adapter in the OF/2 workstation to use by selecting the Relative adapter fields. A relative adapter number of 0 indicates that the primary Token-Ring Adapter card

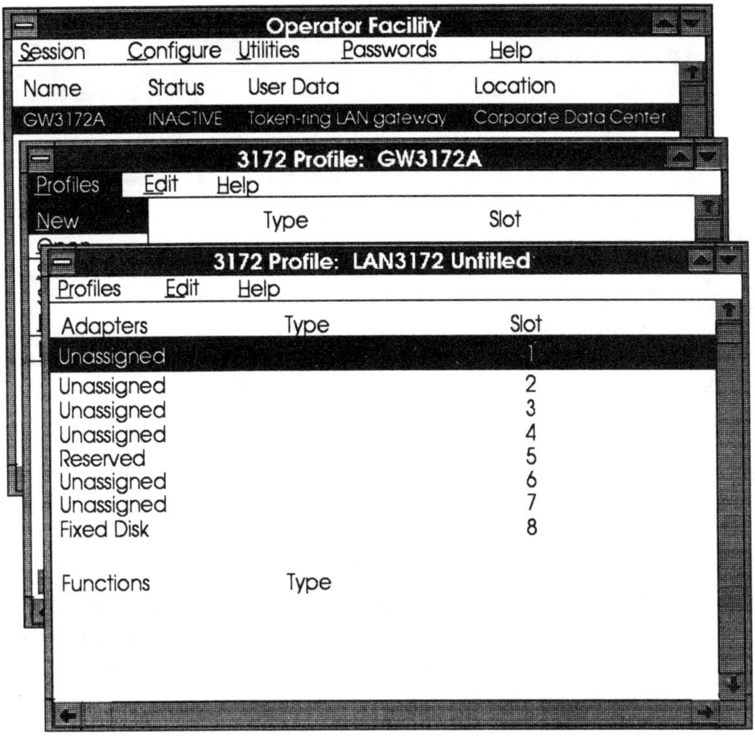

Figure 11.8 The OF/2 screens for defining a 3172 Profile.

in the OF/2 workstation is to be used to access the IBM 3172 being defined. Selecting relative adapter 1 indicates that the alternate Token-Ring Adapter card is to be used by the OF/2 workstation to connect to the IBM 3172 being defined. The User data field may be used to describe the IBM 3172 and its function while the Location field is used to indicate the location of the IBM 3172 within the network. Selecting the Add button accepts the definition and places the end user back at the Operator Facility primary window. The name chosen for the IBM 3172, its user data and location information are displayed on the Operator Facility primary window.

Definition of the adapters is performed by highlighting the newly created IBM 3172 and selecting Configure from the Operator Facility primary window as shown in Figure 11.8. The Profiles option is selected from the Configure menu and displays a new window entitled 3172 Profile: GW3172A. From this window select the Profiles action item and select New from the pull-down menu.

Slot	Adapter
1	Parallel channel adapter.
2	Token-ring 16/4 adpater, Ethernet/802.3 adapter, Token-bus/MAP 3.0 adapter.
3	Token-ring 16/4 adapter, Ethernet/802.3 adapter, Token-bus/MAP 3.0 modem if Token-bus/MAP 3.0 adapter is assigned to slot 2.
4	Parallel channel adapter.
5	None. This slot is reserved.
6	Token-ring 16/4 adpater, Ethernet/802.3 adapter, Token-bus/MAP 3.0 adapter, PC Network adapter.
7	Token-rnig 16/4 adapter, Ethernet/802.3 adapter, token-bus/MAP 3.0 modem if Token-bus/MAP 3.0 adapter is assigned to slot 6, PC Network adapter.
8	None. This slot is resrved for the fixed disk.

Figure 11.9 The adapter slot assignments for the IBM 3172 Model 1.

At this point a new window is displayed entitled 3172 Profile: LAN 3172 Untitled. This menu displays a list of the adapter slots and their current configurations. Since the OF/2 is defining this IBM 3172 for the first time there are no configurations to display. Adapter positions are restrictive and are listed in Figure 11.9.

11.2.3 Defining Channel-Attachments to ICP

During initial configuration of an IBM 3172, all the adapter slots except slot 8 of the model 1 are unassigned. Slot 8 on the model 1 is reserved for the fixed disk controller card. The first channel adapter can be assigned by highlighting the row for slot 1 as illustrated in Figure 11.10. Selecting the Edit function displays a pull-down selection menu. The Add option is selected to add a channel adapter. The resulting window entitled Adapter Type is displayed. The Adapter Type window only shows a list of valid adapter types for the selected slot. In this case, slot 1 was selected, hence, only a single selection is listed. The Parallel Channel Adapter Parameters window is opened by highlighting the Parallel Channel Adapter item and selecting OK as shown in Figure 11.11.

The Parallel Channel Adapter Parameters window allows the end user to enter channel parameters specific to this channel adapter slot. The Name field value is an internal name assigned to the slot. In the sample configuration a 4.5MBps data-stream channel is being used. This is indicated by selecting the 4.5MB data streaming item in the Transfer Mode and Channel Transfer Speed

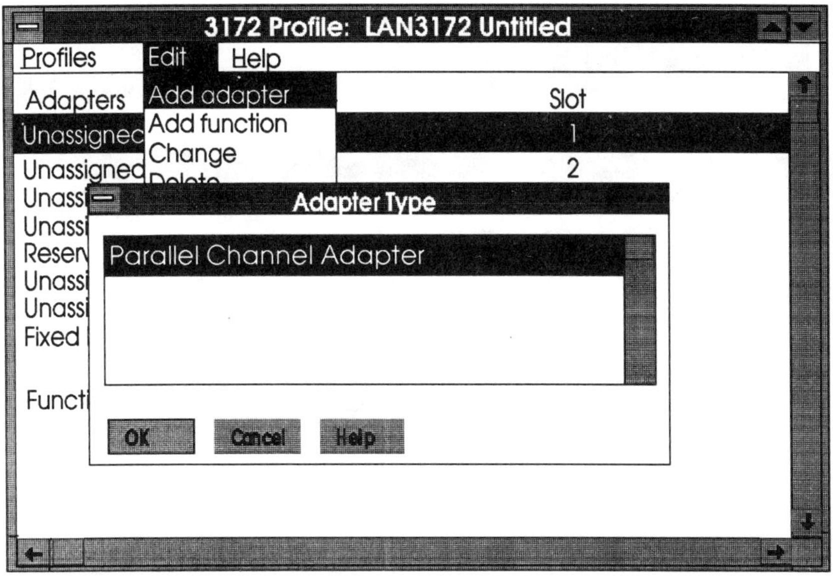

Figure 11.10 The selection screen procedure to define a parallel channel adapter on the IBM 3172 using the OF/2.

field. This channel adapter will also be used as the interface for VTAM V3.4 for SNA management services. This function is indicated by selecting the SNA management services field. Selecting this field requires the VTAM IDNUM field to be specified. This field must match the IDNUM keyword of the switched PU defini-

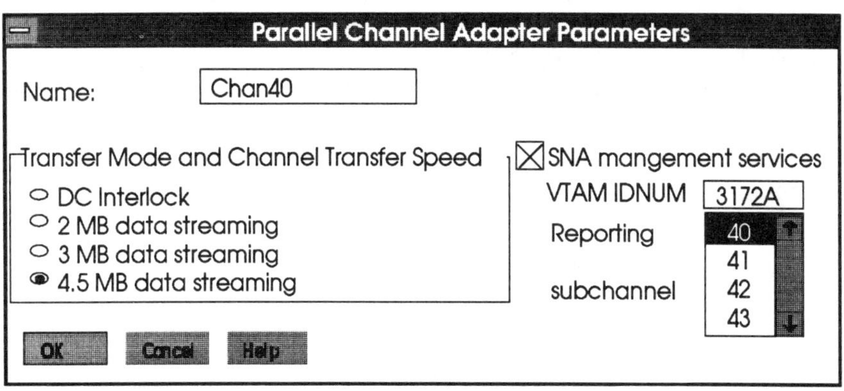

Figure 11.11 The Parallel Channel Adapter parameters for the IBM 3172.

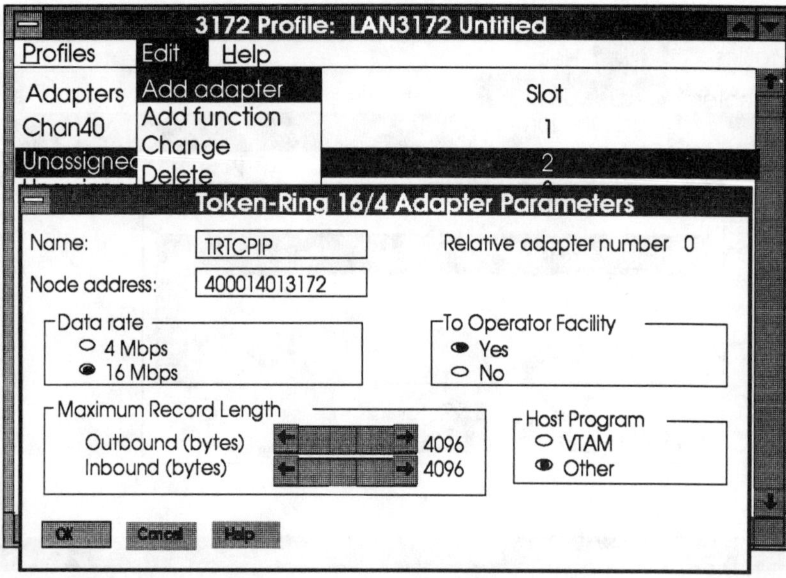

Figure 11.12 The OF/2 defintion screen for the IBM Token-Ring Adapter installed in the IBM 3172.

tion statement that represents the IBM 3172 to VTAM V3.4 on the host computer. The subchannel address associated with the VTAM IDNUM is defined in the Reporting subchannel field. This field is a valid unit address in the address range determined by the operating system IOCP generation. In the example configuration, this value may be any where from 40 to 47. After completing all the fields the OK button is selected and returns you to the 3172 Profile window. This window is now displayed with the name given to the channel adapter in slot 1. The same process may be repeated for a channel adapter installed in slot 4.

Note: It is imperative that adapter cards be installed in the slots that are defined to the ICP. Invalid definitions will result in ICP operational errors.

11.2.4 Defining Token-Ring Adapters to ICP

Token-ring adapters can be installed into a model 1 IBM 3172 in slots 2, 3, 6 and 7. The selection for a Token-Ring Adapter is quite similar to channel adapter selection. The slot to be defined for a Token-Ring Adapter is highlighted and the end user selects the Edit function. The pull-down menu appears and the Add option is selected. This results in the display of the Token-Ring 16/4 Adapter Parameters window as shown in Figure 11.12.

In the upper right-hand corner of the window display is the assigned Relative adapter number. This number is generated by OF/2 during the addition of adapters. The adapter being added here is the first token-ring adapter defined to the IBM 3172 profile, so, it is assigned relative adapter number 0. This number is used later when defining parameters on the host computer.

Again an internal name is entered for the token-ring adapter installed in slot 2. The Name field contains the symbolic name for the adapter. The Node address field is the token-ring local area MAC address assigned to the token-ring adapter. If the default universal address is used then the field would contain the word Universal. In the example, however, a locally administered address is used. The speed at which the attached token-ring network is operating at is defined in the Data rate field. Currently there are only two options: 4Mbps and 16Mbps. The data rate selected affects the maximum record length for inbound and outbound buffers in the IBM 3172.

The Maximum Record Length field determines the size of the inbound and outbound buffer size used by the IBM 3172. If the token-ring data rate is specified as 4Mbps, then the minimum buffer size is 96 and the maximum buffer size is 4464 bytes. A data rate of 16Mbps results in a minimum buffer size of 96 and a maximum of 17960 bytes. The default is 2048 for both inbound and outbound. However, it will not hurt to maximize the buffer size to ensure successful transmission of data between the host computer and token-ring devices.

The To Operator Facility field indicates to the OF/2 whether this token-ring adapter is to be used for the NETBIOS traffic between the OF/2 workstation and the IBM 3172. The Host Program field indicates whether this adapter is to be used by VTAM or one of the other host programs supported, such as, TCP/IP. Selecting Other indicates that a host program other than VTAM will be utilizing this adapter for communicating to and from the mainframe. In the example configuration this token-ring adapter will be used to connect to TCP/IP for MVS on the host computer. These two fields identify how the IBM 3172 is to be managed.

After entering all the fields of the Token-Ring 16/4 Adapter Parameters window the OK button is selected and the 3172 Profile window is displayed. Note that this time the window also includes the token-ring adapter definition for slot 2.

A second token-ring adapter can be defined by going through the

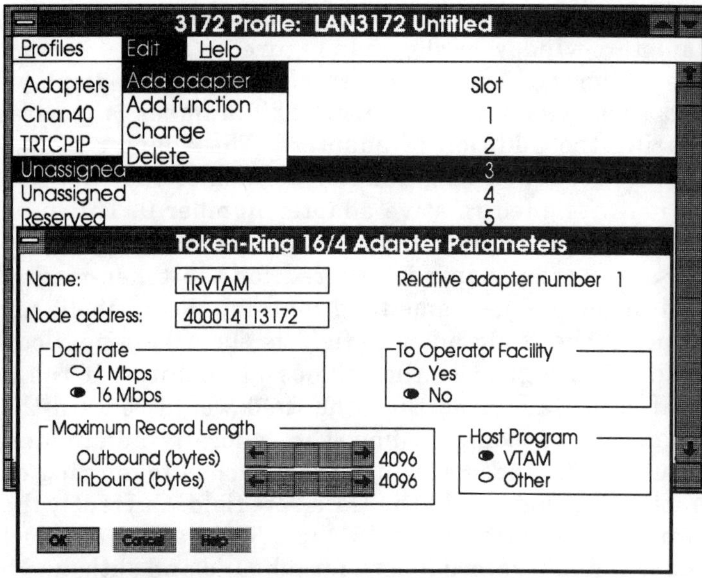

Figure 11.13 The OF/2 definition screen for the second token-ring adapter installed in the IBM 3172.

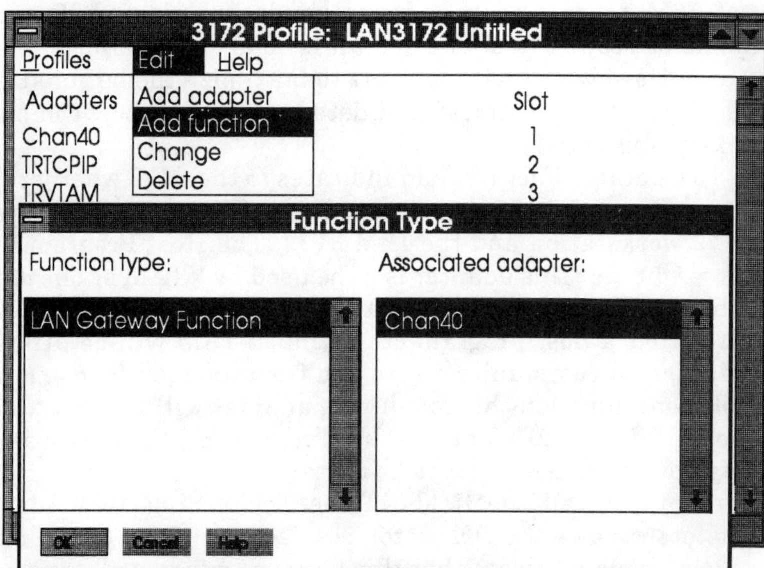

Figure 11.14 The OF/2 function LAN gateway selection screen.

same process just discussed. On this token-ring adapter definition however, a new name and node address is assigned and the host program is VTAM as depicted in Figure 11.13. Also note that the To Operator Facility is defined as No. This is done because the token-ring adapter would be limited to 245 stations acting as SNA physical units rather than the maximum of 255. This is because the OF/2 interface requires ten of these stations. Placing the OF/2 interface on the non-VTAM token-ring adapter does not affect that adapter and add ten more stations to the VTAM adapter.

Selecting OK returns the user to the 3172 Profile window. Again the display is modified to reflect the new configuration in slot 3. The next step in the process is to associate the token-ring adapter addresses and definitions to channel addresses. This is done through the LAN Gateway functional definition.

11.2.5 Defining the LAN Gateway Function

The next step in defining the IBM 3172 is associating the token-ring adapters to subchannel addresses. This is accomplished by the Add function option of the Edit action selection on the 3172 Profile window. Selecting the Add function displays the Function Type window as shown in Figure 11.14. This window displays the available function type. In this case the only option available is LAN Gateway Function. The Associated adapter column in the window lists the channel adapters that are available to associate with the LAN Gateway Function. Since only one channel adapter has been defined then only one selection is possible. Selecting the LAN Gateway Function and the channel listed in the Associated adapter list produces the LAN Gateway Definition window after entering OK.

The LAN Gateway Definition window (Figure 11.15) automatically fills in the Associated adapter name field. The LAN function name field must be entered by the OF/2 operator. This name is the symbolic name given to the LAN Gateway Function being defined. Selecting the Add button presents the LAN Gateway Subchannel Parameters window. This window allows the operator to select the LAN adapter associated with this LAN Gateway Function. Note that the Adapter Type field displays the names of the two token-ring adapters previously defined. Selecting the token-ring adapter labeled TRTCPIP displays a column entitled Subchannels with pairs of subchannel addresses listed. Selecting one of these subchannel address pairs defines the inbound and outbound subchannel addresses that will be used by TCP/IP on the host computer.

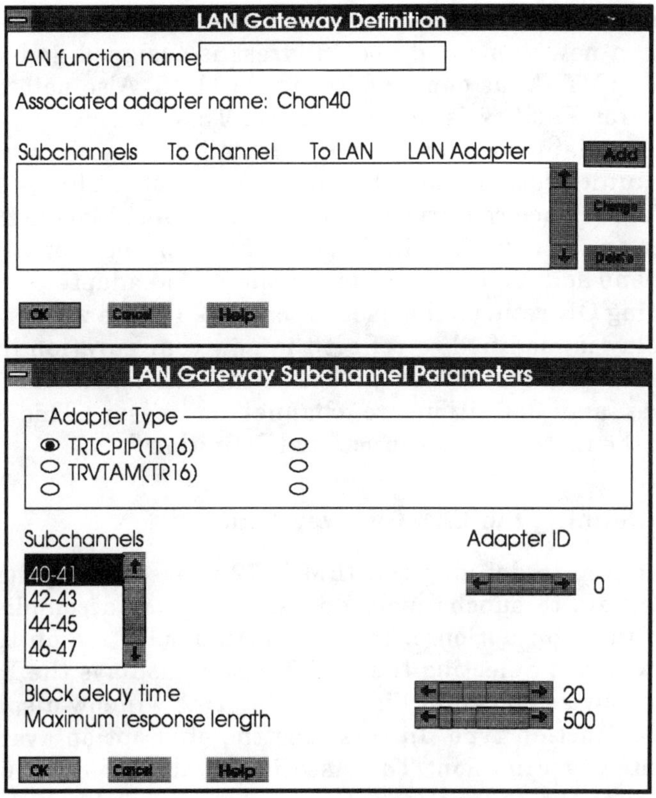

Figure 11.15 LAN gateway defintion screens for channel associations to the token-ring adapters.

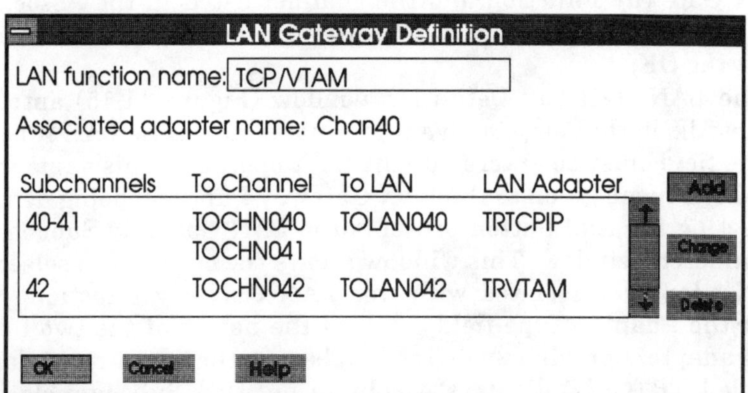

Figure 11.16 The completed LAN gateway defintion screen showing the defined channel addresses with their associated token-ring adapters.

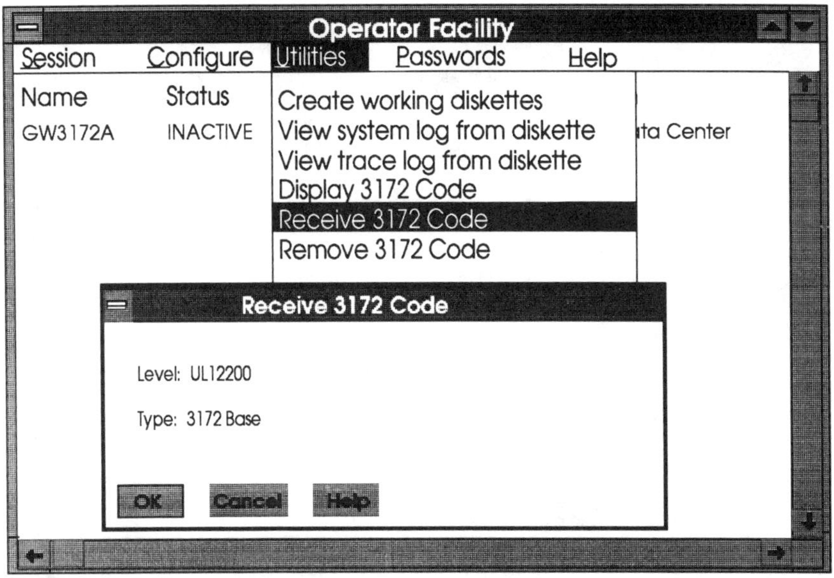

Figure 11.17 The OF/2 utility screen for receiving the IBM 3172 ICP code.

The Adapter ID value is equal to the relative adapter number already assigned by OF/2 during the LAN adapter definition. In the case of TRTCPIP the adapter ID value is 0. Selecting OK returns the operator back to the LAN Gateway Definition window. The process is repeated for the VTAM token-ring adapter. The only difference is that the Subchannels column displays a selection list with only single subchannel addresses. Selecting OK after defining the VTAM token-ring adapter subchannel association results in the LAN Gateway Definition window depicted in Figure 11.16.

At this point the operator can now receive the initial IBM 3172 base code from diskettes and generate the ICP.

11.2.6 Creating the IBM 3172 ICP Working Diskettes

The ICP code delivered with the IBM 3172 must be received into the OF/2 workstation. The ICP code is delivered on diskettes which must be placed into the diskette drive A before starting the receive process. The receive process occurs by selecting Utilities from the Operator Facility main window. A pull-down menu appears with the option Receive 3172 Code as shown in Figure 11.17. Selecting the Receive 3172 Code option displays a window showing the level

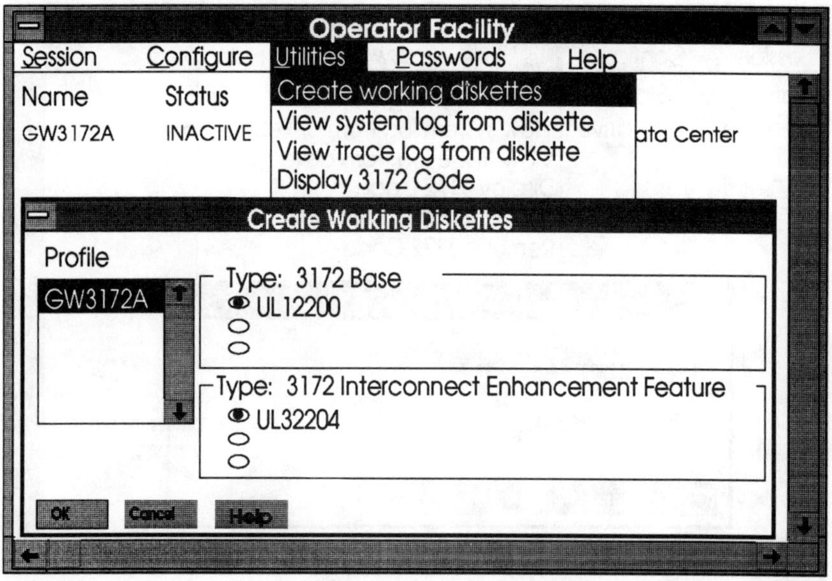

Figure 11.18 The OF/2 utility screen used to create the IBM 3172 working diskettes.

of ICP code to be received and the type of code being received. Selecting the OK button begins the receive process. The interactive displays guide the operator through the complete receive process including receiving the Interconnect Enhancement Feature required for VTAM connectivity. The receive process need only be done during initial installation of the current working release of the IBM 3172 ICP. The receive process must be performed to upgrade to new IBM 3172 ICP releases. Once the ICP code has been received the IBM 3172 working diskettes can be created.

Working diskettes are created for stand alone OF/2 stations every time a new IBM 3172 configuration is necessary. Attached OF/2 stations create working diskettes only on the initial load of the IBM 3172. Three working diskettes are created. The diskettes are created by using formatted OS/2 3.5" 2MB diskettes and the Create Working Diskettes option from the Utilities action on the Operator Facility primary menu as shown in Figure 11.18. The possible IBM 3172 profiles to use are listed in the Profile column of the Create Working Diskettes window along with the 3172 base levels and the 3172 Interconnect Enhancement Feature level of code displayed. Selecting the OK button begins the ICP generation process. The OF/2 guides the operator through the creation of the three working diskettes. The diskettes should be labeled Working diskette 1, 2 and 3. The three working diskettes must be loaded into the IBM 3172.

11.3 LOADING THE IBM 3172 ICP

Before installation and loading the ICP the operator must vary off-line the channel(s) defined on the mainframe to the IBM 3172. This frees the channel and token-ring adapters. A manual load must be performed to initially load the IBM 3172 Interconnect Controller. This is obvious since the ICP was generated on an OF/2 workstation and the information needed by the IBM 3172 is on the diskettes in the form of an ICP load module. For both stand alone and attached OF/2 workstations the initial load process is the same. Subsequent load processes with stand alone OF/2 workstations is the same process as the initial load. Subsequent loads from an attached OF/2 workstation can be accomplished over the token-ring network.

11.3.1 Initial and Stand-Alone ICP Loading

During the installation of the IBM 3172 the IBM CE should have formatted the fixed disk. This is done in preparation for receiving the first ICP load module. Removal of the plastic front panel is

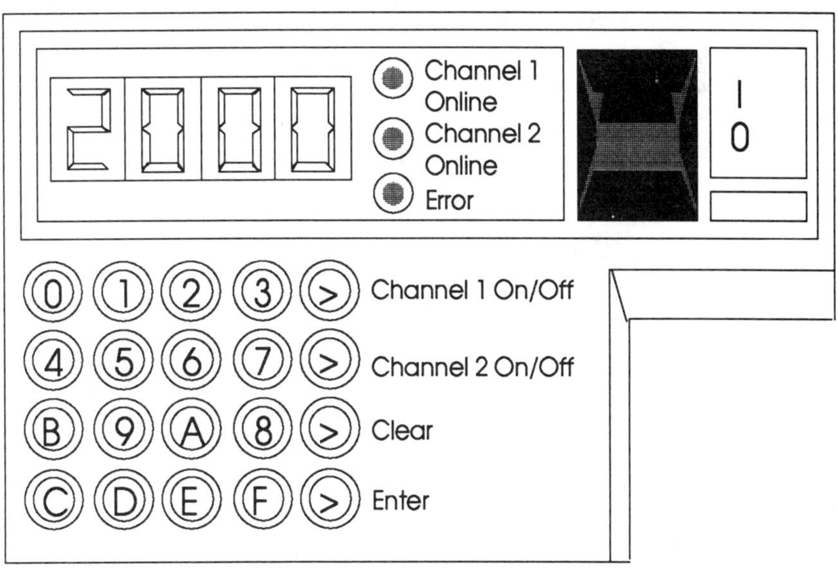

Figure 11.19 The operator display area for the IBM 3172.

necessary to gain access to the diskette drive on the IBM 3172. The ON/OFF switch should be in the OFF position.

The working diskette labeled Working diskette 1 should be placed into the diskette drive with the label facing to the left of the IBM 3172. The ON/OFF switch should now be moved to the ON position to power on the IBM 3172. In a few minutes the number 2000 will appear in the operator display area of the IBM 3172 as shown in Figure 11.19. At this point the operator uses the IBM 3172 key pad to enter the following instruction, CCA, and then presses the Enter key. The IBM 3172 will then display FCCA acknowledging the entered command. The CCA command is repeated and the Enter key is pressed once again to begin the installation of the ICP code. The FCCA characters will return to the display indicating that the process has begun. Completion of this step is indicated when the operator display changes to 0000. The second phase of this step is started after the operator enters the CCD command. Pressing enter displays FCCD on the operator display. The CCD command is entered again and causes code on the working diskette to be copied to the fixed disk on the IBM 3172. The installation of Working diskette 1 is completed when FCCE appears on the operator display.

The diskette labeled Working diskette 2 should now be placed in the diskette drive. The Enter key is pressed to begin copying the code from the diskette to the fixed disk. After a few minutes FCCF appears on the operator display. This indicates that Working diskette 2 has been copied and that Working diskette 3 should now be placed into the diskette drive. Pressing the Enter key one more time begins the copy procedure for Working diskette 3. This last copy step is indicated by FCD0 appearing in the operator display. The diskette is removed and the Clear key is pressed. Successful installation of the ICP code is indicated when 0000 appears on the operator display. Working diskette 3 is removed from the diskette drive and the ON/OF switch is moved to the OFF position.

Loading of the new IBM 3172 ICP occurs when the ON/OFF switch is moved to the ON position. A few minutes will pass before 200*x* appears on the operator display. The *x* digit represents the number of sub channels not active for LAN connections using Parallel Channel Adapters. In the example configuration this value would appear as 2003. As each channel-to-LAN connection is activated the *x* value is reduced by 1 until all channel-to-LAN connections are active. When all sub channels are active 2000 appears on the operator display. The IBM 3172 is now loaded and operational.

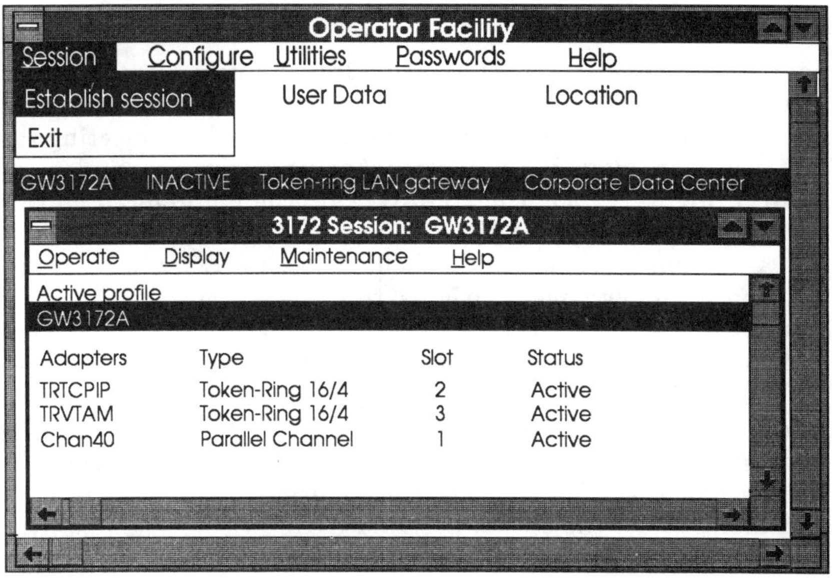

Figure 11.20 The OF/2 screen for establishing a session with an IBM 3172 over the token-ring network.

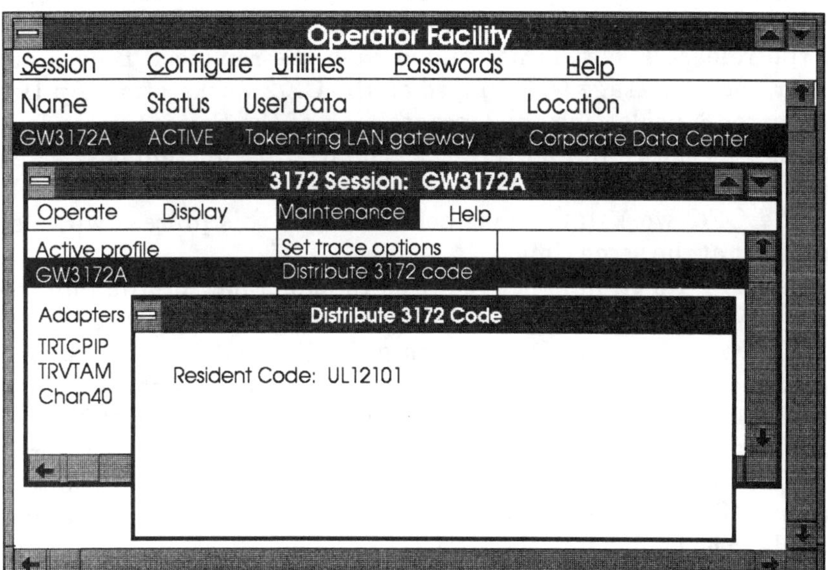

Figure 11.21 The OF/2 screens for distributing new releases of the ICP to the IBM 3172.

11.3.2 Attached ICP Loading

Loading and IPLing the IBM 3172 Interconnect Controller requires a NETBIOS session between the OF/2 workstation and the IBM 3172. A session with an IBM 3172 is started by selecting the Session action from the Operator Facility primary window as shown in Figure 11.20. The IBM 3172 profile highlighted on this window indicates which IBM 3172, managed by this OF/2 workstation, a session is to be established. Selecting Establish session from the pull-down menu begins the process of session establishment.

New release level code can be distributed to the IBM 3172 over the token-ring network after receiving it from the IBM distribution diskettes. Loading the new release level code over the token-ring network is accomplished by selecting Maintenance from the Session secondary window as shown in Figure 11.21. From the pull-down menu select the option Distribute 3172 Code. The resulting display lists the resident code along with the release level of each stored on the OF/2 workstation fixed disk. Highlighting the appropriate release level and selecting OK initiates the transmission of the code over the token-ring network to the IBM 3172.

The new code will not take effect until the IBM 3172 is re-IPLed. During the Initial Program Load (IPL) process the release level of code at both the IBM 3172 and the OF/2 workstation must match. If the release levels do not match then the remote IPL does not occur and a message is displayed on the OF/2 workstation. An IPL is started by selecting the Operate task of the Session secondary window as shown in Figure 11.22. The Re-IPL function is selected to reinitialize the IBM 3172 with the new ICP code. If the profile on the OF/2 workstation has been changed this process will also install it at the same time.

A Re-IPL function is not required to load a new profile into the IBM 3172. This can be accomplished by using the Activate function of the Operate task. After changing the IBM 3172 profile issuing this function causes the OF/2 workstation to activate the profile in the IBM 3172. The profiles must match in order for the IBM 3172 to activate. If the profiles do not match then the OF/2 operator is notified and asked whether the new profile should be transmitted to the IBM 3172. Answering OK to the message causes the new profile to be loaded into the IBM 3172 and an IPL of the IBM 3172.

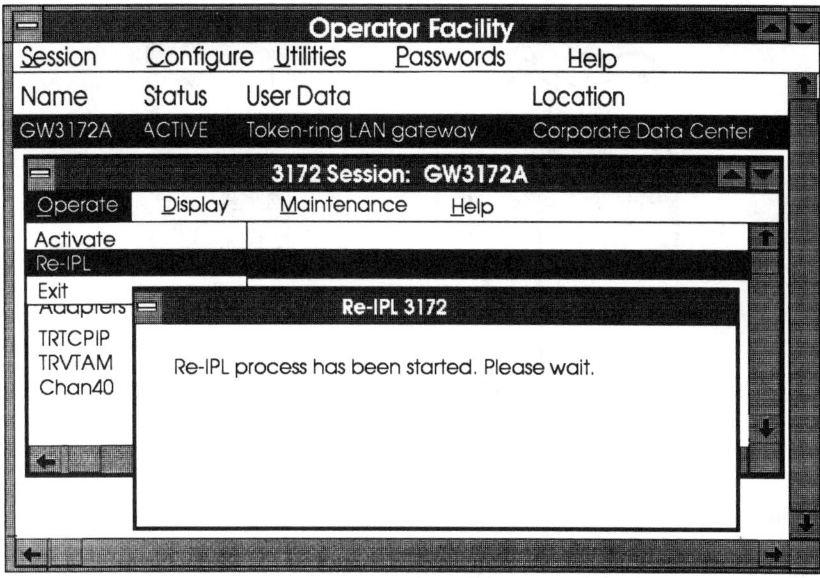

Figure 11.22 TheOF/2 screens for the remote Initial Pogram Load (IPL) function.

11.4 MVS TCP/IP TO TOKEN-RING

Transmission Control Program/Internet Protocol (TCP/IP) is an open communications protocol that provides the means for communication between unlike platforms. TCP/IP is available on all the major platforms in today's multi-platform network environments. Such a networking environment is diagrammed in Figure 11.23.

In this environment a Sun Microsystems Sparc2 workstation is attached to a token-ring network and is using TCP/IP as its communication protocol. Connectivity to the mainframe is provided by an IBM 3172 Interconnect Controller. An IBM 3172 is defined to TCP/IP as a LAN Channel Station (LCS). The channel assigned to the non-VTAM token-ring adapter in the previous discussion is used for the TCP/IP communication. TCP/IP is independent of the physcial transmission media used and therefore can also be used over channel connections to the mainframe.

Recall that two subchannel addresses are assigned by OF/2 during the definition of non-VTAM token-ring adapters. The even numbered channel is used by the IBM 3172 for traffic to the channel and the odd numbered channel is used for traffic to the token-ring network. TCP/IP on the mainframe controls the channel

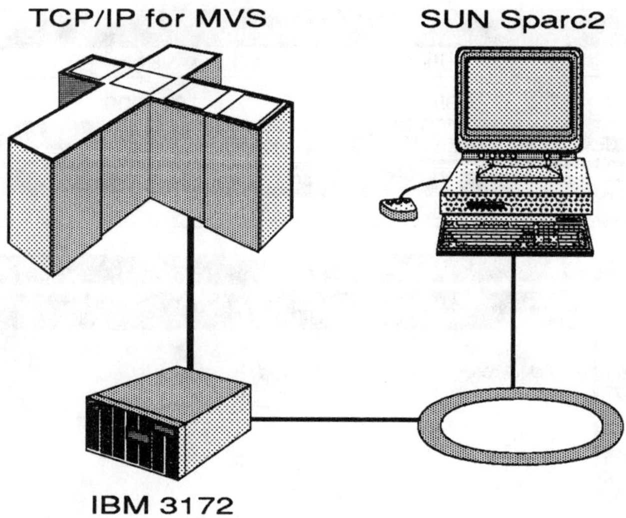

Figure 11.23 A sample token-ring environment for TCP/IP connectivity to the mainframe using the IBM 3172.

```
DEVICE          LCS1        LCS        040
LINK            TRTCPIP     IBMTR      0         LCS1
;
HOME
120.20.10.1     TRTCPIP
;
GATEWAY
;Network        First hop   Driver     Packet    Subnet      Subnet
;                                      size      mask        value
120.20          =           TRTCPIP    2048      0.0.255.0   0.0.10.0
;
START           LCS1
```

Figure 11.24 The TCP/IP defintions for IBM 3172 connectivity.

input/output over the channel. TCP/IP must have definitions that reflect the environment. These definitions are found in the tcpip.TCPIP.PROFILE data set on the mainframe storage device. The tcpip value is the high-level data set name qualifier for this data set. Figure 11.24 illustrates the TCP/IP definitions.

A DEVICE statement is required to define to TCP/IP a LAN Channel Station (LCS). The LCS1 value following the DEVICE operand specifies the TCP/IP name for the LCS. The LCS operand indicates that this DEVICE statement is defining an LCS. The last value on this statement is the even number of the even/odd pair of sub channels defined to the token-ring adapter on the IBM 3172. In this example the value indicates that the subchannel pair is 040/041.

The second TCP/IP statement required to define the IBM 3172 token-ring adapter to TCP/IP is the LINK statement. More than one LINK statement can be associated with a DEVICE statement. The LINK operand is followed by a name describing the link. For our example the link name is TRTCPIP. The IBMTR operand specifies to TCP/IP that the LCS being defined on the DEVICE statement utilizes IBM token-ring network. The following value of 0 is the relative adapter number assigned in the IBM 3172. Recall that the relative adapter number is assigned sequentially by the IBM 3172 during "like-adapter" configurations for each profile in use for an IBM 3172. If the IBM 3172 profile is changed in such a way that the non-VTAM token-ring adapter is defined second then the relative adapter number will change to a 1 and must be reflected on this LINK statement. The last operand on the LINK statement is the name of the LCS device associated with this LINK statement.

In TCP/IP the host address must be defined. More than one address may defined to the TCP/IP host computer, however, in our scenario only one address is necessary. The links can not be shared between multiple host addresses. Therefore, if more than one address is assigned to the TCP/IP host then more than one adapter must be defined in the IBM 3172 for non-VTAM support and associated with a unique device and link name in TCP/IP. The HOME section of the tcpip.TCPIP.PROFILE data set associates the host address with the link name. In our example the host TCP/IP address is 120.20.10.1 and it uses the link named TRTCPIP to send and receive data to other TCP/IP hosts (e.g., Sun Microsystems Sparc2).

The GATEWAY section of the tcpip.TCPIP.PROFILE data set defines to the TCP/IP host the path it is to take to connect to other

TCP/IP hosts in the network. The first parameter is the destination network address with which this host may communicate. The value of "=" for the First hop parameter indicates that connection is made directly from this TCP/IP host without any intervening hosts. The Driver parameter specifies which link is to be used to access the destination network. The packet size parameter defines the largest packet size that can be used over the specified driver. This value should be equal to or less than the inbound/outbound value defined for the adapter in the IBM 3172. In our example the IBM 3172 inbound/outbound frame size defined for TRTCPIP is 4096 and in TCP/IP the largest packet size is only 2048. This satisfies the frame-to-packet size requirement. The Subnet mask of 0.0.255.0 specifies that all subnet addresses in the 120.20 network may be connected over this path. The Subnet value of 0.0.10.0 indicates that specifically only TCP/IP hosts with addresses ranging from 120.20.10.1 to 120.20.10.255 may be connected over this path.

Finally the TCP/IP can define which defined devices to start during TCP/IP initialization with the START statement. The START parameter of this statement is followed by the name of the LCS device. In our working example the device name LCS1 is started at TCP/IP initialization.

11.5 VTAM DEFINITIONS FOR IBM 3172

Connectivity to IBM's Virtual Telecommunication Access Method (VTAM) is used by IBM 3172 to access mainframe applications written to IBM's SNA and execute under VTAM. This SNA application access over token ring through an IBM 3172 requires IBM VTAM V3R4 and higher. This release of VTAM includes a new definition called an external communication adapter (XCA). It is the XCA definition that allows VTAM to define token-ring resources off of the IBM 3172 as switched devices. The importance of this connectivity configuration is the absence of a front-end processor as the SNA VTAM token-ring gateway.

The XCA definition defines to VTAM all down-stream SNA resources attached to the token-ring through the IBM 3172. VTAM still provides the SNA routing, session and data flows as it would under standard SNA environments. The four major types of SNA nodes are supported on the IBM 3172 using the XCA definition. Each adapter installed on the IBM 3172 and configured for VTAM support, without OF/2 support, has a maximum of 255 active SNA physical units. This totals 1020 active SNA physical units per IBM

3172 without OF/2 support. OF/2 on a VTAM supported token-ring adapter takes up 10 of the possible 255, hence, limiting the full capacity support to 1010 active SNA physical units.

11.5.1 Defining the External Communication Adapter

The IBM 3172 Interconnect Controller provides VTAM SNA LAN gateway support with VTAM V3R4. The added functionality is provided by the new VTAM major node External Communication Adapter (XCA). An XCA major node must be coded in VTAM's SYS1.VTAMLST data set for each token-ring LAN adapter that is to be supported by VTAM on the IBM 3172. In our example only one XCA major node needs to be defined to support the SNA LAN gateway. A second XCA major node may be defined to allow the IBM 3172 to be managed by VTAM and a communication network management application on the mainframe. Network management and the XCA major node required are discussed in section 11.6. The XCA major node contains three distinct sections: VBUILD, PORT and GROUP.

An example of an XCA major node is found in Figure 11.25. The VBUILD definition statement identifies this major node to VTAM as an external communication adapter major node by having the TYPE operand value equal to XCA. A single PORT definition statement must be coded for each XCA major node.

The PORT definition statement defines the VTAM host connection to the token-ring network attached to the IBM 3172. The CUADDR keyword defines the subchannel address assigned to the

```
ICLAN1      VBUILD     TYPE=XCA

ICLAN1P     PORT       CUADDR=042,ADAPNO=1,MEDIUM=RING,
                       SAPADDR=4

ICPUGRP     GROUP      DIAL=YES,CALL=IN,ANSWER=ON

ICPULNE1    LINE       ISTATUS=ACTIVE

ICPU01      PU         ISTATUS=ACTIVE

ICPULNE2    LINE       ISTATUS=ACTIVE
```

Figure 11.25 The External Communication Adapter (XCA) defintion for the IBM 3172.

LAN adapter during the IBM 3172 adapter configuration process. Recall that in our scenario the VTAM supported token-ring adapter is defined with subchannel address 042 as the SNA LAN gateway subchannel address. The ADAPNO keyword identifies the relative adapter number generated by the IBM 3172 during the VTAM supported token-ring adapter definition. In our example the relative adapter number generated for this adapter is 1. If a new profile for the IBM 3172 is created and the VTAM supported token-ring adapter is defined second, then this value will change to a 1 and must be changed here in the XCA major node to reflect the new IBM 3172 configuration. The MEDIUM keyword of the PORT definition statement identifies the type of LAN medium attached to the IBM 3172. In our scenario the value will specify RING since we are only concerned with token-ring connectivity. The SAPADDR keyword specifies the service access point (SAP) address for the LAN connection through the IBM 3172. The SAPADDR is used in conjunction with the CUADDR and ADAPNO keywords to route information between the LAN and VTAM.

The keywords and values discussed are required for every XCA major node defining SNA node types 2.0, 2.1, 4 and 5. Each of these SNA node types are defined within the XCA major node.

11.5.2 Defining SNA Node Type 2.0/2.1 in the XCA Major Node

SNA Node types 2.0 and 2.1 provide IBM logical unit access to VTAM applications. Typically, these nodes provide IBM 3270 terminal connectivity to the mainframe. The platform executing these node types are varied. Some platforms that can support these SNA node types are: IBM 3174 Establishment Controllers, IBM AS/400, DOS and OS/2 based personal computers and UNIX based workstations. The hardware platform is not what matters in this type of connectivity. It is the software available on the various platforms that gives them SNA connectivity using SNA node type 2.0 and 2.1. SNA node types 2.0 and 2.1 are also referred to as peripheral nodes.

In Figure 11.26, a typical configuration is diagrammed showing the connectivity of an SNA node type 2.0 and 2.1 device to VTAM on the mainframe using an IBM 3172 as the gateway. These devices must be defined to the XCA major node. Following the PORT definition in the XCA major node will be a GROUP definition statement defining the line groups associated with the SNA node types 2.0 and 2.1 as shown in Figure 11.25.

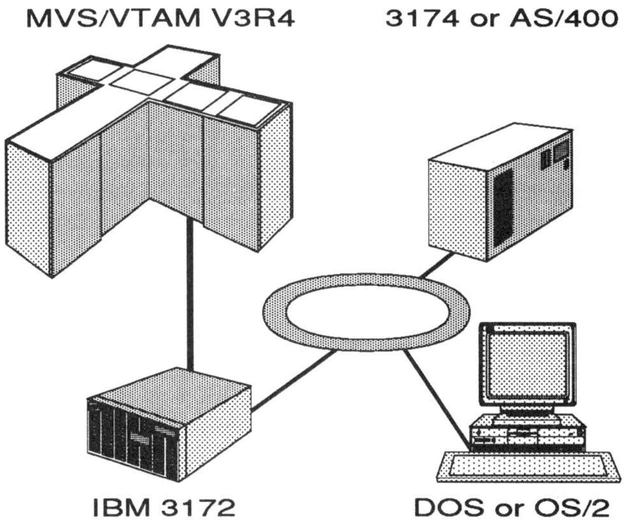

Figure 11.26 An SNA node type 2.0 and 2.1 token-ring connectivity configuration to the SNA mainframe using an IBM 3172.

The SNA node types 2.0 and 2.1 are defined as switched resources to VTAM in the XCA major node. This switched connectivity is specified by the DIAL keyword being equal to the value YES. The CALL keyword value of IN indicates to VTAM that the resources will always initiate the connectivity process. A value of INOUT is also possible but indicates that VTAM, on behalf of an application, may initiate the session to the SNA node type 2.0 and 2.1 device. In current networking environments the CALL=IN operand will suffice. The ANSWER keyword with a value of ON specifies that the switched resource may initiate communications when the line associated with the node is active. The ANSWER and CALL keywords actually apply to the LINE definition statement following the GROUP definition statement but are coded here to reduce repetitive coding of these parameters. The values code on the GROUP definition statement are sifted down to the LINE definition statements that follow. The values may be overridden by coding the keywords on the LINE definition statement. One LINE and one PU definition statement is required for each SNA node type 2.0 and 2.1 resource having connectivity through the IBM 3172.

VTAM requires a switched major node for all switched resources. A sample switch major node for our example is listed in Figure 11.27. The switched major node like the XCA major has a VTAM

```
SWICLAN1    VBUILD    TYPE=SWNET,MAXGRP=1,MAXNO=2

SWICPU01    PU        ADDR=C1,CPNAME=ARDEPT,PUTYPE=2,
                      MAXDATA=1033

ICPATH01    PATH      DIALNO=010440000000005D,
                      GRPNM=ICLAN1G

SWICLU01    LU        LOCADDR=0

SWICPU02    PU        ADDR=C2,IDBLK=017,IDNUM=31741,
                      PUTYPE=2,MAXDATA=265

ICPATH02    PATH      DIALNO=0104400000000017,
                      GRPNM=ICLAN1G

SWICLU02    LU        LOCADDR=2
```

Figure 11.27 VTAM switched major node defining the downstream LAN connections attached to the IBM 3172.

VBUILD statement identifying the type of major node being defined. TYPE=SWNET indicates to VTAM that this major node is defining switched resources. The MAXGRP keyword specifies the number of unique group names defined in this switched major node. The MAXNO keyword defines the number of unique dial numbers in the switched major node.

The PU definition statement defines the SNA switched physical unit attributes. The ADDR keyword defines the switched resources unique SNA station address. The value is the hexadecimal digits ranging from 01 to FF. An SNA node type 2.1 contains a control point function. This function is given a name and the keyword that identifies the name is the CPNAME keyword. This value must match the definition assigned in the node type 2.1. The presence of the CPNAME keyword indicates to VTAM that the physical unit definition is that of a node type 2.1. For node type 2.0 devices the IDBLK and IDNUM values must be defined. The 3-digit hexadecimal IDBLK value is dependent on the type of device being used for the SNA node type 2.1 connectivity. For example, IBM 3174 Establishment Controllers use a value of 017, OS/2 platforms use 05D, DOS platforms use 017. The IDNUM value is assigned by the network administrator and provides a unique 5-digit hexadecimal number for the device. Frequently the device serial number may be used for this number. The PUTYPE keyword for both peripheral types has a value of 2. The MAXDATA keyword defines the largest frame size that can be sent to the device.

The PATH definition statement follows the PU definition statement in a VTAM switched major node. The DIALNO keyword on the PATH definition statement for an IBM 3172 attached resource has the following syntax:

```
aacccccccccc
```

The *aa* is a 2-digit place holder and is not used in the IBM 3172. It may be useful for documentation purposes to assign the relative adapter number to the *aa* position. The remaining 12 characters is the MAC address (i.e., LAA) for the station associated with this definition. The GRPNM keyword value must match the XCA GROUP name associated with the switched peripheral node definitions.

Following the PATH statement is the LU definition statement of the switched major node. This statement defines characteristics of the SNA logical units used on the physical unit. The LOCADDR keyword of the LU definition statement defines the address of the logical unit on the physcial unit. LOCADDR=0 indicates that the logical unit being defined is an SNA LU 6.2 logical unit. LU 6.2 is IBM's peer-to-peer protocol for cooperative processing between applications. This type of logical unit with a LOCADDR=0 can only reside on SNA node type 2.1. This logical unit can initiate sessions without the assistance of VTAM. Instead it utilizes the control point function of SNA node type 2.1. These logical units are also called independent logical units (ILU). A LOCADDR specifying anything greater than 0 is referred to as a dependent logical unit (DLU). Dependent logical units require the assistance of VTAM to establish sessions with other logical units.

SNA node type 2.0 and 2.1 require an XCA major node definition and a switched major node definition. The following sections illustrate the differences when defining SNA node type 4 and 5 connectivity through the IBM 3172 Interconnect Controller.

11.5.3 Defining SNA Node Type 4 in the XCA Major Node

The XCA major node can also include and SNA node type 4 definition along with the node type 2.0 and 2.1 definitions. Figure 11.28 depicts the addition of a node type 4 to the sample configuration. A node type 4 in SNA is basically synonymous with a communication controller executing Network Control Program (NCP). Communication controllers attach to a token-ring network using token-ring interface couplers (TIC). The NCP defines the token-ring interface and assigns a MAC address along with a transmission group num-

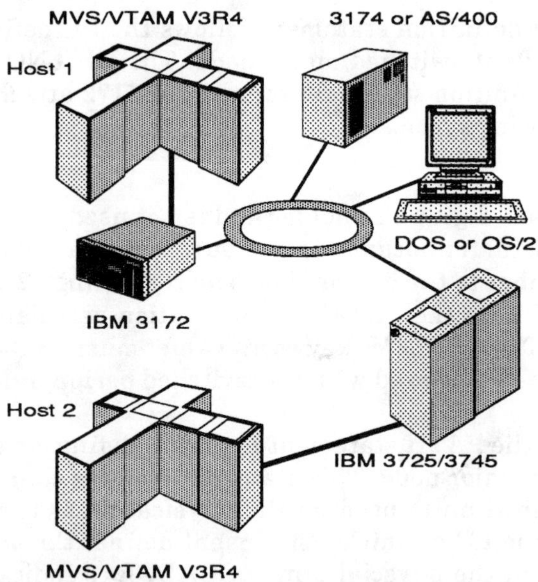

Figure 11.28 The SNA node type 4 connectivity to an SNA mainframe through an IBM 3172.

ber. The transmission group number (TGN) is used in SNA routing. The NCP as well as VTAM is also assigned an SNA subarea number. The subarea number is a network wide unique address for the SNA node type 4. Different SNA node types may access VTAM through an IBM 3172 SNA LAN gateway because each connection is actually viewed as a point-to-point connection. The SNA node type 4 must be controlled (i.e., owned) by an SNA node type 5 VTAM host either through channel attachment, SDLC attachment or token-ring attachment from a channel attached SNA node type 4. SNA node type 4s can not be activated, loaded or dumped connected to VTAM through an IBM 3172.

The sample listing shown in Figure 11.29 shows the addition of the SNA node type 4 and 5 definition to the current XCA major node.

A GROUP definition statement is coded. However, note that the DIAL keyword now specifies a value of NO. This defines to VTAM that this is not a switched definition but a dedicated link definition. Because of this a switched major node is not necessary to define the token-ring attached node type 4 device when using an IBM 3172. The LINE definition statement for a node type 4 definition indicates that the line is using SNA protocols to access the

IBM 3172 over the LAN. The PU definition statement specifies the MAC address of the node type 4 device on the MACADDR keyword. The PUTYPE keyword identifies the device as a node type 4. The SUBAREA keyword defines the node type 4 SNA subarea value assigned to the communication controller and the TGN keyword identifies the link as transmission group number 1. The SAPADDR keyword defines the SAP address of the LAN connection through the IBM 3172.

The NCP in the node type 4 defines its MAC address on the LINE definition statement of the physical GROUP definition statement. The LOCADD keyword is the MAC address associated with the TIC in the communication controller. This LOCADD keyword value must match the MACADDR keyword value in the XCA definition of this node type 4. The ADDR keyword on the PU definition statement of the NCP logical GROUP definition specifies the MAC address of the IBM 3172 VTAM supported token-ring adapter. The

```
ICLAN1      VBUILD    TYPE=XCA

ICLAN1P     PORT      CUADDR=042,ADAPNO=1,MEDIUM=RING,
                      SAPADDR=4

ICPUGRP     GROUP     DIAL=YES,CALL=IN,ANSWER=ON

ICPULNE1    LINE      ISTATUS=ACTIVE

ICPU01      PU        ISTATUS=ACTIVE

ICPULNE2    LINE      ISTATUS=ACTIVE

ICPU02      PU        ISTATUS=ACTIVE

ICNCPGRP    GROUP     DIAL=NO

ICNCPLNE    LINE      USER=SNA,ISTATUS=ACTIVE

ICNCP11     PU        PUTYPE=4,MACADDR=400000374501,
                      SAPADDR=4,SUBAREA=11,TGN=1

ICVTMGRP    GROUP     DIAL=NO

ICVTMLNE    LINE      USER=SNA,ISTATUS=ACTIVE

ICVTM02     PU        PUTYPE=5,MACADDR=400000317202,
                      SAPADDR=4,SUBAREA=2,TGN=1
```

Figure 11.29 The XCA major node defintion with the addition of an IBM 3745 and IBM 3090 token-ring attached through an IBM 3172.

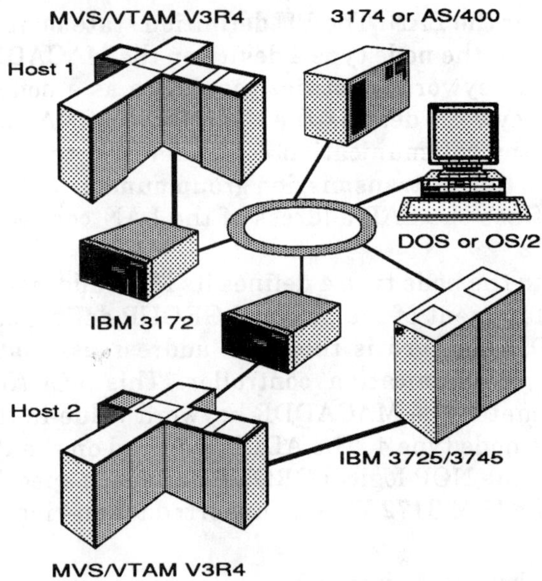

Figure 11.30 The SNA node type 5 configuration with two IBM 3172s devices.

logical line associated with the logical physical unit identifies transmission group number 1 matching the definition in the XCA major node. The NCP token-ring definitions are discussed in chapter 12 Mainframe Connectivity with IBM 3174 and IBM 3745 and OS/2 SNA Gateways.

In the configuration diagrammed in Figure 11.28, SNA routes may be established between all the SNA subareas. SNA routes will utilize the token-ring network as its medium for transmission.

11.5.4 Defining SNA Node Type 5 in the XCA Major Node

IBM's larger mainframe SNA node type 5 devices may now be directly connected over token-ring using the IBM 3172. In Figure 11.30, a second SNA host has been added to the network using a second IBM 3172. The XCA definition defined for Host 1 now includes the definition for Host 2. Note that the SNA node type 5 definition in the figure is comparable to that just discussed for node type 4 connectivity. The differences here are the values specified on the PU definition statement for the node type 5. The MACADDR value specifies the MAC address assigned to the IBM 3172 token-ring adapter defined for VTAM support on the IBM

3172 channel attached to Host 2. The PUTYPE keyword value of 5 indicates that this definition is for an SNA node type 5 resource, namely VTAM on an SNA host computer. The TGN keyword identifies the transmission group number to use when determining SNA routing paths and the SAPADDR value is the service access point on the LAN connection.

11.5.5 Defining a Shared Token-Ring Adapter

The VTAM supported token-ring adapter in the IBM 3172 can be shared between two VTAM host computers. The sharing of the token-ring adapter is accomplished by using two different SAP addresses. In Figure 11.31 the XCA major node definitions for the two SNA VTAM hosts pictured are listed. The SAPADDR keyword

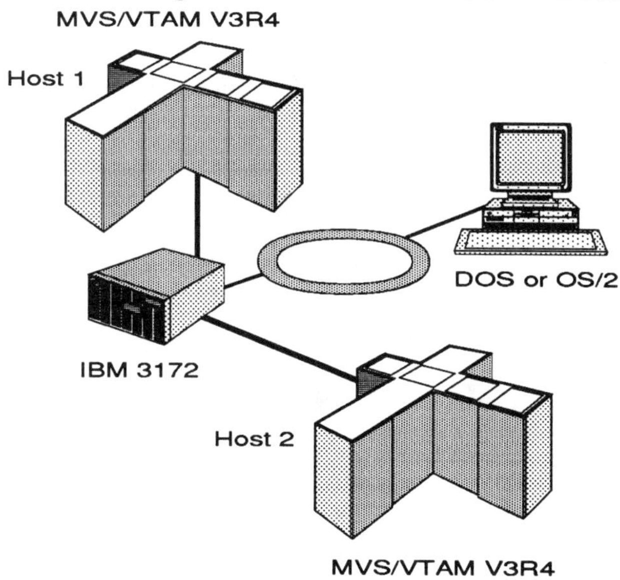

Host 1 XCA definitions

```
ICLANP PORT CUADDR=043,ADAPNO=1,
            MEDIUM=RING,SAPADDR=4
ICVTMP PU   PUTYPE=5,MACADDR=400000317201,
            SAPADDR=8,SUBAREA=2,TGN=1
```

Host 2 XCA definitions

```
ICLANP PORT CUADDR=042,ADAPNO=2,
            MEDIUM=RING,SAPADDR=8
ICVTMP PU   PUTYPE=5,MACADDR=400000317202,
            SAPADDR=4,SUBAREA=1,TGN=1
```

Figure 11.31 A shared token-ring adapter configuration and definitions.

on the XCA PORT definition of each VTAM specify different values. The SAPADDR=4 operand in Host 1 defines the SAP address of the token-ring adapter in the IBM 3172 as Host 1 knows it. Host 2 knows the token-ring adapter in the IBM 3172 as service access point address 8. Note that the IBM 3172 must have two parallel channel adapters installed and configured for this configuration to be valid. The TGN value must be the same if the two VTAMs are to communicate through the IBM 3172. The SAPADDR value found in the PU definition statement of the node type 5 definitions specifies the SAP address defined in the other VTAM XCA definition. The down-stream peripheral node can determine which host to connect with via defining the remote or destination SAP accordingly.

11.5.6 Defining Dual Ring Backup

Dual apex rings provide for bridge, ring and adapter backup. In Figure 11.32 a single VTAM host computer is attached to a single

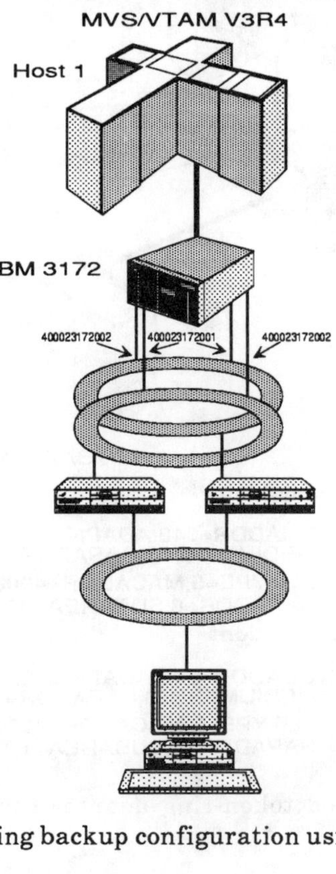

Figure 11.32 A dual- ring backup configuration using an IBM 3172.

IBM 3172. The IBM 3172 has all four token-ring adapters installed and defined to support VTAM. Each apex ring is bridges to the user ring. This configuration provides for two paths from the end user to the VTAM host. It is accomplished by duplicating MAC addresses on the IBM 3172. There are four XCA major nodes needed for this configuration. One for each token-ring adapter on the IBM 3172. Duplicate MAC addressing is achieved during definition of the token-ring adapters on OF/2. Every other adapter is assigned the same MAC address. Every other token-ring adapter is connected to a different apex ring. Thus, duplicate MAC addresses are defined and operable because the duplicated MAC addresses are on different rings adhering to token-ring network architecture of unique addresses on a ring.

The crucial part in this type of configuration is accounting for the maximum support of 255 stations per token-ring adapter. The end user stations access the IBM 3172 token-ring adapters by using the MAC address defined for the IBM 3172 token-ring adapters as their destination MAC address. Deployment of the addresses must be managed carefully to avoid a backup scenario that would necessitate the need of more than 255 stations on a token-ring adapter.

In a similar scenario two IBM 3172s may be used providing the same backup. Figure 11.33 details the single host and dual IBM 3172 with dual apex ring configuration. Four XCA major nodes are still required but note that the CUADDR keywords will specify different channel unit addresses. One channel for each IBM 3172 .

11.6 NETWORK MANAGEMENT SUPPORT WITH THE XCA MAJOR NODE

The IBM 3172 can provide SNA network management support by defining an XCA BOXMGR major node. The IBM 3172 Interconnect Enhancement Feature is required for this functionality. The XCA major node and its associated switched major node is defined like that in Figure 11.34. The MEDIUM keyword value of BOXMGR signifies to VTAM that this major node will be defining the subchannel address dedicated to providing network management. The CUADDR value defined is the dedicated subchannel address. In our scenario, going back to the IBM 3172 OF/2 definitions, subchannel 043 is used for the BOXMGR functions, 042 is used for VTAM connectivity and 040/041 is used for TCP/IP access. The switched major node definition is fairly straightforward. The MAC address of the VTAM supported token-ring adapter is coded

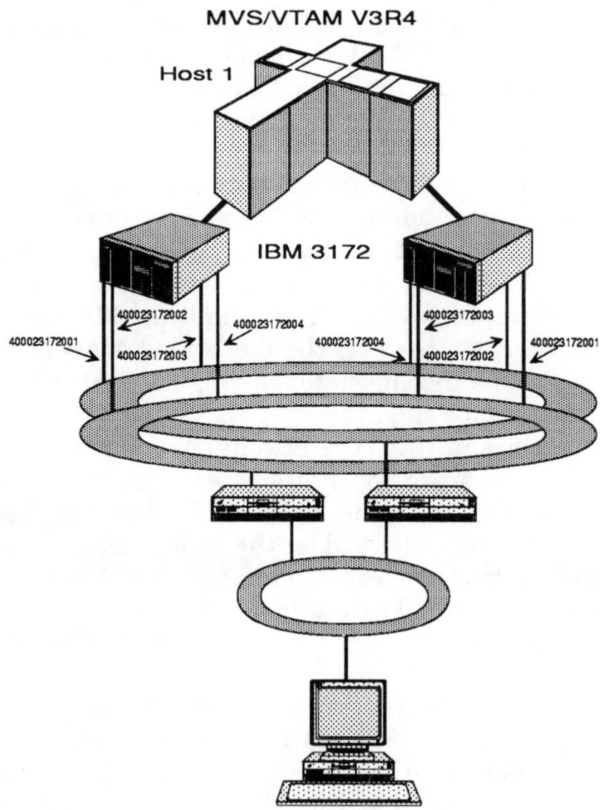

Figure 11.33 A dual-ring dual-3172 configuration.

```
ICMGR1      VBUILD    TYPE=XCA

ICMGR1P     PORT      CUADDR=043,MEDIUM=BOXMGR

ICMGRGRP    GROUP

SWICMGR     VBUILD    TYPE=SWNET

SWMGRPU     PU        ADDR=C1,IDBLK=074,
                      IDNUM=31721,PUTYPE=2,MAXDATA=265

MGRPATH     PATH      DIALNO=0104400031720001,
                      GRPNM=ICMGRGRP

IICMGRLU    LU        ISTATUS=INACTIVE
```

Figure 11.34 A sample BOXMGR major node definition for network management through VTAM.

on the DIALNO keyword in the PATH definition statement of the switched major node. Note that the IDBLK value of an IBM 3172 is 074.

In SNA network management data flows on the VTAM to PU session (i.e., SSCP-PU). The network management unit used is called a Network Management Vector Transport (NMVT). This management unit supports NetView V2 generic alerts, Central Site Control Facility (CSCF) and NetView Asset Manager Vital Product Data (VPD). CSCF can provide the NetView operator with the following information about the IBM 3172 Interconnect Controller:

- Adapter status, number of bytes successfully transmitted from adapter to the transport media
- Number of bytes received successfully from the media by this adapter
- Number of frames successfully transmitted from the adapter to the transport media
- Number of frames received successfully from the media by the adapter
- Number of blocks successfully transmitted from the adapter to the channel
- Number of blocks successfully received from the channel
- Received frames discarded due to lack of buffers
- Frames not transmitted due to media failures
- Number of invalid frames discarded (invalid length)

Vital Product Data can provide the NetView operator with the following data:

- Machine type
- Serial number
- Model number
- Software common name
- Software product level

11.7 SUMMARY

This chapter concentrated on the use and value of the IBM 3172 Interconnect Controller. The examples used demonstrated how to connect token-ring resources to the IBM mainframe without the use of an IBM 3745. The mainframe operating system channel definition requirements were discussed. The IBM 3172 is defined to the operating system as an IBM 3088 Channel-to-channel (CTC) Control Unit.

The generation of the ICPon OF/2 was discussed. The mechanism for transporting and controlling the IBM 3172 over the token-ring network was explained and the NETBIOS parameters that relate to this control were reviewed. The mainframe host support parameters and their relationships to the IBM 3172 configuration were reviewed and discussed for TCP/IP and SNA VTAM connectivity.

Chapter

12

Mainframe Connectivity with IBM Gateways

Token-Ring Networks provide a unique platform for SNA host connectivity. The connectivity is made possible through the Virtual Telecommunications Access Method (VTAM) and the Network Control Program (NCP). These two programs define configuration parameters and characteristics of token-ring devices and how they connect to the SNA host computer. The ability of popular SNA devices to use token-ring, like the IBM 3174 and IBM 37X5 controllers, preserves the investment made by corporations in standard SNA connectivity. Figure 12.1 details a possible configuration for mainframe access using token-ring connectivity.

12.1 IBM's 37X5 LAN GATEWAY WITH NCP

The IBM communication controller line offers token-ring network connectivity support. The IBM 3725 and IBM 3745 communication controllers provide token-ring network connectivity through the NCP Token-Ring Interface (NTRI). This interface is actually firmware (i.e., microcode) that executes in the communication controller token-ring adapter (TRA). Each TRA on an IBM communication

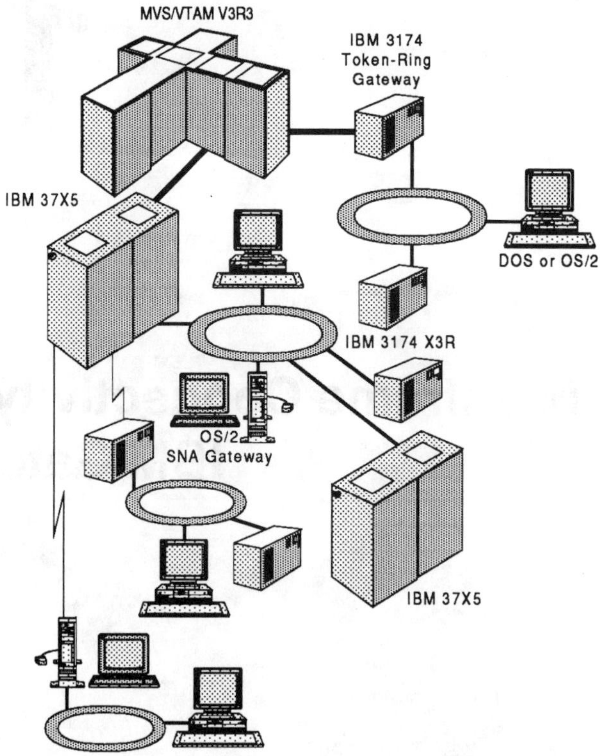

Figure 12.1 A token-ring configuration featuring the three SNA token-ring gateways: the IBM 3174, IBM 3745 and IBM OS/2 SNA Gateway.

controller has two token-ring interface couplers (TIC). The IBM 3725 can only support the type 1 TRA. The type 1 TRA supports a token-ring network data rate of 4Mbps. The IBM 3745 can support both a type 1 and a type 2 TRA. The type 2 TRA supports a data rate of 4 Mbps or 16Mbps. Token-ring stations access the SNA applications residing on the SNA host computer through an IBM 37X5 LAN gateway by specifying the LAA number assigned to the TIC as the destination address. All the parameters and characteristics of the token-ring network connection are specified in the NCP.

12.1.1 NCP OPTIONS and BUILD Definition Statements

The NCP defines the physical as well as the logical token-ring network connections associated with a IBM 37X5 Communication Controller. The OPTIONS and BUILD definition statements of an

```
NCPOPTS        OPTIONS     NEWDEFN=YES
```

Figure 12.2 The NCP OPTIONS and BUILD definition statements and parameters for token-ring specification.

NCP specify generation parameters specific to an NCP supporting token-ring interfaces. This text will discuss only those parameters necessary for token-ring connectivity. For a discussion on some of the other parameters in an NCP consult, *Introduction to SNA Networking: A Guide to Using VTAM/NCP* and *Advanced SNA Networking: A Professionals Guide to VTAM/NCP*.

The OPTIONS statement shown in Figure 12.2, indicates to the NCP generation process certain options specific to the NCP. The NEWDEFN keyword of the OPTIONS definition statement specifies whether NTRI definitions should be generated even if they have not been coded. The BUILD definition statement in an NCP has two keywords that are specific to token-ring. These are the MXRLINE and MXVLINE keywords. The MXRLINE keyword identifies the number of physical lines attached to the TICs. One line for each physically attached TIC. The MXVLINE keyword indicates the number of logical lines associated with the physical lines. These keywords and values are automatically generated when using NCP V5R3 and the *system support program* (SSP) V3R5 and higher. Prior to these releases each physical and logical line definitions would have to be counted manually and the totals then entered on these keywords.

12.1.2 Defining the Physical GROUP Definition Statement

In an NCP, GROUP definition statements are used to define characteristics and parameters commonly found for many different network resources. Token-ring resources connecting to an IBM 37X5 Communication Controller uses the LAA number assigned to the TIC as a destination station address. The physical GROUP definition statement has three keywords that define the physical attributes of the TIC. The three keywords that define the physical attributes are: ECLTYPE, ADAPTER and TRSPEED.

The ECLTYPE keyword identifies the type of connection associated with the TIC being defined in the group. As shown in Figure 12.3, the ECLTYPE keyword has two variables. The first variable

name	GROUP	ECLTYPE=(PHYSICAL|LOGICAL, ANY|PERIPHERAL |SUBAREA), ADAPTER=TIC1|TIC2,TRSPEED=4|16

Figure 12.3 The GROUP defintion statement and format of the ECLTYPE keyword for token-ring specification.

indicates that the group is defining the physical interface attributes to the NCP.

The second variable specifies the type of traffic that will be traveling over the physical connection. The specification of PERIPHERAL in the second variable of the ECLTYPE keyword indicates that the TIC will be supporting peripheral node traffic. Peripheral or boundary network nodes (BNN) support SNA node type 2.0 and type 2.1 connectivity. In a token-ring network these devices are typically IBM 3174 Establishment Controllers with token-ring support or workstations with software that emulate SNA node type 2.0 devices. The SUBAREA value specified for the second variable of the ECLTYPE keyword indicates that the TIC will be supporting communication between SNA subareas. This subarea-to-subarea connection is also referred to as Intermediate Network Node (INN) traffic when the connection involves two or more NCP subareas. Each NCP subarea is therefore referred to as an Intermediate Network Node. The last possible value for the second variable of the ECLTYPE keyword is ANY. Coding ANY indicates that either BNN or INN traffic will be used over the TIC. ANY can be specified only if a type 2 TRA is being used.

The ADAPTER keyword specifies the type of token-ring adapter associated with the GROUP definition. The default is TIC1. TIC1 indicates that TRA type 1 is installed. TRA type 1 can only run at a data rate of 4Mbps. A value of TIC2 indicates that the IBM 37X5 has a type 2 TRA installed. If ANY was coded as the second variable of the ECLTYPE keyword then the ADAPTER value would default to TIC2.

The TRSPEED keyword defines to the NCP the data rate for the TIC. The possible values are 4 and 16. The default is 4Mbps. Token-ring adapter type 1 can only support 4Mbps while type 2 can support both 4Mbps and 16Mbps. The value coded here must equal the data rate of the other token-ring adapters on the same LAN segment.

name	LINE	ADDRESS=(n,FULL),PORTADD=n, LOCADD=4000***abbbbbbb*** [,MAXTSL=692|n] [,RCVBUFC=n]

Figure 12.4 The NCP LINE definition statement for defining token-ring connectivity.

12.1.3 Defining the Physical LINE Definition Statement

Every GROUP definition statement has associated LINE definitions. The LINE definition statement is outlined in Figure 12.4. For a token-ring connection, the physical LINE definition specifies the physical location of the TIC on the IBM 37X5. The physical location is defined on the ADDRESS keyword. In an IBM 3725 this value is related to the TIC's position in the Line Attachment Base (LAB) type C. In an IBM 3745 the value can range from 1088 to 1095. The FULL parameter of the ADDRESS keyword indicates that the TIC can send and receive data simultaneously. This value must be coded for token-ring connections.

An associative mechanism is used to relate the physical token-ring connection to a logical token-ring connection. This is accomplished through the PORTADD keyword. This keyword associates a logical number to the physical line definition for the token-ring connection. The value can range from 0 to 99.

The LOCADD keyword is the token-ring MAC address assigned to the TIC on the IBM 37X5 Communication Controller. The format for the value is 4000*abbbbbbb*. The *a* value can be in the range of 0 to 7. The *bbbbbbb* value can be a combination of numbers with values ranging from 0 to 9. The value coded here is the destination MAC address for token-ring stations to gain access to VTAM and its applications on the SNA mainframe. The LOCADD value of the BNN TIC should be coded on question 107 of an IBM 3174 Establishment Controller configuration.

12.1.4 Defining the Physical NTRI PU

Each LINE definition needs a physical unit definition. Token-ring line definitions are defined as SNA physical unit type 1 resources. The format of this physical unit definition is:

```
name PU PUTYPE=1
```

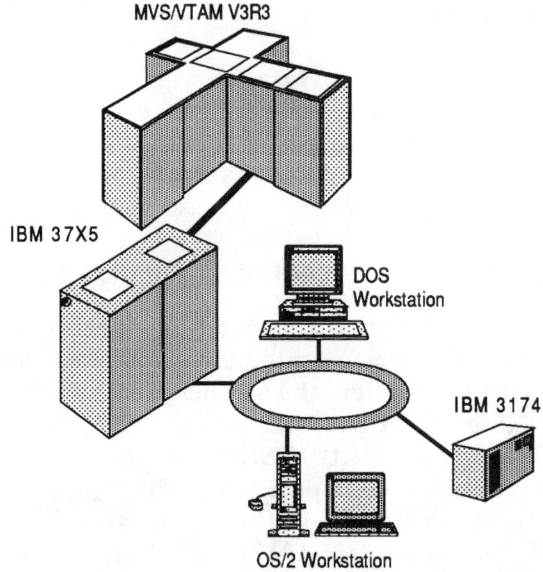

Figure 12.5 The downstream physical unit configuration to an IBM 3745 Token-ring LAN gateway.

12.1.5 Defining a Downstream Physical Unit

Downstream physical units (DSPU) are SNA type 2.0 or type 2.1 nodes that are downstream from a LAN gateway. Figure 12.5 illustrates some possible token-ring network configurations for downstream devices off of an IBM 37X5. Notice that these downstream devices can be either establishment controllers or workstations. The downstream physical unit definitions are defined in the NCP through a logical GROUP definition.

Again an ECLTYPE keyword is used to define the characteristics of the group. Downstream physical units are defined as boundary network nodes and therefore the ECLTYPE keyword will specify LOGICAL as the type of connection being defined and PERIPHERAL as the type of traffic over the TIC being defined. This is shown in Figure 12.6.

The PHYPORT keyword is the link back to the physical LINE definition associated with the TIC. The association is made by coding the PORTADD value specified on the physical LINE definition as the value for the PHYPORT keyword.

The logical lines and physical units are defined using the AUTOGEN keyword. This keyword generates logical line as physical unit

```
TRINNGRP      GROUP      ECLTYPE=(LOGICAL,SUBAREA),
                         PHYPORT=1,SDLCST=(PRIGRP,SECGRP)
```

Figure 12.6 A sample NCP GROUP definition statement for down stream physical units.

pairs based on the number defined on the AUTOGEN keyword. The maximum value is 3000. The NCP builds control blocks to associate VTAM definitions with the logical line and physical unit definitions.

12.1.6 Defining a Token-Ring Subarea Configuration

Logical definitions are also required for specifying INN traffic over token-ring. The ECLTYPE keyword in the logical GROUP definition for INN communications specifies the connection as being logical and the type of connection is set to subarea (Figure 12.6). The PHYPORT keyword relates this logical definition to the physical definition.

The logical LINE definition statement specifies the transmission group number associated with the logical line. Token-ring links between NCP subareas must be single link transmission groups. That is, each token-ring INN link defined between two NCP subareas must have a unique transmission group number.

The logical physical unit definition defines the type of station on the remote TIC. For subarea INN links, the PUTYPE keyword on the PU definition statement is always 4. The ADDR keyword specifies the destination MAC address for which the NCP TIC will establish a session. The ADDR value follows the format *ss*4000*abbbbbbb*. The *ss* value is the SAP of the token-ring defined by this PU definition statement. The *ss* value is always X'04' when the INN link is attached to another NCP. If the INN link is attached to an IBM 9370 host computer, the *ss* value must be a multiple of X'04'. The 4000*abbbbbbb* value must match the LOCADD keyword value of the physical line definition found in the attached NCP subarea. Figure 12.7 lists a completed token-ring definition for both BNN and INN TICs in two NCP subareas.

12.1.7 Defining a Duplicate TIC Configuration

Duplicate TIC addresses are not allowed on the same LAN seg-

```
NCP11:

S11TRGR    GROUP    ECLTYPE=(PHYSICAL,ANY),                    *
                    ADAPTER=TIC2,                              *
                    TRSPEED=16

S11TRLNE   LINE     ADDRESS=(1088,FULL),                       *
                    LOCADDR=400041000111,                      *
                    PORTADD=1,MAXSTL=4096,                     *
                    RCVBUFC=4096

S11TRPU1   PU       PUTYPE=1

S11TRLOG   GROUP    ECLTYPE=(LOGICAL,SUBAREA),                 *
                    PHYPORT=1,SDLCST=(PRIGRP,SECGRP)

S11S12LN   LINE     TGN=11

S11S12PU   PU       PUTYPE=4,ADDR=04400041000121

S11BNN     GROUP    ECLTYPE=(LOGICAL,PERIPHERAL),              *
                    PHYPORT=1,CALL=INOUT,                      *
                    AUTOGEN=140

NCP12:

S12TRGR    GROUP    ECLTYPE=(PHYSICAL,ANY),ADAPTER=TIC2,       *
                    TRSPEED=16

S12TRLNE   LINE     ADDRESS=(1088,FULL),                       *
                    LOCADDR=400041000121,                      *
                    PORTADD=1,MAXSTL=4096,RCVBUFC=4096

S12TRPU1   PU       PUTYPE=1

S12TRLOG   GROUP    ECLTYPE=(LOGICAL,SUBAREA),                 *
                    PHYPORT=1,SDLCST=(PRIGRP,SECGRP)

S12S11LN   LINE     TGN=11

S12S11PU   PU       PUTYPE=4,ADDR=04400041000111

S12BNN     GROUP    ECLTYPE=(LOGICAL,PERIPHERAL),              *
                    PHYPORT=1,CALL=INOUT,AUTOGEN=140
```

Figure 12.7 A completed token-ring NCP defintions for BNN and INN TICs.

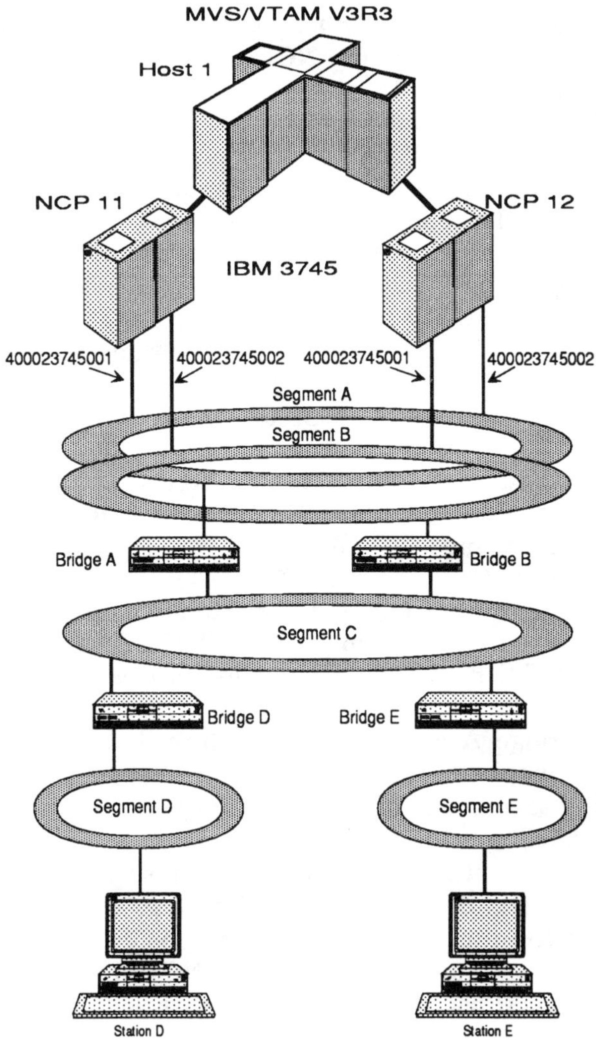

Figure 12.8 A dual ring and duplicate TIC addressing configuration.

ment. Duplication of TIC addresses for IBM 37X5 Communication Controllers is extremely useful for providing alternate paths to the mainframe computer and performance balancing. Duplication of TIC addresses on communication controllers is accomplished using isolation ring segments.

Isolation ring segments are designed using bridges. In Figure 12.8, the two IBM 37X5 Communication Controllers are attached to two different ring segments. The LOCADD values used are

400023745001 and 400023745002, however, be sure to code the 12 digit hexadecimal value in the NCP. Note that the TIC addresses on NCP subarea 11 and 12 are duplicated. The line attaching the TICs to the ring segment represents the MAU and CAU attachments. TIC 400023745001 on NCP subarea 11 is attached to ring segment A and TIC 400023745001 on subarea 12 is attached to ring segment B. The opposite holds true for TIC 400023745002 on the NCP subareas. Ring A and B are connected to another ring segment C by using a dual bridge configuration. Bridge A and B provide the connectivity to the isolation rings that duplicate the TIC addresses on the IBM 37X5 Communication Controllers. Ring segment C is the backbone ring and connects to ring segments D and E using bridges D and E respectively.

In Figure 12.8, Station D defines its destination MAC address as being the TIC address 400023745001. Station E has the destination MAC address as being the TIC address 400023745002. Both stations traverse ring segment C and both may utilize bridge A or B. Recall that IBM Token-Ring Networks utilize source routing and that the path used to the destination is usually the result of the first received frame from an ALL_ROUTES BROADCAST or SINGLE_ROUTE BROADCAST request to locate the destination MAC address.

Suppose bridge A experienced a failure and stations were in session with applications on the mainframe computer. The stations on ring segment D and E would re-connect to the mainframe computer utilizing bridge B and ring segment B. This ability without reconfiguring station destination addresses is made possible through the use of duplicate TIC addressing. The only caution in proceeding with duplicate TIC addressing is ensuring enough capacity on the destination resource (i.e., IBM 37X5) and the intermediate bridge(s) because now the network load has conceivably doubled through these resources.

12.2 VTAM DEFINITIONS FOR IBM 37X5 GATEWAY DSPU SUPPORT

SNA views DSPU token-ring connectivity through the IBM 37X5 gateway as switched or dial connections. VTAM on the SNA host computer defines switched connections using a VTAM switched major node. The switched major node identifies the token-ring station physical units, and their associated logical units, that can "dial" to the mainframe or the mainframe may "call" the stations.

```
TRSWNET    VBUILD   TYPE=SWNET

DSPU1101   PU       IDBLK=017,IDNUM=E1101,MAXDATA=1033,ADDR=C1

TRSWPATH   PATH     DIALNO=0104400031741101

DSPULU01   LU       LOCADDR=02

DSPULU02   LU       LOCADDR=03
```

Figure 12.9 A VTAM switched major node definition for DSPU token-ring resources.

12.2.1 Switched VBUILD Definition Statement

The VTAM switched VBUILD statement defines to VTAM a switched major node definition. The format of the VBUILD statement for defining token-ring resources is listed in Figure 12.9. This format is the same regardless of the token-ring station device type.

12.2.2 Switched PU Definition Statement

The PU definition for token-ring resources uses traditional switched SNA parameters. The PU definition statement itself identifies the station address representing this physical unit. Specific to switched connection is the IDBLK and IDNUM keywords on the PU definition statement as shown in Figure 12.9. These fields together are the unique identifiers of the physical unit and must match the value sent in the PUs exchange identifier (XID). The IDBLK keyword value identifies the actual resource type. For instance an IBM 3174 will use the value 017. The IDNUM keyword value indicates the unique identifier for the resource. The IDNUM value must match the configuration question 215 on an IBM 3174 Establishment Controller. The MAXDATA keyword specifies the largest unit of information that the physical unit can receive. This value must match the value specified on the physical unit definition.

12.2.3 Switched PATH Definitions Statement

The PATH definition statement specifies the LAA address of the station being defined by the PU definition statement. The keyword DIALNO identifies the address of the station. The format of the DIALNO keyword value is *xxyy*4000*abbbbbbb*. The xx value specifies the actual TIC position in the IBM 37X5 Communication Controller. The yy value is the service access point (SAP) for an NCP. The 4000*abbbbbb* matches the MAC address defined on the station. If the station is an IBM 3174 Establishment Controller the value here should match the value defined on the configuration question 380 of the establishment controller.

12.2.4 Switched LU Definitions Statement

The LU definition statement defines the address of the logical unit on the physical unit. The LOCADDR keyword defines the local address of the logical unit. Typically SNA physical units can support up to 255 logical units. For more information of SNA logical unit definitions see *Introduction to SNA Networking: A Guide to Using VTAM/NCP*.

12.3 IBM's 3174 ESTABLISHMENT CONTROLLER GATEWAY CONFIGURATION

The IBM 3174 Establishment Controller can provide two types of token-ring network connectivity. One way is through a local establishment controller (EC) gateway and the second is through a remote token-ring network gateway. Local connection in this context refers to an IBM 3174 channel attached to the mainframe computer, remote indicates that the IBM 3174 is attached to a communication controller using a dedicated communications line.

In both instances the IBM 3174 EC gateway can support up to 250 downstream physical units (DSPU) with up to 255 logical units per DSPU if running with Configuration Support B. Each DSPU appears to VTAM on the mainframe as an SNA node type 2.0. The DSPUs associated with a local IBM 3174 LAN gateway are addressed as if they were "daisy-chained" off of the IBM 3174 EC gateway. Each DSPU off of a local EC gateway is assigned a subchannel address. Remote IBM 3174 EC gateways and their associated DSPUs are viewed by VTAM and NCP as if it were a multipoint communications line. These possible configurations and the ability to theoretically support 63,750 logical units through one IBM 3174 EC gateway provides a robust solution for connecting end users to VTAM applications using token-ring networking.

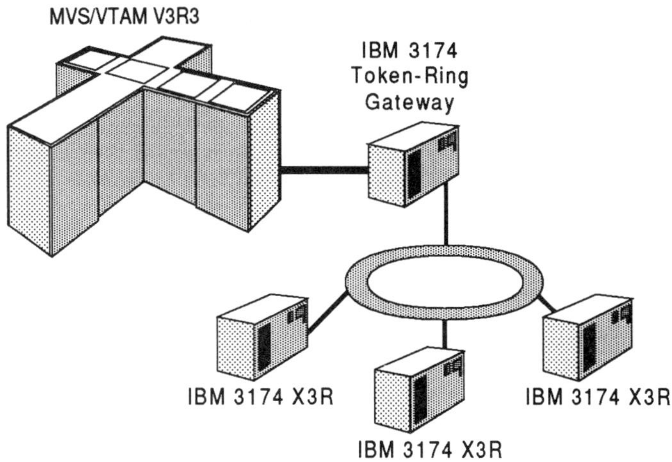

Figure 12.10 The local IBM 3174 Token-ring gateway configuration.

12.3.1 Local 3174 Establishment Controller Gateway

Figure 12.10 illustrates a locally attached IBM 3174 with the token-ring gateway feature installed. Attached to the IBM 3174 EC gateway device are three other IBM 3174 Establishment Controllers. These three devices are the down-stream physical units. All four of these controllers need operating system channel addresses and definitions in VTAM and token-ring specific parameters.

The host operating system on the mainframe computer must define channel addresses for each of the four controllers. It is recommended that the range of addresses be a multiple of 8 ending in either hexadecimal 0 or 7 or F. For VM operating systems the definitions for the four controllers may be coded as:

```
RDEVICE ADDRESS=200,DEVTYPE=3705,
ADAPTER=TYPE4,MODEL=E8,CPTYPE=NCP

RDEVICE ADDRESS=201,DEVTYPE=3705,
ADAPTER=TYPE4,MODEL=E8,CPTYPE=NCP

RDEVICE ADDRESS=202,DEVTYPE=3705,
ADAPTER=TYPE4,MODEL=E8,CPTYPE=NCP

RDEVICE ADDRESS=203,DEVTYPE=3705,
ADAPTER=TYPE4,MODEL=E8,CPTYPE=NCP

RDEVICE ADDRESS=204,DEVTYPE=3705,
ADAPTER=TYPE4,MODEL=E8,CPTYPE=NCP
```

```
RDEVICE ADDRESS=205,DEVTYPE=3705,
ADAPTER=TYPE4,MODEL=E8,CPTYPE=NCP

RDEVICE ADDRESS=206,DEVTYPE=3705,
ADAPTER=TYPE4,MODEL=E8,CPTYPE=NCP

RDEVICE ADDRESS=207,DEVTYPE=3705,
ADAPTER=TYPE4,MODEL=E8,CPTYPE=NCP

RCTLUNIT ADDRESS=200,CUTYPE=3705,FEATURE=256-DEVICE

RCHANNEL ADDRESS=8,CHTYPE=BLKMPXR
```

The address range defined here is indicated by the number of RDEVICE statements and the ADDRESS parameter of the RCHANNEL statement. The address of 207 specifies the highest address defined to the operating system for DSPUs supported by the EC gateway. The RCTLUNIT statement must be defined for the gateway and all DSPUs that will attach to the host via this gateway. The EC gateway definition is identified with the RCTLUNIT statement. The ADDRESS parameter on the RCTLUNIT statement must specify the lowest address in the defined range and it must end with a value of 0. The FEATURE keyword indicates the number of DSPUs available with the gateway feature installed on the IBM 3174. Configuration Support B microcode supports up to 250 DSPUs and is defined to the VM operating system as shown. Configuration Support S supports up to 140 DSPUs (i.e., FEATURE=144-DEVICE).

The VSE operating system identifies the four controllers with the following statements:

```
ADD 200,3791L,EML /* defines gateway */

ADD 201,3791L,EML /* defines DSPU */

ADD 202,3791L,EML /* defines DSPU */

ADD 203,3791L,EML /* defines DSPU */

ADD 204,3791L,EML /* defines DSPU */

ADD 205,3791L,EML /* defines DSPU */

ADD 206,3791L,EML /* defines DSPU */

ADD 207,3791L,EML /* defines DSPU */
```

Again, the address range selected is identified to the system by defining the lowest and highest addresses. For the VSE operating system the lowest address is assigned to the EC gateway. The EML parameter indicates to the VSE operating system that the device will be controlled as if it were an IBM 3274-41A channel-attached cluster controller.

The MVS operating system identifies the four controllers through the input/output system generation and the input/output control program (IOCP) generation processes. The definition statement required for the four controllers under MVS for the system generation process is:

```
IODEVICE ADDRESS(200,8),UNIT=3791L
```

This statement simply defines that starting at address 200 for 8 addresses (i.e., 200-207) there will be 8 3791L (i.e., cluster controllers) attached. The IOCP definition statements needed are:

```
CNTLUNIT CUNUMBR=200,UNITADD=((00,8)),UNIT=3791L,
SHARED=Y,PROTCL=D

IODEVICE ADDRESS=(200,8),UNIT=3791L,STADET=N,
CUNUMBR=200
```

These statements further describe the four controllers and their addresses to the MVS operating system.

In all three operating system definitions eight subchannels were defined even though only four devices are used in the example. This was done to provide growth for four more controllers in the future off of the local EC gateway without requiring changes to the mainframe operating system.

It is during configuration customization of the IBM 3174 that token-ring addresses of devices attached via the services of the EC gateway feature are defined. There are eight key parameters specific to defining EC gateway capabilities to the locally attached IBM 3174. The values of the key parameters are defined during a series of configuration questions in the customization process. During this customization period the IBM 3174 is not available to end users, therefore, it is best to plan ahead for growth and define future DSPUs attached to this IBM 3174 to avoid user outages caused by reconfiguration for the addition of another DSPU.

Question 104 requests the two-digit address of the gateway. A value of 00 is entered based on the operating system examples. This value is the I/O address of the IBM 3174 SNA physical unit.

The next question, question 105 in the configuration process sets the range of I/O addresses to be used and directly indicates the number of expected DSPUs attached to this gateway. A value of 07 is coded to coincide with the example. A value of 00 or one equal to the value defined for question 104 indicates that no DSPUs will be attached to this EC gateway.

Question 150 specifies whether an IBM 3174 using Configuration Support B will include the Token-Ring Gateway feature. A value of 1 is specified to include the token-ring gateway support.

This question does not apply to Configuration Support S.

The MAC address is defined when answering configuration question 900. The 12-digit hexadecimal MAC address is defined according to the following format:

- 4000 is the fixed portion
- *a* must not be greater than hexadecimal 7
- *nnnnnnn* can be any value inclusive of hexadecimal 0 to F
- *ss* the SAP address (Configuration Support B Release 2 or higher)

This MAC address format implies that it is a locally administered address.

Question 908 allows the user to identify the gateway with a unique name that has more meaning to network operations than the MAC address. Configuration Support S allows for up to six characters and Configuration Support B provides for up to eight characters. The significance of this field is made apparent when network alerts are sent to NetView on the mainframe computer. The default name is IBMLAN. It may be prudent to assign the VTAM SNA PU definition statement name in this field if your naming conventions allow.

The data rate of the token-ring must be defined to the IBM 3174 for clocking purposes and is specified on question 911. The default value is 0 but the following values are possible:

- 0 = 4Mbps with normal token release. 4Mbps TRA or 16/4Mbps TRA
- 1 = 16Mbps with normal token release. 16/4Mbps TRA
- 2 = 16Mbps with early token release. 16/4Mbps TRA

The MAC addresses of the DSPUs are defined in question 940 during configuration. The question is actually a panel with four columns. The columns and values entered in each relate the host operating system subchannel addresses to the MAC addresses of the gateway itself and the DSPUs. The number of entries needing this mapping is determined by the difference between question 104 and 105. In the example eight entries are defined. Each entry has the subchannel address already specified. The gateway definition is already entered for question 940 when it is displayed. Column 2 of this question is the more important field for it specifies the MAC address of the DSPU.

The final key parameter is the maximum frame size that can be sent The maximum frame size includes the SNA/SDLC header bytes. The maximum frame size is specified in question 941. The available values are as follows:

- F=0 - 256 bytes
- F=1 - 521 bytes
- F=2 - 1033 bytes
- F=3 - 2042 bytes
- F=4 - 4105 bytes
- F=5 - 8201 bytes

The default value for DSPUs that are actual cluster controllers (i.e., IBM 3174 Establishment Controllers) is the entered value of 3 indicating a maximum frame size of 2042 bytes. However, if the DSPU is actually a workstation (i.e., a PC with Attachmate EXTRA!) then the default entered value is 0 indicating a maximum frame size of 256 bytes.

12.3.2 Local Establishment Controller Gateway Support on the IBM 3174 DSPU

The IBM 3174 DSPU attached to the local token-ring gateway as depicted in Figure 12.10 has five key parameters that define their relationship local token-ring gateway controller. Question 106 in the configuration process of the IBM 3174 DSPU indicates the MAC address of the DSPU. The format is the same as that described previously for the gateway MAC address. Question 107 on the DSPU specifies the MAC address of the local token-ring gateway. The value coded here must match the value coded on question 900 of the EC gateway configuration. Question 380 is the maximum frame size that can be sent from the EC gateway to the DSPU. This value must match the maximum fame size specified on question 941 on the EC gateway configuration. Question 382 on the DSPU configuration specifies the maximum frame size the DSPU can send to the EC gateway. It is best to make the values of 380 and 382 the same for performance measurement purposes. Question 384 on the DSPU configuration indicates the data rate of the token-ring. The available values here are the same as described previously for the EC gateway. The value coded for question 384 must however match the value coded on question 911 of the EC gateway.

12.3.3 Local Establishment Controller Gateway Support for DSPU Workstations

By now it should be obvious that there are certain parameters that are constant with any type of connection between a DSPU and an EC gateway. The same holds true if the DSPUs are personal computers or workstations executing a DOS SNA emulator, OS/2 Communication Manager, or a UNIX workstation with an SNA emulator. Since the key parameters have been discussed they will not be discussed in detail here. It is sufficient to say that any station on a token ring that has local SNA token-ring access support must have the following parameters defined and synchronized with the EC gateway: EC gateway address (i.e., destination address), station address, frame size, data rate.

12.3.4 VTAM Local Establishment Controller Gateway Definition

VTAM residing on the SNA host computer defines a physical unit for the EC gateway and each DSPU. The definitions are stored in a file, usually named SYS1.VTAMLST, on the SNA mainframe. Each entry in the file is a VTAM major node. The EC gateway is defined in a VTAM local major node. The major node is defined as local by using the VTAM definition statement VBUILD. The format of the local VBUILD definition statement is:

```
name VBUILD TYPE=LOCAL
```

The *name* parameter is an optional unique name assigned to the major node definition. It is the TYPE keyword that indicates to VTAM that this major node defines channel-attached devices.

The PU definition statement specifies the channel unit address (CUA) and other parameters that describe characteristics of the physical unit and its associated logical units. There must be at least one LU definition statement coded for each PU definition statement. The LU definition statement will not be discussed since it is irrelevant for establishing SNA connectivity through the EC gateway. The format of the PU definition statement is:

```
name PU CUADDR=xxx,.....
```

The *name* parameter on this statement is required and uniquely identifies the channel-attached resource to VTAM. The CUADDR keyword is the channel unit address associated with the physical unit being defined. The value coded here must match a value coded

LCLGW	VBUILD	TYPE=LOCAL
DSPU01	PU	CUADDR=201, ...
DSPU0101	LU	LOCADDR=02
DSPU02	PU	CUADDR=202,...
DSPU0201	LU	LOCADDR=02
DSPU03	PU	CUADDR=203,...
DSPU0301	LU	LOCADDR=02

Figure 12.11 The VTAM definition for local DSPU controllers through an IBM 3174 Token-Ring Gateway.

in the operating system. A PU definition statement is defined for the EC gateway and for each DSPU defined by the EC gateway. Figure 12.11 provides a completed look at the VTAM definitions and parameter associations for establishing SNA connectivity through a local EC gateway.

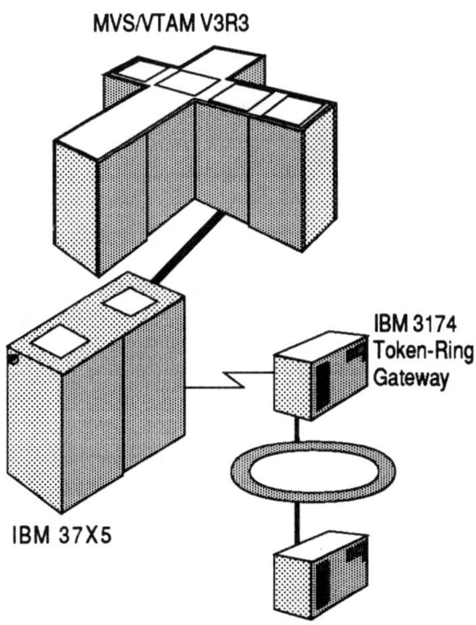

Figure 12.12 The remote IBM 3174 Token-Ring Gateway configuration.

12.3.5 Remote 3174 EC Gateway

Remote 3174 EC gateway configurations are termed remote because they are connected to an IBM 37X5 Communication Controller using a dedicated communications line or a switched communications line as shown in Figure 12.12. The parameters and questions during configuration used for remote EC gateways are the same as those for local EC gateways. The main difference when defining the token-ring gateway function are the answers to questions 104 and 105 and a new question that requests a group poll address.

The configuration questions 104 and 105 asked for remote EC gateways are similar to local EC gateway configuration questions but the values have different meaning. Question 104 on the remote EC gateway inquires about the SNA SDLC address assigned to the remote EC gateway. This value is a 2-digit hexadecimal value. It must not match any DSPU SNA SDLC address. Question 105 defines the highest SNA SDLC address that will use the remote EC gateway function to gain access to the SNA host computer. The value here defines the range of SNA SDLC addresses associated with DSPUs.

Question 900 on the remote EC gateway configuration specifies the MAC address of the remote EC gateway. Again, the value follows the format described for the local EC gateway.

The data rate on the token-ring is defined on question 911 for the remote EC configuration. The values available for this field are the same as those described for the local EC gateway.

The IBM 37X5 polls all devices attached and active to it. In this configuration the SDLC link is treated as if it were a multipoint line configuration. Each PU on the line must be polled by the communication controller. The polling caused by this could be excessive stress on the remote EC gateway. This potential problem has been alleviated in Configuration Support B and question 912. A group poll address is defined so that only one poll is necessary to poll all the devices. The value coded here must be less than the value coded in question 104 or greater than the value coded in question 105.

Question 940 on the remote EC gateway configuration maps the SNA SDLC address to the MAC address rather than the channel unit address to the MAC address as found on the local EC gateway configuration.

The definitions for the DSPU off of the remote EC gateway are no different than that described for a DSPU off of a local EC gateway.

```
ECGWLINE      LINE    ADDRESS=(000,HALF),...
ECGWPU        PU      ADDR=C1,GP3174=CF,SECNET=NO
ECGWLU01      LU      LOCADDR=02
DSPU01        PU      ADDR=C2,SECNET=YES
DSPU0101      LU      LOCADDR=02
DSPU0102      LU      LOCADDR=03
```

Figure 12.13 The remote IBM 3174 Token-Ring Gateway and DSPU definitions in an NCP.

12.3.6 NCP Remote Establishment Controller Gateway Definition

Communication lines are defined to the NCP using a LINE definition statement. The format of the LINE definition statement is:

```
name LINE ADDRESS=(nnn,FULL|HALF),LNCTL=SDLC, DIAL=YES|NO
```

The *name* parameter is a unique name associated with the defined line. The ADDRESS keyword defines which port address (e.g., nnn) the communication line is physically attached. The FULL|HALF parameter indicates whether the communication line can send and receive data simultaneously (i.e., FULL) or serially (i.e., HALF). The LNCTL keyword specifies that the communication line is using IBM's SDLC protocol. The DIAL keyword indicates whether the communication line is a dedicated line (i.e., DIAL=NO) or a switched line (i.e., DIAL=YES).

Each LINE definition statement in a NCP must have at least one PU definition statement. For a remote EC gateway there will be several PU definition statements. The format of the NCP PU definition statement is:

```
name PU ADDR=xx,GP3174=xx,MAXDATA=nnn,SECNET=YES|NO
```

The name parameter is required and defines a unique name to the physical unit being defined. The ADDR keyword specifies a unique SNA SDLC address for this communication line. In a true SDLC multipoint configuration this address would be used as the polling address for the physical unit. Since this is a token-ring environment the GP3174 keyword specifies the group poll address used to poll all the DSPUs including the remote EC gateway. The GP3174 keyword should be defined on each PU definition statement that is to respond to the group poll. The group poll is only used when there is no specific data directed towards a physical unit. The MAXDATA keyword defines the largest frame that the NCP can send to the remote EC gateway. This value should not exceed the maximum frame size value specified on question 941 on the EC gateway configuration. The SECNET keyword indicates to the NCP whether the resource is actually attached through a secondary network. The value of SECNET for the remote EC gateway must be NO and must be set to YES for the DSPU definitions. Figure 12.13 shows the configuration and the appropriate parameters for each resource.

12.4 IBM's OS/2 SNA GATEWAY CONFIGURATION

OS/2 Extended Edition V1.3 and OS/2 Communication Manager provide a function similar to the IBM 3174 EC gateway. An OS/2 SNA gateway is perceived as a cluster controller. The logical units attached to this cluster controller are LAN workstations. As shown in Figure 12.14, the OS/2 SNA gateway can connect the workstations to the SNA mainframe through a local EC gateway, an IBM 37X5 gateway or by using a communications line. The requirements on the EC gateways are no different than previously discussed and therefore will not be described in this section. OS/2 SNA gateways create the mapping of SNA logical unit addresses to the workstation MAC addresses.

12.4.1 OS/2 SNA Gateway through a Local 3174

The destination MAC address of the OS/2 SNA gateway for connectivity to the SNA mainframe must specify the local EC gateway address. This is defined on the destination address field under IBM Token-Ring Network 3270 Profile-Connection. The address defined here must match the address defined on question 900 of the EC gateway configuration. This same address is defined on the destination address field of the SNA Feature Profiles-SNA Gateway Profiles-Host Connection.

The address of the OS/2 SNA gateway is defined on the LAN Feature Profiles address field. This is the MAC address of the OS/2 SNA gateway and should be entered on the appropriate entry for question 940 of the EC gateway configuration. Remember that the OS/2 SNA gateway MAC address will be mapped to an operating

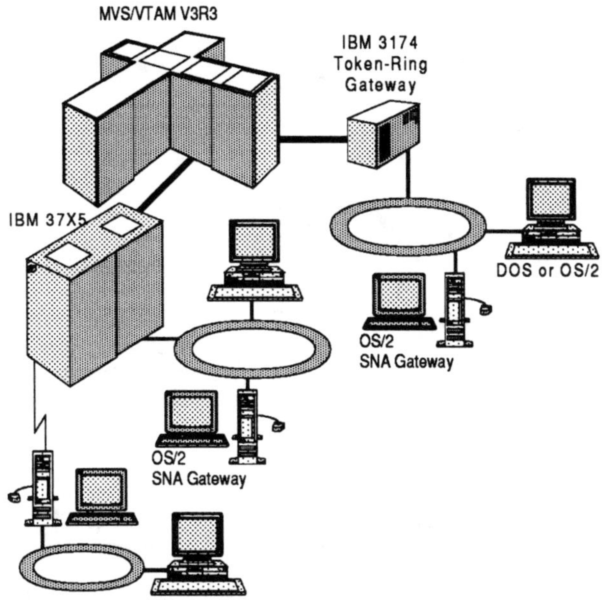

Figure 12.14 The IBM OS/2 SNA Gateway configuration.

system channel unit address through the EC gateway.

Each workstation that requires SNA mainframe access is assigned an SNA LU local address on the OS/2 SNA gateway. This is done through the SNA Feature Profiles-SNA Gateway Profiles-Workstation LU Profile fields. The first field assigns an SNA LU local address. This address can be in the range of hexadecimal 02 to FFF. The value coded here must have an equivalent LU definition statement in the VTAM local major node definition on the SNA mainframe file SYS1.VTAMLST. The parameter in the VTAM local major node is the LOCADDR keyword of the LU definition statement. The second field is the workstations MAC address and is coded on the destination address of the Workstation LU Profiles. A Workstation LU Profile must be created for each workstation that is to gain access to the SNA host computer through the OS/2 SNA gateway.

An OS/2 workstation requiring SNA 3270 connectivity through an OS/2 SNA gateway defines the 3270 Feature Profile-IBM Token-Ring Network 3270 Profile-Connection destination field equal to the MAC address of the OS/2 SNA gateway. The OS/2 worksta-

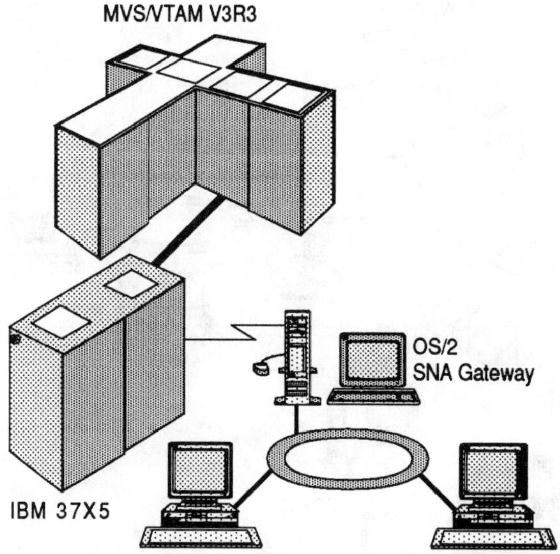

Figure 12.15 The remote OS/2 SNA Gateway configuration using an IBM 3745 Token-Ring Gateway.

tion MAC address is defined on the LAN Feature Profiles address field. When the end user requests a 3270 session the OS/2 Communication Manager contacts the OS/2 SNA gateway to establish an SNA session for the workstation.

DOS workstations may utilize any vendors software that provides for IBM 3270 terminal and printer emulation. The destination address defined for these emulators is the OS/2 SNA gateway MAC address and the DOS workstation MAC address must be defined as either a DXMCxMOD.SYS parameter or as a field on the emulators software configuration program. The IBM 3270 emulator will contact the OS/2 SNA gateway for SNA services.

12.4.2 OS/2 SNA Gateway Through an IBM 37X5 Gateway

All the fields and parameters discussed in the previous section hold true for OS/2 SNA gateway connectivity through an IBM 37X5 gateway. The basic difference is that the destination address defined in the OS/2 SNA gateway is that of the IBM 37X5 TIC as depicted in Figure 12.15. The destination address field of the OS/2 SNA gateway must match the value coded on the physical definition of the peripheral TIC LOCADD keyword in the NCP. The other main difference between connectivity using an EC gateway versus an IBM 37X5 gateway is the need for the unique identifier number (IDNUM) of the OS/2 SNA gateway. Recall that this value is needed because DSPU resources are viewed as switched resources by VTAM. The IDNUM keyword in the VTAM switched major node for the OS/2 SNA gateway must match the SNA Feature Profiles-SNA Base Profile Node ID field. The rest of the parameters discussed in the previous section still hold true and do not change. The only changes required in this configuration are those on the OS/2 SNA gateway.

12.4.3 Remote OS/2 SNA Gateway

This configuration requires changes in the SNA Feature Profiles-Data Link Control (DLC) Profiles section. The key parameters in the SDLC subsection is the local station address. This field must match the ADDR keyword value on the PU definition statement in the NCP that describes the OS/2 SNA gateway. The ADDR value defines the physical unit station address that is used to poll the OS/2 SNA gateway. The other parameters and keywords specific to associating the workstations to LU addresses in the OS/2 SNA gateway do not change. The communications line is defined on the Line type field of the SDLC subsection. This field identifies whether the line is dedicated or switched. A value of non-switched indicates that the connection to the communication controller is over a dedicated line. The maximum RU size field specifies the largest frame that can be sent to the OS/2 SNA gateway from the communication controller. The value coded here plus nine must match the value of the MAXDATA keyword in the NCP. The definition for the OS/2 SNA gateway in the NCP is the same as any other SNA physical unit type 2 node.

12.5 SUMMARY

Connectivity to the SNA mainframe from token-ring network resources is a matter of understanding the simplicity behind establishing sessions between stations. Connecting to the IBM mainframe through an IBM 37X5 gateway requires a Token-Ring Adapter. Each TRA has two token-ring interface couplers (TIC). The TIC is assigned a token-ring network address. It is this address that stations use as the destination address to connect to the SNA mainframe. Connection through IBM 3174 EC gateways is quite similar. Token-ring stations use as the destination address the MAC address of the IBM 3174. Stations down-stream to the IBM 37X5 and IBM 3174 EC gateways that provide full SNA physical unit support are called down-stream physical units (DSPU). Definition of these DSPUs are found in NCP and VTAM and may appear as locally attached, remotely attached or as switched connections.

Appendix

A

Control Field State Variables

Each link station maintains a send state variable, V(S), for the I-format LPDUs it sends and a receive state variable, V(R), for the I-format LPDUs it receives. These two state variables operate independently. It is also necessary for the link station to maintain variables to control XID and TEST exchanges, busy conditions, transmit window size, and checkpointing operations. The following table describes these variables.

Send State Variable	**V(S)**	**V(S) denotes the sequence number of the next in-sequence I-format LPDU to be transmitted on the link. V(S) takes on values sequentially between 0 and 127. The value of V(S) is incremented by one with each successive I-format LPDU transmission on the associated link, but does not exceed the N(R) value of the last received I-format or S-format LPDU by more than the window size (which has a maximum value of 127).**

Receive State Variable	V(R)	V(R) denotes the sequence number of the next in-sequence I-format LPDU to be received on a specific link. V(R) takes on values sequentially between 0 and 127. The value of the V(R) associated with a specific link is incremented by one whenever an error-free, in-sequence I-format LPDU is received whose send sequence number, N(S), equals the value of V(R) for that link.
Last Received	N(R), V(A)	V(A) contains the N(R) value from the last valid I-format or S-format LPDU received. This is used to determine the upper transmit window edge, that is, the value of V(S) at which the link station should stop sending because the window has been reached.
Poll State Variable	V(P)	V(P) denotes the value of V(S) at the time the last I-format or S-format command LPDU with the P bit set to B'1' was transmitted; it is set to the value of V(S). V(P) is used to determine if a frame must be transmitted again when a response LPDU with the F bit set to B'1' is received. If N(R) of the received response LPDU does not acknowledge all frames up to (but not including) the value of V(P), the frames that are not acknowledged must be transmitted again. This variable is necessary only when I-frame transmission is allowed during a checkpoint operation.
Busy State Variable	V(B)	V(B) denotes the ready/busy condition of the local (Lb) or remote (Rb) link stations, or both (LRb) as indicated by RNR, RR, REJ and other related LPDUs.
Final State Variable	V(F)	V(F) is set to the value of the final bit required in the response to the last received command LPDU when the response must be delayed.
Initialization State Variable	V(I)	V(I) denotes the link setup status for local (Llp) or remote (Rlp) link stations, or both (LRlp) as a determined by the source of the link setup initialization. It also denotes that setup is not complete(lSp).

Test State Variable	T(S)	T(S) denotes the link test status (ITp) when a locally initialized test is in process. This variable is required only for link stations that support TEST LPDUs.
ID_Exchange State Variable	X(S)	X(S) denotes the ID_Exchange status for local (IXP) or remote (KXp) ID exchanges or both (IOXp), as determined by the source of the XID initiation. This variable is required only for link stations that support XID LPDUs.
Working Window Size	Ww	Ww is the minimum number of sequentially numbered I-format LPDUs that the link station may have outstanding (unacknowledged) at any given time. Ww is initialized to the value of TW when a link is established. When the dynamic window algorithm is invoked, Ww varies from 1 up to its maximum TW.

Appendix

B

SNA to Token-Ring Communications Protocol

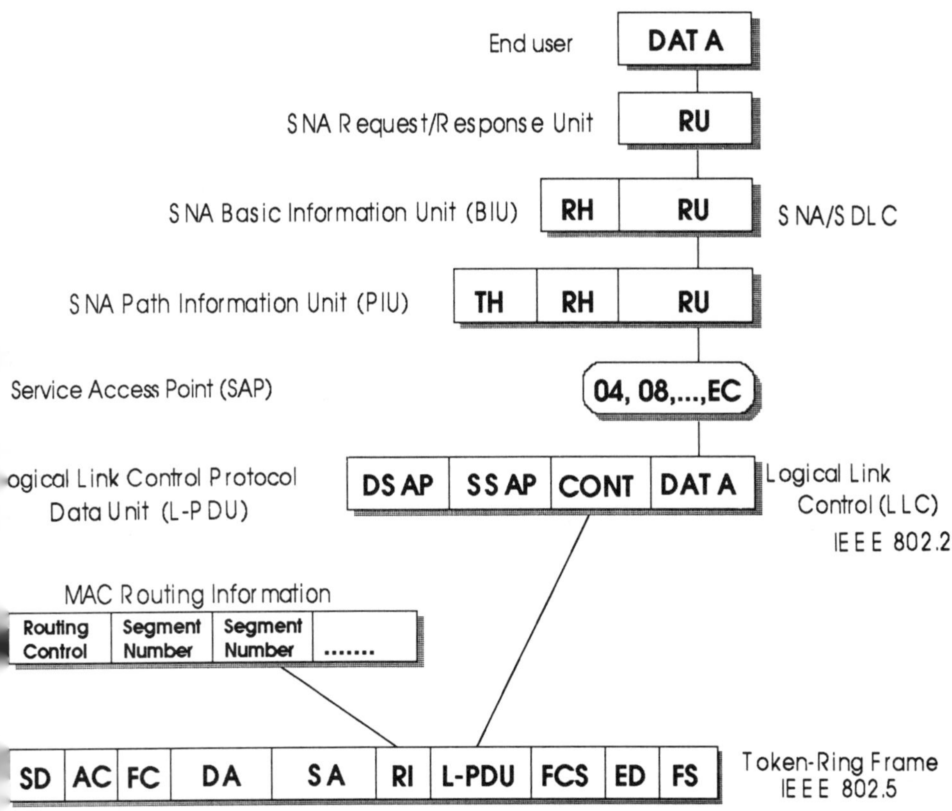

Appendix

C

The Differential Manchester Code

IBM's Token-Ring Network uses the Manchester Differential code to convert the binary data of a MAC frame to electrical signals for transmission over medium.

Each bit of data is made up of two singal elements of opposite polarity. It is the transition from one polarity to another or the lack of the transition determines the bit value to be B'0' or B'1'. This transition is checked at the bit start point. A B'0' is represented when both sides of the start point have opposite polarity (i.e., transition). The same polarity at the start point inidcates a B'1'. A transition at the midpoint the bit value is a valid B'0' or B'1'. If the midpoint has the same polarity then there is a code violation. A J code violation is a postive code violation because there is not transisiton at the start point. The second code violation is denoted as a K code violation. A K code violation is also known as a negative code violation. This is determiend when there is a transition at the start point. Figure C.1 diagrams the signal combinations for the starting and ending delimiters .

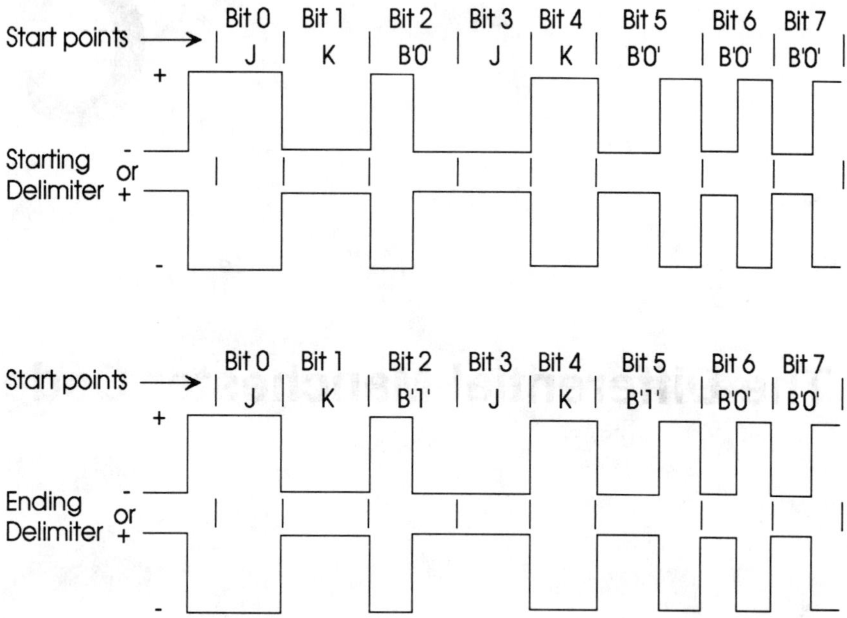

Figure C.1 Signal combinations used to determine the starting delimiter (SD) and ending delimiter (ED).

Appendix

D

MAC Major Vectors

Major Vector Name	Major Vector Identifier
Request REM Status	X'8101'
Report REM Status	X'8102'
Set REM Parameters	X'8103'
REM Parameters Set	X'8104'
REM Parameters Changed Notification	X'8105'
Error Rate Decaying Notification	X'8106'
Preweight Exceeded Notification	X'8107'
Weight-Exceeded Notification	X'8108'
Nonisolating Threshold Exceeded	X'8109'
Forward MAC Frame	X'810A'
REM Error	X'810C'
Receiver Congestion Notification	X'810E'
Receiver Congestion Ended	X'810F'
Beaconing Condition on Ring	X'8110'
Beaconing Condition Recovered	X'8111'

Major Vector Name	Major Vector Identifier
Request RPS Status	X'8201'
Request RPS Status	X'8202'
RPS Error	X'8203'
Report Station in Ring	X'8206'
Report New Active Monitor	X'8301'
Report NAUN Change	X'8302'
Report Transmit-Forward	X'8303'
Request Station Information	X'8304'
Report Station Information	X'8306'
Set Station Parameters	X'8307'
Station Parameters	X'8308'
Removing Ring Station	X'8309'
Ring Station Removed	X'830A'
CRS Error	X'830B'
Downstream Converter Presence	X'8402'
Beaconing Back-up Ring	X'8403'
Request Bridge Status	X'8501'
Report Bridge Status	X'8502'
Set Bridge Parameters	X'8503'
Bridge Parameters Set	X'8504'
Bridge Error	X'8505'
Bridge Parameters Changed	X'8506'
Bridge Performance Threshold Exceeded	X'8507'
Path Trace Report	X'8508'
Bridge Counter Report	X'8509'
Single-Route Broadcast Status Change	X'850A'
Report LRM Parsing Error	X'8603'
LRM Parameters Set	X'8604'
LRM Error	X'8605'
LRM Parameters Changed	X'8606'
Set Reporting Point	X'8607'
LAN Manager Accepted	X'8608'
LAN Manager Rejected	X'8609'
Report LAN Manager Rejection	X'860A'
New Reporting Link Established Notification	X'860B'
Report LAN Manager Control Shift	X'860C'
Report LRM Control Breach Attempt	X'860D'
Close Reporting Link	X'860E'
LRM Terminating	X'860F'
Invalid Request	X'8610'
Set Reporting Point Error	X'8611'

Major Vector Name	Major Vector Identifier
LRM Congestion	X'8612'
Management Servers Present	X'8613'
Alert Transport	X'8701'
Alert Transport Received	X'8702'

Appendix

E

Standardized Group and Functional Addresses

Standardized Group Addresses

Bridge	X'8001 4300 0000'
Bridge management	X'8001 4300 0008'
Load Server	X'8001 4300 0088'
Loadable device	X'8001 4300 0048'
ISO 10589 level-1 Intermediate Stns	X'8001 4300 0028'
ISO 10589 level-2 Intermediate Stns	X'8001 4300 00A8'
FDDI RMT Directed Beacon	X'8001 4300 8000'
FDDI status report frame	X'8001 4300 8008'
OSI Network Layer End-stations	X'8001 D400 00A0'
OSI NL Intermediate stations	X'8001 D400 0020'

IEEE and IBM Functional Addresses

Active Monitor	X'C000 0000 0001'
Ring Parameter Server	X'C000 0000 0002'
Network Server Heartbeat	X'C000 0000 0004'
Ring Error Monitor	X'C000 0000 0008'
Configuration Report Server	X'C000 0000 0010'
Synchronous Bandwidth Mgr.	X'C000 0000 0020'
Locate Directory Server	X'C000 0000 0040'
NETBIOS	X'C000 0000 0080'
Bridge	X'C000 0000 0100'
IMPL Server	X'C000 0000 0200'
Ring Authorization Server	X'C000 0000 0400'
LAN Gateway	X'C000 0000 0800'
Ring Wiring Concentrator	X'C000 0000 1000'
LAN Manager	X'C000 0000 2000'
User-defined	X'C000 0000 8000' through X'C000 4000 0000'

Appendix

F

IBM's Suggested MAC Addressing Guidelines

There is no "right" answer on how to assign locally administered MAC addresses throughout a multisegment LAN. The following appendix provides IBM-supplied examples of addressing structures to show the kind of information that may be provided using locally administered addresses.

IBM local area networks allow the assignment of a twelve-digit hexadecimal address to override the "burned in" adapter address. The locally administered address can range from X'400000000000' to X'4000FFFFFFFF', although some applications and devices limit these addresses to being numeric.

A possible addressing scheme could be:

```
4000XZZZZZZZ
```

Where **X** is a hexadecimal digit representing the device type:

```
0       Gateway or IS server
1       Primary Bridge adapter
2       Secondary bridge adapter
```

3 LAN servers

5 Workstation

ZZZZZZZ A unique identifier

3174 token-ring controllers: With an addressing structure **4000 0BA0 DDDD**, where:

B 3174 machine type

A Model type

- **0** 01L
- **1** 11L
- **2** 03R
- **3** 13R
- **4** 01R
- **5** 11R

DDDD A unique identifier

37XX gateways: With an addressing structure **4000 09AB DDDD**, where:

9 37XX/3172 gateway machine

A Machine type

- **0** 3720
- **1** 3725
- **2** 3725
- **3** 3745
- **4** 3172

B TIC Number

- **0** 1st TIC
- **1** 2nd TIC
- **2** 3rd TIC
- **3** 4th TIC . . . .

DDDD Unique device identifier

IS Servers: With an addressing structure **40000 0EAB DDDD**, where:

E Host/server type

A Type

- **0** AS/400
- **1** 9370
- **2** S/36
- **3** Series 1
- **4** PS/2
- **5** Printer
- **6** RISC/6000

B Adapter Number

- **0** First adapter
- **1** Second adapter

DDDD Unique device identifier

Network Management and Performance: With an addressing structure **4000 0FAB CDDD**, where:

F Network support device

A Device function

- **0** LAN Manager
- **1** Trace and Performance Tool

B Adapter number

- **0** First adapter
- **1** Second adapter

C Device number

DDD LAN segment number

Local Servers: With an addressing structure **4000 3AZZ ZZZZ**, where:

3 Local server

A Sequence number of the server

ZZZZZZ The employee serial number of the server owner

Bridges: With an addressing structure **4000 XABB BCCC**, where:

X Adapter

- **1** Primary
- **2** Secondary

A Remote or local bridge number on the segment

- **0** Remote bridge number 1 on the segment
- **1** Remote bridge number 2 on the segment
- **2** Remote bridge number 3 on the segment
- **A** Local bridge number 1 on the segment
- **B** Local bridge number 2 on the segment
- **C** Local bridge number 3 on the segment

BBB Higher segment number

CCC Lower segment number

Appendix

G

Cable, Closet and Ring Segment Drive Distance and Guideines

This appendix provides guidelines for single- and multiple-wire closets. It covers type 1, type 2 and type 9 cables for 4Mbps and 16Mbps Rings.

Single-Wiring Closet Lobe Lengths in Feet (type 1 or type 2 Cable) for 4Mbps Rings

Number of 8228s	Number of Racks: 1	2	3	4	5	6	7	8	9	10
1	1263									
2	1246	1213								
3	1230	1197	1181							
4	1213	1181	1164	1148						
5	1197	1164	1148	1131	1115					
6	1181	1148	1131	1115	1099	1082				
7	1164	1131	1115	1099	1082	1066	1049			
8	1148	1115	1099	1082	1066	1049	1033	1017		
9	1131	1099	1082	1066	1049	1033	1017	1000	984	
10	1115	1082	1066	1049	1033	1017	1000	984	967	951
11	1099	1066	1049	1033	1017	1000	984	967	951	935
12	1082	1049	1033	1017	1000	984	967	951	935	918
13		1033	1017	1000	984	967	951	935	918	902
14		1017	1000	984	967	951	935	918	902	885
15		1000	984	967	951	935	918	902	885	869
16		984	967	951	935	918	902	885	869	853
17		967	951	935	918	902	885	869	853	836
18		951	935	918	902	885	869	853	836	820
19		935	918	902	885	869	853	836	820	803
20		918	902	885	869	853	836	820	803	787
21		902	885	869	853	836	820	803	787	770
22		885	869	853	836	820	803	787	770	754
23		869	853	836	820	803	787	770	754	738
24		853	836	820	803	787	770	754	738	721
25			820	803	787	770	754	738	721	705
26			803	787	770	754	738	721	705	688
27			787	770	754	738	721	705	688	672
28			770	754	738	721	705	688	672	656
29			754	738	721	705	688	672	656	639
30			738	721	705	688	672	656	639	623
31			721	705	688	672	656	639	623	606
32			705	688	672	656	639	623	606	590
33			688	672	656	639	623	606	590	574

Single-Wiring Closet Lobe Lengths in Feet (type 9 Cable) for 4Mbps Rings

Number of Racks

Number of 8228s	1	2	3	4	5	6	7	8	9	10
1	842									
2	831	809								
3	820	798	787							
4	809	787	776	765						
5	798	776	765	754	743					
6	787	765	754	743	732	721				
7	776	754	743	732	721	710	699			
8	765	743	732	721	710	699	689	678		
9	754	732	721	710	699	689	678	667	656	
10	743	721	710	699	689	678	667	656	645	634
11	732	710	699	689	678	667	656	645	634	623
12	721	699	689	678	667	656	645	634	623	612
13		689	678	667	656	645	634	623	612	601
14		678	667	656	645	634	623	612	601	590
15		667	656	645	634	623	612	601	590	579
16		656	645	634	623	612	601	590	579	568
17		645	634	623	612	601	590	579	568	557
18		634	623	612	601	590	579	568	557	546
19		623	612	601	590	579	568	557	546	535
20		612	601	590	579	568	557	546	535	524
21		601	590	579	568	557	546	535	524	514
22		590	579	568	557	546	535	524	514	503
23		579	568	557	546	535	524	514	503	492
24		568	557	546	535	524	514	503	492	481
25			546	535	524	514	503	492	481	470
26			535	524	514	503	492	481	470	459
27			524	514	503	492	481	470	459	448
28			514	503	492	481	470	459	448	437
29			503	492	481	470	459	448	437	426
30			492	481	470	459	448	437	426	415
31			481	470	459	448	437	426	415	404
32			470	459	448	437	426	415	404	393
33			459	448	437	426	415	404	393	382

Single-Wiring Closet Lobe Lengths in Feet (type 1 or type 2 Cable) for 16Mbps Rings

	Number of Racks									
Number of 8228s	1	2	3	4	5	6	7	8	9	10
1	569									
2	556	523								
3	543	511	494							
4	531	498	481	465						
5	518	485	469	452	436					
6	505	472	456	439	423	407				
7	492	459	443	427	410	394	377			
8	479	447	430	414	397	381	365	348		
9	467	434	417	401	385	368	352	335	319	
10	454	421	405	388	372	355	339	323	306	290
11	441	408	392	377	359	343	326	310	293	277
12	428	395	379	363	346	330	313	297	281	264
13		383	366	350	333	317	301	284	268	251
14		370	353	337	321	304	288	271	255	239
15		357	341	324	308	291	275	259	242	226
16		344	328	311	295	279	262	246	229	213
17		331	315	299	282	266	249	233	217	200
18		319	302	286	269	253	237	220	204	187
19		306	290	273	257	240	224	207	191	175
20		279	263	247	230	214	197	181	165	148
21		253	236	220	204	187	171	154	138	122
22		226	210	193	177	161	144	128	111	95
23		200	183	167	150	134	118	101	85	68
24		173	157	140	124	107	91	75	58	42
25			130	114	97	81	64	48	32	15
26			103	87	71	54	58	21		
27			77	60	44	28	11			
28			50	34	18					
29			24							

Single-Wiring Closet Lobe Lengths in Feet (type 9 Cable) for 16Mbps Rings

Number of Racks (columns); Number of 8228s (rows)

Number of 8228s	1	2	3	4	5	6	7	8	9	10
1	379									
2	371	349								
3	362	340	329							
4	354	332	321	310						
5	345	323	312	301	291					
6	337	315	304	293	282	271				
7	328	306	295	284	273	263	252			
8	320	298	287	276	265	254	243	232		
9	311	289	278	267	256	245	235	224	213	
10	303	281	270	259	248	237	226	215	204	193
11	294	272	261	250	239	228	217	207	196	185
12	286	264	253	242	231	220	209	198	187	176
13		255	244	233	222	211	200	190	179	168
14		247	236	225	214	203	192	181	170	159
15		238	227	216	205	194	183	172	162	151
16		230	219	208	197	186	175	164	153	142
17		221	210	199	188	177	166	155	144	134
18		212	202	191	180	169	158	147	136	125
19		204	193	182	171	160	149	138	127	116
20		186	175	164	153	142	132	121	110	99
21		169	158	147	136	125	114	103	92	81
22		151	140	129	118	107	96	85	74	63
23		133	122	111	100	89	78	67	57	46
24		115	104	93	83	72	61	50	39	28
25			87	76	65	54	43	32	21	10
26			69	58	47	36	25	14		
27			51	40	29	18				
28			34	23	12					
29			16							

4Mbps Allowable Drive Distances in Feet (type 1 or type 2 Cable) without using Repeaters or Converters

Number of 8228s	Number of Wiring Closets										
	2	3	4	5	6	7	8	9	10	11	12
2	1192										
3	1163	1148									
4	1135	1120	1104								
5	1106	1091	1076	1061							
6	1078	1062	1047	1032	1017						
7	1049	1034	1019	1004	989	974					
8	1020	1005	990	975	960	945	930				
9	992	977	962	947	932	916	901	886			
10	963	948	933	918	903	888	873	858	843		
11	935	920	905	890	874	859	844	829	814	799	
12	906	891	876	861	846	831	816	801	786	770	755
13	878	863	848	833	817	802	787	772	757	742	727
14	849	834	819	804	789	774	759	744	729	713	698
15	821	806	791	775	760	745	730	715	700	685	670
16	792	777	762	747	732	717	702	687	671	656	641
17	764	749	733	718	703	688	673	658	643	628	613
18	735	720	705	690	675	660	645	629	614	599	584
19	707	691	676	661	646	631	616	601	586	571	556
20	678	663	648	633	618	603	587	572	557	542	527
21	649	634	619	604	589	574	559	544	529	514	499
22	621	606	591	576	561	545	530	515	500	485	470
23	592	577	562	547	532	517	502	487	472	457	441
24	564	549	534	519	503	488	473	458	443	428	413
25	502	520	505	490	475	460	445	430	415	399	384
26	474	492	477	461	446	431	416	401	386	371	356
27	445	462	448	433	418	403	388	373	357	342	327

4Mbps Allowable Drive Distances in Feet (type 1 or type 2 Cable) with Repeaters or Converters

Number of Wiring Closets

Number of 8228s

0	1	2	3	4	5	6	7	8	9	10	11	12
1	1235											
2	1207	1192										
3	1178	1163	1148									
4	1150	1135	1120	1104								
5	1121	1106	1091	1076	1061							
6	1093	1078	1062	1047	1032	1017						
7	1064	1049	1034	1019	1004	989	974					
8	1036	1020	1005	990	975	960	945	930				
9	1007	992	977	962	947	932	916	901	886			
10	979	963	948	933	918	903	888	873	858	843		
11	950	935	920	905	890	874	859	844	829	814	799	
12	921	906	891	876	861	846	831	816	801	786	770	755
13	860	878	863	848	833	817	802	787	772	757	742	727
14	832	849	834	819	804	789	774	759	744	729	713	698
15	803	821	806	791	775	760	745	730	715	700	685	670
16	774	792	777	762	747	732	717	702	687	671	656	641
17	746	764	749	733	718	703	688	673	658	643	628	613
18	717	735	720	705	690	675	660	645	629	614	599	584
19	689	707	691	676	661	646	631	616	601	586	571	556
20	660	678	663	648	633	618	603	587	572	557	542	527
21	632	649	634	619	604	589	574	559	544	529	514	499
22	603	621	606	591	576	561	545	530	515	500	485	470
23	575	592	577	562	547	532	517	502	487	472	457	441
24	546	564	549	534	519	503	488	473	458	443	428	413
25	485	502	520	505	490	475	460	445	430	415	388	384
26	456	474	492	477	461	446	431	416	401	386	371	356
27	428	445	463	448	433	418	403	388	373	357	342	327

4Mbps Allowable Drive Distances in Feet (type 9 Cable) without using Repeaters or Converters

Number of Wiring Closets

Number of 8228s	2	3	4	5	6	7	8	9	10	11	12
2	794										
3	775	765									
4	756	746	736								
5	737	727	717	707							
6	718	708	698	688	678						
7	699	689	679	669	659	649					
8	680	670	660	650	640	630	620				
9	661	651	641	631	621	611	601	591			
10	642	632	622	612	602	592	582	572	562		
11	623	613	603	593	583	573	563	553	543	533	
12	604	594	584	574	564	554	544	534	524	514	503
13	585	575	565	555	545	535	525	515	505	494	484
14	566	556	546	536	526	516	506	496	486	475	465
15	547	537	527	517	507	497	487	477	466	456	446
16	528	518	508	498	488	478	468	458	447	437	427
17	509	499	489	479	469	459	449	438	428	418	408
18	490	480	470	460	450	440	430	419	409	399	389
19	471	461	451	441	431	421	410	400	390	380	370
20	452	442	432	422	412	402	391	381	371	361	351
21	433	423	413	403	393	383	372	362	352	342	332
22	414	404	394	384	374	363	353	343	333	323	313
23	395	385	375	365	355	344	334	324	314	304	294
24	376	366	356	346	335	325	315	305	295	285	275
25	335	347	337	327	316	306	296	287	276	266	256
26	316	328	318	307	297	287	277	267	257	247	237
27	297	309	299	288	278	268	258	248	238	228	218

4Mbps Allowable Drive Distances in Feet (type 9 Cable) with Repeaters or Converters

Number of Wiring Closets

Number of 8228s	1	2	3	4	5	6	7	8	9	10	11	12
1	823											
2	804	794										
3	785	775	765									
4	766	756	746	736								
5	747	737	727	717	707							
6	728	718	708	698	688	678						
7	709	699	689	679	669	659	649					
8	690	680	670	660	650	640	630	620				
9	671	661	651	641	631	621	611	601	591			
10	652	642	631	622	612	602	592	582	572	562		
11	633	623	613	603	593	583	573	563	553	542	533	
12	614	604	594	584	574	564	554	544	534	524	514	503
13	573	585	575	565	555	545	535	525	515	505	494	484
14	554	566	556	546	536	526	516	506	496	486	475	465
15	535	547	537	527	517	507	497	487	477	466	456	446
16	516	528	518	508	498	488	478	468	458	447	437	427
17	497	509	499	489	479	469	459	449	438	428	418	408
18	478	490	480	470	460	450	440	430	419	409	399	389
19	459	471	461	451	441	431	421	410	400	390	380	370
20	440	452	442	432	422	412	402	391	381	371	361	351
21	421	433	423	413	403	393	383	372	362	352	342	332
22	402	414	404	394	384	374	363	353	343	333	323	313
23	383	395	385	375	365	355	344	334	324	314	304	294
24	364	376	366	356	346	335	325	315	305	295	285	275
25	323	335	347	337	327	316	306	296	286	276	266	256
26	304	316	328	318	307	297	287	277	267	257	247	237
27	285	297	309	299	288	278	268	258	248	238	228	218

16Mbps Allowable Drive Distances in Feet (type 1 or type 2 Cable) without Converters

Number of Wiring Closets

Number of 8228s	2	3	4	5	6	7	8	9	10
2	530								
3	509	492							
4	487	471	454						
5	465	449	432	416					
6	443	427	411	394	378				
7	422	405	389	372	356	340			
8	400	383	367	350	344	318	301		
9	378	361	345	329	312	296	279	263	
10	356	340	323	307	290	274	258	241	225
11	334	318	301	285	269	252	236	219	203
12	312	296	279	263	247	230	214	197	181
13	270	253	236	220	204	188	171	155	138
14	227	211	194	178	161	145	129	112	96
15	184	168	152	135	119	102	86	69	53
16	142	125	109	92	76	60	43	27	10
17	99	83	66	50	33	17			
18	56	40	24						

16Mbps Allowable Drive Distances in Feet (type 1 or type 2 Cable) with Converters

Number of Wiring Closets

Number of 8228s	1	2	3	4	5	6	7	8	9	10
1	569									
2	547	530								
3	525	509	492							
4	503	487	471	454						
5	482	465	449	432	416					
6	460	443	427	411	394	378				
7	438	422	405	389	372	356	340			
8	416	400	383	367	350	344	318	301		
9	394	378	361	345	329	312	296	279	263	
10	372	356	340	323	307	290	274	258	241	225
11	351	334	318	301	285	269	252	236	219	203
12	329	312	296	279	263	247	230	214	197	181
13	253	270	253	236	220	204	188	171	155	138
14	211	227	211	194	178	161	145	129	112	96
15	168	184	168	152	135	119	102	86	69	53
16	125	142	125	109	92	76	60	43	27	10
17	83	99	83	66	50	33	17			
18	40	56	40	24						

16Mbps Allowable Drive Distances in Feet (type 9 Cable) without Converters

Number of Wiring Closets (columns); Number of 8228s (rows)

Number of 8228s	2	3	4	5	6	7	8	9	10
2	354								
3	339	328							
4	325	314	303						
5	310	299	288	277					
6	296	285	274	263	252				
7	281	270	259	248	237	226			
8	266	255	244	233	222	211	200		
9	252	241	230	219	208	197	186	175	
10	237	226	215	204	193	182	171	160	149
11	223	212	201	190	179	168	157	146	135
12	208	197	186	175	164	153	142	131	120
13	180	169	158	147	136	125	114	103	92
14	151	140	129	118	107	96	85	74	63
15	123	112	101	90	79	68	57	46	35
16	94	84	73	52	51	40	29	18	7
17	66	55	44	33	22	11			
18	38	27	16						

16Mbps Allowable Drive Distances in Feet (type 9 Cable) with Converters

Number of Wiring Closets

Number of 8228s	1	2	3	4	5	6	7	8	9	10
1	379									
2	365	354								
3	350	339	328							
4	336	325	314	303						
5	321	310	299	288	277					
6	306	296	285	274	263	252				
7	292	281	270	259	248	237	226			
8	277	266	255	244	233	222	211	200		
9	263	252	241	230	219	208	197	186	175	
10	248	237	226	215	204	193	182	171	160	149
11	234	223	212	201	190	179	168	157	146	135
12	219	208	197	186	175	164	153	142	131	120
13	169	180	169	158	147	136	125	114	103	92
14	140	151	140	129	118	107	96	85	74	63
15	112	122	112	101	90	79	68	57	46	35
16	84	94	84	73	62	51	40	29	18	7
17	55	66	55	44	33	22	11			
18	27	38	27	16						

Appendix

H

LAN Network Manager Commands Supported by NetView

ADAPTER COMMANDS

OBJECT	ACTION	PARAMETERS	
ADP	ADD	NAME=<ADAPTER NAME>	ADDR=<ADAPTER ADDR>
ADP	DELETE	ADP=<ADAPTER>	CONFIRM=Y|N
ADP	QUERY	ADP=<ADAPTER>	SEG=<SEGMENT NUMBER>
ADP	LIST		
ADP	REMOVE	ADP=<ADAPTER>	SEG=<SEGMENT NUMBER> CONFIRM=Y|N
ADP	SET	ADP=<ADAPTER>	MONITOR=Y|N
ADP	SET	ADP=<ADAPTER>	TRACE=Y|N
ADP	SET	ADP=<ADAPTER>	PLUG=<WALL PLUG NUMBER>
ADP	SET	ADP=<ADAPTER>	IAU=<IAU NUMBER>
ADP	SET	ADP=<ADAPTER>	LOBE=<LOBE NUMBER>
ADP	SET	ADP=<ADAPTER>	MOD=<LOBE ATTACHMENT MODULE>
ADP	SET	ADP=<ADAPTER>	TIME=<TIME AUTHORIZED>
ADP	SET	ADP=<ADAPTER>	DAY=<DAY AUTHORIZED>
ADP	SET	ADP=<ADAPTER>	LOCATION=<ADAPTER LOCATION>
ADP	SET	ADP=<ADAPTER>	USERDATA=<USER DATA>
ADP	SET	ADP=<ADAPTER>	COMMENT=<COMMENT>
ADP	REG	ADP=<ADAPTER>	CONFIRM=Y|N
ADP	DEREG	ADP=<ADAPTER>	CONFIRM=Y|N

<table>
<tr><th colspan="4">BRIDGE COMMANDS</th></tr>
<tr><th>OBJECT</th><th>ACTION</th><th>PARAMETERS</th><th></th></tr>
<tr><td>BRG</td><td>ADD</td><td>NAME=<BRIDGE NAME></td><td>ADP1<ADAPTER> ADP2<ADAPTER> AUTOLINK=Y|N</td></tr>
<tr><td>BRG</td><td>DELETE</td><td>NAME=<BRIDGE NAME></td><td>CONFIRM=Y|N</td></tr>
<tr><td>BRG</td><td>LINK</td><td>NAME=<BRIDGE NAME></td><td>AUTOLINK=Y|N</td></tr>
<tr><td>BRG</td><td>LIST</td><td></td><td></td></tr>
<tr><td>BRG</td><td>QUERY</td><td>NAME=<BRIDGE NAME></td><td></td></tr>
<tr><td>BRG</td><td>SET</td><td>NAME=<BRIDGE NAME></td><td>BDGNUM<BRIDGE NUMBER> CONFIRM=Y|N</td></tr>
<tr><td>BRG</td><td>SET</td><td>NAME=<BRIDGE NAME></td><td>AUTOLINK=Y|N CONFIRM=Y|N</td></tr>
<tr><td>BRG</td><td>SET</td><td>NAME=<BRIDGE NAME></td><td>FORWARD=Y|N</td></tr>
<tr><td>BRG</td><td>SET</td><td>NAME=<BRIDGE NAME></td><td>INTERVAL=<PERFORMANCE INTER-VAL >CONFIRM=Y|N</td></tr>
<tr><td>BRG</td><td>SET</td><td>NAME=<BRIDGE NAME></td><td>LOSTHRES=<LOST THRESHOLD> CONFIRM=Y|N</td></tr>
<tr><td>BRG</td><td>SET</td><td>NAME=<BRIDGE NAME></td><td>SCOPE=SEG1|SEG2 SEG=<SEGMENT NUMBER ADP=<ADAPTER> CONFIRM=Y|N</td></tr>
<tr><td>BRG</td><td>SET</td><td>NAME=<BRIDGE NAME></td><td>SCOPE=HOP1|HOP2 HOPCNT=<HOP COUNT ADP=<ADAPTER>CONFIRM=Y|N</td></tr>
<tr><td>BRG</td><td>SET</td><td>NAME=<BRIDGE NAME></td><td>SCOPE=SGL1|SGL2 SGLROUTE=Y|N ADP=<ADAPTER> CONFIRM=Y|N</td></tr>
<tr><td>BRG</td><td>SET</td><td>NAME=<BRIDGE NAME></td><td>SGLMODE=A|M CONFIRM=Y|N</td></tr>
<tr><td>BRG</td><td>SET</td><td>NAME=<BRIDGE NAME></td><td>LNKPASS0=<REPORT LINK PASSWORD 0> CONFIRM=Y|N</td></tr>
<tr><td>BRG</td><td>SET</td><td>NAME=<BRIDGE NAME></td><td>LNKPASS1=<REPORT LINK PASSWORD 1> CONFIRM=Y|N</td></tr>
<tr><td>BRG</td><td>SET</td><td>NAME=<BRIDGE NAME></td><td>LNKPASS2=<REPORT LINK PASSWORD 2> CONFIRM=Y|N</td></tr>
<tr><td>BRG</td><td>SET</td><td>NAME=<BRIDGE NAME></td><td>LNKPASS3=<REPORT LINK PASSWORD 3> CONFIRM=Y|N</td></tr>
<tr><td>BRG</td><td>SET</td><td>NAME=<BRIDGE NAME></td><td>COMMENT=<COMMENT></td></tr>
<tr><td>BRG</td><td>UNLINK</td><td>NAME=<BRIDGE NAME></td><td>AUTOLINK=Y|N</td></tr>
</table>

<table>
<tr><th colspan="4">CAU COMMANDS</th></tr>
<tr><th>OBJECT</th><th>ACTION</th><th>PARAMETER</th><th></th></tr>
<tr><td>CAU</td><td>LIST</td><td>UNIT=<ACCESS UNIT></td><td></td></tr>
<tr><td>CAU</td><td>QUERY</td><td>UNIT=<ACCESS UNIT></td><td>ATTR=WRAP</td></tr>
<tr><td>CAU</td><td>QUERY</td><td>UNIT=<ACCESS UNIT></td><td>MOD=<MODULE NUMBER></td></tr>
<tr><td>CAU</td><td>RESTART</td><td>UNIT=<ACCESS UNIT></td><td>CONFIRM=Y|N</td></tr>
<tr><td>CAU</td><td>SET</td><td>UNIT=<ACCESS UNIT></td><td>WRAP=M|WRI|WRO|WRIRO CONFIRM=Y|N</td></tr>
<tr><td>CAU</td><td>SET</td><td>UNIT=<ACCESS UNIT></td><td>MOD=<MODULE NUMBER> STATUS=ACT|INACT CONFIRM=Y|N</td></tr>
<tr><td>CAU</td><td>SET</td><td>UNIT=<ACCESS UNIT></td><td>MOD=<MODULE NUMBER> LOBE=<LOBE NUMBER> STATUS=ACT|INACT CONFIRM=Y|N</td></tr>
<tr><td>CAU</td><td>SET</td><td>UNIT=<ACCESS UNIT></td><td>FILE=<FILE NAME> ADP=<ADAPTER> CONFIRM=Y|N</td></tr>
<tr><td>CAU</td><td>DELETE</td><td>UNIT=<ACCESS UNIT></td><td>CONFIRM=Y|N</td></tr>
</table>

EVENT CAU COMMANDS

OBJECT	ACTION	PARAMETERS
EVT	DELETE	CONFIRM=Y|N
EVT	LIST	SDATE=<START DATE> EDATE=<END DATE> STIME=<START TIME> ETIME=<END TIME> MSGID=<MESSAGE NUMBER> SEG=<SEGMENT NUMBER> BRG=<BRIDGE NAME> CAU=<CAU NUMBER> ADP=<ADAPTER>
EVT	QUERY	DATE=<DATE> TIME=<TIME> MSGID=<MESSAGE NUMBER>

HELP COMMANDS

OBJECT	ACTION	PARAMETERS
CMD	HELP	TEXT=<COMMAND>
MSG	HELP	MSGID=<MESSAGE NUMBER>
ITEM	UMDK2	DOCUMENT ID Q568562

LOGGING COMMANDS

OBJECT	ACTION	PARAMETERS
CFGLOG	QUERY	
CFGLOG	SET	SCOPE=ALL|NONE
CFGLOG	SET	SEG=<SEGMENT NUMBER>
SOFTLOG	QUERY	
SOFTLOG	SET	SEG=<SEGMENT NUMBER> SCOPE=ALL|NONE|RESET|LIMITED

NETWORK COMMANDS

OBJECT	ACTION	PARAMETERS
LANMGR	RESTART	CONFIRM=Y|N
CFG	LIST	SEG=<SEGMENT NUMBER>
SEG	STATUS	SEG=<SEGMENT NUMBER>
SEG	TEST	SEG=<SEGMENT NUMBER>

<table>
<tr><th>OBJECT</th><th>ACTION</th><th>PARAMETERS</th></tr>
<tr><td>LANMGR</td><td>RESTART</td><td>CONFIRM=Y|N</td></tr>
<tr><td>CFG</td><td>LIST</td><td>SEG=<SEGMENT NUMBER></td></tr>
<tr><td>SEG</td><td>STATUS</td><td>SEG=<SEGMENT NUMBER></td></tr>
<tr><td>SEG</td><td>TEST</td><td>SEG=<SEGMENT NUMBER></td></tr>
<tr><td>ALTFLTR</td><td>ADD</td><td>ID=<ALERT ID>
ETYPE=PERF|TEMP|IMPN|PERM|UNKN
NAME=<RESOURCE NAME>
ACTION=B|P</td></tr>
<tr><td>ALTFLTR</td><td>ADD</td><td>PROGRAM=<PROGRAM NAME> ROUTINE=<ROUTINE NAME>
PGMSTATUS=ACT|INACT</td></tr>
<tr><td>ALTFLTR</td><td>DELETE</td><td>ID=<ALERT"ID>
ETYPE=PERF|TEMP|IMPN|PERM|UNKN
NAME=<RESOURCE"I ".NAME>
CONFIRM=Y|N</td></tr>
<tr><td>SYSP</td><td>QUERY</td><td>ATTR=ADP|BRG|HOST|MIS|ALTFLTR|CAU</td></tr>
<tr><td>SYSP</td><td>SET</td><td>ADPTNUM=0|1</td></tr>
<tr><td>SYSP</td><td>SET</td><td>DLCLINK=<NUMBER OF LINKS></td></tr>
<tr><td>SYSP</td><td>SET</td><td>RPTLINK=C|01|02|03</td></tr>
<tr><td>SYSP</td><td>SET</td><td>AUTOLINK=ACT|INACT</td></tr>
<tr><td>SYSP</td><td>SET</td><td>BRGPASSWORD=<PASSWORD></td></tr>
<tr><td>SYSP</td><td>SET</td><td>MAXPERF=<MAXIMUM RECORDS IN BRIDGE PERFORMANCE TABLE></td></tr>
<tr><td>SYSP</td><td>SET</td><td>LANNAME=<LAN NAME></td></tr>
<tr><td>SYSP</td><td>SET</td><td>TRACE=ALL|NONE|DEFINED</td></tr>
<tr><td>SYSP</td><td>SET</td><td>MAXEV=<MAXIMUM NUMBER OF EVENTS></td></tr>
<tr><td>SYSP</td><td>SET</td><td>AGEOUT=<AGE OUT TIMER></td></tr>
<tr><td>SYSP</td><td>SET</td><td>RESYNC=<RESYN TIMER></td></tr>
<tr><td>SYSP</td><td>SET</td><td>MONITOR=ACT|INACT</td></tr>
<tr><td>SYSP</td><td>SET</td><td>MONADP=<ADAPTERS MONITORED IN ONE INTERVAL></td></tr>
<tr><td>SYSP</td><td>SET</td><td>MONRETRY=<RETRIES NUMBER BEFORE SENDING ALERT></td></tr>
<tr><td>SYSP</td><td>SET</td><td>LTIMEOUT=<LOCAL TIME OUT></td></tr>
<tr><td>SYSP</td><td>SET</td><td>RTIMEOUT=<REMOTE TIME OUT></td></tr>
<tr><td>SYSP</td><td>SET</td><td>AUTO=ACT|INACT</td></tr>
<tr><td>SYSP</td><td>SET</td><td>BEACTIME=<AUTO-RETRY ON BEACONING TIME INTERVAL></td></tr>
<tr><td>SYSP</td><td>SET</td><td>BEACRETRY=<AUTO-RETRY ON BEACONING NUMBER OF RETRIES></td></tr>
<tr><td>SYSP</td><td>SET</td><td>CAU=ACT|INACT</td></tr>
<tr><td>SYSP</td><td>SET</td><td>UNAUADP=R|A</td></tr>
<tr><td>SYSP</td><td>SET</td><td>UNAUTIME=R|A</td></tr>
<tr><td>SYSP</td><td>SET</td><td>ADPMOVE=R|A</td></tr>
<tr><td>SYSP</td><td>SET</td><td>UNAUBRG=R|A</td></tr>
<tr><td>SYSP</td><td>SET</td><td>REMOVE=F|L</td></tr>
<tr><td>SYSP</td><td>SET</td><td>CAUPASSWORD=<CAU PASSWORD></td></tr>
<tr><td>SYSP</td><td>SET</td><td>PGMSTATUS=ACT|INACT</td></tr>
<tr><td>SYSP</td><td>SET</td><td>PROGRAM=<PROGRAM NAME> ROUTINE=<ROUTINE NAME>
PGMSTATUS=ACT|INACT</td></tr>
<tr><td>SYSP</td><td>SET</td><td>COMMENT=<COMMENT></td></tr>
</table>

Appendix

I

IBM's Token-Ring Network Bridge Program Parameters

Local Bridge Function Installation Parameters		
Description	**Default Value**	**Valid range**
Locally Administered Address	**000000000000**	**400000000001-40007FFFFFFF**
Shared RAM Address	**0000**	**Primary Adapter RAM address=D800 Secondary Adapter RAM address=D400**
Early Token Release	**Y**	**Y or N**

Local Bridge Function Configuration Parameters		
Description	**Default Value**	**Valid Range**
Bridge Number	1	0-9, A-F
LAN segment number adapter 0	001	001-FFF
LAN segment number adapter 1	002	001-FFF
Frame forwarding active	Y	Y or N
Bridge Performance Threshold	10	0-9999
Restart on error	Y	Y or N
Drive for memory dump on error	0	0, A, B, C, D
Drive for error log	0	0, A, B, C, D
Hop count limit	7	1-7
Single-route broadcast (selection mode)	M (manual)	M (manual) A (automatic)
Single-route broadcast acitve (manual mode)	Y	Y or N
Automatic single-route broadcast: Bridge label Path cost	 8000 0000000	 0000-FFFF 00000000- FFFFFFFF
Parameter server	Y	Y or N
Error monitor	Y	Y or N
Configuration report server	Y	Y or N
Link password 0	00000000	
Link password 1	00000000	
Link password 2	00000000	

Remote Bridge Function Installation Parameters		
Description	**Default Value**	**Valid Range**
Locally Administered Address	000000000000	400000000001- 40007FFFFFFF
Shared RAM Address	0000	Adapter RAM address=D800
Early Token Release	Y	Y or N

Remote Bridge Function Configuration Parameters		
Description	**Default Value**	**Valid Range**
Bridge Number	1	0-9, A-F
LAN segment number (primary bridge half)	001	001-FFF
LAN segment number (secondary bridge half)	002	001-FFF
Frame forwarding active	Y	Y or N
Maximum frame size	0	0, 1, 2, 3
Bridge Performance Threshold	10	0-9999
Telecommunications link error threshold	0	0-9999
Restart on error	Y	Y or N
Drive for memory dump on error	0	0, A, B, C, D
Drive for error log	0	0, A, B, C, D
Hop count limit	7	1-7
Single-route broadcast (selection mode)	M (manual)	M (manual) A (automatic)
Single-route broadcast acitve (manual mode)	Y	Y or N
Automatic single-route broadcast: Bridge label Path cost	 8000 0000000	 0000-FFFF 00000000-FFFFFFFF
Parameter server	Y	Y or N
Error monitor	Y	Y or N
Configuration report server	Y	Y or N
Link password 0	00000000	
Link password 1	00000000	

Remote Bridge Function Communications Adapter Configuration Parameters		
Description	**Default Value**	**Valid Range**
Line data rate	None; user must provide value	9600-1344000
Electrical interface	None; user must provide value	1, 2, 3
Communications adpater transmit buffer size	0	0-65535
Bridge mode	0	1, 2

Appendix

J

Acronyms and Abbreviations

AC	**Access Control**
ANSI	**American National Standards Institute**
APPC	**Application Program-to-Program Communication**
APPN	**Advanced Peer-to-Peer Network**
ASCII	**American Standard Code for Information Interchange**
BNN	**Boundary Network Node**
bps	**bits per second**
Bps	**Bytes per second**
CATV	**Community Antenna TeleVision (Cable TV)**
CAU	**Controlled Access Unit**
CCITT	**Comite Consultatif International Telegraphique et Telephonique (International Telegraph and Telephone Consultative Committee)**
CF	**Control Field**
CIM	**Computer-Integrated Manufacturing**
CRC	**Cyclic Redundancy Check**

CSMA/CD	Carrier Sense Multiple Access with Collision Detection
CUT	Control Unit Terminal
dB	decibel
DFT	Distributed Function Terminal
DLC	Data Link Control
DSAP	Destination Service Access Point
DSPU	Downstream Physical Unit
DTE	Data Terminal Equipment
EBCDIC	Extended Binary Code Decimal Interchange Code
ED	Ending Delimiter
FC	Frame Control
FCS	Frame Check Sequence
FDDI	Fiber Distributed Data Interface
FS	Frame Status
ICS	IBM Cabling System
IEEE	Institute of Electrical and Electronic Engineers
INN	Intermediate Network Node
IML	Initial Microprogram Load
IPL	Initial Program Load
IO	Input/Output
IP	Internet Protocol
ISO	International Standards Organization
IWS	Intelligent Workstation
Kbps	Kilobits per second
KBps	Kilobytes per second
LAM	Lobe Attachment Module
LAN	Local Area Network
LED	Light Emitting Diode
LLC	Logical Link Control
LPDU	Logical Link Control Protocol Data Unit
LU	Logical Unit
MAC	Media Access Control
MAP	Manufacturing Automation Protocol
MB	Megabytes
Mbps	Megabits per second
MBps	Megabytes per second
MFI	Mainframe Interactive
MMS	Manufacturing Messaging Services
MVS	Multiple Virtual Storage
NADN	Nearest Active Downstream Neighbor
NAUN	Nearest Active Upstream Neighbor
NCP	Network Control Program
NFS	Network File System
NTRI	NCP Token-Ring Interface

OSI	Open Systems Interconnection
PBX	Private Branch Exchange
PC	Personal Computer
PDU	Protocol Data Unit
PHY	Physical Layer
PMD	Physical Medium Dependent
PU	Physical Unit
RAM	Random Access Memory
RF	Radio Frequency
RFC	Request For Comment
RH	Request/Response Header
RI	Routing Information
RR	Receive Ready
RU	Request/Reponse Unit
SA	Source Address
SAP	Service Access Point
SD	Starting Delimiter
SDLC	Synchronous Data Link Control
SMT	Station Management
SSAP	Source Service Access Point
TCP	Transmission Control Protocol
TH	Transmission Header
TIC	Token-Ring Interface Coupler
TR	Token-Ring
TRA	Token-Ring Adapter
TRM	Token-Ring Multiplexor
TRSS	Token-Ring Subsystem
XID	Exchange Identifier

Glossary

access control byte The byte following the start delimiter of a token or frame that is used to control access to the token-ring network.

access priority The maximum priority that a token can have for the adapter to use it for transmission.

access unit A unit that allows multiple attaching devices access to a token-ring network at a central point. Some times these devices may also be referred to as a concentrator.

acknowledgment In data communications, the transmission of characters from the receiving device indicating that data sent has been received correctly.

active (1) Operational. (2) Pertaining to a file, page, or program that is in main storage or memory, as opposed to a file, page, or program that must be retrieved from auxiliary storage. (3) Pertaining to a node or device that is connected or is available for connection to another node or device.

active monitor A function in a single adapter on a token-ring network that initiates the transmission of tokens and provides token error recovery facilities. Any active adapter on the ring has the ability to provide the active monitor function if the current active monitor fails.

active program Any program that is loaded into memory and ready to be executed.

active session The session in which a user is currently interacting with the computer.

adapter address Twelve hexadecimal digits that identify a LAN adapter.

adaptive routing A method of routing packets of data or data messages in which the system's intelligence selects the best path. This path might change with traffic patterns or link failures.

adaptive session-level pacing A form of session-level pacing in which session components exchange pacing windows that may vary in size during the course of a session. This allows transmission within a network to adapt dynamically to variations in availability and demand of buffers on a session-by-session basis. Session-level pacing occurs within independent stages along the session path according to local congestion at the intermediate nodes.

address (1) A character or group of characters that identify data source or destination or a network node. (2) The destination of a message sent through a communications system. In computer network terms, it is a set of numbers that uniquely identify a workstation on a LAN.

adjacent In a network, pertaining to devices, nodes, or domains that are directly connected by a data link or that share common control.

adjacent link station A link station directly connected to a given node by a link connection over which network traffic can be carried.

adjusted ring length (ARL) In a multiple-wiring-closet ring, the sum of all wiring closet-to-wiring closet cables in the main ring path less the length of the shortest of those cables.

Advanced Peer-to-Peer Networking (APPN) An extension to SNA featuring (a) greater distributed network control that avoids critical hierarchical dependencies, thereby isolating the effects of single points of failure; (b) dynamic exchange of network topology information to foster ease of connections and reconfiguration, adaptive route selection, and simplified network definition; (c) automated resource registration and directory lookup. APPN extends the LU 6.2 peer orientation for end-user services to network control; APPN also uses LU 6.2 protocols on its own control point sessions that provide the network control.

Advanced Program-to-Program Communication (APPC) (1) The general facility characterizing the LU 6.2 architecture and its various implementations in products. (2) Sometimes used to refer to the LU 6.2 architecture and its product implementation as a whole, or an LU 6.2 product feature in particular, such as an APPC application program interface.

alert A message sent to a management services focal point in a network to identify a problem or an impending problem.

algorithm A prescribed finite set of well defined rules or processes for the solution of a problem in a finite number of steps. In normal English, it is the mathematical formula for an operation, such as computing the check digits on packets of data that travel via packet switched networks.

all-routes broadcast frame A frame that has bits in the routine information field set to indicates the frame is to be sent to all LAN segments in the network. The destination address is not examined and plays no role in bridge routing.

all-stations broadcast frame A frame whose destination address bits are set to all ones. All stations on any LAN segment on which the frame appears will copy it. It is independent of all-routes broadcasting.

application A program or set of programs that perform a task.

application program interface (API) The formally defined programming language interface that allows a programmer to write to the interface.

application transaction program A program written for or by a user to process the user's application; in an SNA network, an end user of a type 6.2 logical unit.

applications layer The seventh and highest layer of Systems Network Architecture (SNA) and Open Systems Interconnection (OSI). It supplies functions to applications or nodes allowing them to communicate with other applications or nodes.

APPN end node A type 2.1 end node that provides full SNA end-user services and supports sessions between its local control point (CP) and the CP in an adjacent network node, to dynamically register its resources with the adjacent CP (its network node server), to send and receive directory search requests, and to obtain management services; it can also attach to a subarea network as a peripheral node.

APPN intermediate routing The capability of an APPN network node to accept traffic from one adjacent node and pass it on to another, with awareness of session affinities in controlling traffic flow and outage notifications.

APPN intermediate routing network The portion of an

APPN network consisting of the network nodes and their connections.

APPN network A type 2.1 network having at least one APPN node.

APPN network node A type 2.1 (T2.1) node that, besides offering full SNA end-user services, provides intermediate routing services within a T2.1 network, and network services to its local LUs and attached T2.1 end nodes in its domain; it can also attach to a subarea network as a peripheral node.

APPN node An APPN network node or an APPN end node.

asynchronous transmission A method of data transmission which allows characters to be sent at irregular intervals by preceding each character with a start bit, and following it with a stop bit. No clocking signal is provided. This is in contrast to synchronous transmission.

attenuation A decrease in magnitude of current, voltage, or electrical or optical power of a signal in transmission between points. It may expressed in decibels or nepers.

back-up server A program or device that copies files so at least two up-to-date copies always exist.

backbone A LAN, a WAN, or a combination of both dedicated to providing connectivity between subnetworks in an enterprise-wide network. Subnetworks are connected to the backbone via bridges and/or routers and the backbone serves as a communications highway for LAN-to-LAN traffic.

backbone LAN segment In a multisegment LAN configuration, a centrally located LAN segment to which other LAN segments are connected by means of bridges or routers.

backup path In an IBM Token Ring Network, an alternative path for signal flow through access units and their main ring path cabling.

balun Balanced/unbalanced. An impedance matching transformer. Baluns are small passive devices that convert the impedance of coaxial cable so that its signal can run on twisted-pair wiring. They are used often so that IBM 3270-type terminals, which traditionally require coaxial cable connection to their host computer can run on twisted pair.

bandwidth The range of electrical frequencies a device can handle.

beacon A token-ring frame sent by an adapter indicating that it has detected a serious ring problem, such as a broken cable or a multistation access unit. An adapter sending these frames is said to be beaconing.

bisynchronous transmission Also called BISYNC. A data character-oriented communications protocol developed by IBM for synchronous transmission of binary-coded data between two devices.

bit Abbreviation for binary digit. The smallest unit of information (data) and the basic unit in data communications. A bit can have a value of 0 or 1.

bit rate The number of bits of data transmitted over a communications line each second.

BNC. A bayonet-locking connector for slim coaxial cables.

bps (bits per second) A measurement of data transmission speeds.

bridge (1) An interface connecting two similar local area networks. (2) A device that connects two local area networks. It performs its functions at the data link control (DLC) layer.

bridge ID The bridge label combined with the adapter address of the adapter connecting the bridge to the LAN segment with the lowest LAN segment number.

bridge label A two-byte hexadecimal number that the user can assign to each bridge.

bridge number The bridge identifier that the user specifies in the bridge program configuration file. The bridge number distinguishes between parallel bridges.

broadcast The simultaneous transmission of data to more than one destination.

broadcast message A message from one station sent to all other users. On a token- ring LAN, the destination address is unspecified, thus all devices receive the message.

brouter In local area networking a device that combines the dynamic routing capabilities of an internetwork router with the ability of a bridge to interconnect local area networks.

BSC (Binary Synchronous Communication) A set of IBM operating procedures for synchronous transmission used in teleprocessing networks.

buffer In data transmission, a buffer is a temporary storage location for information being sent or received. Usually located between two different devices that have different abilities or speeds for handling the data.

bus A network configuration in which nodes are interconnected through a bi-directional transmission medium.

byte A binary character operated upon as a unit and usually shorter than a computer word. It is eight consecutive bits representing a character.

cable loss The amount of radio frequency signal attenuation caused by a cable.

cable riser Cable running vertically in a multi-story building to serve the upper floors.

campus A networking environment in which users — voice, video and data — are spread out over a broad geographic area, as in a university, hospital, medical center, etc. There may be several LANs on a campus. They will be connected with bridges and/or routers communicating over telephone or fiber-optic cable.

carrier A wave or pulse train that may be varied by a signal bearing information to be transmitted over a communication system.

class of service (COS) A designation of the transport network characteristics, such as route security, transmission priority, and bandwidth, needed for a particular session. The class of service is derived from a mode name specified by the initiator of a session.

CMIP (Common Management Information Protocol) A protocol formally adapted by the International Standards Organization used for exchanging network management information over OSI. Typically, this information is exchanged between two management stations. It can be used to exchange information between an application and a management station. Though designed for OSI networks, it is transport independent. Theoretically, it can run across a variety of transports, including IBM's SNA.

CMOT (CMIP over TCP/IP) The use of CMIP over a TCP/IP based transport.

coaxial cable A cable composed of an insulated central conducting wire wrapped in another cylindrical conducting wire. The whole thing is usually wrapped in another insulating layer and an outer protective layer. A coaxial cable has great capacity to carry great quantities of information. It is typically used to carry high-speed data and in cable TV.

communication The transmission and reception of data.

communication adapter A circuit card with associated software that enables a processor, controller, or other device to be connected to a network.

communications line The physical link (such as wire or a telephone circuit) that connects one or more workstations to a communications control unit or that connects one control unit to another.

Communications Manager A component of OS/2 Extended Edition that lets a workstation connect to a host computer and use the host resources as well as the resources of other personal computers to which the workstation is attached, either directly or through a host.

communication network management (CNM) The process of designing, installing, operating and managing distribution of information and control among user of communication systems.

communications port (1) An access point for data entry or exit to or from a communication device such as a terminal. (2) On a personal computer or workstation, a synchronous or asynchronous serial port to which a modem can be attached.

composite end node To a type 2.1 node, a group of nodes that appears to be a single end node.

concurrent Pertaining to the occurrence of two or more activities within a given interval of time.

CONFIG.SYS A file that contains configuration options for and OS/2 program or DOS program installed on a workstation or personal computer. It defines the devices, system parameters and resource options of a workstation or personal computer.

connectionless service A networking node in which individual data packets in a local area network traveling from one point to another are directed from one intermediate node to the next until they reach their ultimate destination. The receipt of a transmission is typically acknowledged from the ultimate destination to the point of origin.

control point (CP) A component of a node that manages resources of that node and optionally provides services to other nodes in the network.

control vector One of a general class of RU substructures that has variable length, is carried within some enclosing structure, and has a one-byte key used as an identifier.

controller A unit that controls input/output operations for one or more devices.

conversation A logical connection between two transaction programs using an IBM LU 6.2 session.

corporate network May also be called an internetwork or a wide-area network or enterprise network. A network of networks that connects most or all of a corporation's local area networks. Connections between networks and LANs are made with bridges and routers.

CRC (Cyclic Redundancy Check) A process used to check the integrity of a block of data.

data circuit-terminating equipment (DCE) The equipment installed at the user's premises that provides all the functions required to establish, maintain, and terminate a connection for data transmission, and the signal conversion and coding between the data terminal equipment device and the line.

data communication The transmission and reception of data.

data link A physical link, like a wire, that connects one or more devices or communication controllers.

data link control (DLC) (1) The physical means of connecting one location to another for the purpose of transmitting and receiving data. (2) In SNA, the second layer of the seven-layer architecture. (3) In OSI, the second layer of the seven-layer architecture.

datastream (1) All data transmitted through a data channel in a single read or write operation. (2) A continuous stream of data elements being transmitted, or intended for transmission, in character or binary-digit form, using a defined format.

dependent logical unit (DLU) An LU controlled by an SNA host system.

destination In a network, any point or location, for example, a node, a station, or a terminal, to which data is to be sent.

destination address That part of a message which indicates for whom the message is intended. Synonymous with the address on an envelope. IBM Token-Ring Network addresses are 48-bits in length.

device (1) An input/output unit such as a terminal, display, or printer. (2) In computers it may be used for direct access storage (e.g., hard disk).

differential Manchester encoding A transmission encoding scheme in which each bit is encoded as a two-segment signal with a signal transition (polarity change) at either the bit time or half-bit time. Transition at a bit time represents a 0. No transition at a bit time indicates a 1.

diskless workstation A workstation without a hard disk or diskette drive.

distributed processing A network of computers such that the processing of information is initiated in local computers, and the resultant data is sent to a central computer for further processing with the data from other local systems. A LAN is an example of distributed processing.

domain In IBM's SNA, a host-based systems services control point (SSCP), the physical units (PUs), logical units (LUs), links, link stations and all the affiliated resources that the host (SSCP) controls.

downloading The act of receiving data from one computer into another.

downstream physical unit (DSPU) A controller or a workstation downstream from a gateway that is attached to a host.

early token release This is a method of token passing which allows for two tokens to exist on the network simultaneously. It is used on 16Mbps token-ring networks.

end user The ultimate source or destination of application data flowing through a network. An end user can be an application program or a human operator.

end-node domain An end-node control point, its attached

links, and its local LUs.

error rate In data transmission, the ratio of the number of incorrect elements transmitted to the total number of elements transmitted.

file A set of related records treated as a unit.

file server A device which serves as a central location for commonly used files by everyone on a LAN.

frame check sequence In a token ring LAN, a 32-bit field which follows the data field in every token ring frame.

frame A group of bits sent serially (one after another). It is a logical transmission unit.

front end processor Off loads line control, message handling, code conversion, error control and routing of data from the host computer. IBM's 3725, 3745 are examples of front end processors. Also known as a communication controller.

functional address In IBM network adapters, this is a special kind of group address in which the address is bit significant, each "on" bit representing a function performed by the station (e.g., active monitor, ring-error monitor, LAN error monitor or configuration report server).

gateway A functional unit that connects two different computer network architectures.

gateway function (1) A capability of a subarea node to provide protocol support to connect two or more subarea networks. (2) The component that provides this capability.

group address In a LAN, a locally administered address assigned to two or more adapters to allow the adapters to copy the same frame.

group SAP A single address assigned to a group of service access points (SAPs).

half-session A session-layer component consisting of the combination of data flow control and transmission control components comprising one end of a session.

hard error An error condition on a network that requires the source of the error to be removed or that the network be reconfigure before the network can resume reliable operation.

header The portion of a message that contains control information for the message. Usually find at the beginning of a frame.

hertz (Hz) A unit of frequency equal to one cycle per second.

hexadecimal A numbering base where 4 bits are used to represent each digit. The digits can have one of 16 values, 0, 1, 2,..., 9, A, B, C, D, E, F.

hierarchical network A multisegment network configuration providing only one path through intermediate segments between source segments and destination segments.

hop In token-ring networking, the connection between ring segments. The connection is usually made using bridges.

hop count The number of ring segments spanned to establish a session between two workstations. In IBM token-ring networks the maximum is seven.

host node (1) A node at which a host computer is situated. (2) In SNA, a subarea node that contains an SSCP.

host system (1) A data processing system that is used to prepare programs and the operating environments for use on another computer or controller. (2) The data processing system to which a network is connected and with which the system can communicate.

IEEE 802 IEEE committee on local area networks.

IEEE 802.1 IEEE standard for overall architecture of LANs and inter networking.

IEEE 802.2 IEEE data link control layer standard used with IEEE 802.3, 802.4, 802.5.

IEEE 802.3 IEEE carrier-sense multiple access with collision detection (CSMA/CD). A physical layer standard specifying a LAN with a CSMA/CD access method on a bus topology. Ethernet and Starlan both follow subsets of the 802.3 standard. Typically they transmit at 10Mbps.

IEEE 802.4 IEEE physical layer standard specifying a LAN with a token-passing access method on a bus topology. Used with Manufacturing Automation Protocol (MAP) LANs. Typical transmission speed is 10Mbps.

IEEE 802.5 IEEE physical layer standard specifying a LAN with a token-passing access method on a ring topology. Used by IBM's Token-Ring Network. Typical transmission rates are

4Mbps and 16Mbps.

impedance The combined effect of resistance, inductance, and capacitance on a signal at a particular frequency.

independent logical unit (ILU) In SNA, a logical unit that does not require assistance from an SSCP to establish and LU-LU session.

Institute of Electrical and Electronic Engineers (IEEE) A publishing and standards-making body responsible for many standards used in LANs.

International Standards Organization (ISO) An international standards-making body for creating internationally accepted standards. One such standard is Open Systems Interconnection (OSI).

jitter Undesirable variation in the arrival time of a transmitted digital signal.

LAN adapter A circuit board installed in workstations that connects the workstation with the LAN media.

layer In networking architectures, a collection of network processing functions that together comprise a set of rules and standards for successful data communication.

leased line A dedicated communications link usually owned by a telecommunications provider that charges for the use of the line.

lobe A term used to describe the connection from a workstation to a token ring concentrator such as a multistation access unit.

local area network (LAN) A network of two or more computing units connected to share resources over moderate sized geographic area such as an office, a building or campus.

locally administered address (LAA) An adapter address that the user can assign to override the universally administered address (UAA).

logical connection In a network, devices that can communicate or work with one another because they share the same protocol.

logical link The conceptual joining of two nodes for direct communications. Several logical links may be able to utilize the same physical hardware.

logical link control (LLC) A protocol developed by the IEEE 802 committee, common to all of its LAN standards, for data link-level transmission control; the upper sublayer of the IEEE Layer 2 (OSI) protocol that complements the media access control protocol; IEEE standard 802.2.

logical link control protocol (LLC protocol) In a local area network, the protocol that governs the exchange of frames between data stations independently of how the transmission medium is shared.

logical unit (LU) An access port for users to gain access to the services of a network.

LU-LU session In SNA, a session between two logical units in an SNA network. It provides communication between two end users, or between an end user and an LU services component.

MAC frame Frames used to carry information to maintain the ring protocol and for exchange of management information.

MAC protocol The LAN protocol sublayer of data link control (DLC) protocol that includes functions for adapter address recognition, copying of message units from the physical network, and message unit format recognition, error detection, and routing within the processor.

medium access control (MAC) A media-specific access control protocol within IEEE 802 specifications. The physical address of a station is often called the MAC address.

mesh network. A multisegment network configuration providing more than one path through intermediate LAN segments between source and destination LAN segments.

mips Million instructions per second. A measure of computer speed.

modem (modulate/demodulator) A device that converts digital data from a computer to an analog signal that can be transmitted on a telecommunication line and converts the received analog signal to digital data for the computer.

multiple-domain network In SNA, a network with more than one SSCP. In APPN, a network with more than one network node.

NAU In SNA, network addressable unit. In APPN, network

accessible unit.

NetBIOS (Network Basic Input/Output System) Provides an interface to allow programs to operate the token-ring adapter in a personal computer or workstation.

NetView An IBM communication network management product.

network addressable unit (NAU) It is the origin or destination of data transmitted by the path control layer. Synonymous with network accessible unit.

network A group of nodes and the links interconnecting them.

network management The conceptual control element of a station that interfaces with all of the architectural layers of that station and is responsible for the resetting and setting of control parameters, obtaining reports of error conditions, and determining if the station should be connected to or disconnected from the network.

network management vector transport (NMVT) One of the SNA formats used for the transmission for communications and systems management data.

node A device connected into a network.

node type The classification of a network device based on the protocols it supports and the network addressable unit it can contain.

noise. A disturbance that affects a signal and that can distort the information carried by the signal.

non-broadcast frame A frame containing a specific destination address and that may contain routing information specifying which bridges are to forward it. A bridge will forward a non-broadcast frame only if that bridge is included in the frame's routing information.

Open Systems Interconnection (OSI) The only internationally accepted frame work for communication between two systems made by different vendors. It is a seven-layer architecture developed by ISO.

operating system A software program which manages the basic operating of a computer system.

pacing In data communications a technique by which receiving the receiving device controls the rate of transmission of a sending device to prevent overrun.

parallel bridge One of the two or more bridges that connect the same two LAN segments in a network.

physical unit (PU) The component that manages and monitors the resources of a node.

port A physical connection to the link hardware. May also be referred to as an adapter.

print server A computer or program providing LAN users with access to a centralized printer.

protocol The set of rules governing the operation of functional units of a communication system that must be followed if communication is to be achieved.

repeater A device inserted at intervals along a circuit to boost, and amplify a signal being transmitted.

ring error monitor (REM) A function that compiles error statistics reported by adapters on a network, analyzes the statistics to determine probable error cause, sends reports to network manager programs, and updates network status conditions. It assists in fault isolation and correction.

ring in (RI) The receive or input receptacle on an access unit or repeater.

ring out (RO) The transmit or output receptacle on an access unit or repeater.

route An ordered sequence between origin and destination stations that represent a path in a network between the stations.

router An intelligent device that connects two LAN segments which use similar or different architectures at the network layer.

segment In IBM Token-Ring Network, (1) A portion of a LAN that consists of cables, components or lobes up to a bridge. (2) An entire ring without bridges.

segment number The identifier that uniquely distinguishes a LAN segment in a multisegment LAN.

server A computer providing a service to LAN users. Services may be a shared file.

service access point (SAP) The point of access to services provided by the layers of a LAN architecture.

session A connection between two stations that allows them to communicate.

single-route broadcast The forwarding of specially designated broadcast frames only by bridges which have single-route broadcast enabled. If the network is configured correctly, a single-route broadcast frame will have exactly one copy delivered to every LAN segment in the network.

soft error An intermittent error on a network that causes data to be transmitted more than once to be received.

source routing A method used by a bridge for moving data between LAN segments. The routing information is embedded in the token.

source routing transparent (SRT) bridge A combination bridge utilizing IBM's source routing mechanism along with transparent routing mechanism.

station An input or output device that uses telecommunications facilities.

subarea A portion of an SNA network consisting of the subarea node and any attached resources to that node.

subarea address A value defined to identify the subarea node and is placed in the subarea address field of the network address.

subarea network The interconnection of subareas.

subarea node A node that used subarea addressing for routing.

switched line A telecommunications line in which the connection is established by dialing.

symbolic name A name that may be used instead of an adapter or bridge address to identify an adapter location.

synchronous data link control (SDLC) A bit-oriented synchronous communications protocol developed by IBM.

system services control point (SSCP) A function within IBM's VTAM that controls and manages an SNA network and its resources.

Systems Network Architecture (SNA) IBM's seven-layer

networking architecture.

T1 A digital transmission link with a capacity of 1.544 Mbps.

telephone twisted pair (TTP) One or more twisted pairs of copper wire in the unshielded voice-grade cable commonly used to connect a telephone to its wall jack. It is also known as unshielded twisted pair (UTP).

token A sequence of bits passed from one device to another on the token-ring network that signifies permission to transmit over the network. It consists of a starting delimiter, an access control field, and an end delimiter.

token passing In a token-ring network, the process by which a node captures a token, inserts a message, addresses the token and adds control information and then transmits the frame and then generates another token after the original token has made a complete circuit.

token ring A network with a ring topology that passes tokens form one attaching device to another.

token-ring interface coupler (TIC) The hardware interface for connecting front end processors and controllers to a token-ring network.

token-ring network A network that uses a ring topology in which tokens are passed in a sequence from one node to another.

topology The physical or logical arrangement of nodes in a computer network.

Transmission Control Protocol/Internet Protocol (TCP/IP) A set of protocols that allow cooperating computers to share resources across a heterogeneous network.

transmission group (TG) A single link or a group of links between adjacent nodes logically grouped together. In SNA these nodes are adjacent subarea nodes. In APPN, it is a single link.

transparent routing A method used by a bridge for moving data between two networks through learning the station addressees on each network.

twisted pair A transmission medium that consists of two insulated conductors twisted together to reduce noise.

type 2.0 (T2.0) node A node that attaches to a subarea

type 2.0 (T2.0) node A node that attaches to a subarea network as a peripheral node and provides full end-user services but no intermediate routing services.

type 2.1 (T2.1) node An SNA node that can be configured as an end point or intermediate routing node in a T2.1 network, or as a peripheral node attached to a subarea network. It may act as an end node, network node or intermediate node in an APPN network.

type 4 node An SNA subarea node that provides routing and data link control functions for a type 5 node. Type 5 nodes control type 4 nodes.

type 5 node An SNA subarea node that contains an SSCP and controls type 4 and type 2 SNA node types.

universally administered address (UAA) The address permanently encoded in an adapter at the rime of manufacture. All universally administered addresses are unique.

unnumbered acknowledgment (UA) A data link control command used in establishing a link and in answering receipt of logical link control frames.

unshielded twisted pair (UTP) See telephone twisted pair.

Virtual Telecommunications Access Method (VTAM) A set of programs that control communication between nodes and application programs in SNA.

wide area network (WAN) LAN segments bridged or routed using communication lines increasing the geographic size of the LAN.

workstation A terminal or computer attached to a network.

Bibliography

Suggested IBM Manuals

Local Area Network

GG24-3178	**IBM Local Area Network Concepts and Products**
SC30-3383	**IBM Local Area Network Technical Reference**
GG24-3398	**IBM Multisegment LAN Design Guidelines**
GG24-3338	**LAN Server Guide**
S33F-9428	**IBM OS/2 LAN Server V1.3 Network Administrator's Guide**
GG24-3506	**IBM OS/2 LAN Server V1.2 Planning and Installation Guide**

Token-Ring Network

SC30-3374	**IBM Token-Ring Network Architecture Reference**
GA27-3677	**IBM Token-Ring Network Introduction and Planning Guide**
GG24-3291	**IBM Installation Guide Lines for the Token-Ring Network Products**
31G6960	**IBM Token-Ring Network Bridge Program V2.2 User's Guide**
G3738	**IBM Education — Planning Complex Token-Ring Networks**
G3723	**IBM Education — Token-Ring Problem Isolation Workshop for Host Connection**

Network Services and Support

SC52-1110-00	**IBM SAA Networking Services/2 Installation and Network Administrator's Guide**
GG66-3120-00	**IBM 3172 Interconnect Controller Technical Overview/Installation Guide**
GA27-3867	**3172 Interconnect Controller Planning Guide**
SC30-3543	**3172 Interconnect Controller Program User's Guide Version 2.1**

SC23-0468	Using the IBM 3172 Operator Facility/2
SK2T-1995	Learning About NetView Operation
SC31-6053	NetView V2R2 7Operation
GG24-3569	VTAM V3R4 Planning Guide for New Functions
SC31-6434	VTAM Network Implementation Guide V3 R4 for MVS/ESA, VM/SP and VM/ESA
SC31-6438	VTAM V3R4 Resource Defintion Reference
SC30-3447	NCP, SSP and EP Resource Definition Guide
SC30-3448	NCP, SSP and EP Resource Definition Reference

Miscellaneous

0-07-051143-8	Ranade, J., Sackett, G., *Advanced SNA Networking: A Professional's Guide to VTAM / NCP*, McGraw-Hill, New York, 1991
0-07-051144-6	Ranade, J., Sackett, G., *Introduction to SNA Networking: A Guide to VTAM / NCP*, McGraw-Hill, New York, 1989
0-8306-3424-X	Hordeski, M., *Microcomputer LANs*, 2nd Edition, TAB Professional and Reference Books, Blue Ridge Summit, PA, 1990
0-07-046455-3	Naugle, M., *Local Area Networking*, McGraw-Hill, New York, 1991

Index

Access control function, 170–173
  control profile, 171, 173
  group access list, 171
  local administrator, 170
  network administrator, 170–171
  resource protection, 171
  universal access permissions, 171–173
  user, 170
  user access list, 171
Access priority, 65–66
Active monitor, 64
ADAPTER command, 149
Additional servers, 161
Address Filter Program, 210, 212–213
Addressing (*see* Token-ring addressing)
Advanced Peer-to-Peer Communication (APPC), 96
Affinity group, 94–95, 98, 111–112
Alerter service, 174–176
  alerter, 176
  alertnames, 174
  diskalert, 175
  erroralert, 174, 175
  logonalert, 175
  sizalertbuf, 176
Aliases, 163, 164
All-stations broadcast token-ring addressing, 51
Alternate routing, 100
API (Application Program Interface), 128
APPC (Advanced Peer-to-Peer Communication), 96
Application Program Interface (API), 128
Asset Management, 222
Automatic ring reconfiguration, 82, 83

Backbone ring configuration, 112, 115–117
Basic transmission unit (BTU), 28
Beaconing adapter, 197
BIA (burned-in address), 51, 101
BPDU (bridge protocol data units), 58–59
Bridge, 48, 52–60
  IEEE standards, 52–55, 59
  LAN Bridge, 86–87
  parallel routes, 59
  reinitialization, 197–198
  source routing, 52–55
  source routing transparent, 59–60
  spanning tree algorithm, 56–59
  token bridge, 91
  transparent, 55–56
  (*See also* Token-Ring Network Bridge Program)
BRIDGE command, 149–151
Bridge congestion, 114, 197
Bridge number, 52, 196
Bridge protocol data units (BPDU), 58–59
Brouter, 61
BTU (basic transmission unit), 28
BUILD, 258–259
Burned-in address (BIA), 51, 101
Bus LAN topology, 42, 44–45

Cable, 71–75
  coaxial, 70, 72
  comparison table, 72
  Multistation Access Unit and, 74, 77, 79
  optic fiber, 73–74, 110
  parallel pairs, 74
  patch, 75, 76, 79

Cable (*Cont.*):
- plenum, 72
- riser, 72–73
- telephone twisted pair, 73, 74
- twisted pair, 71–75
- types, 74

Cabling System, 69, 71, 74, 75
Carrier sense multiple access/collision detection (CSMA/CD), 10
CAU (*see* Controlled Access Unit)
Central server, 94
Central Site Control Facility (CSCF), 222, 255
Centralized backbone configuration, 108, 109
Channel-to-channel adapter (CTCA), 221
Channel-to-channel (CTC) Control Unit, 217, 219, 222
Client/server, 96
CLIST (Command Lists), 133
Cloud concept, 122–123
Cluster controller, 120
Clustered bridge distributed backbone configuration, 109
CMIP (Common Management Information Protocol), 147
CNM (Communications Network Management), 128, 129, 132
Coaxial cable, 70, 72
Collapsed backbone configuration, 106–108
Command Lists (CLIST), 133
Common Management Information Protocol (CMIP), 147
Common User Access (CUA), 142
Communication Manager, 278
Communications adapter transmit buffer size default values, 207
Communications Controller, 90–91, 100, 258, 259
- connectivity options, 91
- SNA gateway connectivity, 118–120
- support, 118, 119

Communications Manager, 187–189, 191, 224
Communications Network Management (CNM), 128, 129, 132
Components, 69–92
- Communications Controller, 90–91, 100, 118–120, 258, 259
- copper repeater, 76–78

Components (*Cont.*):
- Interconnect Controller, 88–89, 100, 118, 122–123
- LAN Bridge, 86–87
- LAN Channel Station, 87–88, 239, 241
- optical fiber converter, 80–81
- optical fiber repeater, 78–79
- SNA and, 89–91
- test connector, 79
- token bridge, 91
- token-ring media, 70–75
- (*See also* Controlled Access Unit; Establishment Controller; Multistation Access Unit; Token-Ring Network Bridge Program)

Controlled Access Unit (CAU), 47, 81–83, 102, 141, 146–147
- automatic recovery, 82, 83
- LAN design, 107, 110
- LAN Network Manager and, 144–15
- lobe attachment module, 81–82
- MAC address, 82–83
- optical fiber converter, 80–81
- primary-in adapter, 83
- primary-out adapter, 83
- ring-in port, 80–81
- ring-out port, 80–81
- secondary adapter, 83

Converter, 110
Copper repeater, 76–78
CRC (cyclic redundancy checking), 61–62
Cross-over patch cable, 75, 76, 79
CSCF (Central Site Control Facility), 222, 255
CSMA/CD (carrier sense multiple access/collision detection), 10
CTC (Channel-to-channel) Control Unit, 217, 219, 222
CTCA (channel-to-channel adapter), 221
Cyclic redundancy checking (CRC), 61–62

Data Channel Interlock (DCI), 219
Data-grade media (DGM) shielded twisted pair, 70–71
Datagram, 19
DCI (Data Channel Interlock), 219
Departmental ring segment, 112
Departmental server, 94
Designated bridge, 57, 58
Designated port, 57, 58
Destination service access point (DSAP), 19–20

DGM (data-grade media) shielded twisted pair, 70–71
Disk server, 95–96
Distributed backbone configuration, 108–110
Distribution panel, 69
DLR (*see* DOS LAN Requester)
Domain, 160, 161, 164, 165
Domain controller, 160–161
DOS LAN Requester (DLR), 159–160, 162, 166, 169, 184–186, 224
  hardware requirements, 184
  implementation from OS/2 LAN Server, 187, 192
  LAN Support Program, 185–186
  NETBIOS, 186, 189, 190, 210
  Remote Initial Program Load screen, 193
  software requirements, 184
DOS Remote Initial Program Load (RIPL), 162, 166, 173–174, 181
  DOS LAN Requester screen, 193
  implementation from OS/2 LAN Server, 187, 192–194
Downstream physical unit (DSPU), 90, 121–122
  mainframe connectivity, 262–263
    with Establishment Controller, 268, 273, 274
    with VTAM, 266–268
Drive distances, 77, 78, 301–313
DSAP (destination service access point), 19–20
DSPU (*see* Downstream physical unit)
Dual backbone configuration, 116–117
Dual backbone ring configuration, 109, 110, 119–120
Dual ring backup, 252–254
Dumb terminal, 100, 120
Duplex backbone configuration, 116, 117
Duplicate token-ring interface coupler, 263, 265–266

EC (*see* Establishment Controller)
ENA (extended network addressing), 12
Enterprise Systems Connection (ESCON), 217, 219–220
Establishment Controller (EC), 89–90, 100, 118, 120–122, 130
  mainframe connectivity, 268–278
    with downstream physical unit, 268, 273, 274
Establishment Controller (EC) (*Cont.*):
    local, 269–274, 278–280
    remote, 268, 275–278
    with VTAM, 274–275
Ethernet, 4, 87, 88, 123
Extended network addressing (ENA), 12
External communication adapter (XCA), 242–244
  network management support, 253–255
  SNA Node Type 2.0/2.1 definition, 244–247
  SNA Node Type 4 definition, 247–250
  SNA Node Type 5 definition, 250–251
External resources, 164, 165

FDDI (fiber distributed data interface), 4, 89
FDP (field-developed programs), 132
Fiber distributed data interface (FDDI), 4, 89
Field-developed programs (FDP), 132
File server, 95–96
Filtering database, 55–56
Filtering programs, 210–213
  Address Filter Program, 210, 212–213
  Link Limiting Filter Program, 210, 211
  NETBIOS Filter Program, 210–212
Frame, 28
Frame size, 204
Functional token-ring addressing, 51, 296

Gateway, 48, 100
  SNA gateway connectivity, 118–125, 278–281
  (*See also* Mainframe connectivity with gateways)
GMF (NetView Graphic Monitor Facility), 136–137
GROUP, 259–260, 262, 263
Group token-ring addressing, 50, 295
Guest account, 163

Hierarchical network, 2, 3
High availability, 98, 116, 120–122, 124

ICP (*see* Interconnect Control Program)
IEEE standards:
  bridge, 52–55, 59
  local area network, 4, 10, 14, 17, 18
  logical link control, 11, 18–27
  medium access control, 11, 18, 27–38
  Token-Ring Profile panel, 189, 190

Individual token-ring addressing, 50
Info/Master, 128
Information/Management, 128
INN (intermediate network node), 89
Input/Output Configuration Program (IOCP), 217–220
Institute of Electrical and Electronic Engineers Computer Society (*see* IEEE standards)
Interconnect Control Program (ICP), 221–235
  channel-attachments definition, 226–228
  computer definition, 224–226
  LAN Gateway function definition, 224, 230–233
  load, 235–239
    attached, 235, 237, 238
    initial, 235–236
    manual, 235
    stand-alone, 235–236
  Operator Facility/2, 221–224
  support, 222, 223
  Token-Ring Adapter definition, 228–231
  working diskettes creation, 233–235
Interconnect Controller, 88–89, 100, 118, 122–123
  configuration, 123, 124
  support, 121, 123
  (*See also* Mainframe connectivity with Interconnect Controller)
Intermediate network node (INN), 89
Internet protocol (IP) router, 52
IOCP (Input/Output Configuration Program), 217–220
IP (Internet protocol) router, 52
ISDN Terminal Adapter, 85
Isolated dual host-ring configuration, 119, 120

Jumper, 69

LAA (locally administered token-ring addressing), 50–51, 91, 118
LAM (lobe attachment module), 81–82
LAN (local area network), 1–10
  benefits, 8
  IEEE standards, 4, 10, 14, 17, 18
  LAN-to-WAN connectivity, 91
  NetView support, 134–135
  network, 2–3
LAN (local area network) (*Cont.*):
  private branch exchange comparison, 4–6
  wide area network and, 6–7
LAN Bridge, 86–87
LAN Channel Station (LCS), 87–88, 239, 241
LAN commands, 148–149
  ADAPTER, 149
  BRIDGE, 149–151
  QNETWORK, 150–151
  RESETLAN, 151
  SEGMENT, 152
LAN design, 105–125
  logical topology design, 105, 111–117
    multisegment LAN design, 112–117
    user segment, 111–112
  physical topology design, 105–110
    backbone design, 106–110
    multiple floor ring configuration, 105–106
  SNA gateway connectivity, 118–125
  (*See also* LAN planning)
LAN Gateway mainframe connectivity, 222, 268
  Interconnect Control Program function, 224, 230–233
  with Network Control Program, 257–266
    BUILD, 258–259
    downstream physical unit definition, 262–263
    duplicate token-ring interface coupler definition, 263, 265–266
    GROUP, 259–260, 262, 263
    LINE, 261–263
    NTRI PU, 261
    OPTIONS, 258–259
    token-ring subarea definition, 263, 264
LAN Manager, 141, 142
LAN Network Manager, 102–103, 128, 131, 133, 134, 141–146
  communication flow, 147
  Controlled Access Unit management, 144–145
  NetView connectivity, 143, 144, 315–318
  standards, 142–143
LAN planning, 8–10, 93–104
  affinity group, 94–95, 98, 111–112
  applications, 97

LAN planning (*Cont.*):
backbone ring design, 96, 98–99
backup, 96, 100–101
corporate objectives, 8, 9, 96, 103
design criteria, 93–94
end-user requirements, 8, 9, 97–99
future growth, 96, 103
high availability, 98, 116, 120–122, 124
information collection, 96–98
migrations, 96, 103
network management, 9, 10, 96, 102–103
network resource naming standards, 96, 101
performance, 97–98
physical requirements, 97
recovery, 96, 100–101
security, 9–10
server, 94–96
SNA connectivity, 96, 99–100
special functions, 9
systems management, 96, 103
traffic flow and control, 96, 102
workstations, 9
(*See also* LAN design)
LAN segment, 47–49, 196
LAN Services, 184
LAN Station Manager, 102–103, 141, 146–147
fields, 146
LAN Support Program, 169, 185–186
LAN topologies, 42–49
bus, 42, 44–45
mesh, 42–43
multisegment, 47–49
ring, 42, 45–47
star, 42–44
star-wired ring, 46–47, 69
tree, 45
LCS (LAN Channel Station), 87–88, 239, 241
LINE, 261–263
Link Limiting Filter Program, 210, 211
Link stations, 42
LLC (*see* Logical link control)
Lobe attachment module (LAM), 81–82
Local area network (*see* LAN)
Local bridge configuration, 195–201
Local server, 94
Locally administered token-ring addressing (LAA), 50–51, 91, 118
Logical link control (LLC), 11, 18–27, 195
acknowledged connectionless, 18–19
classes, 19
connection oriented, 18
connectionless operation, 18
protocol data unit, 19–27
Logical link control protocol data unit (LPDU), 19–27
control field, 21–27
information format, 21–23, 26–27
supervisory format, 21–23
unnumbered format, 21–26
destination service access point, 19–20
format, 21
source service access point, 20
Loop configuration, 112–114
LPDU (*see* Logical link control protocol data unit)
LU, 268

MAC (*see* Medium access control)
Mainframe connectivity with gateways, 257–282
configurations, 257, 258
downstream physical unit, 266–268
Establishment Controller, 268–278
LAN Gateway, 257–266, 268
Network Control Program, 257–266, 268, 277–278
OS/2 gateway, 278–281
VTAM, 266–268, 274–275
Mainframe connectivity with Interconnect Controller, 215–256
access methods, 215, 216
Interconnect Control Program, 221–235
load, 235–239
network management support, 253–255
networking architecture, 215–217
operating systems, 215–221
channel attachment, 217, 218
device definitions, 220–221
Input/Output Configuration Program, 215, 217–220, 222
Multiple Virtual Storage, 216, 217, 220–221, 239–242
Virtual Machine, 216, 217, 220–221
TCP/IP, 215, 217, 222
VTAM, 215, 217–220, 222, 242–253
Management Information Base (MIB), 147
Master-slave relationship, 2, 3
MAU (*see* Multistation Access Unit)

Media (*see* Token-ring media)
Medium access control (MAC), 11, 18, 27–38, 195
  addressing, 27, 297–300
  frame copying, 27–28
  frame delimiting, 28
  frame format, 28–38
    access control field, 28–30
    destination address, 30–31
    ending delimiter, 28, 35–37
    frame check sequence, 28, 35
    frame control field, 28, 30
    frame status field, 29, 37–38
    information field, 35
    reserved bits, 38
    routing information field, 32–36
    source address, 31
    starting delimiter, 28, 29
  frame recognition, 28
  frame status, 28
  network concepts and, 49, 50, 52, 57, 61–67
  priority management, 28
  routing, 28
  timing, 28
  token management, 28
Mesh configuration, 112, 114–115
Mesh LAN topology, 42–43
MIB (Management Information Base), 147
MSNF (multi-system networking facility), 12, 127
Multiple Virtual Storage (MVS), 216, 217
  device definitions, 220–221
  Input/Output Configuration Program definitions, 219–220
  TCP/IP to token ring connectivity, 239–242
Multisegment LAN topology, 47–49
Multistation Access Unit (MAU), 7, 47, 75–76
  cable and, 74, 77, 79
  LAN design and, 108
  network concepts and, 66
  optical fiber converter, 80–81
  ring-in port, 75–76, 80–81
  ring-out port, 75–76, 80–81
Multi-system networking facility (MSNF), 12, 127
MVS (*see* Multiple Virtual Storage)

Naming standards, 96, 101
NAUN (nearest active upstream neighbor) address, 64, 65, 67, 83
NCCF (Network Command Control Facility), 132–133
NCP (*see* Network Control Program)
NCP Token-Ring Interface (NTRI), 257
Nearest active upstream neighbor (NAUN) address, 64, 65, 67, 83
Neighbor notification, 64–67
Net Logon, 176–178
  backup, 176–178
  member server, 176, 177
  primary server, 176, 177
  pulse parameter, 177
  User Profile Management, 176–177
Net/Master, 128
NETBIOS, 186, 189, 190, 210, 223, 224
NETBIOS Filter Program, 210–212
NetView, 127–129, 131–135, 142, 255
  Command Facility, 148
  LAN Network Manager connectivity, 143, 144, 315–318
  LAN support, 134–135
  NetView Hardware Monitor, 132–134
  Network Command Control Facility, 132–133
  as network manager, 141, 148–157
    LAN ADAPTER command list, 149
    LAN BRIDGE command list, 149–151
    LAN generic command, 148–149
    LAN QNETWORK command list, 150–151
    LAN RESETLAN command list, 151
    LAN SEGMENT command list, 152
    problem determination scenario, 152–157
NetView Asset Manager Vital Product Data (VPD), 255
NetView Command Facility, 132–133
NetView Graphic Monitor Facility (GMF), 136–137
NetView Hardware Monitor, 132–134
  display example, 134
  recommended action screen, 135
Network, 2–3
  hierarchical, 2, 3
  peer, 2–3, 41
Network architecture, 11–39
  open systems, 16–18
  Open Systems Interconnection, 11, 14–18, 135, 139, 147

Network architecture, Open Systems Interconnection (*Cont.*):
- logical link control sub-layer, 11, 18–27
- medium access control sub-layer, 11, 18, 27–38
- (*See also* Systems network architecture)

Network Command Control Facility (NCCF), 132–133
Network concepts, 41–67
- access priority, 65–66
- active monitor, 64
- bridge, 48, 52–60
- brouter, 61
- LAN topologies, 42–49
- medium access control and, 49, 50, 52, 57, 61–67
- Multistation Access Unit and, 66
- neighbor notification, 64–67
- ring station, 41
- router, 48, 52, 60–61
- token claiming, 62–63
- token passing ring protocol, 61–62
- token-ring addressing, 49–51
- token-ring attachment process, 66–67
- unidirectional communication, 41–42

Network Control Program (NCP), 11–12, 91, 118, 122
- mainframe connectivity, 215, 247, 257, 268
  - LAN Gateway, 257–266
  - remote Establishment Controller gateway, 277–278

Network design (*see* LAN design; LAN planning)
Network Logical Data Manager (NLDM), 132
Network management, 141–157
- LAN Network Manager, 102–103, 128, 131, 133, 134, 141–146
- LAN Station Manager, 102–103, 141, 146–147
- NetView, 141, 148–157

Network management architectures, 127–140
- NetView, 127–129, 131–135, 142, 255
- Open Network Management, 127–130, 141
- SNA network services flow, 130–132
- SystemView, 135–139, 141, 142, 148

Network Management Productivity Facility (NMPF), 132
Network management support with external communication adapter, 253–255
Network Management Vector Transport (NMVT), 131, 132, 134, 255
Network Problem Determination Application (NPDA), 132–134
NLDM (Network Logical Data Manager), 132
NMPF (Network Management Productivity Facility), 132
NMVT (Network Management Vector Transport), 131, 132, 134, 255
Nodes, 42
NPDA (Network Problem Determination Application), 132–134
NTRI (NCP Token-Ring Interface), 257
NTRI PU, 261
Null token-ring addressing, 51

OF/2 (*see* Operator Facility/2)
Open Network Management (ONM), 127–130, 141
- entry point, 128–130, 135
- focal point, 128–129, 135
- service point, 128, 130, 135
- services flow, 131
- structure, 128, 129

Open systems, 16–18
Open Systems Interconnection (OSI), 11, 14–18, 135, 139, 147
- LAN segment connection, 48
- layers, 15, 16
  - application layer, 16
  - data link layer, 16, 49
  - network layer, 16
  - physical layer, 16, 70
  - presentation layer, 16
  - session layer, 16
  - transport layer, 16
- logical link control sub-layer, 11, 18–27
- medium access control sub-layer, 11, 18, 27–38

Operator Facility/2 (OF/2), 221–224
- attached, 222–223
- computer definition, 224–226
- stand-alone, 222

Optic fiber, 70–72
Optic fiber cable, 73–74, 110
Optical fiber BNC-to-biconic patch cable, 75
Optical fiber converter, 80–81

Optical fiber repeater, 78–79
OPTIONS, 258–259
OS/2 Extended Edition (EE), 141–143, 159, 222, 224, 278
OS/2 gateway, 118, 124–125, 278–281
  through communications line, 278, 281
  configuration, 125, 278, 279
  through local establishment controller, 278–280
  through Token-Ring Gateway, 278, 280–281
OS/2 LAN Requester, 166, 169, 182–183
  functions, 182–183
  hardware requirements, 183
  implementation to OS/2 LAN Server, 187, 189–192
  logon screen, 191
  software requirements, 183
OS/2 LAN Server, 159, 162, 168–182
  access control function, 170–173
  Add User screen, 191
  alerter service, 174–176
  configuration, 160
  DOS Remote Initial Program Load, 173–174, 193
  functions, 169
  hardware requirements, 182
  implementation from DOS Remote IPL Service, 187, 192–194
  implementation to DOS LAN Requester, 187, 192
  implementation to OS/2 LAN Requester, 187, 189–192
  Net Logon, 176–178
  print spooling, 170
  replicator service, 178–181
  resource sharing, 169
  software requirements, 182
OSI (*see* Open Systems Interconnection)

Parallel bridge configuration, 112, 114
Parallel pairs cable, 74
Parallel routes bridge, 59
Passive wiring concentrator (PWC), 75
Passwords, 163
Patch cable, 75
  cross-over, 75, 76, 79
PATH, 267–268
Path cost, 57, 200, 201, 206
Path information unit (PIU), 14
PBX (private branch exchange), local area network comparison, 4–6
Peer network, 2–3, 41
PIU (path information unit), 14
Plenum cable, 72
Port identifier, 57
Presentation Manager, 222
Print server, 94–95
Print spooling, 170
Private branch exchange (PBX), local area network comparison, 4–6
PU, 267
PWC (passive wiring concentrator), 75

QNETWORK command, 150–151

Radial hierarchical wiring, 46–47
RCS (remote configuration support), 89
Real time interface coprocessor (RTIC), 85
Record Formatted Maintenance Statistics (RECFMS), 134
Remote bridge configuration, 196, 201–207
Remote configuration support (RCS), 89
Remote dial support, 207–210
Remote initial program load (*see* DOS Remote Initial Program Load)
Repeaters, 10
Replicator service, 178–181
  benefits, 178
  exportlist parameter, 179
  exportpath parameter, 179
  extent parameter, 180
  guardtime parameter, 180, 181
  importlist parameter, 179
  importpath parameter, 179–180
  integrity parameter, 181
  interval parameter, 180–181
  replicate parameter, 179
  subdirectory configuration, 181
Request unit (RU), 134
Requester (*see* Server/requester environment)
Requester workstations, 162
RESETLAN command, 151
Resource sharing, 159, 169
Restructured Executive Executable (REXX), 133
Ring Error Monitor Facility, 121
Ring LAN topology, 42, 45–47
Ring number, 52
Ring parameter server (RPS), 67
Ring station, 41

RIPL (*see* DOS Remote Initial Program Load)
Riser backbone configuration, 108–109
Riser cable, 72–73
Root bridge, 57
Root path cost, 57
Root port, 57
Router, 48, 52, 60–61
(*See also* Bridge)
RPS (ring parameter server), 67
RTIC (real time interface coprocessor), 85
RU (request unit), 134

SAA (Systems Application Architecture), 135, 142
SAP (service access point), 19, 20, 27
SDLC (Synchronous Data Link Control), 89, 118
SEGMENT command, 152
Serial configuration, 112, 113
Server, 94–96
affinity group, 94–95, 98, 111–112
central, 94
client/server, 96
configuration, 95
departmental, 94
disk, 95–96
file, 95–96
local, 94
print, 94–95
Server/requester environment, 159–194
additional servers, 161
aliases, 163, 164
domain, 160, 161, 164, 165
domain controller, 160–161
DOS LAN Requester, 159–160, 162, 166, 169, 184–186
DOS Remote Initial Program Load, 162, 166, 173–174, 181
external resources, 164, 165
guest account, 163
implementation, 187–194
Communications Manager LAN profiles, 187–189
DOS Remote IPL Service from OS/2 LAN Server, 187, 192–194
OS/2 LAN Server to DOS LAN Requester, 187, 192
OS/2 LAN Server to OS/2 LAN Requester, 187, 189–192
LAN Support Program, 169, 185–186
network administrator, 167–168
Server/requester environment (*Cont.*):
OS/2 LAN Requester, 166, 169, 182–183
OS/2 LAN Server, 159, 162, 168–182
passwords, 163
planning, 166
requester workstations, 162
shared network resources, 163, 164
system administrator, 165–167
user, 163
user ID, 163
Service access point (SAP), 19, 20, 27
Shared network resources, 163, 164
Shared token-ring adapter, 251–252
Single backbone configuration, 115, 116
Single backbone-dual riser configuration, 109
Single ring backbone configuration, 106, 107
SMF (System Management Facility), 134
SNA (systems network architecture), 11–14, 148
characteristics, 13
components and, 89–91
LAN segment connection, 48, 96, 99–100, 141
layers, 13–14
data flow control, 14
data link control, 14, 49
path control, 14
physical control, 14, 70
presentation services, 16
transaction services, 13
transmission control, 14
local area network and, 2, 6–9
SNA gateway connectivity, 118–125, 278–281
Communications Controller, 118–120
Establishment Controller, 118, 120–122
Interconnect Controller, 118, 122–123
OS/2, 118, 124–125
remote, 278, 281
SNA Network Interconnection (SNI), 12, 14, 127
SNA network services flow, 130–132
SNI (SNA Network Interconnection), 12, 14, 127
Source routing bridge, 52–55
all-routes broadcast, 52–53
single-source, 53–55
Source routing transparent (SRT) bridge, 59–60

Source service access point (SSAP), 20
Spanning tree algorithm bridge, 56–59
  blocking, 56
  bridge protocol data units, 58–59
  designated bridge, 57, 58
  designated port, 57, 58
  forwarding, 57
  learning, 57
  listening, 56–57
  path cost, 57
  port identifier, 57
  root bridge, 57
  root path cost, 57
  root port, 57
  unique bridge identifier, 57
SQL (Structured Query Language), 139, 142
SRT (source routing transparent) bridge, 59–60
SSAP (source service access point), 20
SSP (system support program), 259
Star LAN topology, 42–44
Star-wired ring LAN topology, 46–47, 69
Structured Query Language (SQL), 139, 142
Synchronous Data Link Control (SDLC), 89, 118
System administrator, 165–167
System Management Facility (SMF), 134
System support program (SSP), 259
Systems Application Architecture (SAA), 135, 142
Systems network architecture (*see* SNA)
SystemView, 135–139, 141, 142, 148
  application dimension, 136–139
    business management, 137
    change management, 137
    configuration management, 137–138
    operations management, 138
    performance management, 138–139
    problem management, 139
  data dimension, 136, 139
  end-use dimension, 136–137, 142

TCP/IP (Transmission Control Program/Internet Protocol), 88, 122, 123
  mainframe connectivity, 215, 217, 222
  token-ring, 239–242
Telecommunications link error threshold value defaults, 204
phone twisted pair (TTP), 5, 70–72
Telephone twisted pair cable, 73, 74
Test connector, 79
TGN (transmission group number), 248
TIC (*see* Token-ring interface coupler)
Token bridge, 91
Token claiming, 62–63
Token passing ring protocol, 61–62
Token-Ring Adapter (TRA), 91, 118, 228–231, 257–258
  shared, 251–252
Token-ring addressing, 49–51
  all-stations broadcast, 51
  functional, 51, 296
  group, 50, 295
  individual, 50
  locally administered, 50–51, 91, 118
  naming standards, 96, 101
  null, 51
  universal, 50–51, 101
Token-ring attachment process, 66–67
  duplicate address check, 66
  lobe testing, 66
  monitor check, 66
  neighbor notification participation, 66–67
  request initialization, 67
Token-Ring Gateway, 278, 280–281
Token-ring interface coupler (TIC), 7, 91, 118–120, 247
  duplicate, 263, 265–266
Token-ring media, 70–75
  cable types, 71–75
  coaxial cable, 70, 72
  data-grade media shielded twisted pair, 70–71
  fiber optic, 70–72
  telephone twisted pair, 70–72
Token-Ring Network Bridge Program, 84–86, 91, 195–213
  domains, 161
  filtering programs, 210–213
  local bridge configuration, 195–201
  parameters, 319–321
  remote bridge configuration, 196, 201–207
  remote dial support, 207–210
Token-ring network design (*see* LAN design; LAN planning)
TRA (*see* Token-ring adapter)
Transmission control program/internet protocol (*see* TCP/IP)
Transmission group number (TGN), 248

Transparent bridge, 55–56
Tree LAN topology, 45
TTP (telephone twisted pair), 5, 70–72
Twisted pair, 5, 70–72
Twisted pair cable, 71–75

UCW (Unit Control Word), 217
Ugly plug, 81
UNC (Universal Naming Convention), 163
Unique bridge identifier, 57
Unit Control Word (UCW), 217
Universal Naming Convention (UNC), 163
Universal token-ring addressing, 50–51, 101
Unshielded twisted pair (UTP), 5, 70–72
UPM (User Profile Management), 170, 176–177
User, 163, 170, 171
User ID, 163
User Profile Management (UPM), 170, 176–177
UTP (unshielded twisted pair), 5, 70–72

VBUILD, 267
Virtual Machine (VM), 215, 217, 220–221
Virtual Machine/Enterprise System Architecture (VM/ESA), 221
Virtual Machine/Extended Architecture (VM/XA), 221
Virtual Machine/System Product (VM/SP), 220–221
Virtual Telecommunications Access Method (*see* VTAM)
VM (Virtual Machine), 215, 217, 220–221
VM/ESA (Virtual Machine/Enterprise System Architecture), 221
VM/SP (Virtual Machine/System Product), 220–221
VM/XA (Virtual Machine/Extended Architecture), 221
VNCA (VTAM Node Control Application), 132
VPD (NetView Asset Manager Vital Product Data), 255
VTAM (Virtual Telecommunications Access Method), 11–13, 89, 118, 122–123, 129–131, 143, 144
  mainframe connectivity, 215, 217, 218, 222, 268, 274–275
    with downstream physical unit, 266–268
    dual ring backup, 252–254
    external communication adapter, 242–251
    with gateways, 257
    Input/Output Configuration Program definitions, 219–220
    with Interconnect Control, 242–253
    shared token-ring adapter definition, 251–252
  Primary Program Operator, 132–133
VTAM Node Control Application (VNCA), 132

WAN (wide area network):
  LAN-to-WAN connectivity, 91
  local area network and, 6–7
Wiring closet, 69, 77
Wiring concentrators, 69, 70

XCA (*see* External communication adapter)

Yellow cross-over patch cable (YCP), 75, 76, 79

ABOUT THE AUTHOR

George Sackett is president and chief consultant with ASAP Technologies, Inc., in Rutherford, New Jersey. He is a columnist for *Enterprise Systems Journal* and writes feature stories for *Network World*. He is also coauthor of *Introduction to SNA Networking* and *Advanced SNA Networking*, both published by McGraw-Hill.